Software Engineering Measurement

Software Engineering Measurement

JOHN C. MUNSON, PH.D.

CRC Press
Taylor & Francis Group
Boca Raton London New York

CRC Press is an imprint of the
Taylor & Francis Group, an **informa** business

AN AUERBACH BOOK

CRC Press
Taylor & Francis Group
6000 Broken Sound Parkway NW, Suite 300
Boca Raton, FL 33487-2742

First issued in paperback 2019

© 2003 by Taylor & Francis Group, LLC
CRC Press is an imprint of Taylor & Francis Group, an Informa business

No claim to original U.S. Government works

ISBN-13: 978-0-8493-1503-9 (hbk)
ISBN-13: 978-0-367-39537-7 (pbk)

Visit the Taylor & Francis Web site at
http://www.taylorandfrancis.com

and the CRC Press Web site at
http://www.crcpress.com

Dedication

This book is dedicated to my wife, Mary. She has endured much.

Contents

Preface

This is a book about software measurement. It is not a book about software metrics. There are many of those books. The world is populated with metricians who are eager to build new rulers. The act of applying the metrics is called software measurement. Measuring software, however, will produce data, not information. We must have a reason to measure. We need to know what the data produced by the measurement process really tell us about the software. And we will need to know the essential difference between measuring the complexity of the software application and the complexity of the programming language metaphor.

Measurement, it seems, is a necessary condition for a scientific discipline but not a sufficient condition. Researchers and practitioners need training in the use of this measurement data to validate the theories of computer science. That is what motivated me to write this book.

There are three fundamental questions that remain unanswered after all these years of software development and measurement. First, exactly how do you get the measurement data? Second, how to you convert the data from the measurement process to information that you can use to manage the software development process? Third, how do you manage all of the data? These are the fundamental issues that this book was written to resolve.

Let us start with the first question: how do you get data? I have worked with members of the IEEE 982.1 Standards Committee on the *Dictionary of Measures to Produce Reliable Software*. Some of the measurement data relates to the measurement of faults. Very well. What is a fault? Exactly what is a fault? Where is there a standard for recognizing faults in C code? How will I count faults? The committee produced a glib document in which faults figured heavily but never got around to telling us what a fault is. Looking further, we discover that the basis of software science measures is operators and operands. N_1 is, for example, the total number of operators in a program. Very well. Exactly what is an operator? You might well have some C code and want to count operators in this code. You will not learn how to do this from IEEE 982.1. What you need is a list of things in C that are operators and things that are operands. Oddly, the National Institute of

Standards and Technology resolutely maintains its independence from software measurement standards. You will learn in this book what operands are and how to count them. There is a standard for C code measurement. This standard is here for its value in showing just what a standard should look like. Once you have seen such a standard for one programming language, it is easy to generalize this standard to other language contexts. In early England, a foot was the length of the current king's foot. Big king, big foot. Little king, little foot. Once the English finally nailed down the standard for a foot, commerce was made so much easier.

Finally, the astonishing volumes of data that result from the measurement process lead to the death of many software measurement programs. If we have not thought out in advance just how we are going to use measurement data, we will literally be overwhelmed. We might, for example, be working with a software system consisting of 10,000 modules with a total of one million lines of code. Typically, the developers for this system will reside in many different sites remote from each other. On a good day in this software system maybe as many as 100 of the program modules will change. Every time a module is changed, it should be remeasured. Each time it is measured we might collect as many as 30 different data points. That is 3000 data points per day that have to go somewhere. Further, if we are monitoring the activity of the software during test (and we certainly should), the monitoring activity may produce more than a gigabyte of data per second (1 Gbps). If the software is tested for several hundred hours, we will drown in the data long before the test activity is complete. Or, we will just simply not measure the test outcomes and hope for the best (which is neither science nor a sound engineering practice). This book will show how data are reduced to manageable quanta of information. It will talk to the management of the measurement data.

The second question — How do we convert data to information? — is central to the failure of many measurement programs. Many software development organizations have thought to do engineering with their software processes. The act of measurement is central to this engineering process. To get measurements, the thing to do is to buy measurement tools. That is a mistake. If we will take the time to reminisce, we will find in our memories the days in first and second grade when we were taught how to use a ruler and a thermometer. It took quite a bit of teaching for these measurement skills to be acquired. A measurement tool, in and of itself, produces data. We can imagine giving a micrometer to an aborigine from deepest New Guinea. He would probably use this device to decorate either his nose or his ear. The act of measurement is alien to him. So it is also with the software developer. No one has ever shown him or her how to use measurement tools. They run the measurement tools and decorate their offices with the pictures from measurement tools just as the aborigine would decorate himself with the micrometer. These pictures are the measurement data. They have no meaning to the software developer, just as the micrometer has no meaning to the aborigine.

There is probably no harm done in the aborigine putting the micrometer through a hole in his nose. There is very often great damage done when software developers are led to inappropriate conclusions about the data they have obtained on projects they have measured. For example, if we track fault data very carefully by developer, we will find that the best developers contribute a disproportionate number of faults to the code. It seems reasonable, then, that we should sack the most experienced people and our total fault count would drop. If we look further into the problem, the reason for this observation becomes obvious. We give novice developers easy jobs. We give experienced developers heinous problems to solve. If the novices were working on the same problem, their fault introduction rate would be very much higher than the experienced developers. W. Edwards Deming often maintained that people without training in statistics should not be allowed to possess data because it could be so easily misused. This book is designed to teach software developers what the tools measure and what can be done with the data they produce to convert it into meaningful and valid information. The statistics necessary to perform this conversion will be supplied.

Measurement process issues are also given a fair amount of attention throughout the book. Over the years, I have discovered that if measurement processes are not automated, they simply do not occur. Thus, there is a heavy bias given to automating and hiding the measurement activity itself. When, for example, a program module is checked out of a source control system, updated, and placed back in the code repository, the source control system should invoke a measurement tool that will measure the code and record that data in the measurement database unseen to the developer. The second feature that we will address is the measurement process improvement process. Once the measurement processes are in place and everything is simmering on the back burner, the measurement tools can be refined and new tools can be added to the process.

To build better software technology we will certainly need to do better engineering. Our engineering processes are limited by our measurement technology. The Industrial Revolution was not the result of the steam engine, as is the popular belief. The Industrial Revolution was the direct result of precision manufacturing, which was only possible with precision measurement.

Underlying the development of any software system is a software process. This process must be monitored continuously, just like any other manufacturing process. Steel mills are heavily instrumented. Every part of the steel-making process is continuously monitored and measured; so, too, should software processes. We should measure each change to the software specifications, design, and code. We should monitor both the activity of the test process and the activity of the code as it is executing. Finally, the software systems produced by this process should be continuously monitored when they are deployed.

Computer security and reliability concerns dominate our world. Millions of dollars are being spent trying to secure software systems. The problem is that these systems are essentially running out of control. There are no monitoring systems built into the operating software to watch what it is doing when it is running. Novice hackers very easily hijack these unmonitored systems. A system is easily hacked when no one is minding the store. We do not have a computer security problem. We do have a software control problem. If suitable instrumentation is placed into the systems that we develop, their activity can be monitored in real-time. We can detect code that is being attacked. We can detect code that is likely to fail. We can block the hacker and his inroads to the system if we are monitoring our software systems. We can fix a software system before it breaks if we are monitoring that software system. We just have to know what to watch for and how to instrument properly.

I have used this material in a graduate-level course on software engineering measurement. It presumes the level of academic preparation of a typical computer science student. Most of these students have had at least some background in statistics. Where I know that background to be missing, I attempt to fill in the holes. There is also an appendix on statistics that should also be useful in this regard. Where possible, I have created simple examples to show some of the measurement concepts. I have also integrated data and observations from my years of measurement practice in industry.

My overall objectives in creating this opus are to (1) develop an understanding in the reader about measuring software, (2) foster a more precise use of software measurement in the computer science and software engineering literature, (3) demonstrate how one can develop simple experiments for the empirical validation of theoretical research, and (4) show how the measurement data can be made into meaningful information.

One of the most inappropriate terms ever used for a discipline was the term "computer science." There has been, historically, practically no science in computer science. This is not surprising, in that the majority of the early pioneers in computer software were drawn from mathematics and philosophy. These pioneers had very little or no training in scientific methodology. They were very good at creating mathematical systems. They had neither the skills nor the training nor the interest in the empirical validation of theoretical constructs. As a result, the field of computer science has much theory and little or no real science. The programming language C++ is an example of this folly. What would ever possess a rational human being to construct a safety-critical software system around a programming language with an ambiguous grammar and no standard semantics?

Modern physical sciences are based primarily on the observation and measurement of physical phenomena. Theories survive only insofar as they can be validated empirically. A considerable amount of effort is devoted to the act of measurement in the training of a new physical scientist. In chemistry, for example, one of the first courses that a potential chemist will take is a course in quantitative analysis. The objective of this course is to train the incipient chemist in basic laboratory measurement techniques. A student in computer science, on the other hand, is typically never contaminated with any course that will permit measurement and assessment of any abstract constructs.

The training of a modern computer scientist is very similar to the training of a theological student in a seminary. Students are exposed to courses such as Dogma 1 (Structured Programming), Dogma 2 (Object-Oriented Programming), Dogma 3 (The Lambda Calculus), etc. The basis of theological study is faith. Theological students are never offered a shred of scientific evidence that any of the constructs they are asked to learn have proven useful in any context. That is not what theology is about. Computer science students are never offered a shred of empirical evidence that any of the constructs that we present to them are valid. They are taught to *believe* that structured programming is somehow *good*, that object-oriented design is really *great*. The use of the words "good" or "great" suggests to a scientist that there must be some criterion measure (or measures) that can be established that would permit structured code (whatever that might be) to be measured against code that is unstructured (whatever that might be). A scientist would set about to define criterion measure(s) for goodness and then conduct experiments to test for the superiority (or lack thereof) of structured programming or the clear benefits derived from object-oriented design. It is interesting to note that in the particular case of structured programming, if the criterion measure is runtime efficiency, for example, structured code will generally result in much slower execution times than unstructured approaches in solving problems of substantial complexity. We will pay a price for program structure.

It is important to understand the limitations of our software developers as they graduate from college. Above all, they are not trained in science. I am very familiar with this educational system, having taught computer science for more than 30 years. Odds are that typical computer science students will never have designed or conducted an experiment of any type, or collected any data about a program or its operation. They will never have been introduced to the notion of measurement. It would never occur to them that a good algorithm might lead to very poor system performance. They will have had no training in statistics or in the interpretation of scientific data. They cannot do science and, as a result, they cannot recognize good science.

This book is the product of many years of work in the software measurement business. While there are quite a few books on the subject of software metrics, there are none about the measurement activity itself. There seems to be a great deal of interest in the creation of new metrics for software development. Anyone, it seems, with a computer and a word processor can become an expert in the area. There is, however, little science that generates from all this activity. This book discusses the conduct of scientific inquiry in the development and deployment of software systems.

Acknowledgments

The research described in this book was carried out at the University of Idaho, Jet Propulsion Laboratory (JPL), California Institute of Technology, at the IBM Federal System Division and subsequently at Loral Space Information System, and at the Storage Technology Corporation. The work at the University of Idaho was partially supported by a grant from the National Science Foundation. Portions of the work performed at JPL were sponsored by the U.S. Air Force Operational Test and Evaluation Center (AFOTEC) and the National Aeronautics and Space Administration's IV&V facility.

Special kudos go to Dr. Allen Nikora of the Jet Propulsion Laboratory; Ted Keller, now of IBM Global Services; and Richard Karcich, now at Sun Microsystems. They have provided the opportunity to investigate and analyze large systems.

Chapter 1
The Goals of Software Engineering Measurement

Everybody talks about the weather but nobody does anything about it.
Everybody talks about bad software but nobody does anything about it.

1.1 SOFTWARE ENGINEERING MEASUREMENT

In the engineering of any hardware system, the term "best engineering practice" is repeatedly applied to all aspects of the development of the system, whether it be a bridge, an automobile, or a large building. Best engineering practice embodies a long tradition of experimentation, analysis, and measurement. It is the application of scientific principles to the solution of a complex hardware design and development project. At the core of the best engineering practice is measurement and empirical validation of design outcomes. This will be the goal in this book. We seek to develop a measurement methodology for the abstract systems that make up the world of computer science and engineering, and use these measurements to build a measurement based on *best software engineering practice*.

1.1.1 The Measurement Process

The field of software engineering has evolved quite recently from the very young discipline of computer science. To distinguish between these two disciplines it will be useful to observe the relationship between the disciplines of physics and mechanical engineering. Physics seeks to develop a theoretical foundation for the laws of Nature as we are capable of observing them. Mechanical engineering is the discipline of applied physics. The basic principles of physics are applied to solve real problems in the physical world. Computer science embodies the theoretical foundations for computers and computation. The field of software engineering is, then, the applied discipline of computer science.

Empirical validation is the basis for all science. All theory is validated through the conduct of experiments. Numerical results are derived from

1

experiments through a rigorous measurement process. For an experiment to be meaningful, it must be reproducible. That is the difference between science and religion. Miracles are not reproducible. You are either privy to the execution of one or you are not. It is kind of a one-shot thing. The standard for science is much more demanding. The numerical outcomes of a scientific experiment are reported in terms of numerical values in units of measures shared by a common scientific community. This is possible because there are standards for the measurement units. So valuable are these standards that they are husbanded by national and international governments. If you need to know, for example, exactly what one meter is to ten decimal places, the National Institute for Standards and Technology (NIST) will tell you. NIST will also share this value with other researchers. In this way, the measurements taken by one group of scientists can be very accurately reported to any other. This is the essence of science.

It is interesting to note that NIST does not maintain any standards for software measurement; nor, for that matter, does any other national standards organization. This makes it difficult to impossible to share experimental results among the community of scholars in computer science that wish to engage in the practice of science. We could, for example, measure the kernel of the Linux operating system. It is written in the C programming language. We might choose to enumerate the number of statements in the source code that comprises this system. In the absence of a standard for counting these statements, this turns out to be a very difficult and ambiguous task. Even if we were successful in this counting exercise, there is no way that our results can be shared with our colleagues throughout the world. Each of these colleagues could enumerate the statements in the same Linux kernel and arrive at a very different number. The principal thrust of this book, then, is to lay the basis for measurement standards so that we can begin to share our experimental results in a meaningful way.

The next thing that will be of interest in the measurement process is that the attributes that we are measuring will have some validity in terms of a set of real-world software attributes. In the early days of psychology, there emerged a branch of inquiry called phrenology. In this discipline, the structures of the human subjects' skulls were carefully measured. Certain values of particular structures were thought to be related to underlying psychological constructs such as intelligence. That is, one could deduce the intelligence of a subject by measuring the structure of his head. These measurements were standardized and were quite reproducible. One experimenter could measure the same subject and get the same attribute values as another experimenter with some degree of accuracy. The problem with the science of phrenology is that the measures obtained from the skull did not correlate well with the attributes such as intelligence that they were thought to be related to. They lacked validity.

As we learn to measure software for scientific purposes, we will thus be concerned with two fundamental measurement principles:

1. The measurements must be reproducible. That is, there must be a standard shared by the software community.
2. The attributes being measured must be valid. They must yield true insights into the fundamental structure of the object of measurement.

1.1.2 We Tried Measurement and It Did Not Work

In our many years of working in software measurement, we have frequently interviewed software development organizations on their various attempts at instituting software metrics programs. Most will say that they have tried measurement and it did not work. Now, this is all very interesting. If you were to meet someone who was holding a ruler and this person said, "I've tried this ruler and it didn't work," you probably would not think to criticize the ruler. Rulers are passive, inanimate objects. If a ruler is not working correctly, it will most certainly not be the fault of the ruler. We would immediately turn our attention to the person holding the ruler who is unable to make it work. The ruler did not work properly because it was not being used properly. The same is true for software measurement techniques. If they are not working (yielding results) in a software development organization, it is probably not the fault of the metrics themselves.

It is possible to measure all aspects of software development. It just takes training. That is what this book is about: to show what there is to measure and how to go about doing this measurement. However, we will not be able to use measurement tools with which we are familiar. A ruler, for example, will not work for most software applications. Because software and software processes are abstract, we will require new tools and new ways of thinking to measure these abstractions. Fortunately, much of this ground has been plowed for us in the social sciences. Practitioners and scientists who function in the social science world also deal with abstractions. Consider the notion of a human intelligence quotient, for example. This is clearly an abstract attribute of all functioning human beings. For a large part of our efforts in measurement, we will draw from the experience of psychologists and sociologists. After all, programmers (as psychological entities) are working in teams (as sociological entities) to produce abstract objects called programs.

1.1.3 Problems in Software Measurement

Whenever we attempt to measure something, we really get more than we bargained for. In addition to the true value of the attribute that is being measured, Nature provides additional information in the form of noise. Quite simply, we wish to exercise control over the amount of noise that Nature is providing. In a practical sense we cannot realistically expect to eliminate all noise from this process. It would be too expensive. Instead, we will set tolerances on this noise and operate within the practical limitations of these tolerances. If we wish to measure the size of a book to see whether it will fit in our bookcase, we would probably be satisfied with a ruler that would let us measure the size of the book to the nearest half-centimeter. A very cheap ruler would be most satisfactory for this purpose. If, on the other hand, we wanted to measure the diameter of an engine crankshaft to fit a new crankshaft bearing, we would probably want an instrument that could measure to the nearest 1/100 of a millimeter. Again, we must accept the proposition that we can never know the true value of the attribute that we wish to measure. Our focus should be on how close to the true value we really need to come in our measurement. We will pay a price for accuracy. We could buy a scale that would be sufficiently accurate to measure our weight changes at a molecular scale. The cost of this knowledge would be astonishing. The scale would be very expensive. Realistically, if we merely want to establish whether we are losing or gaining weight on our new diet, a scale that is accurate to ±10 grams would be more than adequate for our purposes. We could also buy this scale with out-of-pocket cash instead of having to mortgage our house and our future to know our weight at the molecular level. Understanding the economics of the contribution of noise will be the first thing we will have to solve in our software measurement processes.

We can only control noise in the measurement process if we understand the possible sources of this information. In some cases it will be relatively simple to establish what the possible sources of variation in measurement might be. If we buy a cheap ruler for measuring distances, the printed marks on the ruler will be fat and fuzzy. The width of the printed marks, the variation in the thickness of the marks, and the distance between the marks will all contribute to measurement noise. If our ruler has marks at 1-millimeter intervals, then the best we can hope for is an accuracy of ±0.5 millimeter. If the ruler is made of metal, its length will vary as a function of temperature. If the ruler is made of cloth, then the length of the ruler will vary directly with the amount of tension applied to both ends during the measurement process.

One of the greatest problems of measurement in software engineering is the abysmal lack of standards for anything we wish to measure. There are no standards for enumerating statements of C code. There are no standards for measuring programmer productivity. We have no clear concept of how to measure operating system overhead. NIST is not motivated to establish standards for software measurement. We are on our own. This is perhaps the greatest obstacle that we will have to overcome in software engineering measurement. We have no basis for communicating the results of our scientific investigations in that everyone is measuring the outcomes of these investigations with different standards and measurement tools.

1.1.4 The Logistics of Software Measurement

We have recently witnessed the efforts of a number of large software development organizations to begin measurement programs for their software development. They have all come up against the real problem of measurement. The most unexpected problem in measurement is dealing with the volume of data generated from a typical measurement application. The focus within these organizations is on the measurement tools, as if the tools in and of themselves will provide the solution to measurement efforts. This is rather akin to the idea that the tools make the craftsman. That is, one can become a good carpenter if one simply has the tools of the trade. The truth is that a good carpenter can do even marvelous carpentry with the most primitive tools. Training to become a carpenter is a long process. Training to become a mechanical engineer is also a long process. One cannot hope to buy some software measurement tools and become an expert in software measurement. The logistical and statistical issues that surround the measurement process should be the central focus — and not the tools.

Consider a system of 100 KLOC (thousand lines of code) with approximately 200 lines per program module. This system will have approximately 1000 program modules. If we measure the system on 20 distinct attributes, then we will have a 1000×20 data matrix containing 20K data points for one measurement effort. Now, if we consider that most systems in development will change materially each week, they will require new measurement every week. The data bandwidth from the measurement process for one software development project is substantial. The substantial flow of new data from the measurement process is one of the major problems encountered by software metricians. This is generally the reason that most measurement efforts fail. They simply produce too much data and not enough information.

Just having taken measurements on a system does not constitute a measurement process. It merely generates data. These data must somehow be converted into information. This is the role of statistics. The use of statistics permits us to understand just what these data are telling us about our processes. There is just no way that we can make rational interpretations of hundreds of thousands of measurements taken on all aspects of the software development process and reasonably hope to understand or make sense out of the mass of data.

1.2 THE RATIONALE FOR EFFECTIVE MEASUREMENT

We have long passed the point where craftsmanship can play a significant role in software systems. It would appear that a small group of people could design, build, operate, and maintain a software system of about 100 KLOC. Much beyond this critical value, the process rapidly decays. No one person can completely understand the entire system. The software becomes beset with performance, reliability, and maintenance problems. Just about every industry has encountered this same problem. A team of three or four people could hack together an early Wright or Curtiss aircraft. As the aircraft became more complex, however, the hacking was rapidly replaced with basic engineering discipline. Detailed designs were developed for the new, more complex aircraft. Tight manufacturing controls were exercised to make sure that all of the pieces integrated smoothly into a working aircraft. Experiments were conducted to study the best aerodynamic characteristics of the wings of the vehicle. What is astonishing about the software development enterprise is that it has taken so long to perceive the need for simple engineering discipline in the development of these systems.

1.2.1 Achieving Software Quality

Software quality does not happen by accident. It does not happen by investing tremendous resources in the problem. And, it most certainly does not happen by espousing meaningless metaphors or sloganeering. Software quality happens by design.[1] For our purposes, we insist that the first step in any effort at quality improvement begin with the institution of a measurement program. We can institute a host of new quality improvement processes; but until we have the ability to measure with some degree of accuracy certain relevant quality criteria, we cannot hope to improve our existing processes. It is quite possible the new "Quality Improvement Program" that we just bought from the "Software Quality Improvement Consulting Company" might well have had an adverse effect on our overall software development process. If we are not measuring, we will never know. Spending money to solve software quality problems is not the answer. Unfortunately, it is much easier to throw money at the problem than to do the necessary work to achieve engineering discipline in the process.

It is clear that all software development is accomplished by a software development staff. Unfortunately, it is possible to obtain an undergraduate degree in computer science at just about any major university in the world and never once be exposed to the fact that people write software. If there are faults in the code, people put them there. If the design is bad, people made it so. If the requirements are faulty, the requirements analysts created these faults. Processes that people follow permit them to make errors that, in turn, result in faults in the products. People are the real problem, yet we know so little about them. To achieve any real progress in the area of software quality, we are going to have to learn a little about how people tick.

1.2.1.1 Software Quality Objectives. At the core of a set of software quality objectives should be a research effort focused on the factors that we can control in the software development process. We really do not know a great deal about this process. The field abounds with ad hoc studies, speculative conjectures of software quality, and models of capability and maturity. There is very little science that has been done in the area. We simply do not know why programmers put faults into code, but we can learn. Therefore, our foremost quality objective will be to do science. We must learn to measure people, processes, products, and environments. We must conduct the necessary science to understand how these domains interact to product good software. It will not be necessary to reinvent the wheel. There are excellent role models for the conduct of scientific inquiry in the fields of chemistry, biology, psychology, and the many engineering disciplines. Not much is known about software quality. The path to enlightenment is clear; many other disciplines have found the way.

The real tragedy in software development organizations today is that there is no learning in the system. If a good software system is accidentally designed and built, no one will know why this happened. It will not be possible to leverage this success on future projects unless very accurate measurement records are kept. If a lousy software system is designed and built, and this is a far more likely outcome, it will not be possible to learn from our mistakes unless very accurate measurement records are kept. If an engineering firm consistently designed and built bridges that systematically fell apart when they were placed in service, that firm would rapidly be sued out of existence. A good engineering firm can learn from both its successes and its (limited) failures.

It seems clear, then, that there are five simple software quality objectives. They are as follows:

1. Learn to measure accurately people, processes, products, and environments.
2. Learn to do the necessary science to reveal how these domains interact.
3. Institutionalize the process of learning from past mistakes.
4. Institutionalize the process of learning from past successes.
5. Institutionalize the measurement improvement process.

1.2.1.2 Control of the Software Development Environment. Control is the key to quality software development. The more unconstrained degrees of freedom there are in the software development process, the more opportunity there will be for unexpected outcomes. From a statistical perspective, each unconstrained degree of freedom on a programmer is a source of uncontrolled variation in the development process. If a programmer is simply slavishly mapping a design to a particular programming metaphor, such as Java, then the effect of the programmer will be minimal. Every programmer should produce essentially the same code for the same design. If, on the other hand, the design is vague and ambiguous, there will be plenty of opportunity for a programmer to make interpretations of what was meant by the designer. Each programmer looking at the same design will produce different code that will function differently. The programmer is now a main player in the development process. A good programmer will produce clean, efficient, fault-free code. A bad programmer will produce code that is at once clumsy and fault ridden. This potential source of variation in code development is an anathema to the creation of software quality.

Individuality is the key to software craftsmanship. It has no real place in modern software development. Modern software systems must be engineered; they can no longer be crafted. They are much too complex for any one craftsman to understand. Furthermore, computer software is now playing a vital role in embedded software systems in items used in daily life. Its operation must be guaranteed and its safety assured. Individuality is not a desirable trait in engineered software systems. It will result in uncontrolled sources of variation in the software development process. The development of rigorous control systems for the software development process is a necessary but not sufficient condition for the attainment of quality software. A measurement-based feedback control system is a sufficient condition for the attainment of processes that will produce quality software.

1.2.2 Deming and the Software Development Process

W. Edwards Deming played a very influential role in the recovery of the Japanese manufacturing industry. His message was a very simple one, so simple, in fact, that it still eludes most of the manufacturing industry in America. It is totally unknown in the software development industry. We must learn not to focus on the products that we are making. Rather, we must learn to focus on the processes that are making these products.

As we evaluate these processes, we must learn to look beyond measures of central tendency to evaluate processes. We might learn that the average widget that we are manufacturing arrives at the end of a production line with five defects. That is an interesting fact but it has little value to us as information. Suppose, on the other hand, that we know that all widgets have five defects and that there is no variation in this number. We could probably go back down the assembly line and identify the precise source of these five defects and correct the problem. If there is little or no variation in the defect count, we have a problem that we can solve. If, on the other hand, some widgets have no defects while others have 20 or more defects, now we have a real problem. We are accidentally building good widgets and we do not know why. It will be very difficult to find and fix the manufacturing processes that are introducing the defects. The essence of

Deming's message to the manufacturing community was: the real information is in the variance of the measurement.

One of the greatest obstacles to the development of successful engineering programs in software development environments is slogan-based engineering effort. There are numerous opportunists in the field of software. They persistently exploit the simplicity and ignorance of the software development community. Each of the sloganeers has an N-point methodology that will surely lead to the software development nirvana. If you do Practical Software Measurement (PSM), then surely science and engineering discipline must follow. If you join the teaming masses of software developers in the new science of requirements phrenology, function point analysis, then surely this must be engineering. An automobile engineer does not become an engineer because he joined the Society of Automotive Engineers (SAE). He also cannot expect to become an engineer just because he purchased a set of SAE wrenches. The engineering discipline requires many years of education and training. Engineers learned many generations ago that slogans do not build solid bridges. Solid engineering practice builds solid bridges.

If we are going to do software engineering, then we are going to have to listen to such pundits as Deming.[2] His message was a simple one, and a very unpopular one. We are going to have to work hard to achieve reasonable quality in manufacturing processes. It is so much easier to search for a miracle than it is to begin the serious work of a measurement-based engineering discipline. Ford Motor Co. did not build better cars because it posted signs throughout its facilities that said "Quality is Job 1." Ford built better cars because it either did so or lost its market share to the Japanese automobile makers who learned the quality engineering discipline from Deming. In the last analysis, it is probably easier and cheaper to build a quality automobile than it is to build one of lesser quality. The inertia of bad manufacturing practice was very great. It took an outside force (the Japanese) to execute the change. The inertia of bad software development practice is also very great. The industry awaits the stimulus of a country dedicated to the principle of quality software to provide the necessary impetus to produce quality software.

1.2.3 The Role of Statistics in Software Engineering

One of the most powerful tools available to a software engineer is that of statistics. Unfortunately, the typical undergraduate or graduate student has had little or no exposure to this discipline. It would appear that the world of computer science and software engineering is strictly a deterministic one. In this model, it is possible to describe in a deterministic manner exactly what code will be executing in an operating system at any moment, given any number of arbitrary inputs. That is probably true. It is theoretically possible to run the Universe backwards. That is, once we establish the precise location and velocity of each atom in this universe at any instant we could work backwards through time where the atom came from through all of its possible encounters with other atoms. The fundamental premise of the deterministic model is that we can know and observe Nature directly.

The fundamental premise of statistics is that we cannot know or understand Nature directly. We can conduct observations, perform experiments, and learn what we need to know at predetermined levels of confidence or certainty. The important notion is that it is not necessary to know exactly what Nature is about, only to have a good idea what she is up to. Sometimes, Nature is not eager to disclose some of her secrets to us. To this end we will formulate hypotheses about the phenomena we investigate. We can then test our hypotheses with carefully controlled experiments. Nature is not devious; she is not duplicitous. Our experimental process will reveal what we wish to know. The very worst thing that we could do is to make assumptions about Nature's secrets. The experimental method is the only way we can learn what we wish to know about Nature. The discipline of statistics will provide very useful tools to aid us in the discovery process. These statistical analysis tools we will find to be vital in the conversion of data to information.

1.3 MEASUREMENT ACROSS THE LIFE-CYCLE MODEL

Software measurement activities can and should occur throughout the software life cycle. Software requirements are very good leading indicators of the software development cost. Software design measurements will permit evaluation of design alternatives. Measuring the test activities will give great insight into the adequacy of the test process and the expected time to produce a software product that can meet certain quality standards.

We do not have unlimited resources to invest at every stage in the software life cycle. We are constrained by staff hours, hardware resources, and staff capabilities. A good measurement program will permit the optimal allocation of these limited resources to produce the best possible product within the timeframe and with the resources available.

Perhaps the most important contribution that can be made by an effective software measurement program is that a historical database of software development experience can be established. The best estimator of future software development costs is historical data. The best estimator of software reliability and quality is also data from previous software development projects.

1.3.1 Operational Requirements Specification

The requirements specification process is vital to the success of a software development organization. One of the principal products that emerges during this phase should be a cost estimate of the software development project. Unfortunately, it is very easy to underestimate the effort necessary to develop a new software product. That, in turn, means that it is very easy for software development organizations to lose their shirts in underbudgeted and underfunded development projects.

It is clear that the costs of a project will be directly related to the complexity of the project. This complexity clearly begins to emerge during the requirements engineering process. What is missing is a clear-cut method of effectively estimating project complexity from the requirements themselves. In most organizations, however, there is a wealth of historical data from previous projects. The nice thing about a finished product is that it is a done deal. At the conclusion of a project, most of the managers turn their attention to the new threat to their corporate future, the new XYZ project. And this is where the problem lies.

When a project is finished, it should be mined for its historical value. At the end of the project, we will know exactly how much it cost to develop. If we have kept good records, we know where the major cost centers were in the development and where the major concentrations of effort were. In particular, we would know how much time was devoted to design, to coding, to testing, to documentation, to training, etc. We would also have at our disposal a complete requirements document for the entire project. With the historical data from our most recent project and others that preceded it, we can learn to measure and quantify specific requirements attributes.[3] We can then use these measurements to develop predictive models for software costing. The essence of scientific software engineering is that it allows us to learn from the past and then use this information to create a better future.

In most software development organizations, the path from requirements to design to code seems to be a one-way street. The requirements process is merely a way to prime the code development pump. Once we begin to develop the actual code from a preliminary sketch of the requirements, the requirements are never revisited. We will learn that the software requirements specification process is vital to the understanding of the system that we are developing, as well as its maintainability.

If we are to build and maintain a requirements system, we must learn to partition this specification process into three distinct compartments. The first compartment is the user's view of the system; this we will call the operational specification. The interesting thing about software design and

11

development is that there are no real constraints placed on us for the virtual environments that we may create for the user. We can take a basic accounts receivable system and build a nice, warm, cozy, user-friendly system, or we can build a very ornery, cold, user-hostile system. The operational requirements will articulate the operations that the user will perform to interact with the software. They deal only with what the system will do — not how it will be done.

One of the most important concepts that will emerge from the requirements specification process is the notion of requirements traceability. Each operational specification will map to specific code modules. Each code module can be traced to specific operations. We will be able to devise a system that will permit the requirements specification to be kept current with the evolving code base.

1.3.2 Design

Having a good clear idea about what the system we are going to build is to do for the customer, we can then set about to talk about how we are going to implement this system. This leads directly to the development of the high-level design of the system and a very precise description of the functionality of the system. Each user operation will be implemented by a very precisely defined set of system functionalities. Each functionality will be employed in one or more operations. There is a precisely defined mapping between the operational specifications and the functional specifications.

Knowing how we are going to build the system in the high-level design specification, we then have to decompose each functionality into one or module specifications. This constitutes the low-level design stage. Each module specification will detail completely how its piece of functionality will be achieved. It will contain the algorithm necessary to implement its task, and it will completely specify all the data to be used in this process. At this stage, we will be able to implement our first automated measurement systems. We will be able to measure and evaluate different design alternatives. We can understand the nature of the system that we are building before it is actually committed to source code.

During the design process, the overall structure of the program begins to emerge. Its basic functionalities are parsed into software modules. These software modules are then structured into a call graph that will detail the interactions among the modules. The data elements used within the modules are made explicit, as is the data being exchanged among modules on the module interface. In essence then, many salient features or attributes of the evolving program are made explicit during the design process.

The key feature of the design process will center on the notion of requirements traceability. The fundamental purpose of the software design process is to map user operational requirements to system functional requirements to software code elements. During the design process, the structure of the program with regard to control flow complexity and data complexity will clearly emerge. These program characteristics will be remarkably easy to identify and measure. If we are sufficiently careful during this phase, we will be able to model, with some precision, the operational performance characteristics of the system we are designing.

It is quite possible, indeed very easy, to design a system that cannot be tested or maintained. It is vital that we learn to identify those design characteristics that will lead to testable and maintainable software.

1.3.3 Coding

Coding is perhaps the easiest phase of the entire life cycle to measure and assess. For this reason, the literature is replete with measurement studies. We can watch programmers do their work and measure the time it takes to code. We can measure the products of their efforts in volume of code generated. We can measure the total number of problems (faults) they have created in their programming efforts. Unfortunately, as we will see, much of what we have learned about this process is, at best, misleading and, at its worst, dead wrong.

At the coding phase, the code has yet to have a life of its own. Our focus on this phase will initially be on the static properties of the code itself. We will learn to enumerate things about the code, such as the number of lines of source code, the number of statements, etc.

1.3.4 Test

Just as the coding process lends itself to measurement activities, so does the test activity. We can easily count the number of problems found when running the code. We can also measure the test effort in terms of human resources spent on this task.

During the test phase, our focus will shift to measuring aspects of the running code. In this sense we will learn to measure code dynamics, exactly what the code is doing when it is executing. Each test activity will have its own outcome. It will exercise a subset of program modules. Some tests will be good tests; they will expose potential problems in the code. Some tests will be bad; they will exercise code that has already been exercised or they will touch only those code modules not likely to contain faults.

We must learn to establish reasonable goals for the test process. With modern software systems, the number of different states that these systems can get into is impossibly large. We must accept the fact that we cannot find and remove all of the faults that a system might have. What we do care about is that the system we build will not fail when it is deployed. Different users will use our systems in different ways. Different uses of the software will, in turn, exercise different system features and consequently different code modules. Therefore, a vital part of the test process will be to determine how our customers will use the system. Once we have a good idea about how it will be used, we can then devote our test effort to ensuring that the system will perform reliably within this framework.

1.3.5 Maintenance

In the academic preparation of future computer scientists and software engineers, there is a tendency to ignore the maintenance phase altogether. In fact, it is very easy for these students to get the impression from their training that this is the information technology (IT) equivalent of janitorial service. Nothing could be further from the truth. For modern software projects, more than 80 percent of the total life-cycle costs will be allocated to this phase. It is also clear from this figure that the vast majority of jobs in this commercial sector will also be in software maintenance.

Because the focus of most IT development managers is strictly on the development side, there is little interest in what happens to a software product after it is placed into the customer's hands for the first time. Because software development technology is primarily based on the principle of craftsmanship and not on the basic principles of manufacturing technology, the vast majority of delivered software falls far short of any standards currently applied to manufactured goods. These software projects are fraught with flaws. They have been lovingly (or not so lovingly) crafted by a handful of developers who are the only ones who really understand the product functionality. When future problems arise with these systems, they require a phenomenal amount of human effort to fix. Central to this problem is the very simple notion of requirements traceability. We must learn to deduce the functionality of a software system by looking at the code. This is quite the wrong way to develop software. The structure and the functionality of the system should be specified outside the code. This, we will come to learn, is the essence of software maintainability. Software requirements traceability and maintainability are one and the same thing.

1.4 REASONABLE AND ATTAINABLE GOALS FOR SOFTWARE MEASUREMENT

A child must learn to crawl before he walks. He must learn to walk before he runs. So it will be for an incipient software measurement program. We must learn to crawl first. At the outset, the complexity of the measurement problem space appears astonishingly large. There are many *products,* such as requirements, design, and code. Each of these products was produced by a *process,* in a development *environment,* by *people.* It is very difficult to measure a software process. This is not a good place to start. It is very dangerous to measure people. This measurement data is so easily misused. Until we have gained some real sophistication in measuring people and process, we will have little success in trying to measure aspects of the software development environment.

Our objective is not to do software measurement. We must learn to build reliable software measurement process based on valid software measurement tools. If we try to do too much too soon, we will likely fail. Basically, software engineering measurement is not a resource issue; it is a commitment issue. We are going to build a measurement process that will generate great volumes of data. These data must be converted to information that can be used in the software development decision-making process. The principle is a simple one. Even a small amount of measurement data that can be converted to useful information is better than large volumes of measurement data that have little or no information value. We must begin with simple tools and focus most of our attention on the measurement and management processes. We must remember that we learned how to measure distances in the first grade with a very crude ruler. Our teachers did not give us micrometers to learn measurement. Ultimately, we learned that our rulers could be used to quantify size attributes of the objects in our environment. These rulers, in fact, had utility beyond their obvious use as bludgeons that we could use on our classmates.

A very simple rule for the software engineering measurement process is that we must learn to walk before we run. Let us work out a very simple process to begin a measurement program within our software development organization.

At the outset we will focus our efforts on building our first measurement tool. We will identify a very small set of metrics that we know will yield useful information about our software development process. There is no quality in quantity. A small working set of good metrics will yield far more information than a large set of metrics of questionable validity. In Chapter 5 we describe a very simple set of such metrics. We will not convene a panel of metrics experts to tell us what to do. We must learn this ourselves. That is part of the process. It turns out that the processes surrounding the measurement activity are far more important, initially, than the measurements themselves. We will build, or cause to be built, a simple measurement tool that will collect the necessary metrics we have decided to incorporate in our initial working set. We will then validate that the tool does exactly what it is supposed to do.

Now the real fun begins. A modern software system is a very complex organism. It is rapidly evolving. New pieces are being added continually. Existing components are being changed almost constantly. Some dysfunctionality will be removed from time to time. Our measurement of the system must be *timely*. We must be able to know its measured attributes as it is right now. We must figure out a way to integrate the measurement of this code into the development process. It is clear that if we are forced run our measurement tool as a separate measurement exercise, this measurement process is destined to fail. It must occur automatically and invisibly.

Let us observe that essentially all modern software systems are placed under some type of configuration control system, such as SCCS or RCS, at their inception. Whenever a developer wishes to change a module, it must be checked out first. After the changes are made, the module can then be checked back into the system. This is a very good place to insert the measurement tool. We can simply trap the update to the configuration control system and measure the new code module with changes. We will have integrated our measurement tool into the existing process so that it occurs automatically. It is not necessary that the developer know anything about this process; it is part of the software manufacturing process.

It is clear that if there is a lot of code churn, there will be a lot of measurement activity. This measurement activity will create a lot of data. This data must go to some repository. The next logical step in the measurement process is to design a measurement database that will capture this data as it is generated. There are any number of database management systems that are well suited for this task. We will design our measurement tool to interface with the appropriate database management tool to update our measurement database. Now the data are generated automatically and placed into a repository automatically. Measurement will happen without human intervention.

The next step in the measurement process is the conversion of measurement data to information that can be used by the managers of the software development process. It is clear that our database system will probably have a simple query language such as SQL (structured query language) that will allow us to summarize the information in the database. We now have at our disposal a system that allows us to see the changes being made to the code base in a very timely fashion. We could know, for example, how many lines of code had been added or changed in the last five minutes. The query language capability of the database is an invaluable aid in the transformation of data to information.

We now have crossed some of the most difficult hurdles in the software measurement process. We now have a software measurement system. It will invisibly chug away at its measurement task. The data will go to a measurement database where it can be converted to information. We accept the fact that measurement is an integral and continuous part of the software development process.

There are any number of directions that we can now go that will begin to flesh out our measurement database. Perhaps the next logical step is to accumulate information on software quality. We will next probably begin to interface our problem tracking system with our measurement database. All failure events, as they are assigned tracking numbers, will be recorded in our database. As the failures are traced to specific faults in specific code modules, the fault data is also stored in our management database. New code and code changes are attributable to people. It is appropriate that we begin to collect data on exactly who is making changes to the code base. As each code element, subsystem, and system is tested, the code activity for the test suite can be recorded in the measurement database. We can know where the problems in the code are and how well we have tested for them. We know that each code module implements a specific design element. Each design element, in turn, implements a specific requirement. It is appropriate that we also manage these design and requirement specifications in our database. Each test case exercises a specific functional system requirement. Test cases should also be managed by our measurement system. Now, for the first time, we are in a position to begin the engineering and testing of our software systems. We will just have the beginnings of a primitive engineering measurement system.

Now begins the most important part of the entire measurement process. We are going to institutionalize the process of measurement process improvement. The more we really learn about software development processes, people, products, and environments, the more questions we will have for which we seek answers. That is the essence of science. Each new thing we learn will create a flurry of new questions. For example, software faults are clearly inserted into the code by developers for reasons that can be known. Some faults are because of the complexity of data structures. Other faults are attributable to the complexity of control flow. We should be able to measure the code base and determine where these types of faults are likely to be found by code module. If we cannot make good predictions of where faults might be found with the data we have at our disposal, then we can design experiments to find new metrics that will allow better fault prediction. We can then test and validate our new metric candidates. The software measurement tool can then be modified to incorporate the new validated metrics. This tool can be modified without impact to the measurement process. No one will know that a change has occurred. We have institutionalized the measurement process; it is part of the system.

Next, we might well observe that there are sources of unexplained variation among programmers with respect to certain types of software faults. We will now design experiments to understand why programmers make certain types of errors. The data, in turn, will permit us to assign developers to tasks where they can be most productive. In short, the measurement database allows us to manage our resources.

1.5 SUMMARY

It has often been said, quite incorrectly, that the steam engine ushered in the age of industry. It did not. The ruler, precision measurement tools, and manufacturing processes governed by precise measurement made the steam engine possible. The basic principles of the steam engine were available to Aristotle and Michelangelo. They just could not have crafted the devices to the tolerances necessary to make them work very well. Up until beginning of the industrial age and the Industrial Revolution, all machines were hand-built by craftsmen. A gunsmith lovingly crafted each rifle. The parts of his rifle were built by hand to work together; they were not interchangeable with parts from any other rifle made by him or any other gunsmith. In fact, the entire rifle could be crafted without a single measurement tool. The Industrial Revolution began when parts made by many different individuals could work interchangeably and when there were precise specifications (designs) for these parts. The beginning of the industrial age was also the end of the age of the craftsman.

The overwhelming majority of software development projects are staffed by craftsmen. Each module of code is handcrafted by a software developer. We cannot measure his or her efforts. We typically do not have any real specifications for the module thus crafted. And, it would be next to impossible to integrate this module in a similar system being crafted by another "codesmith." We will soon enter the industrial age of computer software development. It will be driven by the same force as the Industrial Revolution: engineering principles based on measurement technology.

A criticism of the great industrial society that we have built is that we have been homogenized. Every rifle manufactured on a single assembly line looks just like every other one produced by that assembly line. If they are of high quality, there will be very little variation in their composition, for that is one the central attributes of quality. In the good old days — and there is some real dispute about how good they were — each rifle had its own character. You could learn how to shoot with your rifle and then it became part of you. The main problem with this world of yesteryear was that if you bought a rifle from a good craftsman, you had a good chance of getting a fine rifle. On the other hand, if you bought a rifle from bad craftsman, it could kill you outright. Our current software development practices are very similar to this world of yesteryear.

At the core of each software development organization is a group of practiced and disciplined software craftsmen. Each of these craftsmen sits at his or her shop (cubicle), handcrafting his or her part of the *objet d'art*. Periodically, these craftsmen gather in the commons (meeting room) to talk about how the pieces they are crafting will fit together (design reviews). When each craftsman has finished his or her piece of the system, the pieces will be cobbled together to see what happens when electricity is put through it (first build). Those pieces that seem to cause the system to break will be tossed back to the offending craftsman, who will pound on them, file them some more, and sand them a bit. The pieces are then put together a second time to see if they work any better after their rework (second build). This process is repeated until the system seems to work acceptably well.

Stagecoaches were built in this manner. Clipper ships were built this way. Castles were built this way. Cathedrals were built this way. Jet aircraft are not built this way but the avionics that control the jet aircraft are built this way. Nuclear reactors are not built this way but the control systems for these nuclear reactors are built this way. We build very complex systems, the hardware of which is designed according to best engineering practices and we power these systems with software control systems that are hand-crafted like flintlock rifles. These systems are truly anachronisms. The time has come to incorporate best engineering practice into software development.

References

1. Juran, J.M., *Juran on Quality by Design: The New Steps for Planning Quality into Goods and Services,* Free Press, New York, 1992.

2. Deming, W.E., *Out of the Crisis,* MIT Press, Cambridge, MA, 2000.

3. Munson, J.C. and Coulter, N.S., "An Investigation of Program Specification Complexity," *Proceedings of the ACM Southeastern Regional Conference,* April 1988, p. 590–595.

Chapter 2
The Conduct of Scientific Investigations

Lemmingineering *n*: the process of engineering systems by blindly following techniques the masses are following without regard to the appropriateness of those techniques.

2.1 THE PRINCIPLES OF SCIENTIFIC INVESTIGATION

Engineering as a discipline has at its foundation the application of the principles of science to solve real problems in a real world. Empirical investigations serve to drive the engineering process. Structural engineers can design and build a good bridge because they understand the structural properties of the elements they will use to build the bridge. The structural properties of the materials used in bridge building were developed over years of measurement, testing, and analysis.

The engineering discipline presumes the application of an underlying science based on hypothesis, measurement, and experimentation. Software engineering is a very young discipline based on the tacit theoretical foundation of computer science. That software engineering is an engineering discipline is still an aspiration in part because computer science is not yet a science. We have yet to master the process of validating our theories of computation and software development in the laboratory.

The current best practice in software development appears to be software lemmingineering. We tend to follow the *experts* without ever asking if we want to go where this leader is taking us. We tell ourselves that if everybody else is taking a certain path, it must be the right way to go. However, we do not even ask if the leaders know where they are going. The path to our current state-of-the-art of software development is littered with examples of the application of lemmingineering methodology. Consider the example of computer-aided software engineering (CASE) tools. Not long ago, every software development organization had to have CASE tools or they were considered clearly out of the mainstream. There were major worldwide conferences on CASE tools. Everybody who was anybody was using CASE tools because everyone else was using them. What was missing was the empirical validation that CASE tools somehow enhanced the software development process or the products developed under CASE tools were superior to those that were not. The use of CASE tools just felt right. In addition, everyone was doing it. Thus, there must be some good in it.

2.2 MEASUREMENT

Despite the fact that the theoretical foundation for software measurement lies in measurement theory, both practitioners and researchers have largely ignored this fact. The result is that much published work in software measurement is theoretically flawed. Some of this material may even be quite misleading. Let us begin our inquiry into software measurement with a brief look at the notion of measurement.

Measurement is the process by which numbers or symbols are assigned to objects, either real or abstract, that we observe in our intellectual environment. These objects we refer to as entities. An example of a real object is a person (human being) or an automobile. An example of an abstract object is a sorting algorithm. Each *instance* of these objects has certain properties or attributes. The car in my driveway is an example of an instance of the entity automobile. Each instance of the entity automobile would have the attributes of manufacturer (Ford, Chevrolet, etc.), size (compact, mid-size, van, etc.), weight, horsepower, etc. Measurement is also a process for standardization whereby we can make statements of equivalence among objects of many different types.

The process of identifying the attributes of an abstract object, on the other hand, is not nearly so simple. This fact is regrettable, in that most of the objects we will have to deal with in software engineering are abstract objects (i.e., requirements specifications, design rules, computer programs, software processes). Most of us have little or no training in the determination of the properties (attributes) of abstract objects. Thus, it will be very difficult for us to measure these attributes.

Measurement, in the most general sense, is the mapping of numbers (symbols) to attributes of objects in accordance with some prescribed rule. The property of the entities that determines the mapping according to that rule is called a *magnitude*, the measurable attribute. The number assigned to a particular object by the mapping rule is called its *measure,* the amount or degree of its magnitude. The mapping rule will define both the magnitude and the measure. The mapping must preserve intuitive and empirical observations about the attributes and entities.

Not all of these mappings are without ambiguity. In earlier, more simple times, the attribute gender of a person would map into one of two categories (male or female), corresponding to the physical properties of the individual. With our new understanding of genetics, the world is not so simple. In addition to males and females, we also now recognize super-males with XYY chromosomes and super-females with XXX chromosomes. What is really interesting is that sometimes a complete understanding of these attributes is vital, such as in sporting events; while at other times, it is irrelevant, such as assigning genders to restroom facilities.

Very frequently among the practitioners of software measurement in software engineering, the following question is asked: "What software metrics should we be using?" Or, "What is the *best* metric to use?" Let us rephrase these questions in a slightly different context. Suppose we were to ask an automotive engineer, "What is the best measure for this car?" Or, "What are the metrics I should use for this car?" Such questions would seem foolish to the automotive engineer. The engineer would know that each automobile has multiple attributes, all of which are necessary to describe the automobile. Red might be our favorite color. We would probably not use this as a sole criterion in the purchase of an automobile. Ferraris come in red, as do Fiats. There are enormous differences between these two types of vehicles with respect to other attributes, such as cost and performance.

2.2.1 Primitive and Derived Measurements

There are basically two types of measurement that we might employ in the software engineering discipline: primitive measures and derived measures. A primitive measurement is one that presupposes no others. It is atomic. It measures a single identifiable attribute of an entity. A derived measurement is one that is obtained from primitive measures through numerical calculation, or possibly indirect observation.

In the field of software metrics, Maurice Halstead, a pioneer in the field of software measurement, identified four primitive measures of a program. He observed that program tokens (terminal symbols in the syntax of the programming language) could be grouped into one of two classes: operators or operands. From this observation he then identified four primitive measures of these operators and operands as follows:

1. η_1, the number of unique operators in the program
2. η_2, the number of unique operands in the program
3. N_1, the total operator count
4. N_2, the total operand count

From this set of metric primitives, he then went on to create a set of derived measures. A subset of these derived metrics is as follows:

$\eta = \eta_1 + \eta_2$, the vocabulary size of a program
$N = N_1 + N_2$, the program length

$V = N \log_2 \eta$, the program volume

$\hat{N} = \eta_1 \log_2 \eta_1 + \eta_2 \log_2 \eta_2$, the estimated program length

There are many more of these derived metrics. It would be a waste of good paper to list any more of them. It is not clear just precisely what program attributes they are actually measuring, nor did Halstead attempt to validate the constructs that these metrics purported to measure.

Yet another context for the concept of a derived measurement is the circumstance when we are unable to measure directly an attribute we wish to know the value of. A case in point is the determination of the weight of individual gas molecules. We cannot determine these directly, but we may do so by employing Avogadro's law: that equal volumes of all gases, at the same temperature and pressure, contain equal numbers of molecules. We can take a gas whose molecular weight is known, weigh a sample of this gas, and then weigh a sample of a gas of equal volume whose molecular weight is not known. We can then derive the weight of the unknown gas by multiplication.

The most important thing we must know about derived metrics is that we cannot add apples and oranges. A new metric simply cannot be derived from two or more simple metrics. We recognize this fact in several aspects of our daily life. We do not recognize this fact in our analysis of software engineering problems. Consider the case of the city of Gold Hill, Colorado. Outside the town there is a sign that reads:

Gold Hill	
Established	1859
Elevation	8463
Population	118
Total	10440

This is really a funny sign. It is obvious to us that the Total is meaningless. Now consider the following example from function point analysis.

Unadjusted Function Point Count	
Number of external input types	i
Number of external output types	o
Number of inquiries	e
Number of external files	p
Number of internal files	f
Total	$4 \times i + 5 \times o + 7 \times p + 10 \times f$

Apparently the folks in Gold Hill do not have a lock on humorous metrics.

2.2.2 Scales

Some measures are intrinsically qualitative in nature. They will cause the mapping of an entity into a set of mutually exclusive classes. Automobiles, for example, can be seen to have the manufacturer attribute. This attribute may have one of the distinct values of Ford, Toyota, Chrysler, etc. Other types of measures will result in the assignment of a number or quantity for that attribute. Some of these numerical assignments will simply allow us to order instances of each entity. Other numerical assignments will allow us to perform arithmetic on the measures.

A *scale* of measurement determines the actual assignment of the numbers and symbols by the rules. The term "scale" may be taken to be the measuring instrument or the standard of measurement. It determines what operations among the numbers (symbols) assigned in a measurement will yield results significant for the particular attribute being measured. There are essentially two classes of scales: scales of intensive (qualitative) and extensive (quantitative) measurement. Qualitative scales permit us to determine, at most, a degree of the relationship between two or more instances of an entity. Quantitative scales, on the other hand, permit us to answer questions of how much or how many.

2.2.2.1 Qualitative Measurement Scales. The *nominal scale* is one in which numbers (symbols) are assigned only as labels or names. The mappings on this scale are into mutually exclusive qualitative categories. An instance of the entity automobile may be perceived to belong to exactly one of the classes of automobile manufacturer. An instance of a human being will have the sexual property of male or female. Eye color and political affiliation are other examples of measures defined on a nominal scale.

Measures defined on nominal scales do not permit the use of arithmetic operators or relational operators. In this new age, one could get into serious trouble by presuming that males were in some sense better than females. Furthermore, the sum of two males is not a female. Sometimes, numbers will be used to represent this assignment. For example, we might let a variable $x_1 = 0$ represent the observation that a particular instance of the entity person is a male. Similarly, we might also let $x_2 = 1$ represents the observation that a particular instance of the same entity is a female. It would not be politically correct (nor accurate) for us to present the fact that $x_1 < x_2$.

Sometimes, these nominal scales lurk in the guises of numbers. In particular is the case of Social Security numbers. This personal attribute is strictly nominal. That someone has a Social Security number less than mine carries no essential information. Similarly, the numerical difference between two such numbers has no meaning. This fact is lost on many computer analysts and programmers who employ numerical conversions on these nominal data.

The *partially ordered scale* orders some relatively homogeneous subset of objects. The movie rating scale (G, PG-13, PG, R, and X) is an example of such a scale. The assignment of movies to each of these groups largely depends on preference dictated by cultural imperatives. In the United States, it is thought that children should be shielded from aspects of human sexuality. The exposure of gratuitous violence to these same children is not thought to be important. Other more pacific cultures might well accept human sexuality as quite normal and regard gratuitous violence as something to shield their children from. These people would rate the very same movies that we have classified to be X-rated as suitable for teenagers (PG-13) as long as these movies were free from violence. Similarly, the assignment of a person on the political scale of liberalism is very much a matter of perspective. A conservative politician to me might well be your view of a liberal renegade. It is also most unfortunate that this type of scale dominates the current standard for employee evaluation, the assessment of the worth of computer software, etc.

The *ordinal scale* provides for the numerical ordering of a set of objects, although this may be a weak ordering with the same number being assigned to two or more elements of the set. We generally associate this scale with the concept of ranking. With this scale it is possible to take a set of programs and rank them according to some criterion, such as cost, performance, or reliability. The ordinal scale allows us to use the set of relational operators ($<, \leq, =, \neq, \geq, >$) on the rank attributes of objects assigned values on an ordinal scale. Thus, it is possible to say that program A performs better than program B. Further, measures defined on this scale exhibit transitivity. Thus, if $A > B$, and $B > C$, then $A > C$.

What is lacking from the ordinal scale is some sense of the distance between objects of differing ranks. That is, if programmer A is the fifth ranked programmer in a company, programmer B is the sixth ranked programmer, and programmer C is the seventh ranked programmer, the differences between A and B may be inconsequentially small whereas the differences between B and C may be very large. If we are able to make such assertions that the differences between the sets of programmers are meaningful, then the scale is not just ordinal but constitutes an *ordered metric*. Not only are the objects ordered, but also the intervals between them are at least partially ordered.

Computer programmers can be assigned into classes of novice, programmer, lead programmer, and team leader. The presumption here is that a programmer at a given level can consistently perform a given programming task better than a programmer of lower rank. If we can establish that lead programmers consistently excel over programmers, whereas programmers generally excel over novices, then we are well on the way to establishing an ordered metric.

2.2.2.2 Quantitative Measurement Scales. The *interval scale* is a scale that provides equal intervals from some arbitrary numerical point on the scale. An example of such a scale is the Fahrenheit (or Centigrade) temperature scale. Neither of these scales has an absolute zero point. While there is a 0° point on the Fahrenheit scale, a negative temperature does not represent the loss of anything nor does a positive temperature represent a gain in anything.

Interval scales do make use of the arithmetic operators (+, −). If the high temperature today is 60° and yesterday's high was 50°, then I can assert with meaning that today it is 10° warmer than yesterday. As an aside, it is interesting to note that multiplicative relationships can be used on the sums (differences) of these same temperatures. Thus, the difference in temperature between 50° and 70° is twice as great as the difference between 50° and 60°.

The *ratio scale*, on the other hand, does have an absolute zero point. The multiplying and exponentiation operators (×, ÷, ↑) can be used with measures on this scale. It is also true that any of the relational operators and adding operators can also be used. A ratio scale, for example, can be used to define the amount of money in my bank account. In this case, there is real meaning to the statement that I have a −$50 in my account. I am over-drawn. I owe the bank $50. If I have a current balance of $500, then the bank owes me $500. Further, if someone else has $1000 in his or her account, then he or she has twice as much as I do. If another individual has $5000 in his account, he has an order of magnitude more money than I do.

It is interesting to note that as I drive to my home, a measure of *distance* may be obtained from those little mileage signposts on the road. All of these signposts are measured from the southwest point in my state. This measure of distance is defined on an interval scale. The only zero on this scale is a very long distance from my home. My *velocity* relative to my home will be defined on a ratio scale. As long as I am driving toward my house, this velocity will be positive. As soon as I begin to drive away from my house, this velocity will be negative. If I stop, it becomes zero.

2.3 MEASUREMENT ISSUES

It is pretty easy to get measurement data. However, it is relatively difficult to obtain accurate and precise measurement data. For every measurement activity, the errors of measurement must be carefully identified and controlled. From a basic engineering viewpoint, it will be impractical to obtain nearly perfect measurements in most cases. We only need to measure accurately enough so that the measurements do not induce functional problems in the task for which the measurements are necessary. To dress appropriately for today's weather, we only need to know the temperature outside (±2 to 3°C). For weather forecasting purposes, we might well need to know the temperature accurately (to within ±0.01°C). Very different measurement tools will be used to collect each of these measurements, a household thermometer being very much cheaper than the electronic version needed by the weather bureau.

2.3.1 Accuracy and Precision

There are two distinct issues that we must deal with in the measurement problem, both related to the fact that we will always be limited in our knowledge of the exact value that an attribute may have for each and every instantiation. Our measurements will only be as good as our measurement tools. Thus, the terms "accuracy" and "precision" are important to us. When we discuss the accuracy of a particular measurement, we will mean the closeness of that answer to the correct (and possibly unknowable) value. Precision, on the other hand, refers to the number of significant digits in our estimate for a population value. For example, the number 3.10473423 is a very precise estimate of the value of π; however, the number 3 is a much more accurate estimate. This very simple concept is lost on many practitioners of the black art of computer science. The literature in this area is replete with tables of very precise numbers. Little consideration, however, is given to the accuracy of these same values.

2.3.2 Measurement Error

There are many possible ways that our attempts to measure will be thwarted by Nature. It seems that there will always be a noise component in every signal provided by Nature. There are two classes of errors in measurement that we must understand: *methodological* errors and *propagation* errors. Methodological errors are a direct result of the noise component introduced by the method of collecting the measurements. Propagation errors are cumulative effects of error in measurement when accuracy suffers as result of repeated computation.

There are three distinct sources of methodological errors. First, there is the error that will be introduced by the measurement tool itself. The marks on an ordinary ruler, for example, are not exactly one millimeter apart, center to center. Further, the width of the marks may vary, causing us to misjudge proximity from one mark to another. Second, there are errors that are inherent in the method itself. Earlier, the value π was discussed. Any value of π that we use in a calculation will always represent an approximation.

A third source of methodological error is a modern one. Computers now perform all of our calculations. These computers can only store a fixed number of digits for any one calculation. If, for example, we have a computer that will store a 24-bit mantissa for floating point calculations, then this machine can precisely represent only $n\log_2 10 = 24$ or $n = 7$ decimal digits. The circumstance may arise that we have a measurement that is precise to ten decimal digits; but as soon as we store this on our hypothetical computer, we will now only have a measurement with seven digits of precision. The imprecision here is due to a type of rounding, namely truncation. Sometimes we seek to capture a more accurate value through symmetric rounding by adding the decimal value 5 to the least significant decimal digit before the truncation.

Measurement without error will occur only in an ideal world. As mortals, we do not live in this ideal world. Thus, when we perform measurements, we must understand and want to know just exactly how much error there will be. We see that our measurement x^* is the sum of two terms, as follows: $x^* = x + \varepsilon$, where x is the actual value of the variable as it exists in nature, and ε is the sum of the error components or the *absolute* error. Many times, it will be useful to talk about the *relative* error introduced by the measurements. This relative error is ε/x^*. For our purposes, the relative error will be a more useful index, in that it shows us how far we have actually deviated from the actual or true value. A relative error of 1 in 100 is far worse than a relative error of 1 in 10,000. From another perspective, if we had an absolute error of measurement of 0.01, then for measurement on the order of 100,000 this would not be a problem. If, however, our measurements were on the order of 0.001, an absolute error of 0.01 would be devastating.

It is also possible to characterize relative error in terms of x if we are assured that ε is substantially less than x, as follows:

$$\frac{\varepsilon}{x^*} = \frac{\varepsilon}{x+\varepsilon} = \frac{\varepsilon}{x}\left(\frac{x}{x+\varepsilon}\right)$$

Observe that:

$$\frac{x}{x+\varepsilon} = 1 - \frac{\varepsilon_x}{x} + \left(\frac{\varepsilon_x}{x}\right)^2 - \cdots$$

Then:

$$\frac{\varepsilon}{x^*} = \frac{\varepsilon}{x} + O\left(\frac{\varepsilon}{x}\right)^2$$

which is to say that $\varepsilon/x^* \approx \varepsilon/x$ when the relative error squared is negligible.

It is most important to understand that the measurement is an estimate of a value known only to Nature. We must factor this into our thinking whenever we engage in the act of measurement.

2.4 MEASUREMENT STANDARDS

When setting out to measure something, we must have some tool with which to perform the measurement. If we want to measure the length of an object, then we will seek out a ruler or a tape measure. The tool we use for the measurement of length is a copy of a *standard* measure of length, an instrument maintained by a bureau of standards somewhere. The whole purpose of the standard unit of measure is that all of us who have copies of this standard can measure the length attribute of items in our environment. We can then communicate with each other about our measurements and have these communications be meaningful. If a colleague were to send us the measurements of his desk in centimeters, we would have an excellent idea of the size of this desk. Further, if he were to measure all of the components of the desk and transmit those measurements to us, then we could build a replica of his desk. If, on the other hand, we maintained our own ideas of what a centimeter is according to our own standard, then our replica desk would be an inaccurate representation of the original. It would certainly be correctly proportioned, but not a faithful reproduction. Science depends on this ability to measure and report our observations according to a standard.

Sometimes, an apparent standard must be reevaluated. We may think that we have a standard defined, only to find that it is fraught with ambiguity. Consider the rule for mapping people into categories of sex. It seems so obvious. However, in recent Olympic Games, it became apparent that there were some very masculine-looking women competing in the women's athletic events. Visual appearances are not enough to separate individuals into two mutually exclusive sets of sexuality. We find, by examining the chromosomes of the broad spectrum of individuals in our society, that there are males, females, super-females, and super-males. Even more confusing is the fact that we can find that Nature has assigned male genitalia to chromosomal females. Although it seems too obvious at the outset, developing a standard for measuring the sexuality of humans is a very complex issue.

Another interesting measurement problem is that of eye color. The color of my eyes may map into any one of several categories, depending on the observer. They are reported on my driver's license as hazel color. There is, however, no referent standard for hazel eye color. Hazel, it turns out, is a transition color between blue and green. We are left with the inevitable questions as to just when are not quite blue eyes to be classified as hazel eyes. If it were indeed imperative that the color of my eyes be reported exactly, we could report with some degree of accuracy the average wavelength in angstroms of a reflected white light from the iris of my eyes.

In the world of the physical sciences, if it becomes necessary to obtain an accurate measurement of the length of a meter, a standard meter is maintained by the National Institute of Standards and Technology. There is no such measurement body for the measurement of software. Anyone who wishes can construct a metric analyzer and go into the measurement business. The problem with this unstructured approach is that there are just about as many ways to measure a single program as there are tools. Each measurement derived by each tool can be slightly different. Within a fixed application, this circumstance may be not be a problem. This environment, however, is not conducive to the practice of science. When research results are reported in the literature based on these multiple tools, seldom, if ever, is it possible to replicate precisely the results observed by one experimenter.

A ready example of this standards issue can be found in the enumeration of operators and operands in a language such as C. Consider the case in which a call is made to a function `foobar` that will return a value of `float`. On the one hand, the call to `foobar` looks like an operand. We could count it as an operand. On the other hand, `foobar` represents an action on its own operands (arguments). In this case we could count `foobar` as an operator. The truth of the matter is that it is both. When we encounter `foobar`, we should increase the operand count by one and the operator count by one. In that we do not have standard definitions of just how these and other operands and operators should be enumerated in C, the measurements produced by any C metric analyzer must be regarded as imprecise.

Another problem in the enumeration of Halstead's unique operator count, η_1 in the analysis of C language programs, for example, can be found in the enumeration of the "+" operator.[1] Generally, when this token is found for the first time, the unique operator count is increased by one and subsequent occurrences of "+" are ignored. The C language, however, permits operator overloading. Thus, the single operator "+" can be used in several different semantic contexts. It can have integer operands, in which case it represents integer addition. It can have real operands, in which case it is a floating point addition operation. It can have two operands as a binary operator and it can have one operand as a unary operator. Each semantically different context for the "+" operator must be enumerated separately. The failure to account for operator overloading will obscure dramatic differences between program modules. From a statistical perspective, the variance in η_1 among program modules will be artificially small. Modules may appear to be very similar when, in fact, they are very different.

Yet another measurement problem is created in different styles of programmers. Just as operators can be overloaded, operands can also be overloaded. In the good old days, FORTRAN programmers were very concerned about the space that their programs would occupy. There was great incentive to define a minimum of identifiers and use them for everything. A single integer, `I`, might be used as a loop counter, then as a variable in which a summation is computed, and then again as a loop counter. This single integer has been overloaded. It has served many semantically different functions. On the other hand, we can conceive of a programmer trained in a COBOL environment. In this environment, all program variables tend to be tightly controlled as to function. A single variable will always be used in the same context. In this case, there will be little or no operand overloading. If these two programmers set about to write the identical program in a common language such as C, it is possible that their programs would differ only in the operand counts for the programs. Thus, the net effect of operand overloading is that an external source of variation is introduced into the measurement process. This is the variation due to differences in the programmers, not in differences intrinsic in the problem to be solved. If we do not control for the effect of these differences among programmers in our efforts to model with metrics, then this operand overloading problem will be present in the form of pure noise in the model.

2.4.1 Sources of Noise in the Measurement Data

When we wish to quantify a particular attribute for a member of a population, we, for the most part, never really know the true value of this attribute. Only Nature knows the true value of the attribute. The very best that a metrician can provide is an estimate of this value. Nature will have taken the true value and added in additional information in the form of noise. Suppose, for example, that we wish to know the height of Mabel, a person on our software development staff. The more we study this simple problem, the more improbable the measurement task seems. First of all, Mabel is a living organism. The physical composition of her body is changing continually. This means that her height is really changing continually as well. If and when we actually get a measurement on this attribute, it will represent the height attribute in Mabel only at an instant in time. Unfortunately, Nature is also acting to disguise Mabel's height. Mabel's height will vary as a function of the curvature of her spine, among other things. The curvature of Mabel's spine may well have to do with her attitude. Today, Mabel may be depressed. Her shoulders sag. She stands slumped over. This may cause us to measure her to be at least one centimeter shorter than if she were feeling chipper. Nature knows that Mabel is depressed. Nature does not share this information with us. We can never really know Mabel's real height because of this lack of candor on the part of Nature. The very best we can do is to get a viable estimate of this height. We should be smart enough to ask the right question, which is, "What kind of accuracy do we need for our estimate of Mabel's height?"

The information that Nature withholds or adds to our measurement is called noise. Sometimes, the noise component will be sufficiently large as to obscure the attribute that we really wish to measure. It is not difficult to produce an example of this degree of noise contribution. Suppose we want to measure the time it takes for a developer to implement a given design element in a predetermined programming language. To get this measurement, most development organizations simply start the clock running when the developer is tasked with the assignment and stop the clock when he or she has completed the task. The difference between the two clock values is taken to be the development time. The actual development time will be a small fraction of the time reported by the developer. Let us partition the time that actually elapsed into realistic components.

40 percent surfing the Web
10 percent reading and responding to personal e-mail
20 percent communicating with peers in chat rooms on the Web
 5 percent restroom breaks
 2 percent discussion of the latest Dilbert comic strip with colleagues
 5 percent informal inter- and intracube conversation
 5 percent design review meetings
 2 percent staff meetings
11 percent coding

In this case, the signal component of the measurement of development time with respect to this one person consists of 82 percent nonproductive time or noise. What is even worse is that the distribution of activity for this person may well vary from this base level. Given a personal crisis in his or her life, the actual coding time may well fall below 11 percent.

In this not-so-extreme example, we think we are measuring programmer productivity. What we are actually measuring is the recreational use of computer and office facilities by the programmer. If we really want a good estimate of programmer productivity, we will first have to devise a good way of measuring it. It should be quite clear that simply looking at the programmer's reported hours is a very unsatisfactory measure of productivity. These data are almost pure noise. Conclusions based on those noisy data will be equally worthless. We must first devise a means of extracting the signal component from the noise component. Alternatively, we might elect to constrain the noise component.

First, consider extracting the actual number of hours that a programmer is on task. The objective here is to extract the signal component from the noise through the use of some type of filter. Perhaps the simplest filter would be to install a closed-circuit television camera and measure — unobtrusively — exactly what the programmer was doing during the time he was actually occupying his office. We could then monitor the activity of this person and, over time, develop a measure of central tendency (such as the average) and an assessment of the variability of this estimate of the time spent in programming activity.

The second alternative is to move to constrain nonprogramming activity on the part of the programmer. The first step would be to ban all Internet Web access and severely restrict the use of the company intranet. The second step would be to ban all chat room activity. The third step would be to restrict e-mail to the local intranet and then only for company business. The fourth step would be to provide close supervision to ensure that conversations with colleagues were restricted to programming activity. These are very draconian measures. They would, however, dramatically increase the signal component in the reporting of employee programming effort.

Many companies collect enormous amounts of "metrics" data. These data are very similar in content to the programmer productivity example above. They are essentially of no value because the metrics are an end in and of themselves. There is astonishingly little interest in how the data are collected, what the possible source of noise in the data might be, or how reliable the data collection process might be. The numbers appear to speak for themselves. Unless some real provisions are made prior to the collection of the data for the control of extraneous sources of variation, it will be reasonable to assume that the data are essentially worthless. Management decisions based on these data will be misguided and equally worthless.

2.4.2 Reproducibility of Measurements

The essence of scientific reporting is the principle of reproducibility of experimental results. Results of experiments must be reported precisely and accurately. The defining standard for this level of reporting is that another investigator should be able to repeat the study and get absolutely the same result that was reported. There is a real paucity of such reporting standards in the computer literature. For example, the lines of code (LOC) metric is commonly used in the literature as a measure of program size. We might read an article about an experimental system consisting of 100 KLOC of C code. When we begin to analyze this result, some questions come to mind immediately. First, the prefix "K" could mean 1000 LOC. We very frequently use this same prefix "K" to mean 1024 or 2^{10} units. Did the author of the study count 100,000 LOC or did he count 102,400 LOC? Now we turn our attention to exactly how the LOC was enumerated. In the UNIX environment, a logical record (line) is a string delimited by a <CR>. To enumerate LOC, did the author simply count <CR>s for a file containing all of the C code? What about blank lines or comment lines? We could easily opt to report only the actual lines of C code, not including blank lines or comment lines. The main point is that our reporting that we examined a C software system consisting of 100 KLOC gives the reader little reliable information on the size of the system to which we are referring.

Not to belabor the point, but the term "bug" is commonly used in reporting problems encountered in the development of a system. For example, an author might report that 1000 bugs were found and removed in the development of a system. The problem with this statement is that we do not know what a bug means to him. One person's bug is another's lunch. To an Australian aborigine, a grub (bug) is a very tasty treat and an important source of protein. In an abstract sense, bugs found in a program are neither delicious nor nutritious. There is no formal or standard definition of a bug. A bug could be a problem in a requirements specification, a problem in the code, or a very elusive code failure at runtime. We do not know what a bug meant to the author who reported finding 1000 of them. Therefore, we have learned nothing useful from a scientific standpoint in reading about a system that contains 1000 undefined "bugs."

Equally loose standards apply in the personnel area as well. We might read in the literature that a particular system took 10,000 staff hours to develop. We learn even less from this statement. Some basic questions come to mind immediately, to wit:

- Did the 10,000 hours include only programming staff hours?
- Was the requirements specification factored into the 10,000 hours?
- Was the administrative burden factored into the hours, or are we looking at just those staff hours of people actually doing the work?
- What level of granularity of measurement was involved? Did an employee's time get aggregated at a 40-hour workweek, or did the employee actually track the exact time spent working on the project?

The main point here is that learning that a project took 10,000 staff hours to complete provides very little or no useful data about any similar work that we might be performing. We simply do not know what a staff hour means to the author of the study, nor are we typically informed of this in the literature.

Much of the basic work in software reliability is of no scientific value whatsoever. There are two fundamental reasons that this literature is flawed. First, the basic unit of interest to the software reliability community is the failure of a system. Unfortunately, we are never told just what a failure is. There is no standard for reporting failure events. In most cases, a failure is simply the catastrophic collapse of a functioning software system. This is not necessarily a good basis for the concept of a failure. A system could easily return an erroneous result and keep executing, quite happily, and producing consistently bad data. There is simply no standard definition for the software failure event. Therefore, when someone reports a failure in the literature, we do not know what this means to him. Second, much of the literature is based on a measure of time between failure events. There are two problems here. First, if we can not agree on what a failure is in the first place, then it will be somewhat difficult to recognize when one occurs. Second, in very complex modern software systems, a failure can occur many days before it has destroyed enough of the user's files or transactions to be made manifest and counted. Thus, the measure of "time between failure" really has little or no scientific validity.

2.5 PRINCIPLES OF EXPERIMENTATION

Much of what we *know* about the software development process is based on invalid or incomplete information. It is not surprising that we build unreliable and insecure software systems. We know very little about what we will need to know to improve our software development process. Our entire focus at this stage in the evolution of software development should be on research and experimentation. We are going to have to build a scientific basis for software development technology. The main driver for this discovery process will be the measurement methodology. Our experiments will be very simple but our focus on data collection methodology will be intense.

To understand how quality software might be developed, we must first learn to identify the possible sources of variation in this development. Operational definitions of processes and products must be carefully constructed in a manner that will permit accurate and reliable measurements. Levels of quantification and the quality of measurement processes must be carefully understood. In the development of a new field of software measurement, we must learn how to emulate the conduct of inquiry of those physical, natural, and social sciences that have been around for many years. Software development processes very closely resemble the field of alchemy, the precursor to the science of chemistry. One of the guiding objectives of the typical alchemist was the painless conversion of lead to gold. If they could but find the magic formula for this transformation, they could be wealthy people. Current software development practices are hilariously close to this same pursuit. If we can but pass our source code and high-level designs through a magic filter, then we can finally realize the "gold" of maintainable and fault-free code. The problem is one of finding the right magic. We should know by now that there is no magic. There is no real substitute for hard work. It is very hard work to lose weight. It requires substantial discipline and restraint. It is far easier to search for a pill or magic elixir that will substitute for discipline and willpower.

We would like to pull back from the wild enthusiasm of unstructured search for gold and begin to learn from the history of the origins of other sciences. The conduct of our inquiry will thus be constrained to two fairly common approaches to scientific investigation: *ex post facto* and *experimental*. What little structured inquiry that does exist in the fields of computer science and software engineering is generally governed by the *ex post facto* approach. In this method of inquiry, it is customary to compare two known software development techniques with respect to some characteristic. For example, we might compare an object-oriented (O-O) programming approach with a traditional non-object-oriented approach to a software development scenario. If we were to find that the O-O method yielded a significant difference between these two approaches with regard to the maintainability of the resulting software, this evidence would then be used to support our conclusion that the O-O method of software development is in some sense superior to traditional software development practices.

Much of the research literature in support of the *cleanroom* software development method is *ex post facto* research. The salient feature of *ex post facto* research is that we are obliged to analyze data that already existed *before* we ask the research question. Little or no effort will have been made to control extraneous and possibly quite relevant sources of variation in the data. The one thing that can certainly be said about the cleanroom procedure is that it is quite labor intensive in the early phases of the life cycle. It is quite possible, for example, that software generated by the cleanroom technique has fewer faults than other code only because of the intensity of the focus on the problem at a very early stage. Perhaps any other arbitrary *ad hoc* software development technique would do equally well if a similar investment of time were made in the initial life cycle using this new technique. We just do not know. We do not know because the necessary experiments with scientific controls have not been used to test this hypothesis.

The paradigm for experimental research is very different. We will perform an experiment to collect data that is central to the questions we wish to answer. In formulating an experiment, we will attempt to identify all of the sources of variation in a set of variables that we will *manipulate* during the experiment and a set of variables that we will *control* during the experiment. If we have designed a good experiment, the variations that occur in the manipulated variables will be attributable to the effect of the experiment. Extraneous influences on these variables are carefully controlled. The data we collect for the experiment will be generated only after we have asked the question. Those data are like chewing gum; they can be used once and only once. They have been created for the purposes of a single experiment and have no real value outside the context of that experiment. Once we have completed the experiment and analyzed the data, they should be discarded. We have gotten the good out of it.

As a simple example of experimental conduct of inquiry, consider the possibility that there are measurable differences between classes of programmers. Specifically, we wish to know whether there is a gender difference between male and female programmers. An *ex post facto* approach to this question would allow us to look at our existing database to see what we could find there that might answer this question. We would find, for example, data on the productivity of each of our programmers as measured by the number of lines of code they contributed to each project. We could then split these observations into a set of values for the male programmers and the set for female programmers. The literature is replete with such studies. It is quite possible that our staff of female programmers has been recently hired due to a push from the Equal Employment Opportunity Commission. This being the case, when we examine the differences between female and male programmers, we will certainly learn that the male programmers are more productive. What we are really measuring by analyzing the existing productivity data is differences in programmer tenure. Most of the females are recent hires; they are novices. The males, as a group, have been around much longer; we would expect them to be more productive.

2.5.1 Hypothesis Formulation

The conduct of scientific inquiry is an iterative process. At the heart of this process is a theory that we think will help us explain our universe. To test the validity of our theory, we will conduct a series of experiments to test various aspects of the theory. Each experiment will test a discrete component of the theory. The experiment begins with the formulation of a hypothesis. Nature has the knowledge to do real good software development. She will disclose these secrets to us through a guessing game. The way this guessing game works is as follows:

1. Watch Nature at work.
2. Identify a discrete process in Nature that we would like to explain.
3. Make an educated guess as to what Nature is up to.
4. Formulate a hypothesis about how and why this process acts the way it does.
5. Conduct an experiment to test the hypothesis.
6. Accept or reject the hypothesis.
7. If we accept the hypothesis, it then becomes a *fact* or a *law*.
8. Revise our notion of how Nature works.
9. Go to Step 1.

Research, then, is an iterative process. There is no end to the process. The absolutely most important aspect to the research process is that we learn to listen to Nature. Hypotheses are not sacred cows. The very worst thing that we could do is to try proving our hypotheses correct. Hypotheses are trial balloons. They are conjectures. They may be wrong.

2.5.2 Hypothesis Testing

Each hypothesis that we formulate must be tested for validity. That is what an experiment is designed to do. There are two possible outcomes for each experiment. First, we can find that the data suggest that our hypothesis is correct. In this case, the hypothesis is now no longer conjectural; it is a fact or a law. Subsequent hypotheses will have as their foundation this new law.

There is a tradition among statisticians that we couch our hypotheses in negative terms. Instead of stating that there will be an observable treatment effect between an experimental and a control group, a null hypothesis will be used instead. In this sense, the null hypothesis, represented as H_0, will state that there is no observable difference between a treatment group and a control group for the experiment. If we conduct the experiment and find this to be the case, we will accept the null hypothesis, H_0. If, on the other hand, we do find a significant difference between the control and the treatment group in our experiment, we will reject H_0 in favor of the alternate hypothesis H_1, which says that there is a significant difference between the experimental and treatment groups.

Hypothesis formulation is usually not a problem in the conduct of scientific inquiry. Once the research pump is primed by the first experiment, new hypotheses flow quite naturally from the experiment. It is appropriate to think of an experiment not in terms of closure but rather in terms of opening a research area. Generally, a successful experiment will yield far more questions than answers. Essentially, the more we learn, the more we will understand how little we really know. The real problem in the experimental process is the actual test of the hypothesis. Many times, the effects we are trying to assess are tenuous. The signal component will be well disguised in the noise. Statistics will be a tool that we will use to make decisions on outcomes based on the uncertainty of signal recognition.

2.5.3 Type I and Type II Errors

When conducting an experiment, we are really playing a two-person, zero sum game with Nature. Nature knows *a priori* what the outcome of our experiment will be. We do not. From Nature's point of view there are two states for our experiment: either H_0 is true or it is false. We, on the other hand, can either accept H_0 as a result of our experimental observations or we can reject this hypothesis. There are two ways that we can get the right result. If H_0 is false and we choose to reject this hypothesis, then we will have a correct result. Also, if H_0 is true and we choose to accept this hypothesis, then we will again have a correct experimental outcome. There are two different ways that we can arrive at exactly the wrong conclusion. If H_0 is known by Nature to be true and we reject H_0, then we will have committed a Type I error. If, on the other hand, H_0 is false and we accept H_0, then we will have made a Type II experimental error. These experimental outcomes are summarized in Exhibit 1.

Exhibit 1. The Experimental Paradigm

	H_0 True	H_0 False
Reject H_0	Type I error	Correct decision
Accept H_0	Correct decision	Type II error

Type I and Type II errors are not equivalent. In most circumstances, we would much rather make a Type II error than a Type I error. In making a Type II error, we will simply assume that there is no experimental effect when Nature knows that there really is. The implications of the Type I error are much greater. Nature knows that there is no experimental effect of our treatment. We will learn, from our experiment, quite incorrectly that there is an experimental effect. We will base our future actions on this conclusion and cause harm as a result. The consequences of such a decision in a safety-critical application can be great. If, for example, a new drug is being tested to treat a particularly virulent form of cancer, H_0 will state that there is no significant drug effect while H_1 represents the alternate hypothesis that there is. If a Type I error is made, H_0 will be rejected in favor of the alternate hypothesis. Nature knows that the drug is ineffective but the experiment has shown that it will have a significant effect as a cancer treatment. Based on this experimental evidence, drug companies will market the drug as a successful cancer-treating agent, which it is not, and many cancer patients will be treated with a drug that has no effect. Had a Type II error been made in the same experiment, a drug that had potential as a cancer treatment would be eliminated from consideration by the experiment. This is a far more conservative strategy.

2.5.4 Design of Experiments

The design of experiments is a very complicated and involved process. It can only be performed by statisticians who have had substantial training in the area. It would never occur to us individually to try to remove our own appendix. It takes surgeons a very long time to learn how to do surgery. One cannot simply read a book and go to work with a knife to extract appendixes, or kidneys, or whatever. It should be equally clear that the design of experiments should be left to someone who has been trained to do this work. What we need to know most about the design of experiments is that only professionals should perform this work. If you select a good surgeon for your surgery, your chances of survival are enhanced. If you find a good statistician, your chances for doing good science will improve as well.

We live in a very complex, multivariate world. There is no way in the world that a couple of paragraphs in this or any other text could begin to explain the complexities of the design of software experiments. It is very important to understand our own limitations. It is equally important that we can recognize the need for professional help in our conduct of inquiry. The consequences of making bad decisions in software development are becoming dire. As more safety-critical systems using embedded software systems are being developed, the more important it is that we understand exactly what it is we are about when developing the software for these systems.

The most important thing to know about the design of experiments it that this activity must be performed *before* the data are collected — not afterward. Once we have formulated our hypothesis, then and only then will we seek the aid of a statistician to help design our experiment.

2.5.5 Data Browsing: *Ex post facto* Research

The most prevalent form of investigation in software engineering and in computer science is *ex post facto* analysis. In this case, data are analyzed after they have been collected, the collection generally being done by someone else. We do not have precise knowledge about the circumstances of data collection, either in regard to validity or reliability. This form of research is tantamount to beating the data with a statistical stick. If you beat it hard enough, you are almost certain to find that for which you are looking. This, of course, was a guiding principle behind the Spanish Inquisition. The unfortunate subjects of the inquisition were beaten and tortured until they were willing to say whatever was necessary to end their misery. Exactly the same principle drives *ex post facto* investigations. Modern statistical software packages in the hands of inadequately trained researchers become instruments for data torture. These statistics packages should be treated like a surgeon's instruments. They should only be used by people with the necessary training in statistics. It is far too easy to torture the data with these tools until the data scream to validate our favorite hypothesis.

There is, however, a role for *ex post facto* investigation. It is not a scientific one. It is an intuitive one. While it would be very bad form for *ex post facto* data to be analyzed and reported as scientific evidence, these same data will disclose their intrinsic sources of variation. These data can be of real value in the formulation of a solid hypothesis for subsequent experimentation. So very much of science hinges on the emergent event and intuition. *Ex post facto* data can be very useful for data exploration. There are a host of statistical techniques, such as factor analysis, that can disclose some very interesting interactions among the sources of variation in the data. We will use the insights provided by these techniques to guide our scientific intuition.

We must learn to treat experimental data as if they were very fragile. They can be used once and only once and must then be discarded. In the normal course of conducting an experimental inquiry, a hypothesis will be formulated, an experiment will be designed, the experiment will be conducted, and the data will be collected. Finally, the data will be analyzed only in the context of the specified experimental design. This experimental design will be completely specified before the data are collected. The analysis of the data specified by the experimental design will suck all of the juice out of the data. There will be nothing of value left in the data once they are analyzed.

Finally, we would never consider using data for our science that we did not personally collect. We just do not know where these data have been or with whom they have been. It would be very unsafe science to consort with data of uncertain origin.

References

1. Halstead, M.H., *Elements of Software Science*, Elsevier, New York, 1977.

Chapter 3
Measuring Software Development

3.1 MEASUREMENT DOMAINS

The ultimate focus of software engineering measurement will be on the software product, the source code program itself. The actual program *product* is, however, very strongly influenced by the software engineering *process* used to created it; the *people* involved in the specification, design, coding, and testing of the product; and the *environment* in which those people and processes were operating. It will be our task to develop measurement methodologies for each of these measurement domains.

The first and most important realization that we must come to is that we are working with a multivariate problem. There is no single best measure of a program. There is no single best measure of a requirements analysis. There is no single best measure of a software process.

Measurement of software systems is a multivariate problem. To characterize any of the products, people, processes, or environments, we will have to measure a number of attributes simultaneously. For example, consider the case of two programs. Program A has 100 lines of code; Program B has 500 lines of code. On the surface, it would appear that Program B is the more complex of the two because it is exactly five times longer than Program A. Now let us measure the if statement complexity of these two programs. We discover that Program A has an if statement complexity of 20, whereas Program B has an if statement complexity of 8. This means that there are many more distinct paths in Program A than in Program B. In this circumstance, Program A would be considered by most software developers to be far more complex than Program B.

Now suppose that we measure the number of cycles in the control flow graph representation of both programs. This count will correspond directly to the number of loops in the programming language of both programs. Under this count let us suppose that there are eight such loops in Program B and none in Program A. The numerical relationship between the two programs is now not so clear. It is generally such circumstances that cause software developers to seek to simplify their world. They now seek to choose one of the three measures of the program as being the *best* metric. This is somewhat like trying to find the best metric for a person. People have many attributes. We must understand them all in order to represent the person from whom these metrics are drawn. People are short and tall, smart and dull, thin and heavy, light and dark; but people are none of these one at a time. People have each of these attributes at once. There are multiple simultaneous attributes for people and there are multiple simultaneous attributes for programs. We would not think to characterize a person by a single attribute, nor should we try to characterize a program by a single attribute.

Perhaps one of the most destructive notions ever created was that the software development process was an art. We see continual reference to the "art of programming" or the "art of software testing." For there to emerge a real discipline of software engineering, there must be a science of programming, a science of design, and a science of testing. One of the basic principles of science is that a theory can be validated empirically through the scientific method. A hypothesis is formulated based on theoretical considerations. An experiment can be designed to test the hypothesis. Measurements are taken on the phenomenon whose existence (nonexistence) is being postulated. The measurements are analyzed. The hypothesis is accepted or rejected. The theory is thus validated or invalidated. The operant term in this process is the concept of measurement. For there to be a science, there must be measurement.

There are several tangible products of the software development process. The software development process begins with the software requirements specification (SRS). This SRS is the leading indicator of the product that is to be built. There are many measurable attributes of the SRS that can be identified.[1] The next physical product in the evolving software system is the software design. This design may take many different forms. It can be a set of design specifications on printed paper, a set of files as output from a CASE tool, or a high-level source document in a program design language. After the design details of the program have been fleshed out, the source code representing this design is then constructed. Perhaps it is worth noting here that there is not just one set of source code. A source code program will continually evolve over its lifetime. At the point that it stops evolving, it will be retired. Last, but certainly not least among the potentially measurable software products, is the set of software system documentation. These products are tangible objects. Their measurement is fairly well defined.

From the standpoint of the software development process we would like to begin our science by identifying those attributes for which valid and reliable measures can be defined. We will learn to treat with great suspicion those concepts that do not lend themselves to measurement. If we carefully examine the circumstances of software development, we can construct a taxonomy of measurable software attributes that fall into four basic categories as follows: *people* attributes, *process* attributes, *product* attributes, and *environment* attributes. We can define metrics on specific properties within each of these attribute domains.

In the initial stages of the development of a software measurement program, the emphasis should not be on gathering data from a large number of metrics from each of the four measurement domains. Instead, the focus should be on the measurement processes.

3.1.1 People Metrics

We very often forget or most certainly suppress the fact that computer software is designed and built by people. We seldom, if ever, mention this fact in our undergraduate and graduate computer science curricula. Computer programs have algorithms and data structures. Somehow these algorithms and data structures are scrunched together and computer programs happen. Anyone who has ever taught programming courses realizes that there are an astonishing number of different ways to solve the same problem using different algorithms and different data structures. Some students can find the essence of the problem and produce very elegant, simple programs. Other students seem determined to make a mountain out of a molehill. They produce hundreds of lines of labyrinthine logic whose real functionality may never be known but seems to produce the required result. Very simply put, people design and develop programs. If you want to understand the software development process, it is vital to understand the people performing the work.

Measuring people is one of the most important things we can learn to do in understanding the software development process, and it is also the most difficult. With the exception of a brief excursion into this arena in Chapter 4, we will not devote further attention to measuring people in this book. Measuring people is a tar pit. It will trap the unwary, the novices, and suck them down into certain doom. As much as we would like to know about how our developers function, we must learn to walk before we can run. People metrics require very special knowledge about how people work and what makes them tick. The typical software practitioner simply does not have the educational background in psychology or sociology to attempt this very difficult feat.

A little story is in order here. Sometime in the past we were invited into a software development organization at the XYZ Company to work with its development staff to build a model for mapping from software code complexity measures to software faults. In general, this is a fairly easy task. A very small set of valid software metrics can reasonably account for more than 70 percent of the observed variation in recorded software faults.

When we attempted to replicate this result at the XYZ Company, we could only account for about 20 percent of the variation in the fault data with the canonical software metrics, a most unusual result. A careful inspection of the fault data appeared to suggest that there were substantial differences in how faults were reported by different developers. Some seemed to have far fewer faults than others. Also, the fault rates did not seem to correlate with the tenure of the developers. Sometimes, novices have a much greater fault rate than do more experienced developers.

It became clear that there were real differences among the developers on the rate at which they were reporting faults. In this case, the developers themselves were an uncontrolled source of variation in the modeling problem. The noise they created simply obscured the relationship between the fault data and the software metric data. To control for the constant differences among the development staff in their reporting rates, simple dummy variates were introduced into the model for each developer, save one. (It is not important to understand just what a dummy variate is at this point.) A model was then constructed using the dummy variates and, lo and behold, we were then able to account for the traditional 70 percent variation in software fault data. The coefficients of the dummy variates, in essence, represented the constant difference in reporting rate of each developer.

The results of the research were presented to a committee of software development managers for the project that was being studied. The stated objective of this meeting was to work to achieve a better reporting method for software faults so that we could get better measurement data for software faults. During the course of the meeting, several of the managers wanted to know why the model was so complex and what the individual elements of the model were. When the coefficients of the dummy variates were presented, we suggested that these coefficients, in fact, represent the differences in reporting rates among the developers. The managers then understood that there were vast differences in the rates that the developers were reporting. Some, it was clear, seldom reported problems in their code.

The developers then wanted to know the name of the most egregious violator, the person with the highest coefficient. We made the mistake of sharing this information with the group. It was Sally M. They then sent someone to get Sally M so that they could discuss this with her. When Sally came into the room, a kangaroo court of managers was convened to discuss Sally's failure to report software faults. A conviction was soon forthcoming from this impromptu court. Sally flew into a towering rage and allowed she knew very well that the managers were factoring the fault data into their annual evaluations. Those programmers who reported faults honestly were penalized for their honesty. After some further discussions among the managers, Sally then allowed that she no longer wished to work for the XYZ Company. Sally then left the room to clean out her desk, and the managers continued their discussion. Sally was one of their best software engineers. She had been with the company for years and had an enormous number of implicit software requirements stored in her head for projects on which she had worked. Her loss to the XYZ Company was going to have serious repercussions. The managers now looked for the cause of the problem. It was decided then and there that everything had been just fine until we created the problem. We were asked to surrender our security badges and never darken the halls of the XYZ Company again.

Here was a very classic case in which the managers learned the wrong thing from the data. The wide variation in the reporting rates was not a people metric; it was, in fact, a measure of the failure of a software process. There was a software fault reporting process in place but there was no clear standard for the reporting process. Further, there was no audit function in place to ensure that all faults were reported and that they were reported in the same manner. Many of the faults were repetitive. Divide by zero faults were very common. There was no process in place to ensure that the range of all denominators be checked prior to divide operations. There was no learning from previous mistakes. Developers in that organization are probably still introducing divide faults into their code, only to spend agonizing hours finding them again.

Some people will do a very good job at software development activities and some will not. This people dimension is perhaps the least understood of all the relevant components of the software development process. In general, the people involved can be assembled into two major groups. First, there are the analysts who are responsible for the formulation of the requirements specifications. Then come the people responsible for software design. The design products are used by programmers to create source code. The resulting code is tested by a software test group. Finally, the software is placed into service and becomes the responsibility of a software maintenance staff. Each of the individuals comprising the different groups will have very different characteristics. That is, a person who really likes software maintenance work and is very good at it is probably a very different person from someone who excels in software specification or design.

Learning to measure people is a very difficult and complex task. If we are not careful and conscientious in the measurement process, we can learn exactly the wrong thing from our measurements. This is not new ground that needs to be plowed. There is a veritable wealth of information about the measurement of people that can be drawn from the fields of psychology, sociology, and human factors engineering. Subsequent to this chapter, there will be very little or no mention of the measurement of the people domain. This is not because this domain is not important. It is very important, and perhaps the most important domain. To do measurement on this domain will require very much more expertise in psychology and sociology than the typical software engineer will be exposed to.

Much of the data that we will collect about people will, at first, seem to be counterintuitive. For example, if we track the rate of fault insertion by years of experience with the company, we will invariably find a strong positive relationship between these two attributes. At face value, it would appear that the best way to control faults and lower the overall rate of fault insertion is to sack the older and more experienced developers. If we look further into this problem, we will discover that the overall complexity of the code modules created by the experienced developers is far greater than the complexity of code modules being worked on by the novices. Their tasks are not equal. If the novices were assigned to the complex module design and coding tasks, their rate of fault insertion would be very much greater than the experienced developers. Similarly, if the experienced developers were working on the same code base that the novices were working on, their rate of fault insertion would be very much lower than that of the novices.

W. Edwards Deming maintained that only managers who had a sufficient background in statistics should be allowed access to raw data.[2] Without sufficient preparation in statistical analysis, it is particularly easy to extract the wrong information from raw data. The above example is but one of a myriad of similar circumstances that arise on a daily basis. Many times, the mere perception that they are being monitored will change people's behavior. In some organizations, for example, there are efforts afoot to measure programmer productivity. One such measure is to simply count the lines of code (LOC) that each programmer produces each week. Once the programmers know that they are going to be evaluated by their LOC productivity, the number of comments in the code begins to rise dramatically. Also, the number of language tokens per line can also be expected to drop. In a sense it is a bit like the measurement problems of quantum mechanics. The very act of measurement alters the attribute being measured.

Like computer programs, people have attribute domains. Some of these domains are relevant to the task of software development and others are not. It is possible to list some relevant people attributes that can be measured. These are as follows:

1. Age
2. Gender
3. Number of computer science courses
4. Number of courses in the application domain
5. Date of employment at the company
6. Experience in the programming languages
7. Technical training

This is not intended to be an exhaustive list of people attributes but rather to indicate that there are attributes that may be measured for each of the people in the software process. They are also typical of data that can be kept on the software development staff by the human resources organization. These measures can potentially be used in models of software quality or productivity. What is important is that we must be very careful to establish standards for any measurements that we do make on people variables. This is the most difficult part of measuring people attributes.

From the above list of attributes, we will start with the first attribute, age. It is always bad to define a variable named age. These data will be accurate at the time of employment and become increasingly inaccurate as more time elapses. It would be far better to know a person's birth date than it would be to know their age at employment. From the birth date it will always be possible to work out their age at any time in the future. Now to the birth date field itself. The normal form that such dates are kept in is MMDDYYYY. This definition will allow us to compute how old a developer is to the nearest day. For all practical purposes, this resolution is too great. The birth year probably will give us the resolution that we need for any analysis of our developers. It is highly unlikely that we will need to know age differences to greater than ±6 months. Now that we know our needs, we will only record birth year. We simply do not need to know more than that.

Next on the list of people attributes is gender. This attribute will have the value of male or female. The real question is why we need to know the gender of a developer. It is clear that the human resources organization will have to know this for EEOC reporting but it is not at all clear that these data will be meaningful in the context of the software development environment. Such data would be useful if (1) there were known differences between males and females, (2) these differences were quantified by task, and (3) the organization was structured to exploit these differences. Quite simply, there is not sufficient experimental data at our disposal to suggest that we could begin to make effective use of the gender attribute. We will delete it from our list of people attributes we will measure.

The third item on the list is the number of computer science courses that a developer has completed. There are a couple of major problems with this attribute measure. As we will learn in the next chapter, there may or may not be predictive validity to this attribute. It might well be that exposure to varying levels of the computer science curriculum is not related to software development in any way. Without the science to back up the fact that good developers also have lots of computer science (software engineering) courses, we simply cannot consider this to be a valid attribute. The second problem with this attribute is that not all computer science courses are equal. Graduate computer science curriculum content is very different from upper-division university curriculum content. Also, lower-division computer science curriculum content is materially different from both graduate and upper-division undergraduate curriculum content. Quite a number of people would suggest that the curriculum content of computer science courses at the Massachusetts Institute of Technology is very different from that of the computer science courses at Jadavpur University of Calcutta. Simply counting computer science courses will probably do nothing more than introduce an uncontrolled source of variation in any attempt to use this attribute in modeling.

For application programming, it might well make a difference if the application developers are founded in the discipline. For example, if the application under development is an accounting package, it might be useful for the developers to have a background in the accounting discipline. The fourth people attribute will enumerate the number of courses that a developer has had in the discipline of the application. The course content issue raised above is just as relevant here as it was for the discipline of computer science. Although there is probably less variability in the course content of accounting courses from one university to another than there is in computer science, it is still a substantial factor. There are probably no experimental data available to support the conclusion that a person with an accounting background will do better at writing accounting applications than a person without such a background. Without such evidence at hand, there would be little reason to support maintaining data on this attribute. Finally, it is quite possible that developers will be shifted from one project to another during the course of their careers. A person who started work writing COBOL accounting applications may well be writing Java applications for Web infrastructure applications today. Thus, the fourth people attribute is probably not usable or relevant for any modeling purpose.

Another common practice is to record the date of employment at the company. The same issues of granularity of measurement obtain here as in the case of birth date. In this case we will probably compute the length of service in months. We can make a clear case for being able to resolve this attribute at the month level of granularity. This means that the date of employment will be defined as MMYYYY. Unfortunately, this information is not particularly relevant. If the developer first joined the company as an unskilled employee on the production floor, graduated from that to foreman, and from that to tester and then to programmer, this employee may have been with the company for 20 years or more but will have done development for no more than 1 year. Hence, there is probably little value to the date of employment attribute.

Programmer experience is an interesting attribute. It seems so relevant; however, there are a couple of problems with this attribute. First, there are hosts of programming languages in use today. Probably more have been used in the past. This is not a single attribute. We will need to record experience in Java, FORTRAN, COBOL, JOVIAL, NELIAC, LISP, SLIP, HAL/S, ALGOL, Basic, etc. Perhaps the greatest difficulty with programmer experience is that we will probably learn nothing from it. We have all met developers who are hopeless, regardless of the number of years of experience in the language. A real geek with 2 weeks of Java is probably to be preferred to a programming hack with 20 years of experience.

The final attribute goes to the heart of company training programs. Many software development organizations have available to employees some type of technical vitality program. It is the stated purpose of these programs to provide the employees with a broader educational exposure, to update their skills with new technology, and a host of other very laudable and lofty goals. Kudos are given to employees for participating in these programs. The basic assumption underlying the technical vitality attribute is that the more technical training a person has had, the more valuable he or she will be to the company. Again, there is little evidence to support this conclusion. There is probably an inverse relationship between developer productivity and this attribute. We have taught any number of such training courses. For the typical older developer, they are a very pleasant and viable alternative to real work.

We have now worked our way through the list of people attributes. Except for the first attribute, there is not much in the way of functional information in any of these attributes. Many of them will bring more noise with them than signal. Although the list of people attributes chosen for this discussion is rather limited, the same considerations apply to just about any other list that we might wish to construct. The conclusion is obvious. We know very little about which human attributes are really relevant to the products that they make, to the environments that they are capable of working in, or to the processes that will make them productive. We are going to have to learn to measure people. This will be the biggest challenge in the development of an effective software engineering measurement program. It is important that we learn to do this measurement. People clearly do the design and development, yet we know so little about how they do it. The very best we can do at the present time is to build models that control for the effects of people. We will not be able to build good models that incorporate people attributes because our knowledge of these attributes is so weak.

3.1.2 Process Metrics

Software is developed through a sequence of steps that constitute the underlying software process model. We can measure certain aspects of that process. We might, for example, wish to measure the rate at which software faults are introduced and removed by the development process. We might wish to characterize the process in terms of the number of unre-

51

solved problems that are extant in the software in development. Some notable process attributes include:

- Rate of programmer errors
- Rate of software fault introduction
- Rate of software failure events
- Number of software change requests
- Number of pending trouble reports
- Measures of developer productivity
- Cost information
- Software process improvement (SPI) costs
- Return on investment (ROI)

The above list is not intended to be exhaustive, merely indicative. The important thing to note is that the process variables tend to deal primarily with cost and rate data.

3.1.3 Product Metrics

As was stated earlier, there are several tangible products of the software development process. These are, in part

- The software requirements specification
- The high level design
- The low level design
- The source code
- The test cases
- The documentation

A software system is a rapidly evolving and dynamic structure. All of the products of this development process are in a constant state of flux. In fact, when a system finally reaches a point where it no longer changes, it will probably be replaced. The world that we live in is a rapidly changing place. Software that does not adapt becomes obsolete.

There are clearly many more products than the short list given above. Again, it was not our intention that this list be exhaustive, just illlustrative. Much of our measurement methodology will be devoted to understanding this domain more completely. We will return to the subject in rather more detail in Chapter 5.

3.1.4 Environment Metrics

Environment metrics will quantify the attributes of the physical surroundings of the software development organization. This will include all pertinent aspects of the environment that relate to development. The operating system environment for the design and development of the systems has great bearing on project outcomes. The rate of personnel turnover in programmers and managers will clearly be measurable and worthwhile knowing. If a programmer is assigned to a complicated task and is repeatedly interrupted with meetings, by colleagues, or other distractions, he or she will probably make substantial errors in the programming task. Some pertinent environmental attributes that can be measured are as follows:

- Operating system
- Development environment
- Operating environment
- Administrative stability (staff turnover)
- Machine (software) stability
- Office interruptability
- Office privacy
- Library facilities
- Rendezvous facilities

Again, this is not intended to be an exhaustive list. It merely indicates the types of attributes that might potentially impact the software development process.

3.2 MODELING: MAPPING AMONG MEASUREMENT DOMAINS

There are clearly four distinctly different measurement domains. We would like very much to understand the complex relationships among these four domains. Much of what we wish to know about good software construction will be determined by the mappings that we will make between the four domains. Good programmers, for example, will follow good programming processes that will, in turn, produce good programs. Unfortunately, certain types of programmers will follow good development processes that will yield very bad programs.

The process of building strong functional (and useful) relationships among the four measurement domains will be governed by a distinct set of statistical procedures that will allow us to discover these relationships. This process is called statistical modeling. It is the subject of Chapter 7.

3.3 THE PROCESS OF SOFTWARE MEASUREMENT

Sometimes, software developers are very confused as to why they are measuring software. Metrics are dutifully collected and stored about programs, processes, people, and environments. These measures are similar to one-hand clapping — there is no opposing hand to make a sound. When measurements are being used effectively, we will use these measurements to map from one of the four taxonomic measurement domains to another for the purposes of developing predictive models and also for modifying the software development process.

In recent years, the focus of software development has shifted to understanding the software process. We now understand that programs evolve from a process milieu. Just as there is a software development process, there is a corresponding software measurement process. We should not think of measurement as an unpleasant activity that we will do but once and be done with it. Software systems are rapidly developing entities. Their characteristics change over time.

The measurement circumstances are rather like measuring a child. It would be unthinkable to measure the height of a human child at two years and then presume that we now know all there is to know about that person. Human beings grow until they reach maturity. Then, after a period of some years, they begin to shrink again. Programs are similarly dynamic. In their early evolutionary stages, these programs are relatively simple. As time progresses and we begin to get a better handle on just exactly what the customer really wants, these simple programs grow quite complex. As the programs age, unwanted or unused functionalities are trimmed from them and then the programs may become less complex. But the bottom line is that programs are dynamic objects. We must then conceive of a measurement process so that we can understand the program as it is now.

3.4 SUMMARY

Much of the focus of this book will be on software products. This does not mean that process, people, and environment metrics are not important. Much of what we need to know in these areas is simply not known. There has been a lot of activity in reporting aspects of software processes and also about programmer/developer activity. However, there has been very little real scientific research activity in these fields. It is the real purpose of this book to show how to measure, how to build a measurement program, how to manage the measurement data, and how to institutionalize the improvement of this measurement program. Much of what we need to know about software development we will have to learn. What is worse, we are going to have to do this ourselves. It is not possible to buy engineering discipline. It is not possible to buy a miraculous measurement program. We cannot contract with someone to have our baby for us. We are going to have to do the work ourselves. We will learn that getting babies is not all that bad. There are aspects of this process that can be genuine fun.

References

1. Munson, J.C. and Coulter, N.S., "An Investigation of Program Specification Complexity," *Proceedings of the ACM Southeastern Regional Conference,* April 1988, pp. 590–595.
2. Deming, W.E., *Out of Crisis*, Massachusetts Institute of Technology Center for Advanced Engineering Study, Cambridge, MA, 1993.

Chapter 4
Validation of Software Measures

4.1 UNDERSTANDING WHAT IS BEING MEASURED

It is very easy to think of attributes of computer software products or processes that can be measured. It is also very easy to identify properties of people and programming environments that can easily be measured. Measurement in and of itself is not the real problem. The real problem is identifying meaningful attributes to measure and then finding measurement processes to produce reliable and reproducible assessments of these attributes. One attribute, for example, that we could measure for each of our software developers is that of height. Clearly, every one of our developers occupies some physical space in this universe, so we should be able to measure the height of these people handily. Indeed, there are plenty of tools that we have at hand that will provide satisfactory measurement data for us once we have decided what level of accuracy is required. If we only require accuracy to ±1 centimeter, we could easily acquire a suitable measurement tool, a tape measure, obtained from the local hardware store to do the job for us.

We have now identified an attribute of our developers, height, that we can measure. We have also identified a tool that will provide suitable measurements of that attribute. It is now possible to collect data on all of our developers and save these data for posterity. Unfortunately, nothing will have been gained by this measurement process. A developer's height is probably not related to his programming skills in any way. Knowledge of a developer's height will not give us insight into any of his skills and abilities with regard to programming. Height is not a *valid* measure of developer ability, productivity, or skill. We will insist that all measurements we collect about people, processes, products, and environments have validity with regard to one or more criterion measures that we wish to understand.

Yet another dimension to our problem relates to the mechanism of collecting the data. It is possible to identify an attribute that has face validity yet no reasonable means of quantifying the attribute values. An example of such an attribute would be programmer aptitude. Some programmers write really good code while others cannot code their way out of a bushel

55

basket. Anyone who has ever worked with programmers can attest to this fact. This, then, is a reasonable attribute for us to know. We have only to be able to measure it. Different people have different notions of what good code is so we will attempt to control for these differences by having multiple judges rate the ability of each programmer. By doing this we hope to avoid individual biases introduced by each of the judges. In essence, we want a *reliable* assessment of the programming ability of each programmer. It is clear that we can ask each judge to assign a number (e.g., 1 through 5) to each programmer. A good programmer will receive a value of 5. A bad programmer will receive a value of 1. If all judges assign the same value to each programmer, then the rating scheme will be reliable. If, on the other hand, there is substantial variation among the judges as to programmer ability, then the ratings that we receive will be unreliable.[1]

There are two criteria, then, that we must have for our measurements. First, the attributes being measured must contribute to our understanding of the criterion attributes. The attributes being measured must be valid. Second, the measurement data must be reproducible. Different judges looking at the same attribute will assess it in the same manner. The measurements must be reliable. To assist our understanding of the validity and reliability of measurements, we will borrow heavily from the psychological testing discipline.

4.2 CRITERION-ORIENTED VALIDITY

It is unfortunate, but most of what we would like to know about a person who is interviewing with us for a job as a programmer simply cannot be gleaned from the interview process. We would like to know if this person can write good code. We would like to know if this person has been a consistent high producer of code. We would like to know if this person will work well on a software development team. These attributes are the programmer quality attributes. These are the things that we would really like to know about our programmer before we make a commitment to hire this person. They are our *criterion* attributes. The interesting thing about criterion attributes is that we can, for the most part, only know them after the fact. The very thing that we wish to know, we cannot know. We can, however, learn from the past. We have probably hired many programmers in the past. Some of these programmers will have been good programmers and others were probably marginal. We need to identify attributes of these programmers that we can measure and select a subset of these attributes that can be shown to be related to our criterion measures. We can then use the historical data to identify programmer attributes that are related to our criteria, measure our existing staff to determine the degree of relationship between each of the identified attributes and one or more of the programmer criterion measures, and build a working set of attributes that we can use to identify potentially good programmers from a set of potential candidates.

4.2.1 Predictive Validity

It is clear that we can use the historical data at our disposal to develop relationships among measurable programmer attributes and programmer criterion measures. We might speculate, for example, that a programmer's IQ is a good predictor of her programming skills. This is a reasonable hypothesis. Critical reasoning skills are a necessary attribute of programming. IQ is quite possibly a good measure of these reasoning skills. We cannot, however, speculate about this relationship or suppose that it holds. We must conduct an experiment to understand the relationship between IQ and good programming skills. As part of this experiment we will choose a set of programmers whose programming ability has been assessed by a team of qualified experts. Assume, for the moment, that these experts can produce a reliable assessment of programmer ability. This means that each of the experts can assign a value from 1 to 5 to a variable skill that represents a fair and reliable assessment of a programmer's actual programming ability as demonstrated at our workplace by past performance. Based on our new skill measure, we can learn which programmers we should have hired and which we should not have hired. Unfortunately, this information is not timely. We would like to know this before we hire a potentially bad programmer.

We would like to develop measures on attributes, such as IQ, that we think are related to the skill variable such that the attribute measures vary directly or inversely with our skill assessment. If we are successful in identifying attributes that are related to the skill variable within the pool of existing programmers, then we can use these attributes to predict the skill variable of new candidates. We can then validate that such a relationship holds in the future by experimentation. That is, we can use our attribute measures to hire only the candidates who score high (or low) on our predictive measures. If our selected attributes do a good job of identifying good programmers, then they will have predictive validity.

Sometimes, the concept of predictive validity and correlation are associated. We will see in Chapter 7 that these are two very different things. A good attribute measure may not have a very good statistical correlation with our criterion measure. The correlation statistic measures only linear relationships between two variables. As an example, a programmer IQ value will probably be a very good predictor of programmer skill. Prospective programmers with a very low IQ score are probably going to have a difficult time finding their way to work, much less solving complex programming tasks. Good cognitive skills are directly related to the programming activity. However, there is probably a point of diminishing returns.

Extremely bright people are challenged only once by complicated problems. Programming is often a very repetitive activity. It readily loses its charm to very bright people who do not like the constraints of a typical programming job. They will probably not do well in the long haul as production programmers. We will learn this when we conduct our validation study.

We will not reject IQ as an attribute measure to predict our criterion measure of skill because there is a nonlinear relationship between IQ and skill. Quite the contrary, there is probably a strong quadratic relationship between IQ and skill. We will probably learn to eliminate people from our candidate pool that have IQ scores less than 110 and greater than 135. The IQ attribute will probably have very good predictive validity for skill but it will not be a linear relationship.

4.2.2 Concurrent Validity

We would very much like to have a test of programmer aptitude. High scores on our test of aptitude measure would then indicate that we can identify those potential employees who would make good employees. The problem with developing such an instrument and ensuring that it is working correctly is to evaluate a group of incoming employees with our instrument and then wait 10 to 20 years to get some long-term data on how well these employees really did in our organization. In most cases, we simply cannot wait that long to find out whether our instrument really did allow us to discriminate between potentially good programmers and those who would not succeed in this role.

We can use our existing staff of programmers to validate that the instrument of programmer aptitude we have developed really does work. Within the framework of our current staff, we probably have a full range of successful to not-so-successful programmers. This group of programmers can be used to validate the instrument. They will allow us to establish concurrent validity. We can administer our test of programmer aptitude to them. To the extent that the scores from our programmer aptitude test correspond with the evaluation of our programming staff, the new instrument will have concurrent validity. We will not have to wait 10 to 20 years to see whether the test will discriminate between good programmers and poor ones.

4.3 CONTENT VALIDITY

The act of judging the adequacy of content for a potential measure is called *content validation*. The notion of content validity is particularly critical in the evaluation of people. The typical computer science student will perform very well on the mathematical and reasoning sections of the typical standardized tests used in universities (e.g., the SAT or the GRE). These same students do not do very well on the verbal sections of these same standardized tests. Typically, the verbal scores are not good predictors of a student's success as an undergraduate or graduate student, yet they are part of the composite score of the student's test. In this case, the verbal sections of these tests do not have good content validity, in that for most purposes, it is quite OK for programmers and computer science students to be functionally illiterate.

Return, for a moment, to the construction of a test of programming ability. Content validity will be very difficult to achieve in a general instrument of programming ability. The reason for this is quite simple. There are many different types of programming languages and environments. A programmer who really likes to code in C++ or Java would probably not like to code in COBOL. A programmer who likes to write compilers would probably die if asked to work on an accounts receivable package. The act of writing code to perform complex numerical analysis requires deep and abiding knowledge of the underlying mathematics. There is no universal programming task. There can be no universal test of programming aptitude. No matter what his score on a test of aptitude, if we ask a programmer to do a job that he does not understand in an unfamiliar language environment, this person will not do well at his new task.

4.4 CONSTRUCT VALIDITY

Not all metrics measure what their names imply. Each metric seeks to quantify an underlying construct. We can easily believe that the lines of code (LOC) metric measures the size of a program at least on one of the attribute dimensions of size. The presumption is that if we know the LOC value of a program module, then we will learn something about the amount of raw programmer effort that was expended on that module. In this sense, LOC is a good measure of the size construct. Other metrics, such as Halstead's effort measure, have little or nothing to do with the actual developer effort construct that they purport to measure.

Many software development organizations have developed their own *ad hoc* programmer aptitude tests. In these test scenarios, a potential hire is asked to write a program to solve a well-defined but complex algorithm. After the victim has completed the exercise, his or her efforts will be evaluated as to whether the program actually works, how good the solution was, and also how many mistakes were made in the effort. The resulting program would typically be, for example, 50 to 60 LOC. The supposed underlying psychological construct for this exercise is programmer ability. Unfortunately, this type of exercise does not have construct validity. It will not test what its designers think it is testing, for a number of reasons. First, a good programmer can be expected to produce no more than n clean lines of code per week, where n is a function of the language and the complexity of the problem being solved. Whatever the value of n is for a given organization is certainly well below the 50 LOC that the potential hire is expected to produce on the spot. Second, typically, most software development time will be spent in design and just simply understanding what the task at hand is. Coding is simply the act of translating a design to a particular programming language. There will be no time for such introspection in the brief interval that the hapless interviewee will have to demonstrate his or her ability. Third, most good programmers are very careful and highly methodical. They do not simply sit at a computer terminal and hack code. This is a most atypical code development scenario.

These *ad hoc* programming tests are probably really good in their ability to identify hackers; that is the real construct that the tests measure. In the vast majority of software development organizations, a hacker will not do well in the long run. Good programming skills probably include substantial attention to design detail, the ability to work within a team, and considerable social skills. Modern software systems are designed and built by very large development organizations, possibly distributed throughout the world. There is really no place in such an organization for a lone wolf, a code jockey. Yet, this is the very thing that most locally developed programming aptitude tests do, in fact, measure.

4.5 EMPIRICAL VALIDITY

The concept of the empirical validity of a metric relates to two distinct considerations, both based on the statistical notion of variability. First, a metric must identify a unique source of variation not already present in any other metrics that we might be using. Second, this new source of variation will serve to explain additional variation in one or more of our criterion measures. Third, the metric must vary as a function of concomitant variation in a criterion measure. Both of these considerations may be determined only through the experimentation process. We must design, develop, and conduct carefully controlled experiments for our test of empirical validity. This is a time- and resource-consuming process. We have often witnessed attempts to circumvent the application of scientific methodology in the validation of metrics. The most common means is to hire a metric expert or a panel of metric experts to identify the appropriate metrics to use in an organization. Much of the measurement process is counter-intuitive. Things just do not work the way we think they should. The use of statistics and sound scientific experimental methodology will provide the best opportunity to identify a viable working set of metrics for all of our measurement domains.

In short, a new metric will contribute to a significant increase in the proportion of variation that we observe in a criterion variable. If, for example, we are attempting to validate a new complexity metric for prediction of software faults, then the fault prediction model of complexity metrics on faults must be significantly better with addition of the new metric. A good example of the validation process can be found in a recent work by Anger et al.[2] or in our own work on the validation of the data structures metric.[3]

As we learn to apply this empirical validation process, we soon discover that only a limited subset of the existing metrics meets these new criteria. As we will see in Chapter 5, the Halstead software science metrics are a good example of this.[4] Consider the case of Halstead's program vocabulary, $\eta = \eta_1 + \eta_2$. From the standpoint of linear modeling, we simply cannot use the value of η because it is a linear compound of two other metrics, η_1 and η_2. We observe a similar circumstance with McCabe's cyclomatic complexity, which is the sum of nodes and edges in a control flowgraph representation of a program. The metric primitives of Nodes and Edges contain all of the information. It is clear that a metric that is a simple linear derivative of two other metrics cannot identify new sources of variation different from the metrics that comprise the new metric. In essence, if you know that a person has change amounting to 25 cents in one of his pants pockets and 50 cents in the other pants pocket, you will learn nothing new from my telling you that he has 75 cents in his pants pockets.

The world we live in is not a simple one. There is no one number that can characterize a human being. Human beings have many different attributes, such as height, weight, age, race, gender, hair color, eye color, and an astonishing array of genetic attributes. Each of these attributes can be measured individually. Samples from individuals measured for a single attribute follow some type of univariate probability distribution (probably not the normal distribution). Height, in and of itself, is not a good characterization of a person. To characterize a person more completely, we are going to have to have measures on a plethora of attribution dimensions, *simultaneously*. Realistically, we must learn to deal with the world as it really is. It is a multivariate world. A command of multivariate statistical analysis is vital to our understanding of this world. In all likelihood, our criterion measures are also multivariate in nature. We would like our software to be maintainable, reliable, secure, and demonstrate survivability, all at once. Our studies of empirical validity will most certainly not be a matter of simple correlation between a single metric and a single criterion measure. These empirical validation investigations will be complex multivariate experimental designs.

4.6 RELIABILITY

Validity is a necessary but not sufficient condition for a good metric. The numbers that we produce when we measure a given attribute should not vary as a function of time, of the observer, or of the context. It is clear that LOC is a good measure of program size. It will be possible to specify how the measurement of LOC should occur in such a manner that any observer of the same program would count it in exactly the same way. We could, for example, specify that our LOC metric, when applied to a file containing C code, would simply enumerate the number of carriage return characters in that file. Thus, LOC has good validity and it can be reliably measured.

Many metrics that are collected about people and processes are highly subjective. Each rater who evaluates a particular attribute will arrive at a different numerical value. The function point metric is a very good example of this. The function point metric is used to assess, among other things, the complexity of a set of software specifications. In theory, they provide an estimate of the relative size of a software system based on the functionalities in the specification of that system. The notion of function points has spawned an entire mystical society of software developers who have built a pseudo-science around these improbable measurements. For our purposes, function points have one very serious drawback: they are intrinsically unreliable. Different people evaluating the same system will arrive at different numbers for the same specification.

Just because a rater is able to attach a number to a specific specification attribute does not mean he will be likely to reproduce exactly that number at some future time, or that another observer of the same system will likely produce the same number or one close to it. The missing piece of research on function points relates to the reliability of the technique. We can derive an estimate for the reliability of function point ratings by different judges from a classic paper by Ebel[1] in the psychometric literature. His definition of the reliability of ratings is based on the analysis of variance among raters evaluating the same system. Consider a hypothetical experiment involving three raters who will all evaluate the same four software specifications. Exhibit 1 reveals the outcome of this hypothetical experiment. We can see, for example, that Rater 1 found a function point count of 31 for System 1 and Rater 2 found 55 function points in the same system.

To begin our analysis of variance, we need to compute the sums and the sum squared for each rater across all systems and for each system across all raters. From the work by Ebel, we can compute the reliability of the ratings as:

$$r = \frac{M_{\bar{x}} - M}{M_{\bar{x}} + (k-1)M}$$

where k is the number of raters, $M_{\bar{x}}$ is the system mean square, and M is the error mean square. The computation of the reliability for our hypothetical function point experiment is shown in Exhibit 2. For this experiment, the reliability of the ratings was 0.655.

Exhibit 1. Hypothetical Function Point Scores

	Rater 1	Rater 2	Rater 3	Sum	Sum^2
System 1	31	55	35	121	14641
System 2	42	36	37	115	13225
System 3	14	18	17	49	2401
System 4	22	21	30	73	5329
Sum	109	130	119	358	35596
Sum2	11881	16900	14161	42942	

Exhibit 2. Computation of the Reliability of Ratings

Total sum of squares	12274.0
Average sum squared	10680.3
Sum of squares	
For raters	55.2
For systems	1185.0
For total	1593.7
For error	353.5
Mean square	
For systems	395.0
For error	58.9
Reliability	0.655

If the reliability of the rating scheme is very low, as it is in our example, then this is indicative that the judges themselves are a significant source of variation in the ratings. In a highly reliable rating system, the reliability value will also be very high. In essence, the error mean square term is very small in relation to the mean square error of the systems being measured. The source of this error variation is the difference in the judges' rating for the same systems.

Given that there are no standards for essentially any measurement that will be performed by human raters, the reliability of such data will always be low. We have no real good notion of what constitutes a good developer, for example. If we ask three different managers to evaluate the performance of a single developer, we will likely get three very different perceptions of the same individual. The reason for this is that we simply do not have viable evaluation templates or standards to use in this process. Each of the raters will be using a different construct to evaluate the developer. One rater might simply look at productivity as measured by LOC as a means of rating the developer. Another might look at productivity in terms of lines of clean and tested code, as opposed to raw productivity. Yet another manager might factor elements of collegiality into his evaluation process.

It is really pretty easy to identify metrics that are unreliable. They will be derived from unconstrained judgments of the raters. If the evaluation process is controlled by a very well-defined standard, then there will be no opportunity for variation among the raters. The standard is a good one if it converts the human observer into an automaton. The same observer on different occasions would evaluate the same event and get exactly the same value for each observation. Different observers applying the same standard would get exactly the same value for the same event.

References

1. Ebel, R.L., Estimation of the Reliability of Ratings, *Psychometrica*, 16(4), 407–424, December 1951.

2. Anger, F.D., Munson, J.C., and Rodriguez, R.V., Temporal Complexity and Software Faults, *Proceedings of the IEEE International Symposium on Software Reliability Engineering 1994*, IEEE Computer Society Press, Los Alamitos, CA, 1994.

3. Munson, J.C. and Khoshgoftaar, T.M., The Measurement of Data Structure Complexity, *Journal of Systems and Software*, 20(3), 217–226, March 1993.

4. Halstead, M.H., *Elements of Software Science*, Elsevier, New York, 1977.

Chapter 5
Static Software Measurement

5.1 INTRODUCTION

We can measure a software system in exactly two different ways. We can measure static software attributes of the requirements, the design, and the code. We can also measure the system as it is running. We will learn very different things from each of these types of measurements. Static code attributes will let us learn much about the structure of a system, how it is built, and where the problem areas in the code base might be. We will use our static software observations to learn about the quality of the system. Dynamic source code measurement, on the other hand, will allow us to observe a system when it is running and draw useful conclusions about the efficacy of the test process, the reliability of a system, its availability, and its robustness. We can also predict how a typical user might employ the system and validate this prediction in practice.

The key to software measurement is in understanding just precisely what each of our measurements is telling us about the quality, reliability, security, or availability of the software we are measuring. It is possible to identify a vast number of properties of a program that can be measured.[1,2] The real science is to determine which attributes are meaningful in terms of the software development. We could easily measure the height of all entering freshmen at a university. We could also weigh them. We could count the number of bumps on their skulls. And we could store all these data in a database. But we find that there is very little or no information in these measures. What we are trying to ascertain from the vitals on the entering freshmen is who will succeed academically and who will choose to tank. The height measure on these students will not be a good predictor for academic success, nor will the number of skull bumps probably tell us much about a person's academic future.

We have learned, in the software development arena, to expect miracles. If we were just to find the right CASE tools, the path to complete harmony and fine software would instantly emerge. If we were but to institute the new XYZ process, conveniently packaged and distributed by the XYZ Corporation, we would then produce fine software. In short, we have been told that we can buy into the right tools and implement a new (unproven) methodology and all will be well. Oddly enough, no one has ever been reinforced by having such a miracle happen, but our faith in the process persists. There seems to be a persistent expectation that some miracles will happen if we buy a few metric tools. But, again, no miracles are forthcoming.

Doing science is very hard work. At the foundation of science is a core of measurement and observation. We uncover new truths through a rigorous process of experimentation and investigation. We invest heavily and happily in the measurement process in the name of science in the fields of medicine and in mechanical engineering, among others. There are no miracles in true science. There is only a continuing process of measurement and careful observation. If we are to further our understanding of the software development and evolution processes, then we, too, must stop looking for miracles and start doing some hard measurement and experimentation. We will begin that process by trying to find out what it is that we should be measuring.

Within the vast panoply of metrics available to the software developer, most lack sufficient content validity to provide utility in the measurement process. They are of limited utility at best. They propose to disclose certain properties of the software but lack the fundamental experimental research behind them to validate the claims made about them. A very good example of this is the cyclomatic complexity number $V(g)$ of a program module. The metric is calculated from the relationship $V(g)$ = Edges − Nodes + 2, where Nodes and Edges are derived from a flowgraph representation of the program module.[3] Cyclomatic complexity is supposed to be a measure of the control complexity of a program module. As will be demonstrated later, when this metric is studied in conjunction with measures of lines of code and statement count, it is usually highly correlated with these measures of module size. In essence, $V(g)$ is a measure of size. If, on the other hand, we look at the metric primitives Nodes and Edges, we find that they measure something else altogether.[4] These two metric primitives do, in fact, measure control flow complexity.

So, our first criterion in selecting those metrics is content validity. The metric must measure the attributes that it is supposed to measure. A major objective in the formulation of a software measurement program is to identify a working set of metrics with experimentally (scientifically) derived content validity.[5,6] A metric will not be useful just because a software engineering *expert* says it is. It will be useful because it reveals information about the very attributes we wish to understand. Expert opinion is not the same as scientific validity.

The second criterion in the selection of a metric is that it is related to a quality criterion we wish to understand. Again, if we are interested in estimating the fault-proneness of a module, we will carefully select a working set of static metrics that have demonstrated potential in this regard.[7-10]

The third measurement criterion is that there be a standard for the metric. There are, for example, many published studies in software maintenance that use two apparently simple metrics: line of code and statement count. For a programming language like C or C++, these metrics can be defined in an astonishing number of different ways. The National Institute of Standards and Technology does not maintain measurement standards for computer software. Thus, when we read a study about a C program consisting of 1500 statements, we really do not have a good idea of just how the value 1500 was obtained. If we are unable to identify a standard for a metric we wish to use, then we must publish our own. The essence of this standard is reproducibility. Another scientist can read our standard, apply it in the measurement of code, and get exactly the same results that we would have gotten had we measured the same code.

The fourth measurement criterion is that all measurements be at the same level of granularity. The top-level granularity of measurement would by the system level. An example of such a metric is total program module count. At the lowest level of granularity, we might wish to enumerate the number of characters in C statements. Because of our interest in measuring both the static and dynamic properties of software, the most relevant level of granularity to this enterprise is the module level, where a module is a C function or a C++ method.

It is not an objective of this chapter to enumerate all possible static source code metrics. There have been masterful attempts by others to do that.[1] Our main goal is to identify a working set of software metrics that will typically explain more than 90 percent of the variation in software faults of a software system. Each of these metrics has been chosen because it adds unambiguously to our understanding of software faults. The main purpose of this chapter is to show the process whereby each of the software attributes was specified and then show how it can be unambiguously measured. Once we clearly understand how each attribute is defined and how measures for that attribute can be developed and validated, there are literally no bounds to the extent that we can increase our knowledge about the source code, the processes that led to the creation of the source code, and the quality of the source code when it is placed into service.

5.2 PRIMITIVE MEASURES OF SOURCE CODE

Before discussing the process of measuring source code, it will be useful for us to identify precisely what our objectives are in doing so. There are really two different aspects of a program when a developer writes it. First, the developer must interact with the programming language metaphor. Second, the developer must specify the actions that the code will take at runtime. In C++, for example, a developer must come to grips with the notion of objects and their instantiation. At runtime, however, a program is nothing more than an ordered sequence of machine-level instructions. The programming language metaphor will vanish when the code is compiled. The real value in measuring aspects of the programming language metaphor has to do with the interaction of this metaphor with the developer's psychological attributes. We choose, in this chapter, to discuss only those code attributes that persist through the compilation and result in actual machine code. This is not because we do not regard the measurement of attributes of the language metaphor as important. They are. Most of our recent work has focused on the software that it actually executing. Therefore, we admit to a distinct bias in measuring those source code attributes that persist at runtime.

As established in Chapter 3, we will conduct all of our measurements on program modules. The notion of a module, of course, will vary from one programming language to another. In the case of the C programming language, the choice is simple. A module is a C function. The measurements for a program, then, will be the sum of the modules of a program. That is, if we have a program consisting of five modules, each of which has exactly 100 lines of code (whatever that might mean), then the program will have exactly 500 lines of code in it.

The basis of Halstead software science metrics was that a compiler would process the source code to produce an object program.[11] In the process of doing this, the compiler would have to resolve all tokens established during the process of lexical analysis into one of two distinct classes. A token is an operator or it is an operand. Further, each of these counts for a program could be tallied in two distinct ways: total operators (operands) and unique operators (operands). All other metrics would be derived from these primitive measures.

Our research has shown that Halstead's primitive measures of operator and operand count account for substantially all of the variability among programs in the set of Halstead software science metrics.[5] That is, there is little or no information in the measures of program vocabulary, effort, etc. What is important about Halstead's work in metrics is the fact that the metrics were derived from the language constituents that the compiler would work with to transform the program from a higher-level language to the appropriate machine code. Very simply, the higher-level language was an intermediate representation of the operations necessary to solve a computational problem on a computer. Higher-level language abstractions would be transformed into sequences of code to operationalize these concepts.

We think that this approach is a very good idea. Very little is known about the psychological processes that surround the act of programming. Metrics based on *elementary mental discriminations* made by the programmer are suspect at best. On the other hand, quite a bit is known about how compilers transform higher-level language abstractions into machine code. Constructs and activities in this process are quite measurable.

5.2.1 Measures of Program Size

Software developers and testers are often required to measure software attributes to control, predict, or manage the software process and the software products. Although suggestions might be found regarding the measurement of source code, there is not a set of precise definitions or standards to evaluate source code attributes for any language. The National Institute of Standards and Technology does not deem this standardization to be within its purview. The conflict that arises from the lack of standards is that different measurement tools produce different values for the same program attributes for identical programs. In essence, each measurement tool developer is defining his own *de facto* metric standard. Most metric tool developers are very careful not to disclose the precise method of enumeration by which metric values are obtained by their tools, almost as if a trade secret would be disclosed by such a revelation.

In essence, it is not possible in the current environment to conduct scientific inquiry into any investigations involving source code measurement. We can build our measurement tools to conduct our own private inquiries, but we certainly cannot share these results in the scientific literature. For there to be science, there must be repeatability of results. It is of little or no value to us to learn that the average program module size as reported in the literature was, say, 150 statements. There are no clear rules for the enumeration of statements. We will never be able to reproduce even the simplest investigation because we are all using different rulers for our measurements.

5.2.1.1 Compiler Directives. Our stated measurement objective will be to measure source code attributes that persist through the compilation process to execution. Therefore, all compiler directives must be resolved before the measurement process can begin. The rationale for this is quite simple. The `include` compiler directive can dump several hundred lines of code into a program module when it is resolved by the compiler preprocessor in charge of these things. Very simply, the measurement process can be applied only to post-processed source code. None of our measurements will be taken on compiler directives. They must be resolved, not measured, before the source code measurement process can begin. They are part of the programming language metaphor.

There is very little real science in the literature on programming language practice. There is clear evidence that global variables are bad programming practice. They are bad because a significant number of the total fault population for a given program will be attributable to errors by developers in changing the values of these variables. In the C programming language, we will choose to treat global variables as if they are compiler directives. All global definitions will be mapped into the individual program modules within the scope of the definitions.

5.2.1.2 Style and Statement Metrics. A programmer may have a strong influence over the manner in which a program is constructed. Some programmers use many comment statements to document their activities. Other programmers think that their code must be self-explanatory. Some programmers tend to write very short statements while others might implement the same design specification in very few lines (which generally creates a particular type of C code known as write-only code). Some programmers are very terse in their use of declarations. Other programmers will be very expressive with their use of declared variables. The first class of metrics we wish to define are those that relate to the frequency of use of comments, executable program statements, and nonexecutable statements.

Comments can be represented in many different ways in various programming languages. In some languages, they must be on a separate line by themselves. In others, they may be embedded in a line containing executable code. The rules for comments vary considerably. In the C programming language, we will identify a comment by the token triple </*> <string> <*/>. Each occurrence of this token triple will cause our Comment metric to be incremented by one. Global comments will not be counted. For example, in the C programming language it is possible to put multiple C modules (functions) into one file. Comments can be placed anywhere in this file. We will choose to ignore those that are not physically contained in a program module. We are interested in enumerating only comments that are specific to a particular module. Global comments do not meet this criterion; they are clearly outside the scope of any function module.

Enumerating the number of comments in a programming language is not necessarily a meaningful exercise. Developers tend to put comments into code because they have been told to do so and their compliance with this requirement will be measured by the Comment metric. If a program module is designed correctly, it will contain no comments at all. Each program module should reflect exactly one design element. This design element will partially implement a particular functionality. Thus, the documentation for a program module should be maintained in the design, and not in the code. The name of the developer and the names and dates of the subsequent developers and program modifications should be maintained by the configuration control system. This leaves little or no reason for commented code.

Perhaps the most common program attribute being measured today is the number of lines of code, LOC, in a program. This metric is used everywhere and formally defined nowhere. A very simple definition of LOC in the UNIX environment is the number of logical records in a source code file. In the case of UNIX, a logical record is delimited by <CR>. If we choose to measure LOC in this manner, it will automatically include the number of lines that contain comments only. It will also include lines that contain only white spaces, which in the UNIX environment are <SPACE> and <TAB>. If we are using LOC as a measure of programmer productivity, a wise programmer will be sure to include plenty of comments and blank lines in his program. Perhaps the best way to count LOC is to eliminate lines that contain only comments and lines that contain only white spaces. If we choose to enumerate LOC prior to invoking the compiler preprocess to resolve the compiler directives,LOC will reflect these compiler directives which represent a dialog between the programmer and the compiler. If we want to enumerate LOC after the preprocessor has been invoked, then we find that the preprocessor has taken some serious liberties with the number of logical source records in the post-processed code. In either case, LOC is one of the most misleading measurements that we could hope to get on a program. As a measure of size it can be misleading. We might potentially learn the wrong thing about what we seek to know through the use of this metric.

Another metric that clearly contributes to our confusion about the actual size of a program is the KLOC metric. When we are measuring the number of memory locations in a computer system, the prefix "K" clearly means 2^{10} (or 1024). In most cases when someone reports that her program is 10 KLOC, the value of K is probably 10^3 (or 1000). This is a small point. These two values differ by only about 2 percent. The obfuscation possible in the determination of LOC is certainly much larger than this.

The next program size attribute that we would like to measure is the number of executable statements, which we will denote by the Exec metric. This is a very difficult attribute to define and to measure. We can measure it in any number of ways. The fact that there are many different ways to measure Exec does not mean that it is of no value. What is important is that we specify exactly how we choose to measure it and report this unambiguously. We will, of course, meet this ambiguity criterion if a colleague in another part of the world can measure the same source code that we measured and get exactly the same result.

For our measurement of the Exec attribute, we will require that the source code artifact being measured actually change the state of the machine at runtime in order for a statement to increment the statement count. It is clear that the statement

    count = count + 1;

is an executable statement. It is also clear that:

    int a;

71

is not an executable statement. It is not completely clear whether

　　int a = 1;

is executable. If the integer a is to receive a value of 1 whenever the block containing the declaration is entered, then this is clearly an executable statement and the Exec count is incremented by one when this statement is encountered. The runtime effect of each statement within a programming language metaphor must be carefully examined to prepare the rules for the computation of Exec.

Sometimes, we really do not know what will happen to certain constructs such as the initialization example above. This is particularly true of the C++ metaphor. The syntax for C++ is fraught with ambiguities, and the semantics of the language are more or less at the mercy of the group who wrote each C++ compiler. Thus, many times, we will be forced to create test cases to determine just how the system works. The question at hand is, in the construct

　　int a = 1;

does the variable a get its value from the compiler at compile time or is it reset at runtime? If a receives a new value every time the block that contains this declaration is entered at runtime, then this declaration should be enumerated as an executable statement.

Because we really do not know the answer to this question, let us conduct a test. Consider the following C program:

```
main ()
{
  void test (void);
  test ();
  test ();
}
void test (void)
{
  int i = 0;
  i++;
  printf ("%d \n," i);
}
```

If the compiler initializes the location i to 0 during compilation, then the program should print first 1 and then 2. When we run the program, we find that it prints 1 and then 1. It is now obvious that the initialization is taking place at runtime. Thus, this declarative statement must be counted as an executable statement.

In general, the character ";" is used to delimit statements in the C programming language. The Exec metric is incremented by one every time a semicolon is found at the end of a statement that has been identified as executable. This is not always clearly the case. Consider the following `for` statement:

```
for (i = 1; j = i<50; i++) k + = j;
```

There are clearly four executable statements within this one construct. They are:

```
1. i = 1
2. j = i<50
3. i++
4. k + = j
```

Three of these statements are delimited by semicolons. One (i++) is delimited by the token <)>.

Now consider the following program segment from a C program module:

```
i = j + 1;
{
   int a = 1, b = 1;
   k = a + b + I;
}
```

Now it should be clear that there is yet another statement delimiter. It is the token <,>. The statement delimited is:

```
a = 1
```

in that it is clear to us from our previous example that this declaration is, in fact, executable.

A statement, so far, can be delimited by the tokens <;>, <)>, and <,>. But, we are not finished yet. It turns out that a compound statement delimited by <{> and <}> is also a statement. There are two types of compound statements: those with declarations in them (blocks) and those without. The difference is that a block will create an activation record when it is entered at runtime. It has execution consequences. A compound statement merely brackets statements for the compiler. The braces have no runtime consequences. Thus, the program segment shown above should increment the Exec count by five.

The rules for counting statements can be very complicated. In some programming language metaphors such as C++, the rules for counting statements are astonishingly complex. Unless we have access to the precise set of counting rules, we do not really learn much when they report to us that they have a C program containing 100 statements. We have included in Appendix 2 a standard for the measurement of statements in the C programming language. The purpose of including this standard is that it is a reference point. If a metrician wishes to enumerate certain constructs differently, he need only reference this standard and indicate the modifications that he has made to it. The real role of this standard is to serve as a reasonable template for the creation of similar standards for the C programming language and other programming languages. Maybe if we as an emerging science are lucky, the National Institute of Standards and Technology will choose to embrace software measurement technology as well, and then set and maintain these standards.

Nonexecutable statements represented by the metric NonExec are present in variable declarations, structures, unions, enumerated declarations, and type definitions. If a variable is declared, the declaration is considered a nonexecutable statement. It should now be clear that in languages derived from Algol, compound statements are nonexecutable statement and will cause NonExec to be incremented, whereas blocks will cause Exec to be incremented. If a statement does not modify the runtime environment in any way, then it will be a nonexecutable statement. Comments are not nonexecutable statements. Some sample code and how nonexecutable statements are enumerated can be seen in Exhibit 1. Most notable in this exhibit is the construct int i = 3 ;. This single statement is really two distinct statements. There is a nonexecutable component, int i; and there is an executable component, i = 3 ;.

5.2.2 Lexical Metrics

The lexical analysis of a source program module in any language will resolve the strings of characters on the input stream to a sequence of tokens. We can assign the elements of the set of tokens obtained from this lexical analysis of a program module into two mutually exclusive sets. Some tokens will cause action to be taken by the compiler either at compile time or at runtime. These tokens will be called operators. Other tokens represent the operands of the individual operators. These categories were first measured by Maurice Halstead.[11]

There are two distinct ways to enumerate both of the categories of operators and operands. We can count the total times that a particular operator or operand has been used. That is, we can measure the number of operators (or operands) by the cardinality of the set of all operators (operands) found during the lexical analysis of a source program. Alternatively, we can measure the number of distinct operators (operands) by the cardinality of the set of unique operators. Comments are not considered to be either operators or operands.

The count of total operators for a program was denoted by N_1 by Halstead and the total operand count by N_2. This is now fairly standard nomenclature. When Halstead originally conceived these metrics, he thought to apply them only to arithmetic expressions within a program. We are going to stretch the definition a bit of both operator and operand to a much more

Exhibit 1. Nonexecutable Statements

Example	Nonexecutable Statement
`int i;`	1
`int i = 3 ;`	1
`typedef int bool;`	1
`struct time`	3
`    {`	
`        int hour;`	
`        int minute;`	
`};`	
`typedef struct time`	4
`{`	
`        int hour;`	
`        int minute;`	
`} timetype;`	
`timetype a, b, *c;`	

general case so as to cover all tokens in a program, not just those in arithmetic expressions. Consider the following C program:

```
main ()
{
   int a, b;
   a = 1;
   b = 2;
   b + - a;
   printf (%d, b);
   exit;
}
```

There are 30 total tokens in this program; they are as follows:

```
<main>, <(>, <)>, <{>, <int>, <a>, <,>, <b>, <;>, <a>, <
= >, <1>, <b>, < = >, <2>, <;>, <b>, <+ = >, <a>, <;>,
<printf>, <(>, <%d>, <,>, <b>, <)>, <;>, <exit>, <;>, and
<}>.
```

We can now divide this set into the set of operators O_1 and the set operands O_2. The set of operators is:

```
O₁ = {<main>, <(>, <)>, <{>, <int>, <,>, <;>, < = >, <;>,
<+ = >, <;>, <printf>, <(>, <,>, <)>, <;>, <exit>, <;>,
<}>}
```

There are 20 operators. We would say that $N_1 = \|O_1\| = 20$ for this program. The set of operands is:

```
O₂ = {<main>, <a>, <b>, <a>, <1>, <b>, <2>, <%d>, <b>, <a>,
<printf>, <b>, <exit>}
```

Thus, there are 13 operands and $N_2 = \|O_2\| = 13$.

It is interesting to note that the sum of N_1 and N_2 is not equal to 30. This is so in that the intersection set of operators and operands contains the tokens for the three function calls: `<main>`, `<printf>`, and `<exit>`. This is an interesting aspect of the C programming language. Each function call returns a value. Thus, `<printf>` is at once an operator (function call) and an operand (it contains a return value).

The set of unique operators O_3 is:

```
O₃ = {<main>, <(>, <)>, <{>, <int>, <,>, <;>, < = >, <+ =
>, <printf>, <exit>, <}>}
```

The number of unique operators, η_1, is equal to the cardinality of the set O_3. Thus, $\eta_1 = \|O_3\| = 12$. The set of unique operands is:

```
O₄ = {<main>, <a>, <b>, <1>, <2>, <printf>, <%d>, <exit>}
```

The number of unique operands, η_2, is equal to the cardinality of the set O_4 and $\eta_2 = \|O_4\| = 8$.

In a language such as C, an operator may be overloaded. That is, it may be called to serve many different duties. Take, for example, the operator `<+>`. This operator can be used for integer operands or for real operands. Further, it can be used as a unary operator or as a binary operator. In each of these roles it is doing different duty. Consider the case where `<+>` is infixed between two integer operands a + b. The compiler will generate the code for the two operands, a and b, to be added together using binary integer arithmetic. If, on the other hand, a and b are both real operands, then the compiler must generate the code for the two operands to be added using floating point arithmetic. The single operator `<+>` can be used in the following contexts in the C programming language.

As a binary operator:

+	$+_1$	integer
+	$+_2$	short
+	$+_3$	long
+	$+_4$	float
+	$+_5$	double

As a unary operator:

+	$+_6$	all operands

We will not be able to distinguish among these many different contexts during the lexical phase. Indeed, we will only be able to distinguish an integer addition from a floating addition when we have achieved binding between type and each of the operands. Once we are able to type to operands, we can then identify a new metric, η_3. Halstead did not choose to deal

Exhibit 2. Unique Operator—Operand Counts

Example	η_1	η_3

<pre>{
  int i1 = 1,i2 = 2,i3;
  float f1 = 1.1,f2 =
2.2,f3;
  i3 = i1 + i2;
  f3 = f1 + f2;
}</pre>
	8 unique overloaded operators:
	<pre>{
	int
	  =
	  ,
	  ;
	float
	  +
	  }</pre>
		10 unique operators:
		<pre>{
		int
		  =$_1$
		  ,
		  ;
		float
		  =$_2$
		  +$_1$
		  +$_2$
		  }</pre>

with the problem of overloading; he counted only the total operator tokens. We have found this to be incomplete. A C program is far richer in operands, in terms of their runtime consequences, than the η_2 metric would indicate. η_3 is the number of unique operators in a program accounting for overloading. That is, we will count $a +_4 b$ as a floating operation, where a and b are floating point operands. This will differentiate the operator in the expression $i +_1 j$, where i and j are integer operands. An example of the enumeration of the η_3 metric is shown in Exhibit 2.

5.2.3 Control Flowgraph Metrics

The internal structure of a program module will have a great effect on the number of potential faults it might harbor. A module that contains a lot of statements but no predicate clauses (such as in if statements) will be very easy to understand and to program. It will present little opportunity for the designer or developer to stray from the straight line. Another program module with fewer statements but a really complex control structure will offer both the designer and the developer plenty of opportunity to introduce faults. We will model the internal structure of a program module in terms of its control flowgraph.

A control flowgraph of a program module is constructed from a directed graph representation of the program module that can be defined as follows:

- A directed graph, $G = (N, E, s, t)$, consists of a set of nodes, N, a set of edges E, a distinguished node s the start node, and a distinguished node t the exit node. An edge is an ordered pair of nodes (a, b).
- The in-degree $I(a)$ of node a is the number of entering edges to a.
- The out-degree $O(a)$ of node a is the number of exiting edges from a.

The flowgraph representation of a program, $F = (E', N', s, t)$, is a directed graph that satisfies the following properties:

- There is a unique start node s such that $I(s) = 0$.
- There is a unique exit node t such that $O(t) = 0$.
- We will represent both the start node, s, and the terminal node, t, by the symbol ▬▬. All other nodes, n←N', are members of exactly one of the following three categories:

  1. *Processing node*: It has one entering edge and one exiting edge. They represent processing node a, $I(a) = 1$ and $O(a) = 1$. In our diagrams we will represent a processing node as

     [PROC] .

  2. *Predicate node*: Represents a decision point in the program as a result of if statements, case statements, or any other statement that will cause an alteration in the control flow. For a predicate node a, $I(a) = 1$ and $O(a) > 1$. We will represent this by the symbol ◆ .

  3. *Receiving node*: It represents a point in the program where two or more control flows join, for example, at the end of a while loop. For a receiving node a, $I(a) > 1$ and $O(a) = 1$. This will be represented by the symbol ● .

- A set of edges E' connecting the elements of N'.

If (a, b) is an edge from node a to node b, then node a is an immediate predecessor of node b and node b is an immediate successor of node a. The set of all immediate predecessors for node a is denoted as $IP(a)$. The set of all immediate successors for node b is denoted as $IS(b)$. No node may have itself as a successor. That is, a may not be a member of $IS(a)$. In addition, no processing node may have a processing node as a successor node. All successor nodes to a processing node must be either predicate nodes or receiving nodes. Similarly, no processing node may have a processing node as its predecessor.

From this control flowgraph representation, two essential control flow primitive metrics emerge:

1. Number of nodes
2. Number of edges

A path P in a flowgraph F is a sequence of edges, $\langle \overrightarrow{a_1 a_2}, \overrightarrow{a_2 a_3}, ..., \overrightarrow{a_{N-1} a_N} \rangle$, where all a_i ($i = 1,...,N$) are elements of N'. P is a path from node a_1 to node a_N. An execution path in F is any path P from s to t.

The average length of the paths measured in numbers of edges constitutes a second program characteristic. A program that has a large number of relatively short control-flow paths differs greatly in terms of testing or maintenance from one having a few relatively long control-flow paths.

Another very important feature of a flowgraph, the representation of program iteration constructs, must be considered. A program may contain cycles of nodes created by `if` statements, `while` statements, etc. These iterative structures are called *cycles* as opposed to the more familiar concept of a programming loop. A *loop* is simply a cycle of length one (containing one node and one arc). Whether the nodes lie on a cycle relates to the concept of connectedness defined as follows:

- A flowgraph *F* is weakly connected if any two nodes *a* and *b* in the flowgraph are connected by a sequence of edges.
- A flowgraph *F* is strongly connected if *F* is weakly connected and each node of *F* lies on a cycle.

As an aside, all flowgraphs are only weakly connected in that the start node has an in-degree of zero and the exit node has an out-degree of zero. However, a flowgraph may be made strongly connected by inserting an edge, (*t*, *s*), connecting the exit node with the start node.

Any flowgraph can potentially contain weakly connected subsets of nodes that are flowgraphs in their own right. To examine this potential hierarchical structure of the flowgraph representation, the notion of a subflowgraph is essential.

- A *subflowgraph F'* = (*N''*, *E''*, *s'*, *t'*) of a flowgraph *F* = (*N'*, *E'*, *s*, *t*) is a flowgraph if the out-degree of every node in *F'* is the same as the out-degree of the corresponding node in *F* with the exception of the nodes *s'* and *t'*. Further, all nodes in the subflowgraph are weakly connected only to nodes in *N''*.
- A *subflowgraph* of *F* is a subflowgraph with the property that the cardinality of *N''* > 2 and F' ≠ F. That is, the subflowgraph must contain more nodes than the start and exit nodes and cannot be the same flowgraph.

A flowgraph is an *irreducible flowgraph* if it contains no proper subflowgraph. A flowgraph is a *prime flowgraph* if it contains no proper subflowgraphs for which the property $I(s') = 1$ holds. A prime flowgraph cannot be built by sequencing or nesting of other flowgraphs and contains a single entrance and a single exit structure. The primes are the primitive building blocks of a program control flow. In the C language, the prime flowgraphs are the basic control structures shown in Exhibit 3.

The total *path set* of a node *a* is the set of all paths (*s*, *a*) from the start node to the node *a* itself. The total *path count* of a node *a* is the cardinality of the path set of the node; hence, each node singles out a distinct number of paths to the node beginning at the start node and ending with the node itself. The path count of a node simply equals the number of such paths.

Now that we have constructed a practical means of discussing the internal structure of a program module, we will use this methodology to create

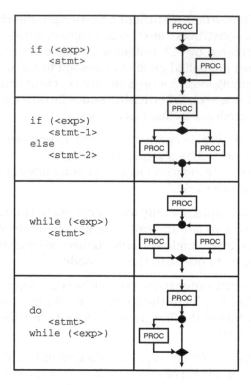

Exhibit 3. Prime Flowgraphs

a program flowgraph for each program module and then enumerate certain characteristics of the flowgraph to represent the control complexity of the corresponding program module.

Converting a C program into its flowgraph representation is not an easy task. We would like to do this in such a manner that the flowgraph we generate from a program would be determined very precisely. That is, any person building a metric tool and following our rules will get precisely the same flowgraph that we would.

First, we will establish that the predicate nodes and the receiving nodes represent points on the flowgraph. That is, they do not represent any source code constructs. All source code will map to the processing nodes.

Because of the complexity of the C grammar, we must decompose switch statements into their component parts before the flowgraph can be constructed accurately. Consider the following C code segment:

```
switch (<exp>)
{
    case <c_exp1> : <stmt>;
```

```
    case <c_exp2> : <stmt>;
    case <c_exp3> : <stmt>;
    default : <stmt>;
}
```

This `switch` statement is functionally equivalent to the following decision structure:

```
if (<exp> = = <c_exp1>)
   goto lab1;
if (<exp> = = <c_exp2>)
   goto lab2;
if (<exp> = = <c_exp3>)
   goto lab3;
else
   goto lab4;
lab1: <stmt>;
lab2: <stmt>;
lab3: <stmt>;
lab4: <stmt>;
lab5:
```

Similarly,

```
switch (<exp>)
{
  case <c_exp1> : <stmt>;
  break;
  case <c_exp2> : <stmt>;
  case <c_exp3> : <stmt>;
  default : <stmt>;
}
```

is equivalent to

```
if (<exp> = = <c_exp1>)
   goto lab1;
if (<exp> = = <c_exp2>)
   goto lab2;
if (<exp> = = <c_exp3>)
   goto lab3;
else
   goto lab4;
lab1: <stmt>;
   goto lab5;
lab2: <stmt>;
lab3: <stmt>;
lab4: <stmt>;
lab5:
```

This new structure is essentially the control sequence that a compiler will generate for the `switch` statement. It is not pretty. The moral to this story

81

is that `switch` statements are probably not a good idea. Nested `if` statements are probably better alternatives.

There are other unfortunate constructs in C that have an impact on the control flow of a program. Expressions that contain the logical operator `&&` are, in fact, carelessly disguised `if` statements. Consider the following C code, for example:

```
if (d > e && (b = foo (zilch)))
    <stmt>;
```

It is clear that the function `foo` may or may not get called and that `b`, as a result, may or may not have its value changed. Thus, whenever we find the logical product operator `&&`, we must break the predicate expression into two or more `if` statements as follows:

```
if (d > e)
    if (b = foo (zilch))
        <stmt>;
```

The same fact is true for the conditional expression. If we were to find the following C code

```
c = a < b ? 5 : 6;
```

we would rewrite this as:

```
if(a < b)
    c = 6;
else
    c = 7;
```

to determine the appropriate flowgraph structure for this conditional expression.

For the sake of simplicity, we will temporarily set aside the rule that a processing node cannot have a processing node as its own successor. We will use this rule to refine the control flowgraph once we have a working model. The following steps will build the initial flowgraph.

1. The opening brace `<{>` and any declarations in a function will automatically constitute the first processing node of the flowgraph. The first node, of course, is the start node, which represents the function name and formal parameter list.
2. Each expression or expression statement will generate a processing node linked to the previous node.
3. All labels will generate a receiving node.
4. All expressions in selection statements (`<if>` and `<switch>`) will be extracted from the parentheses and will constitute one processing node that precedes the predicate node of the selection itself.

5. The `<if>` and `<switch>` will be replaced with a predicate node linked immediately to the next processing block.

6. In the case of the iteration statement `<while>`, three nodes will be generated. First is a receiving node to which control will return after the execution of the statement following the `while` expression. Next, the expression will be extracted and placed in a processing node. Finally, the predicate node will be generated and linked to the next processing node and to the next statement after the `while` group. The last processing node in the structure will be linked to the receiving node at the head the structure.

7. In the case of the `<for>` iteration statement, the first expression in the expression list will be replaced by a processing node followed by a receiving node, and the second (and third) expression(s) will be replaced by a processing node.

8. The `<for>` token will be replaced with a receiving node linked to the next processing node.

9. The `<do><while>` statement will have its predicate node following the statement delimited by `<do>` and `<while>`. First, the `<do>` token will be replaced by a receiving node that will ultimately be linked to the end of the do-while structure.

10. The statement following the `<do>` token, together with the expression after the `<while>` token, will be grouped with the do statement.

11. A `<goto>` statement implies the existence of a labeled statement. All labels will be replaced with receiving nodes. The effect of the `<goto>` is to link the current processing block containing the `<goto>` to the appropriate receiving node.

12. The `<continue>` and `<break>` statements are, in effect, `<goto>` statements to the unlabeled statement at the end of the control structure containing them.

13. All `<return>` statements will be treated as if they were `<goto>` statements. They will link to a receiving node that immediately precedes the exit node. If there is an expression associated with the `return` statement it will create a processing node that is, in turn, linked to the penultimate node. If there is but one return and it is at the end of the function module, then this receiving node with but one link will be removed in the refinement stage.

14. All assignment statements and expression statements will generate one processing node.

15. The declaration list of any compound statement will generate one processing node, which will also contain all executable statements in the declaration list.

After the preliminary flowgraph has been constructed by repetition of the above steps, it can then be refined. This refinement process will consist of:

- Removing all receiving nodes that have but one entering edge
- Combining into one processing node all cases of two sequential processing nodes

When all remaining nodes meet the criteria established for a flowgraph, its structure can be measured.

Exhibit 4 shows a sample C program. The first column of this exhibit shows the original C program. The second column shows the decomposition of this program according to the rules above. In this example, the nodes have been numbered to demonstrate the linkage among the nodes.

In Exhibit 5, there are two figures. The figure on the left shows the graphical representation of the initial program decomposition. This is not a flowgraph. We can find, for example, two processing blocks in a row. There is also a receiving node with one entering edge and one exiting edge. When the surplus processing blocks are combined and the unnecessary processing block removed, we get the final flowgraph shown by the figure on the right in this exhibit.

The Nodes metric will enumerate the number of nodes in the flowgraph representation of the program module. The minimum number of nodes that a module can have is three: the start node, a single processing node, and the exit node. Although it is possible to create a module with just the starting node and a terminal node, it does not make sense for a real system. Modules with just two nodes can be part of a testing environment as stubs but they should not be present in a deliverable product.

If a module has more than one exit point (return), then a receiving node must be created to provide for a single exit node for the structure. This receiving node will ensure that there is a unique exit node. In general, it is not a good programming process to use multiple return statements in a single program module. This is a good indication of lack of cohesion in a module.

The Edges metric will enumerate the edges in the control flow representation of the program module. For a minimal flowgraph of three nodes, there will, of course, be two connecting edges.

A path through a flowgraph is an ordered set of edges $(s,..., t)$ that begins on the starting node s and ends on the terminal node t. A path may contain one or more cycles. Each distinct cycle cannot occur more than once in sequence. That is, the subpath (a, b, c, a) is a legal subpath but the subpath (a, b, c, a, b, c, a) is not, in that the subpath (a, b, c, a) occurs twice.

The total path set of a node a is the set of all paths (s, a) that go from the start node to node a itself. The cardinality of the set of paths of node a is equal to the total path count of the node a. Each node singles out a distinct

Exhibit 4. Sample Program Decomposition

```
int average(int number)              < 0 START NODE int average(int number) >
{                                    < 1 PROCESSING NODE {
    int abs_number;                      int abs_number; LINK 2>
    if (number > 0)                  < 2 PROCESSING NODE (number > 0) LINK 3>
        abs_number = number;         < 3 PREDICATE NODE if LINK 4, 5>
    else                             < 4 PROCESSING NODE abs_number = number; LINK 7>
        abs_number = -number;        < 5 RECEIVING NODE else LINK 6>
    return abs_number;               < 6 PROCESSING NODE abs_number = -number;
}                                        LINK 7>
                                     < 7 RECEIVING NODE LINK 8>
                                     < 8 PROCESSING NODE abs_number;return LINK 9>
                                     < 9 RECEIVING NODE LINK 10>
                                     < 10 EXIT NODE} >
```

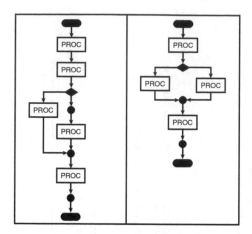

Exhibit 5. Reduction of the Flowgraph

number of paths to the node that begins at the starting node and ends with the node itself. The path count of a node is the number of such paths.

The Paths metric will tally the number of paths that begin at node s and end at node t. Sample enumeration of the Nodes, Edges, and Paths metrics can be seen in Exhibits 6 and 7.

The direct enumeration of paths in a program module may not be functionally possible. Consider the case of a simple if statement. If a program module contains but one if statement, then the number of paths doubles. In fact, the number of paths doubles for each if statement in series. We once encountered a program module that interrogated each bit in a 64-bit status word one bit at a time. This meant that there were a potential 2^{64} = 18,446,744,073,709,551,616 paths through this module. If our metric tool could count 1000 paths per second in the associated control flowgraph, it would take 584,942,417 years to measure this one module. For large program modules, the number of path counts will grow very large. For our measurement purposes, our metric tools put an arbitrary path maximum at 50,000. Common sense should prevail in the design complexity of modules. We think that modules whose path count is in excess of 100 or some other reasonable value, N, should come under the scrutiny of a design review process.

Cycles are permitted in paths. For each cyclical structure, exactly two paths are counted: one that includes the code in the cycle and one that does not. In this sense, each cycle contributes a minimum of two paths to the total path count. The number of cycles in the module flowgraph will be recorded in the Cycles metric. When the path contains control logic, the path count within the module increases.

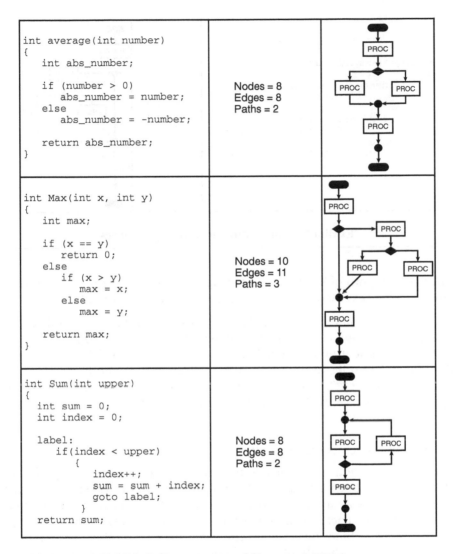

``int average(int number)
{
    int abs_number;
 	
    if (number > 0)
        abs_number = number;
    else
        abs_number = -number;
 	
    return abs_number;
}```
	Nodes = 8
	Edges = 8
	Paths = 2	

``int Max(int x, int y)
{
    int max;
 	
    if (x == y)
        return 0;
    else
        if (x > y)
            max = x;
        else
            max = y;
 	
    return max;
}```
	Nodes = 10
	Edges = 11
	Paths = 3	

``int Sum(int upper)
{
    int sum = 0;
    int index = 0;
 	
    label:
        if(index < upper)
        {
            index++;
            sum = sum + index;
            goto label;
        }
    return sum;```
	Nodes = 8
	Edges = 8
	Paths = 2	

Exhibit 6. Enumeration of Flowgraph Metrics

The MaxPath metric represents the number of edges in the longest path. From the set of available paths for a module, all the paths are evaluated by counting the number of edges in each of them. The greatest value is assigned to this metric. This metric gives an estimate of the maximum path flow complexity that might be obtained when running a module. In the example shown in Exhibit 8 for the Check function, there will be 2^3 (or 8) paths through the structure. The path length is, of course, the number of arcs or edges that comprise the path. Thus, the length of the maximum path is 10.

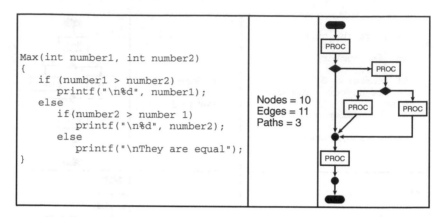

```
Max(int number1, int number2)
{
    if (number1 > number2)
        printf("\n%d", number1);
    else
        if(number2 > number 1)
            printf("\n%d", number2);
        else
            printf("\nThey are equal");
}
```

Nodes = 10
Edges = 11
Paths = 3

Exhibit 7. Enumeration of Flowgraph Metrics

There is one path of length 7, one of length 14, one of length 11, and one of length 17. The average path length, `Average-Path`, is then 12.25.

A cycle is a collection of strongly connected nodes. From any node in the cycle to any other, there is a path of length 1 or more, wholly within the cycle. This collection of nodes has a unique entry node. This entry node dominates all nodes in the cycle. A cycle that contains no other cycles is called an inner cycle. The `Cycles` metric will contain a count of all the cycles in a flowgraph. A sample function with a cycle in its flowgraph is shown in Exhibit 9.

5.2.4 Data Structures Complexity

Our own approach to the problem of measuring the complexity of data structures has been strongly motivated by the work of Halstead and our own work in the analysis of metric primitives. The basis of Halstead's software science metrics was that a compiler would process the source code to produce an object program. In the process of doing this, the compiler would have to resolve all tokens into one of two distinct classes: they were either operators or operands. Further, each of these counts for a program could be tallied in two distinct ways: total operators (operands) and unique operators (operands). All other metrics were derived from these primitive measures.

There are two broad classes of data structures: (1) those that are static and compiled with the source code, and (2) those that are created at execution time. Indeed, it is sometimes useful to model the dynamic complexity of programs.[12,13] It is the purpose of our data structure metric to measure the complexity of static data structures. To a great extent, dynamic data structures are created by algorithms and their complexity will be indirectly measured by the control constructs that surround their creation.

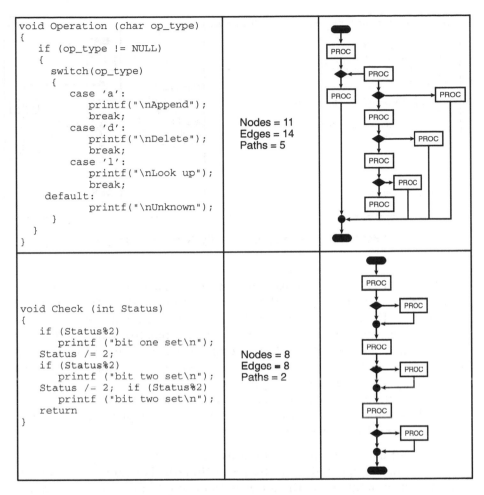

| `void Operation (char op_type)`
`{`
`    if (op_type != NULL)`
`    {`
`      switch(op_type)`
`      {`
`        case 'a':`
`            printf("\nAppend");`
`            break;`
`        case 'd':`
`            printf("\nDelete");`
`            break;`
`        case 'l':`
`            printf("\nLook up");`
`            break;`
`      default:`
`            printf("\nUnknown");`
`      }`
`    }`
`}` | Nodes = 11
Edges = 14
Paths = 5 | |
| `void Check (int Status)`
`{`
`    if (Status%2)`
`      printf ("bit one set\n");`
`    Status /= 2;`
`    if (Status%2)`
`      printf ("bit two set\n");`
`    Status /= 2;   if (Status%2)`
`      printf ("bit two set\n");`
`    return`
`}` | Nodes = 8
Edges = 8
Paths = 2 | |

Exhibit 8. Enumeration of Flowgraph Path Metrics

The data structures used in a program can influence the type of control structures used and the types of operations that can be used. The programming effort, understandability, and modifiability of a program are greatly influenced by the types of data structures used.

There is a definite difference between the complexity of a data structure as it is mapped to memory and its type complexity which are the operations that the machine will use to process data from this structure. The type properties of the structure vanish with the compilation, preserved only in the machine operations on the data. That is, the concept of type is an artifact of the particular programming language metaphor. The data structures persist at runtime. They represent real places in computer memory.

89

```
int find_element(int Array[20], int num)
{
  int counter = 0;
  int found = -1;
  if(counter < 20)
  {

    if (Array[counter] == num)
    {
      found = counter;
      break;
    }
    counter++;

  }
  return found;
}
```

Nodes = 12
Edges = 13
Paths = 4
MaxPath = 17
AvePath = 12.25
Cycles = 1

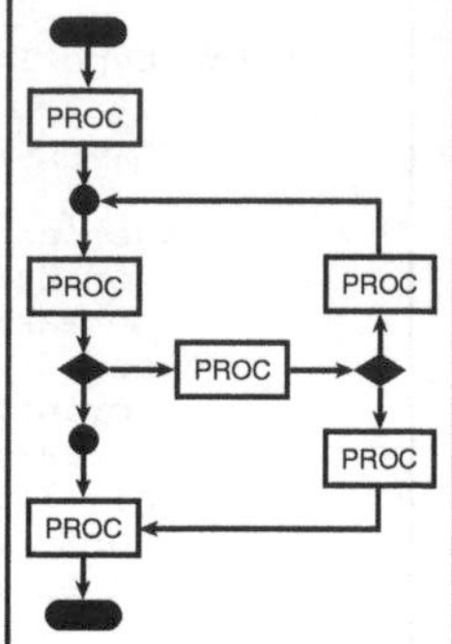

Exhibit 9. An Example of the Cycle in a Flowgraph

The objective of the proposed data structure measure is to obtain finer granularity on the Halstead notion of an operand and the attributes that it might have. The implementation of the notion of an operand by the author of a compiler and the operations needed to manipulate the operand (type) are two different attributes of this operand. Consider the case of an operand that is a scalar. This scalar might have a type of real or integer. On most systems, operands of these two types would occupy four bytes of memory. From the standpoint of managing the physical manifestations of each, they would be identical. The nature of the arithmetic to be performed on each, however, would be very different.

We could live a very long and happy life working with a programming language that supported only integer arithmetic. For those applications that required numbers on the interval from zero to one, we could simply use an additional integer value to store the fractional part of the number. Necessarily, performing arithmetic operations on such numbers would increase the computational complexity. The floating point data attribute greatly simplifies the act of numerical computation for real numbers. However, this type attribute will require its own arithmetic operators distinct from the integer arithmetic ones.

Thus, there appear to be many different components contributing to the complexity problem surrounding the notion of data structures. While they represent abstractions in the mind of the programmer, the compiler must make them tangible. In this regard, there are two distinctly different components of complexity. First, there is the declaration of the object and the subsequent operations a compiler will have to perform to manifest the structure. Second, there are the runtime operations that will manipulate the structure. For the purposes of domain mapping in our complexity domain model, we are interested in the operations surrounding the placement of these objects in the memory map of the object program.

Consider the several aspects of the declaration of an array in C. The declaration of an array, A, would look like this, int A[10]. A reference to the structure represented by A might include a subscript expression in conjunction with the identifier to wit: A[i]. The inherent data structure complexity represented by the subscripted variable would be represented in the increased operator and operand count of the Halstead complexity. The reference to the location, A[i], would be enumerated as two operators, <[> and <]>, and two operands, <A> and <i>. A reference to a simple scalar, say B, would count only as one operand.

The attribute complexity $C(D)$ of a data structure D is the cost to implement a data structure. This cost is closely associated with the amount of information that a compiler must create and manage in order to implement a particular data structure while compiling a program. We would intuitively expect that simple scalar data types are less costly to implement than more complex structures. It would also be reasonable to expect that the attribute complexity of a simple integer would be less than that of a record type.

A simple, scalar data type such as an integer, real, character, or Boolean requires that a compiler manage two distinct attributes: the data type and the address. Actually, the compiler will also manage the identifier, or name, that represents the data structure. However, this identifier will be enumerated in the operand count measure. Thus, the attribute complexity, $C(scalar)$, could be represented in a table with two entries. This structure table will contain all of the data attributes that the compiler will manage for each data structure. We define the structure by the number of entries in this structure table. Thus, the data structure complexity for a scalar will be $C(scalar) = 2$.

To implement an array, a compiler would require information as to the fact that it is an array, the memory location in relation to the address of the array, the type attribute of the elements of the array, the dimensionality of the array, the lower bound of each dimension, and the upper bound of each dimension. The structure table for an n-dimensional array is shown in Exhibit 10.

In the most general sense, the computation of the attribute complexity of an array would then be governed by the formula:

$$C(Array) = 3 + 2 \times n + C(ArrayElement)$$

where n is number of dimensions in the array and $C(ArrayElement)$ is the complexity of the array elements. For some languages, the array elements may only be simple scalars. FORTRAN is an example of such a language. In

Exhibit 10. The Array Structure

Structure: Array
Base Address
Type
Dimensions
Lower Bound #1
Upper Bound #1
Lower Bound #2
Upper Bound #2
•
•
•
Lower Bound #n
Upper Bound #n

the case of other languages, such as Pascal, the array elements may be chosen from the entire repertoire of possible data structures.

Another difference can be found among languages in regard to the bound pairs of the arrays. In languages such as C and FORTRAN the lower bound of the array is fixed. The programmer cannot alter the lower bound. In this case, the compiler will not record or manage the lower bound, and the complexity of arrays in these languages will be:

$$C(Array) = 3 + n + C(ArrayElement)$$

Other kinds of data structures may be seen as variants of the basic theme established above. For example, a string can be considered to be an array of characters. Therefore, we would compute the attribute complexity of the string as a unidimensional array. There are notable exceptions to this view. A string in language such as SNOBOL would be treated very differently. In the case of SNOBOL, there is but one data structure. Both program elements and data elements are represented as strings in this basic data structure.

A record is an ordered set of fields. In the simplest case, these fields are of fixed length, yielding records that are also of fixed length. Each field has the property that it may have its own structure. It may be a scalar, an array, or even a record. The structure table to manage the declaration of a record would have to contain the fact that it is a record type, the number of fields in the record (or alternatively the number of bytes in the record), and the attribute complexity of each of the fields of the record. The computation of the attribute complexity of a fixed-length record would be determined from the following formula:

$$C(Record) = 2 + \sum_{i=1}^{n} C(f_i)$$

where n is the number of fields and $C(f_i)$ is the attribute complexity of field i.

Records with variant parts are a slightly different matter. In general, only one record field of varying length is permitted in a variant record declaration. In this case, the compiler will simply treat the variant record as a fixed-length record with a field equal in length to the largest variant field.

The attribute complexities of subranges, sets, and enumerated data types may be similarly specified. They represent special cases of array or record declarations. In each case, the specific activities that a compiler will generate to manage these structures will lead to a measure for that data type. For example, enumerated data types will be represented internally as positive integers by the compiler. Similarly, a subrange can be represented as a range of integer values, not necessarily positive. The case for sets is somewhat more complicated. A variable with a set attribute is typically represented by a bit array. Each element in the set of declared objects is represented by a bit element in this array. The size of the array is determined by the cardinality of the set.

The notion of a pointer deserves some special attention here. From the perspective of a compiler, a pointer is simply a scalar value. A programmer might infer that the pointer has the properties of the structure that it references. A compiler does not. A pointer is a scalar value on which some special arithmetic is performed. That is all. Hence, a pointer is measured in the same manner as a scalar of integer type. It has a value of 2.

The full effect of a pointer and the complexity that this concept will introduce is, in fact, felt at runtime and not at compile time. A relatively complex set of algorithms will be necessary to manipulate the values that this scalar object may receive. These values will be derived based on the efforts of the programmer and not the compiler. As a result, in this particular model, the complexity of dynamic data structures such as linked lists and trees will be measured in the control structures that are necessary to manipulate these abstract objects.

The data structures complexity of a program module is the sum of the complexities of each of the data structures declared in that module. If, for example, a program has five scalar data items, then the data structures complexity of this module would be 10, or the sum of the five scalar complexity values. If a program module were to contain n instantiations of various data structures, each with a complexity C_i, then the data structures complexity, DS, of the program module would be:

$$DS = \sum_{i=1}^{n} C_i$$

To facilitate the understanding of the calculation of the data structures metric, Exhibit 11 shows a sample C function that will serve to illustrate

Exhibit 11. Sample `struct` Definition

```
void datatest (void)
{
    struct Complex {
        int Field1;
        int Field2;
    } Instance;
    int * Able;
    int Baker [100];
```

this process. In this very simple example, there are three declared variables, `Instance`, `Able`, and `Baker`. The variable `Baker` is an array of integers. It has a structure complexity of 6. The variable `Instance` is of type record. There are two fields in this record that are scalars. The structure complexity of this record is 5. The variable `Able` is a scalar. It is of type pointer. It has a structure complexity of 2. Thus, the DS value for this function is 13.

5.2.5 Coupling Metrics

There are many different attributes that relate specifically to the binding between program modules at runtime. These attributes are related to the coupling characteristics of the module structure. For our purposes, we will examine two attributes of this binding process: (1) the transfer of program control into and out of the program module, and (2) the flow of data into and out of a program module.

The flow of control among program modules can be represented in a program call graph. This call graph is constructed from a directed graph representation of program modules that can be defined as follows:

- A directed graph $G = (N, E, s)$ consists of a set of nodes N, a set of edges E, a distinguished node s, the main program node. An edge is an ordered pair of nodes (a, b).
- There will be an edge (a, b) if program module a can call module b.
- As was the case for a module flowgraph, the in-degree $I(a)$ of node a is the number of entering edges to a.
- Similarly, the out-degree $O(a)$ of node a is the number of exiting edges from a.

The nodes of a call graph are program modules. The edges of this graph represent calls from module to module, and not returns from these calls. Only the modules that are constituents of the program source code library will be represented in the call graph. This call graph will specifically exclude calls to system library functions.

Coupling reflects the degree of relationship that exists between modules. The more tightly coupled two modules are, the more dependent on each other they become. Coupling is an important measurement domain because it is closely associated with the impact that a change in a module (or also a fault) might have on the rest of the system. There are several program attributes associated with coupling. Two of these attributes relate to the binding between a particular module and other program modules. There are two distinct concepts represented in this binding: the number of modules that can call a given module and the number of calls out of a particular module. These will be represented by the fan-in and fan-out metrics, respectively.[14]

The F_1 metric, fan-out, will be used to tally the total number of local function calls made *from* a given module. If module b is called several times in module a, then the F_1 metric will be incremented for each call. On the other hand, the number of unique calls out will be recorded by the f_1 metric. In this case, although there might be many calls from module a to module b, the f_1 metric will be incremented only on the first of these calls. Again, neither the F_1 nor the f_1 metrics will be used to record system or system library calls.

The F_2 metric, fan-in, will be used to tally the total number of local function calls made *to* a given module. If module b is called several times in module a, then the F_2 metric for module b will be incremented for each call. On the other hand, the number of unique calls into module b will be recorded by the f_2 metric. In this case, although there might be many calls from module a to module b, the f_2 metric will be incremented only on the first of these calls. Neither the F_2 nor the f_2 metric will be used to record system or system library calls.

The problem with the fan-in metrics is that they cannot be enumerated from an examination of the program module. We cannot tell by inspection which modules call the `print_record` example of Exhibit 12. The static calls to this module we will have to obtain from the linker as the system is built. Another problem with these metrics stems from the fact that C and languages derived from it have a very poor programming practice built into them. Calls can be made using function pointers. These calls will have to be determined at runtime.

The degree of data binding between a module and the program modules that will call it is measured by the data structures complexity of the formal parameter list. These parameters are not measured by the module data structures complexity metric DS. We will denote the data structures complexity of the formal parameter list by the metric `Param_DS` to distinguish it from the module local data structures complexity DS.

Exhibit 12. Sample Fan-Out

Example	F_1	f_1
`void print_record(long int id)`	Look_up	Look_up
`{`		
`    Record Rec; char pause;`	PutMessage	PutMessage
`    printf("\nEnter new id");`	PutMessage	
`    while (Rec = Look_up(id)) =  = NULL))`		
`    {`		
`        PutMessage("not Found);`		
`        printf("\nEnter new id");`		
`        scanf("%d," &id);`		
`    }`		
`    else`	Total: 3	Total: 2
`    {`		
`        PutMessage("Record Description");`		
`        printf("\n%d:\n\t%s," id, Rec);`		
`    }`		
`getc(pause);`		
`}`		

5.3 MEASURES OF SOFTWARE QUALITY

The majority of software quality attributes relate to the operation of the code in terms of performance, availability, and security, to name but three. There are two aspects of software quality that do represent static attributes: software faults and software maintainability. We can measure maintainability but we cannot measure software faults. If we had a tool that could peruse a source code base and identify faults, the progress that could be made in software development would be astonishing. Sadly, we will only be able to recognize them when they cause problems or through intense scrutiny of individual source code modules.

5.3.1 Software Faults

Unfortunately, there has been no particular definition of just precisely what a software fault is, a problem that we intend to ameliorate.[15] In the face of this difficulty, it has rather difficult to develop meaningful associative models between faults and metrics. In other words, a fault is a physical characteristic of the system of which the type and extent can be measured using the same ideas used to measure the properties of more traditional physical systems. People making errors in their tasks introduce faults into a system. These errors can be errors of commission or errors of omission. There are, of course, differing etiologies for each fault. Some faults are attributable to errors in the specification of requirements; some faults are directly attributable to error committed in the design process; and finally, there are faults that are introduced directly into the source code. We will concern ourselves with source code faults in this chapter.

There are two major subdivisions of faults in our fault taxonomy: faults of *commission* and faults of *omission*. Faults of commission involve deliberate, albeit unwitting, implementation of a behavior that is not part of the specification or design. Faults of omission involve lapses wherein a behavior specified in the design was not implemented. It is important to make these distinctions, especially so the inspection protocol can be used as a checklist for specific faults that have been found in the past.

To count faults, there must be a well-defined method of identification that is repeatable, consistent, and identifies faults at the same level of granularity as our static source code measurements. In a careful examination of software faults over the years, we have observed that the overwhelming number of faults recorded as code faults are really design faults. Some software faults are really faults in the specification. The design implements the specification and the code implements the design. We must be very careful to distinguish among these fault categories.

There may be faults in the specification. The specification may not meet the customer's needs. If this problem first manifests itself in the code, it still is not a code fault. It is a fault in the program specification, or a *specification fault*. The software design may not implement the software requirements specification. Again, these design problems tend to manifest themselves during software testing. Any such design faults must be identified correctly as *design faults*. In a small proportion of faults, the problem is actually a code problem. In these isolated cases, the problem should be reported as a *code fault*.

We observed an example of this type of problem recently in a project on a large embedded software system. The program in question was supposed to interrogate a status register on a particular hardware subsystem for a particular bit setting. The code repeatedly misread this bit. This was reported as a software problem. What really happened was that the hardware engineers had implemented a hardware modification that shifted the position of the status bit in the status register. They had failed to notify the software developers of this material change in the hardware specification. The software system did exactly what it was supposed to do. It is just that this no longer met the hardware requirements. Yet the problem remains on record to this date as a software fault.

It is clear, then, that the etiology of the fault must be determined. It is the subject of this chapter to identify and enumerate faults that occur in source code. We ought to be able to do this mechanically; that is, it should be possible to develop a tool that can count the faults for us. Further, some program changes to fix faults are substantially larger than others. We would like our fault count to reflect that fact. If we have accidentally mistyped a relational operator such as "<" instead of ">", this is very different from having messed up an entire predicate clause from an if statement. The actual changes made to a code module are tracked for us in configuration control systems such as RCS or SCCS as code deltas. All we must learn to do is to classify the code deltas that we make as to the origin of the fix. That is, each change to each module should reflect a specific code fault fix, a design problem, or a specification problem. If we manifestly change any code module, give it a good overhaul, and fail to record each fault as we repaired it, we will pay the price in losing the ability to resolve faults for measurement purposes.

We will base our recognition and enumeration of software faults on the grammar of the language of the software system. Specifically, faults are to be found in statements, executable and nonexecutable. In the C programming language we will consider the following structures to be executable statements:

```
<executable_statement> :: = <labeled_statement> |
<expression> |
<selection_statement> |
<iteration_statement> |
<jump_statement>
```

In very simple terms, these structures will cause our executable statements metric, Exec, count to change. If any of the tokens change that comprise the statement, then each of the change tokens will represent a contribution to a fault count.

Within the framework of nonexecutable statements there is:

```
<declaration> :: = <declaration_specifiers> ;
| <declaration_specifiers> <init_declarator_list> ';'
```

We will find faults *within* these statements. The granularity of measurement for faults will be in terms of tokens that have changed. Thus, if I typed the following statement in C:

```
a = b + c * d;
```

but I had meant to type:

```
a = b + c/d;
```

then there is but one token that I got wrong. In this example, there are eight tokens in each statement. There is one token that has changed. There is one fault. This circumstance is very different when wholesale changes are made to the statement. Consider that this statement:

```
a = b + c * d;
```

was changed to:

```
a = b + (c * x) + sin(z);
```

We are going to assume, for the moment, that the second statement is a correct implementation of the design and that the first is not. This is clearly a coding error. (Generally, when changes of this magnitude occur, they are design problems.) In this case there are eight tokens in the first statement and fifteen tokens in the second statement. This is a fairly substantial change in the code. Our fault recording methodology should reflect the degree of the change. This is not an unreasonable or implausible notion. If we are driving our car and the car ceases to run, we will seek to identify the problem or have a mechanic do so for us. The mechanic will perform the necessary diagnostics to isolate the problem. The fan belt may have failed. That is a single problem and a simple one. The fan belt may have failed because the bearing on the idler pulley failed. We expect that the mechanic will isolate *all* the problems and itemize the failed items on our bill. How much information would we have if the mechanic simply reported that the engine broke? Most of us would feel that we would like to know just exactly what pieces of the engine had failed and were subsequently replaced. We expect this level of granularity in reporting engine problems. We should expect the same level of granularity of reporting on code fixes.

The important consideration with this fault measurement strategy is that there must be some indication as to the amount of code that has changed in resolving a problem in the code. We have regularly witnessed changes to tens or even hundreds of lines of code recorded as a single "bug" or fault. The only really good index of the degree of the change is the number of tokens that have changed to ameliorate the original problem. To simplify and disambiguate further discussion, consider the following definitions.

- *Definition:* A fault is an invalid token or bag of tokens in the source code that will cause a failure when the compiled code that implements the source code token is executed.
- *Definition:* A failure is the departure of a program from its specified functionalities.
- *Definition:* A defect is an apparent anomaly in the program source code.

Each line of text in each version of the program can be seen as a bag of tokens. That is, there may be multiple tokens of the same kind on each line of the text. When a software developer changes a line of code in response to the detection of a fault, either through normal inspection, code review processes, or as a result of a failure event in a program module, the tokens on that line will change. New tokens may be added; invalid tokens may be removed; the sequence of tokens may be changed. Enumeration of faults under this definition is simple and straightforward. Most important of all, this process can be automated. Measurement of faults can be performed very precisely, which will eliminate the errors of observation introduced by existing *ad hoc* fault reporting schemes.

An example is useful to show this fault measurement process. Consider the following line of C code:

```
(1) a = b + c;
```

There are six tokens on this line of code. They are $B_1 = \{<a>, < = >, <b>, <+>, <c>\}$, where B_1 is the bag representing this token sequence.

Now let us suppose that the design, in fact, required that the difference between b and c be computed; that is:

```
(2) a = b — c;
```

There will again be six tokens in the new line of code. This will be the bag $B_2 = \{<a>, < = >, <b>, <->, <c>\}$. The bag difference is $B_1 - B_2 = \{<+>, <->\}$. The cardinality of B_1 and B_2 is the same. There are two tokens in the difference. Clearly, one token has changed from one version of the module to another. There is one fault.

Now suppose that the new problem introduced by the code in statement (2) is that the order of the operations is incorrect. It should read:

```
(3) a = c — b;
```

The new bag for this new line of code will be $B_3 = \{<a>, < = >, <c>, <->, <b>\}$. The bag difference between (2) and (3) is $B_2 - B_3 = \{ \}$. The cardinality of B_2 and B_3 is the same. This is a clear indication that the tokens are the same but the sequence has been changed. There is one fault representing the incorrect sequencing of tokens in the source code.

Now suppose that we are converging on the correct solution; however, our calculations are off by 1. The new line of code will look like this:

```
(4) a = 1 + c — b;
```

This will yield a new bag $B_3 = \{<a>, < = >, <1>, <+>, <c>, <->, <b>\}$. The bag difference between (3) and (4) is $B_3 - B_4 = \{<1>, <+>\}$. The cardinality of B_3 is 6 and the cardinality of B_4 is 8. Clearly, there are two new tokens. By definition, there are two new faults.

It is possible that a change will span multiple lines of code. All of the tokens in all of the changed lines so spanned will be included in one bag. This will allow us to determine just how many tokens have changed in the one sequence.

The source code control system should be used as a vehicle for managing and monitoring the changes to code that are attributable to faults and to design modifications and enhancements. Changes to the code modules should be discrete. That is, multiple faults should not be fixed by one version of the code module. Each version of the module should represent exactly one enhancement or one defect.

We will take a simple example and trace the evolution of a source code program through three successive revisions in the UNIX RCS program. The sample program is from Exhibit 13 (repeated here with added line numbers for future reference).

```
1  int Sum(int upper)
2  {
3     int sum = 0;
4     int index = 0;
5
6     label:
7        if(index < upper)
8           {
9              index++;
10             sum = sum + index;
11             goto label;
12          }
13       return sum;
14  }
```

The program above represents version 1.1 of the program. Successive updates to this will be 1.2, 1.3, etc. The RCS system will keep track of the version number, the date and time of the update, and the author of the RCS activity. An abridged version of the RCS module structure to record these data is shown in Exhibit 13.

Exhibit 13. RCS Header Information

1.4		
date	2005.02.01.22.17.38;	author John Doe;
next	1.3;	
1.3		
date	2005.01.22.22.01.31;	author John Doe;
next	1.2;	
1.2		
date	2005.01.20.21.54.08;	author Sam Lee;
next	1.1;	
1.1		
date	2005.01.15.21.49.29;	author Mary Roe;
next	;	

The odd part of RCS is that the most recent version, in this case 1.4, is kept at the top of the list and the list is numbered chronologically backwards in time. Each version keeps a pointer to the next version in the table.

The actual changes to the source code at each version are shown in Exhibit 14. The RCS program will always keep the most recent version in the file. This is shown in the table entry beginning with, in this case, version 1.4. The second entry in the record for version 1.4 is an entry beginning with the word log and delimited by @s. This is the log comment introduced by the developer. In our proposed model, this log entry would begin with the word "fault" if the version increment were attributable to a fault fix, or the word "change" if it were attributable to a change in design or requirements. The initial log entry, version 1.1, is for neither a change nor a fault fix but is the title of the program.

Following the log entry is the text entry. In the case of RCS, the topmost text entry is the most recent version of the program. Each of the subsequent table entries show the changes that must be made to the most recent program to change it to a previous version. All changes are made, in RCS, by adding or deleting entire lines. Thus, to return to version 1.3 from version 1.4, the text part of record 1.3 tells us to go to line 7 (relative to 1) of the program and delete one line. That is what the line d7 1 tells us. The next text line says that we must add one line, a7 1, again at line 7. The text that must be added is on the following line. Thus, version 1.3 will look like this:

```
1   int Sum(int upper)
2   {
3       int sum = 0;
4       int index = 0;
5
6       label:
7           if(index < = upper)
8               {
9                   index++;
10                  sum = sum + index;
11                  goto label;
12              }
13          update (index);
14          return sum;
15  }
```

Line number 7 has been changed on version 1.3. Let

$$B_2 = \{<\text{if}>, <(>, <\text{index}>, << = >, <\text{upper}>, <)>\}$$

represent this bag of tokens. On version 1.4, the bag of tokens is:

$$B_1 = \{<\text{if}>, <(>, <\text{index}>, <>>, <\text{upper}>, <)>\}$$

Exhibit 14. RCS Text Information

```
1.4
log
@fault: fixed relational operator
@
text
@int Sum(int upper)
{
  int sum = 0;
  int index = 0;
  label:
    if(index > upper)
       {
          index++;
          sum = sum + index;
          goto label;
       }
  update (index);
  return sum;
@
1.3
log
@fault: inserted call to update function
@
text
@d7 1
a7 1
    if(index < = upper)
@
1.2
log
@fault: found a problem with a relational operator
@
text
@d13 1
@
1.1
log
@Initial revision
@
text
@d7 1
a7 1
    if(index < upper)
@
```

The bag difference is $B_2 - B_1 = \{<< = >, <>>\}$. The cardinality of B_2 is 6 and the cardinality of B_1 is 6. The cardinality of the bag difference is 2. Therefore, one token has changed and we will record one fault.

To return to version 1.2 from version 1.3, we see that we must delete line 13. All of the tokens on this line were placed there in remediation of a fault. The bag representing this line of tokens is:

$$B_3 = \{<update>, <(>, <index>, <)>, <;>\}$$

There are five tokens on this line. There was no former version of this line in version 1.2. Therefore, all of the tokens on this line were put into the program to fix a defect in the program. We will then record five faults for this fix.

Finally, to return to the initial version, 1.1, of the program, we must delete line 7 and add a new line represented by the bag

$$B_4 = \{<if>, <(>, <index>, <<>, <upper>, <)>\}$$

This is similar to the transition between versions 1.3 and 1.4. Only one token has changed. We will record one fault for this module version.

5.3.2 Software Maintainability

Our first task in learning to measure the maintainability of software will be to understand the attributes of maintainability that can be measured. It is clear, for example, that source code maintainability is directly related to the linkage between the source and a design. It is very difficult to fix something whose functionality you do not understand. The second attribute has to do with module coupling. If a module is called without arguments from one module, modifying this module will have little impact on the program as a whole. If, on the other hand, a module is called by many modules, calls many others, and has an extensive formal parameter list, then it is clearly woven tightly into the fabric of the program. Any changes to this module will have far-reaching consequences in the program operation. Thus, there are two significant aspects of maintainability that we wish to measure: (1) the ease of modification of the module, and (2) the impact of the module change on the program containing the module.

The principal criterion measure for maintainability will, of course, be the cost in staff resources of making changes to code. We would expect that our measures of maintainability would be directly related to the cost in human resources of making changes to systems.

5.3.2.1 Traceability. Each statement in a programming language can be identified and counted by the set of counting rules established early for the executable statements metric Exec. We will have complete requirements traceability if and only if each source code statement can be mapped directly back to a design element. This will be possible, of course, only if there is an appropriate design database that is maintained as the code base changes. Again, the granularity of measurement will be the program module.

We will have complete requirements traceability if we can directly map each source code statement to a design database element. We will now define a Map metric to measure this mapping. For each module source code statement that is correctly mapped to a design element, we will increment the Map metric for that code module. A maintainable program, under this definition, will have the property that Exec = Map. The traceability of a system is then measured by the relationship between total executable statements and those executable statements that are traceable to design elements; that is:

```
Traceability = Exec - Map
```

5.3.2.2 Coupling. It is clear that the modules that are tightly bound to other program modules will be difficult to modify. There are two distinct attributes that must be considered in this binding. First there is the linkage of each program module to other program modules. We can measure this with the coupling metrics defined earlier. These metrics can easily be classified as measures of program maintainability. If a program module is called by one and only one program module, and calls only one program module, then the impact of any change to this module is probably local to a small number of modules. If the control structure integrating a particular module is tightly woven into the control fabric of other modules, as is the case with the object-oriented programming metaphor, then the impact of modifying a module may be very great.

The second attribute of program module binding is that of data binding between modules. We have accounted for some of this potential data binding in the measurement of data structures in the formal parameter list. The most insidious and dangerous aspect of data binding among program modules deals with global variables. We have seen hundreds of program trouble reports that deal specifically with changes made to global variables with far-reaching side effects in a host of other program modules. In essence, then, the maintainability of a program module is inversely proportional to the amount of data in global variables.

The global data structures attribute Global_DS will be the data structure metric applied to all data identifiers that are declared outside the scope of the current module. In the case of the C (or C++) programming language, if the data declaration for an identifier is not in the function module being measured, then the data structures complexity of this identifier will be used to increase the Global_DS metric for the module.

5.4 SUMMARY

It has not been an objective of this chapter to identify all possible metric primitives for program modules. The metrics defined herein are those that we have found of maximum utility for measuring the activity for program modules. These metrics represent a first step in the development of a software measurement program.

We have found that there are very many program attributes that can easily be counted, such as `Comments` and `LOC`. Enumeration of these attributes for a program will produce data. The problem with these two values is that their information content is negligible. We can learn nothing really useful from them. They are not very useful in predicting software quality attributes. On the other hand, there are other measures of program size, such as total executable statement count, `Exec`, that are good predictors of software quality and are not nearly so dependent on the uncontrolled source of variation of style of individual programmers.

An overriding objective of this book is to focus on the software measurement process. We would expect that this measurement process itself should come under close measurement scrutiny. It should be continually measured and enhanced. The metrics presented in this chapter are intended to be an initial working metric set for the institution of a measurement process. Any measurement process should have at its heart a process for measurement improvement. With this basic set of working metrics, we know that we can account for at least 80 percent of the total variation in software faults, for example. That is quite a bit more information than the vast majority of software managers have at their current disposal. Now we can begin the process of refinement. Careful analysis of software fault data will now tell us what we are missing in the 20 percent of variance for which we cannot account.

References

1. Zuse, H., *Software Complexity: Measures and Methods,* Walter de Gruyter & Co., New York, 1990.
2. Zuse, H., *A Framework of Software Measurement*, Walter de Gruyter & Co., Berlin, 1998.
3. McCabe, T.J., A Complexity Measure, *IEEE Transactions on Software Engineering*, SE-2, pp. 308–320, 1976.
4. Munson, J.C. Software Measurement: Problems and Practice, *Annals of Software Engineering*, 1(1), 255–285, 1995.
5. Munson, J.C., and Khoshgoftaar, T.M., The Dimensionality of Program Complexity, *Proceedings of the 11th Annual International Conference on Software Engineering*, IEEE Computer Society Press, Los Alamitos, CA, 1989, pp. 245–253.
6. Munson, J.C. and Khoshgoftaar, T.M., Regression Modeling of Software Quality: An Empirical Investigation, *Journal of Information and Software Technology*, 32, 105–114, 1999.

7. Khoshgoftaar, T.M., Munson, J.C., Bhattacharya, B.B., and Richardson, G.D., Predictive Modeling Techniques of Software Quality from Software Complexity Measures, *IEEE Transactions on Software Engineering*, SE-18(11), 979–987, November 1992.

8. Munson, J.C. and Khoshgoftaar, T.M., The Detection of Fault-Prone Programs, *IEEE Transactions on Software Engineering*, SE-18(5), 423–433, 1992.

9. Munson, J.C., Software Faults, Software Failures, and Software Reliability Modeling, *Information and Software Technology*, 687–699, December 1996.

10. Munson, J.C. and Khoshgoftaar, T.M., The Detection of Fault-Prone Programs, *IEEE Transactions on Software Engineering*, SE-18(5), 423–433, 1992.

11. Halstead, M.H., *Elements of Software Science*, Elsevier, New York, 1977.

12. Munson, J.C., Dynamic Program Complexity and Software Testing, *Proceedings of the IEEE International Test Conference*, Washington, D.C., October 1996.

13. Munson, J.C. and Khoshgoftaar, T.M., Dynamic Program Complexity: The Determinants of Performance and Reliability, *IEEE Software,* November 1992, pp. 48–55.

14. Henry, S. and Kafura, D., Software Metrics Based on Information Flow, *IEEE Transactions on Software Engineering*, 7(5), 510–518, 1981.

15. Munson, J.C. and Nikora, A.P., Towards a Quantifiable Definition of Software Faults, *Proceedings of the 2002 IEEE International Symposium on Software Reliability Engineering*, November 2002.

Chapter 6
Derived Software Measures

6.1 INTRODUCTION

In Chapter 5 we discussed primitive software metrics. These were atomic measures of a program module. They measured a single program attribute. Derived software measures, on the other hand, are linear and nonlinear composites of metric primitives. We might think to create a new measure of program module size such that Size = Exec + LOC. Unfortunately, life is not that simple. We will not benefit from our new size metric. In fact, we will probably lose information in the sum of module executable statement and lines of code. The metrics Exec and LOC are drawn from different populations. They are measured in different units. And they are also highly correlated. This exercise is somewhat akin to our creating a size measure from human attributes. Consider the following new size measure: Health = Height + Weight. To compute our new Health metric we will measure an individual's height and his or her weight and then add them together. We might speculate that the larger the value of Health, the fewer medical problems an individual will have. Immediately, common sense kicks in. We know that you cannot add these two values. Height is measured in centimeters and weight is measured in kilograms. These two attributes are measured in different units. Finally, the relationship between our new Health metric and a person's actual well-being is purely speculative. The basic principles of science would demand that we validate our Health metric with an empirical investigation before we make any health assertions about our new metric.

We will see this common sense thrown to the winds in just about every derived software metric. Unfortunately, much of the foundation of the field of software metrics is based on such derived metrics. We must first learn what part of the current store of information about software metrics is usable and what is of no particular value or downright wrong. A good place to begin this investigation is with the work of Maurice Halstead and his theory of software science.

6.2 SOFTWARE SCIENCE METRICS

Halstead was one of the pioneers in the field of software measurement. He is responsible for a set of metrics known as the Halstead software science metrics. These metrics can be divided into two distinct sets: primitive metrics and derived metrics. He observed that a compiler could parse program tokens into the two sets of operators and operands. Complicated algorithms could be seen to require more operators and operands than more straightforward algorithms. Hence, the count of operators and operands was quite relevant to the underlying complexity of the program. The Halstead primitives discussed in Chapter 5 are:

- η_1 is the cardinality of the set of *operator* tokens in a program module.
- η_2 is the cardinality of the set of *operand* tokens in a program module.
- N_1 is the cardinality of the bag of *operator* tokens in a program module.
- N_2 is the cardinality of the bag of *operand* tokens in a program module.

These basic metrics are of real value in understanding the complexity of a program. They are really related to software quality criterion measures. We can learn a lot from them. Now the fun really begins and the science ends.

Halstead set about to extract more information from the basic set of metric primitives that he derived from the program tokens, beginning with the follow two new metrics:

- $\eta = \eta_1 + \eta_2$ is defined as the *vocabulary* of the program.
- $N = N_1 + N_2$ is defined as the implementation *length* of the program.

Here, common sense should prevail. If you knew that there are 5000 undergraduates and 1000 graduate students at State University, it would be completely redundant to say that there are 6000 students at State University. There is no new information in their sum. By the same reasoning, there is simply no information in the vocabulary or length of a program. No new sources of variation have been added to these new metrics. We can learn nothing new from their sum.

When all else fails, it is a tradition in the discipline of computer science to take the log to the base two of a value. This will surely create new information content. Observe the following:

- $\hat{N} = \eta_1 \log_2 \eta_1 + \eta_2 \log_2 \eta_2$ is the *calculated length* of the program.
- $V = N \log_2 \eta$ is the *volume* of the program.

Again, there are no new sources of variation being evaluated, nor did we learn anything new. Principal component analysis will show us that $\hat{N}$ and V always vary in the same manner as the metric primitives.

Now it gets really interesting. Two new potential sources of variation enter the problem space. These are:

- $\eta_1{}^*$, the minimum number of unique or distinct *operators* for the algorithm being implemented
- $\eta_2{}^*$, the minimum number of unique or distinct *operands* for the algorithm being implemented

It would appear that we are plowing new ground here. Unfortunately, the new sources of variation introduced by $\eta_1{}^*$ and $\eta_2{}^*$ are probably noise. There are no real precise rules for measuring these attributes. They cannot be measured accurately or unambiguously. They will vary differently from the token primitives but not because they represent new information, only because there are measurement discrepancies in them. There are a host of derived metrics that are based on the new metrics of $\eta_1{}^*$ and $\eta_2{}^*$. They are as follows:

- $V^* = \eta^* \log_2 \eta^*$ is the *potential volume* of the program.
- $V^{**} = (2 + \eta_2{}^* \log_2 \eta_2{}^*)\log_2(2 + \eta_2{}^*)$ is the *boundary volume* of the program.
- $L = V^*/V$ is the *program level* of the implementation of a program.
- $\hat{L} = \dfrac{\eta_1^*}{\eta_1}\dfrac{\eta_2}{N_2}$ is an alternate representation for program level.
- $D = 1/L$ is the *difficulty* in implementing a program.
- $I = \hat{L} \times V$ represents the *intelligence content* of the program.
- $E = V/L$ is the *total number of elementary mental discriminations* required to generate a given program. This is generally called Halstead's *effort*.

These metrics have proven very popular with software metricians over the years. This in itself is a very sad fact. There have been no efforts to validate these metrics. Had there been, they would never have seen the light of day.

Now we move rapidly into the area of pseudoscience. Once upon a time there was a man by the name of Stroud who published an obscure piece of research in an equally obscure journal of psychology. That article was Stroud's only real publication and was dutifully ignored by the psychology community. The work reported by Stroud was purely speculative and certainly not validated empirically. He thought that people could make about ten elementary mental discriminations per second. Unfortunately, we do not know what an elementary mental discrimination was, nor was Stroud able to convey this idea in his article. Halstead found this article in the psychological literature and incorporated Stroud's concept of elementary mental discriminations into his emerging software science metrics. This yields a new set of metrics as follows:

- S is an arbitrary random variable such that $5 \leq S \leq 20$ Stroud moments per second.
- $\hat{T} = E/S$ is the *estimated implementation time* for a program.
- $\lambda = LV^*$ is the *language level* of a program.

- v is a count of the number of *transfers* of control flow both conditional and unconditional in a program.
- $\beta = \dfrac{N}{v+1}$ is the *average block size*.
- E_0 is the mean number of elementary discriminations between potential errors in programming.
- $B = E^{2/3}/E_0$ is the number of delivered errors in a program.
- M is the number of modules in a program.
- $V_m^* = (\eta_1^* + \eta_2^*/M)\log_2(\eta_1^* + \eta_2^*/M)$ is the *individual potential volume* of a program module.
- $V_M^* = MV_m^* + M\log_2 M$ is the *combined potential volume* of a fully modularized program.
- $M = \eta_2^*/6$ is the *ideal* number of modules in a program.

We have every reason to believe that Halstead had his heart in the right place but the overwhelming majority of these metrics are just not woven out of whole cloth. There are some real conceptual problems with those metrics that are associated with the Stroud number, S.[1] Each of the Halstead metrics theoretically represents a unique program attribute. This being the case, there should be a distinct source of variance contributed by each of the metrics when we observe them at work measuring a program. This is simply not the case. The four primitive metrics of operator and operand count account for essentially the variation in all of the rest of the metrics.

6.3 SOURCES OF VARIATION

As we measure software attributes, we can characterize in two different ways the number that we get from each program module that we measure. First, we can look at measures of central tendency such as mean, median, or mode. Unfortunately, there is very little information in these statistics. We could know, for example, that the average Exec for a program module is 1000 executable statements. If we were to know this statistic and the fact that module A had 1010 executable statements in it, we will have to learn little about module A in relation to the rest of the program modules. This information is contained in the measures of dispersion, typically the second moment about the mean or variance. To understand the relationship between module A and all the other program modules, we will need information about the variation among the program modules. If the standard deviation is found to be 5, for example, then module A is fully two standard deviations from the mean. It is large in relation to the other program modules. If, on the other hand, the standard deviation is found to be 20, then we learn that module A is relatively close to the average of all program modules in executable statements. If the variance were 0, then all program modules would have 1000 statements. There would be no information in the knowledge that a module was comprised of 1000 statements. The main

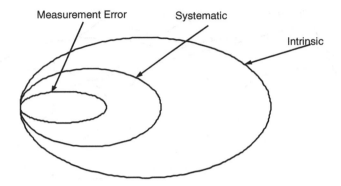

Exhibit 1. Sources of Variation

point here is that the information content on the measure is dependent on its variance.

There are many possible sources of the observed variance in program statements. First, there is the intrinsic variation. Different program modules simply have different numbers of statements in them. Some modules are large and others are small, depending on the module functionality. Second, there are systematic sources of variation that are not intrinsically related to the size of the program module. In this category, we have errors of measurement. If we have people counting statements, they can simply miscount statements. This will induce a source of variation that is related to errors in measurement. There can also be systematic variance induced by differences in people. If there are ambiguities in the standards for defining statements, different people will enumerate statements differently. There will be a source of variance, then, directly related to constant differences among the enumerators. These are summarized in the Venn diagram of Exhibit 1.

If we are measuring both the executable statements and lines of code of a program module, these metrics clearly have a lot in common. They are both measures of the size of a program. As such, they share an element of common variation, as is shown in Exhibit 2. We call this element of shared variance the *covariance*, whereas, the variance term is derived from the second moment about the mean as follows:

$$Var(x) = \frac{1}{n-1} \sum_{i=1}^{n} (x_i - \bar{x})^2 ,$$

The covariance term is derived from the cross-product of two variables and their simultaneous variation as follows:

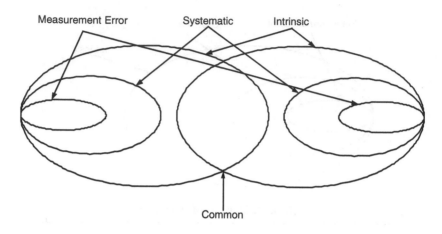

Exhibit 2. Common Variation

$$Cov(x,y) = \frac{1}{n-1}\sum_{i=1}^{n}(x_i - \bar{x})(y_i\bar{y}).$$

If x_i and y_i differ from their respective means in the same way for the same program module, then their element of shared variation is very large. If, on the other hand, knowledge of x does not yield much information about the corresponding value of y for the same module, then their shared variation is very small.

Each attribute that we are measuring has its own mean and variance. It is very difficult to impossible to learn anything about a program module of 75 lines of code whose statement count is 53 by looking at these raw values. If we adjust each for the effect of its own mean and standard deviation, then we can look at these adjusted values and know something about the size of the program module in question. To do this we will convert the raw metric scores to z-scores as follows: $z_i = (x_i - \bar{x})/\delta_x$. Now each of the new z-scores will have a mean of 0 and a standard deviation of 1. Now, if we know that the average lines of code for a module is 85 with a standard deviation of 10 and that the average statement count is 62 with a standard deviation of 7, we can convert the raw scores of 75 LOC and 53 Exec to their corresponding z-scores as follows:

$$z_{LOC} = (75 - 85)/10 = -1.0$$

$$z_{Exec} = (53 - 62)/7 = -1.3.$$

It is now apparent that the program module in question is significantly smaller in both lines of code and executable statements than other program modules. That the z-scores are negative indicates that the values are less than the mean. That they are less than or equal to −1.0 indicates that they are at least one standard deviation below the average module for the system. In that they now have the same underlying distribution, it would make statistical sense to add them together or find their average.

Now that we have adjusted for the effect of the mean and the standard deviation in the creation of z-scores for the lines of code and executable statement metrics, we can now talk about their common variance in terms of the Pearson product moment correlation statistic as follows:

$$r_{xy} = \frac{1}{n-1} \sum_{i=1}^{n} z_x z_y.$$

This new statistic is a measure of the common variation between the variables x and y. It is based on the standardized z-scores. This means that $-1.0 \le r_{xy} \le 1.0$. This new statistic is a measure of the bivariate relationship between two variables x and y.

It would be useful, at this point, to examine some real data with this newly found understanding of variation. Exhibit 3 depicts the basic set of size and control metrics discussed in Chapter 5 for the Space Shuttle Primary Avionics Software System (PASS) Guidance and Navigational Control subsystem. This system was written in a programming language called HAL/S. To collect these data, we wrote a metric analyzer that conformed to the rules articulated in Chapter 5. The means and standard deviations of the various metrics are shown in Exhibit 3. On the surface there are some rather surprising values in this table. For example, the average program module has more than 7300 paths and there is considerable variation in this value. Also, there is substantial variation in the total operator and operand counts among the program modules. Of greater interest to us than the simple variation of each variable is the degree of interrelationship among these variables. To this end, the correlation coefficients for the bivariate relationships among all of the metrics is shown in Exhibit 4. We can see, for example, that there is a strong relationship between Exec and LOC (0.86). That is not surprising. There is also a strong relationship between *Nodes* and *Edges*; again, there are no surprises in this. What we are looking for is a pattern of communality among the variables. There seems to be a cluster of relationships among the size metrics and another among the flowgraph metrics. It turns out that these metrics are all related to one another simultaneously. Their individual bivariate relationships simply do not reveal how all of these metrics interact simultaneously. There is a multivariate relationship among them. We will use a multivariate statistical technique called principal components analysis (PCA) to explore these multivariate relationships.[3]

115

Exhibit 3. Metric Statistics for PASS

Metric	Mean	Standard Deviation
η_1	15.5	13.3
η_2	50.4	70.0
N_1	299.6	593.5
N_2	154.4	289.5
Exec	69.7	130.7
Loc	138.3	229.3
Nodes	34.3	54.5
Edges	43.9	74.4
Paths	7300.8	16667.9
Cycles	1.1	2.9
Maxpath	30.3	25.2
Avepath	46.8	42.5

6.4 THE PRINCIPAL COMPONENTS OF MEASUREMENT

In most linear modeling applications concerned with the mapping of software metrics onto software faults, such as regression analysis and discriminant analysis, each of the independent variables, or metrics, are assumed to represent some distinct aspect of variability not clearly present in other measures. That is, each metric will measure a distinct and unique software attribute. This clearly is not the case. The best case to examine in this regard are the two metric attributes of LOC and Exec. These are clearly related, are highly correlated, and measure almost the same thing. Knowledge of LOC clearly reveals a great deal about the number of executable statements in a program.

The metrics we will collect for most software development applications will be highly correlated. They have a high degree of linear relationship, covariance, to one another. We will use the term *multicollinearity* to describe this linear relationship of shared variance. In cases where there is a high degree of multicollinearity, it will be almost impossible to establish the unique contribution of each metric to the model. One distinct result of multicollinearity in the independent measures is that the regression models developed using independent variables with a high degree of multicollinearity have highly unstable regression coefficients. To circumvent this problem we will employ a statistical procedure called principal components analysis (PCA) to map the metrics into orthogonal attribute domains.[1] Each principal component extracted by this procedure may be seen to represent an underlying common attribute domain. A somewhat more extensive discussion of the foundations of PCA can be found in Appendix 1.

The principle behind PCA is quite straightforward. Assume that we are given a set of n metrics $\mathbf{M} = (m_1,\ldots,m_n)$ having a multivariate distribution with a mean $\mu = \mu_1,\ldots,\mu_n$ and a covariance matrix Σ. The covariance matrix,

Exhibit 4. Correlation Coefficients for PASS Metrics

	η_1	η_2	N_1	N_2	Exec	LOC	Nodes	Edges	Paths	Cycles	Maxpath
η_2	0.78										
N_1	0.62	0.85									
N_2	0.64	0.89	0.99								
Exec	0.64	0.89	0.97	0.96							
LOC	0.61	0.79	0.84	0.83	0.86						
Nodes	0.58	0.66	0.67	0.65	0.71	0.73					
Edges	0.56	0.65	0.66	0.64	0.70	0.70	0.99				
Paths	0.47	0.56	0.50	0.50	0.55	0.53	0.66	0.66			
Cycles	0.39	0.45	0.39	0.40	0.42	0.39	0.63	0.65	0.49		
Maxpath	0.60	0.65	0.60	0.60	0.64	0.65	0.87	0.87	0.70	0.82	
Avepath	0.55	0.63	0.58	0.58	0.63	0.64	0.86	0.86	0.67	0.83	0.99

S, for a sample drawn from this multivariate distribution is a real symmetric matrix and, thus, by the spectral decomposition theorem it can be decomposed as follows:

$$S = PLP'$$

where P is a matrix whose columns are eigenvectors and L is a diagonal matrix of eigenvalues or latent roots of S. Alternatively, we can rewrite this equation as:

$$P'SP = L$$

While there are many solutions to this problem, the principal components factoring technique extracts the eigenvalues from the largest to the smallest, each of which represents the proportion of variance explained by its associated component. Each principal component represents an underlying metric domain onto which each of the raw metrics will be mapped. The relationship between the original set of metrics, M, and the new orthogonal set can be clearly seen by computing the product moment correlation for each raw metric with each new principal component as follows:

$$r_{m_i d_j} = \frac{P_{ij}\sqrt{l_j}}{s_i}$$

where l_j is the eigenvalue of the jth principal component and s_i is the standard deviation of the ith metric.

We have two objectives in mind when we employ PCA. First, we wish to transform our n highly correlated metrics, $M = (m_1,...,m_n)$, into a new uncorrelated set $D = (d_1,...,d_n)$ that we will call *domain* metrics to distinguish them from the raw metrics. Second, we would like to reduce the dimensionality of the problem. That is, we understand intuitively that there really are not n distinct sources of variation in the original set of metrics M. There is probably a smaller number p, $p < n$, of distinct sources of variation within the set of n original raw metrics. We feel certain, for example, that LOC, Exec, N_1, and N_2 all represent a single aspect of the size of a program.

The problem that we would now like to solve is to determine just exactly how many usable sources of variation can be identified in our original set of metrics M. We know that the PCA technique will extract the eigenvalues and the corresponding eigenvectors from the largest value to the smallest value. From a statistical perspective, each eigenvalue, l_i, represents the proportion of variance accounted for by a particular principal component. For example, the proportion of variance accounted for by the first principal component is l_1. Also observe that

$$\sum_{i=1}^{n} L_i = n.$$

Exhibit 5. Principal Components of PASS Metrics

Metric	1	2	3	4	5	Domain 6	7	8	9	10	11	12
η_1	0.73	0.18	−0.61	−0.09	−0.19	0.01	−0.03	0.11	−0.01	0.00	0.00	0.00
η_2	0.88	0.33	−0.21	0.01	0.08	0.01	0.02	−0.28	0.02	0.01	0.00	0.00
N_1	0.87	0.43	0.14	0.09	0.09	0.10	0.01	0.11	0.02	0.06	0.00	0.00
N_2	0.87	0.43	0.08	0.10	0.13	0.10	0.02	0.05	0.10	−0.05	0.00	0.00
Exec	0.90	0.38	0.12	0.06	0.07	0.06	0.02	0.01	−0.16	−0.02	0.00	0.00
LOC	0.86	0.28	0.16	0.00	−0.11	−0.38	−0.08	0.02	0.01	0.00	0.00	0.00
Nodes	0.90	−0.25	0.16	−0.08	−0.29	0.09	−0.06	−0.03	0.01	−0.01	−0.01	0.03
Edges	0.89	−0.27	0.17	−0.06	−0.28	0.13	−0.07	−0.04	0.00	0.01	0.01	−0.03
Paths	0.72	−0.24	0.02	−0.58	0.31	0.00	−0.05	0.02	0.00	0.00	0.00	0.00
Cycles	0.67	−0.55	−0.11	0.37	0.26	0.00	−0.19	0.01	−0.01	0.00	0.00	0.00
Maxpath	0.89	−0.41	−0.04	0.05	0.02	−0.06	0.16	0.03	0.00	0.00	−0.04	−0.01
Avepath	0.87	−0.43	−0.01	0.09	0.02	−0.07	0.19	0.00	0.00	0.00	0.03	0.01
Eigenvalue	8.5	1.6	0.5	0.5	0.4	0.2	0.1	0.1	0.0	0.0	0.0	0.0
% Variance	70.7	13.1	4.6	4.3	3.4	1.7	1.0	0.9	0.3	0.1	0.0	0.0
Cumulative variance	70.7	83.8	88.4	92.7	96.1	97.8	98.8	99.6	99.9	100	100	100

Thus, the first principal component will account for $l_i/n \times 100$ percent of the variation of all n metrics. As the process of extracting each new principal component progresses, more and more of the variation in the original set of metrics is accounted for.

The complete mapping between a set of 12 metrics, **M**, for the modules of the Space Shuttle Primary Avionics Software System and the 12 orthogonal metrics, **D**, is shown in Exhibit 5. To the right of each of the original 12 metrics in this table are the correlation coefficients for that metric with the 12 new orthogonal domain metrics. We can see that beyond the domain metrics 1 and 2, the correlation coefficients are very small.

The penultimate row of Exhibit 5 shows the eigenvalue associated with each new orthogonal domain. The final row of this table shows the proportion of variation contributed by each domain. Again, we can see that this proportion rapidly drops off beyond the first two new metric domains. This can be seen graphically in Exhibit 6, a plot of the eigenvalues.

The PCA technique is an iterative technique that extracts eigenvalues (and eigenvectors) from the largest eigenvalue to the smallest, as can be seen in Exhibit 7. Clearly, there is a point of diminishing returns in this extraction process. What is needed is a stopping rule that would terminate the process of extraction when a *sufficient* number of orthogonal domains have been extracted. There are many such stopping rules, and a number of them are discussed in Appendix 1. For our purposes, we will observe that if we were to perform PCA on completely random data, all of the eigenvalues would be 1.0. That is, $l_i = 1.0$, $\forall i = 1, 2, \ldots, n$. Thus, a very common stopping rule is to extract all principal components whose eigenvalue is 1.0 or greater. For convenience alone, we will employ this stopping rule in our subsequent analysis. This will yield the new factor pattern shown in Exhibit 7.

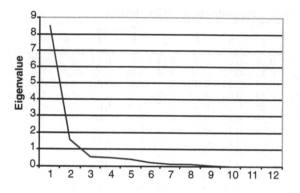

Exhibit 6. Plot of Eigenvalues

Exhibit 7. Two Orthogonal Metric Domains

Metric	Domain 1	Domain 2
η_1	0.73	0.18
η_2	0.88	0.33
N_1	0.87	0.43
N_2	0.87	0.43
Exec	0.90	0.38
LOC	0.86	0.28
Nodes	0.90	−0.25
Edges	0.89	−0.27
Paths	0.72	−0.24
Cycles	0.67	−0.55
Maxpath	0.89	−0.41
Avepath	0.87	−0.43
Eigenvalue	8.5	1.6
% Variance	70.7	13.1

When we examine the contents of Exhibit 7, we can see that all 12 metrics are highly correlated with the new Domain 1 and not well correlated with Domain 2. We have identified two new sources of variation in the 12 metrics but it is difficult to understand what we have found. This is an artifact of the PCA technique. It extracted the new domains based on the principal axes of variation through an orthogonal rotation of the original data axes. To clarify the nature of the two sources of variation, we will now conduct another orthogonal rotation of the two new domain axes, this time in an attempt to redistribute the variance accounted for by each domain equally among the two domains. There are many rotation techniques that can be employed. Some of these are discussed in Appendix 1. The technique of choice in this context will be the varimax orthogonal rotation. The results of the PCA with varimax rotation for the PASS data are shown in Exhibit 8 for the 1115 modules in the PASS GNC system. This table shows the factor pattern loadings for the first two principal components whose eigenvalues are greater than 1.0.

Exhibit 8. PCA of the 12 PASS Metrics

Metric	Size	Control
η_1	**0.66**	0.37
η_2	**0.87**	0.36
N_1	**0.93**	0.28
N_2	**0.93**	0.27
Exec	**0.92**	0.33
LOC	**0.82**	0.38
Nodes	0.49	**0.80**
Edges	0.47	**0.80**
Paths	0.37	**0.66**
Cycles	0.12	**0.86**
Maxpath	0.37	**0.91**
Avepath	0.35	**0.91**
% Variance	44.1	39.7

From Exhibit 8 we can see that most of the information represented by the original 12 metrics can be represented in two distinct metric domains. The raw complexity metrics are clustered into two distinct groups, or orthogonal metric domains. In some cases it is useful to associate names with the domains. The metrics most closely associated with the first domain in this table are those metrics that have the common characteristic of measuring variation in program size. All of these metrics share a common source of variation in the size of a program. Similarly, the metrics associated with the second domain seem to share a common element of control variation. They measure aspects of the program module flowgraph, which represents the control structure of a program.

If we carefully examine the set of 12 measures used above we can observe that there are some conceptual areas of software attributes that are not represented in this set of metrics. For example, there is the matter of data structure complexity. Clearly, there are no measures present in the set for this software attribute. The problem is that we do not know just how many distinct, measurable attributes a software system might have, but we do know that these 12 metrics are only measuring two distinct, uncorrelated attributes.

From the last row in the table in Exhibit 8 we can see that the size metrics account for approximately 44 percent of the variation in the set of 12 metrics. The control metrics account for about 38 percent of the variation in the same set. Altogether, the two new orthogonal domains account for roughly 82 percent of the variation in the original set.

The objective for the next research effort is to begin to build and extend a model for software attributes. This model will contain a set of orthogonal attribute domains. Once we have such a model in place, we would then like to identify and select from the attribute domain model those attributes that are correlated with a software quality measure, such as number of faults. Each of the orthogonal attributes will have an associated metric

121

value that is uncorrelated with any other attribute metrics. Each of these attributes may potentially serve to describe some aspect of variability in the behavior of the software faults in a program module.

6.5 PRINCIPAL COMPONENTS ANALYSIS AS A VALIDATION TOOL

It is very easy to misuse software metrics if we do not understand just exactly what they are measuring. There have been some ill-considered attempts to design software systems based on misleading information derived from metrics. The most notable of these attempts relates to the use of McCabe's measure of cyclomatic complexity $V(g)$ = Edges − Nodes + 2. This metric is a very good example of an inappropriately derived metric. It is a linear composite of the two metric primitives of Edges and Nodes, attributes of the control flowgraph representation of a program module. We would strongly suspect that there is little or no information in $V(g)$ above and beyond the metric primitives. We will see that this is exactly the case.

For some unknown reason, magic values of cyclomatic complexity are now being incorporated into the requirements specifications of some software systems. For example, we might choose to specify that no program module in the software system should have a cyclomatic complexity greater than an arbitrary value of, say, 15. This is a very good example of how software measures might well be misused in the design process. If we base software development decisions on a particular metric, then it really behooves us to validate that metric first.

There are potentially catastrophic consequences associated with this univariate design criterion. First, there is little or no empirical evidence to suggest that a module whose cyclomatic complexity is greater than 15 is materially worse than one whose cyclomatic complexity is 14. Second, and most important, is the fact that if, in the process of designing a software module, we find that the module has a cyclomatic complexity greater than 15, the most obvious and common solution to the problem is to divide the software module into two distinct modules. Now we will certainly have two modules whose cyclomatic complexity is less than 15. The difficulty here is that instead of one program module, we have created two, or possibly three, in its place. This will increase the macro complexity of measures related to complexity. That is, we have decreased cyclomatic complexity but we have increased coupling complexity. The result of the ignorant decision may well be that the total *system* complexity will increase. This, in turn, will probably lead to a concomitant increase in total faults.

Now let us take the first step in the validation process and see whether the $V(g)$ metric does, in fact, contribute new information to our understanding of the complexity of a software module. For $V(g)$ to contribute new information to our understanding of software complexity, we would

Exhibit 9. An Analysis of Cyclomatic Complexity

Metric	Size	Control
η_1	**0.67**	0.35
η_2	**0.87**	0.35
N_1	**0.92**	0.29
N_2	**0.93**	0.28
Exec	**0.91**	0.35
LOC	**0.82**	0.38
Nodes	0.47	**0.83**
Edges	0.45	**0.84**
$V(g)$	0.38	**0.85**
Paths	0.37	**0.65**
Cycles	0.12	**0.84**
Maxpath	0.37	**0.90**
Avepath	0.35	**0.90**

expect that a new source of variation directly attributable to this metric would be visible to us when we perform the PCA on the data containing the new metric. This analysis is shown in Exhibit 9.

From the attribute domain model, we can see that there are many distinct software complexity domains. If we make design decisions on the basis of incomplete measurements, we run the risk of creating bad designs. Design decisions may be made that will reduce a measurement in one domain but this may, in fact, cause a concomitant increase in measures in other complexity domains. The net result of this univariate decision is that the net complexity of the total software system may rise. While it is true that we may have fewer faults associated with aspects of control complexity, we run the risk of increasing the count of faults associated with coupling considerations.

We now turn our attention to the Halstead software science metrics. Essentially, all of the Halstead metrics were derived from the metric primitives of η_1, η_2, N_1, and N_2. It should be clear by now that program vocabulary ($\eta = \eta_1 + \eta_2$) and program length ($N = N_1 + N_2$) do not represent new sources of variation. When we augment our original 12 metrics with these two new metrics and perform the PCA for the new set of 14 metrics, we can clearly see that the new metrics vary in precisely the same way as the metric primitives from which they were derived. The results of this analysis is shown in Exhibit 10.

It should not be necessary to revisit the rest of the Halstead software science metrics. As derivatives of the four metric primitives, we cannot expect them to disclose new sources of variation. As pointed out earlier in this chapter, the exceptions will be the measures of effort that are based on the work of Stroud. The Halstead metrics based on Stroud's work do, in some cases, identify new sources of variation. They will, however, fail to meet our additional requirements for metric validity in that they do not provide predictive validity for our criterion measure of software faults.

Exhibit 10. Halstead Vocabulary and Program Length

Metric	Size	Control
η_1	**0.66**	0.38
η_2	**0.87**	0.36
η	**0.87**	0.38
N_1	**0.93**	0.29
N_2	**0.93**	0.28
N	**0.93**	0.28
Exec	**0.91**	0.34
LOC	**0.80**	0.39
Nodes	0.47	**0.81**
Edges	0.45	**0.82**
Paths	0.35	**0.67**
Cycles	0.13	**0.85**
Maxpath	0.37	**0.91**
Avepath	0.34	**0.91**

6.6 DISCOVERING NEW SOURCES OF VARIATION

One of the fundamental benefits of the PCA technique is that it allows us to identify exactly what it is we are measuring. That is, we can identify relevant sources of variation in our working set of metrics. To date, there are 12 metrics in this working set. It is not clear, at this point, just why we have so many metrics that all seem to measure either size or control characteristics of program modules. Although there are six different measures of program size, they will each contribute meaningfully to our understanding of a criterion measure. We will discuss this further in the next chapter. What we would like to do next is to see if we can expand our knowledge in what we are measuring.

In Chapter 5, a new metric, the data structures metric DS, was introduced. This was an outgrowth of a series of studies to identify new sources of variation, particularly in the area of data structures complexity. The need to measure data structures complexity was driven by an observation that a very large number of program discrepancy reports (DRs) involved programmer misuse or misunderstanding of particular data structures in the HAL/S programming language for the Space Shuttle PASS. We developed several candidate data structures metrics, each of which was believed to measure the observed variability in data structures complexity. Sadly, most of these metrics turned out to be new measures of program size, as is generally the case with unvalidated metrics. One metric, the DS metric presented in Chapter 5, was distinctly different from the other measures of data structures complexity. It behaved in a very different manner from the other 12 measures. The results of the varimax rotation of the PCA with the new DS metric are shown in Exhibit 11. In this exhibit we can see that the DS metric is distinctly correlated with only one of the orthogonal domains. Further, it is really the only metric so correlated. It identifies a new source of variation distinctly different from other measures of size and

Exhibit 11. PCA with the DS Metric

Metric	Size	Control	Data Structures
η_1	**0.67**	0.36	−0.25
η_2	**0.87**	0.36	−0.03
N_1	**0.92**	0.28	0.08
N_2	**0.93**	0.28	0.07
Exec	**0.91**	0.39	0.07
LOC	**0.82**	0.38	0.05
Nodes	0.49	**0.80**	−0.00
Edges	0.47	**0.81**	0.01
Paths	0.36	**0.66**	0.01
Cycles	0.17	**0.86**	0.03
Maxpath	0.37	**0.91**	−0.00
Avepath	0.35	0.91	0.01
DS	0.05	0.03	**0.98**
% Variance	40.6	36.8	8.0

control complexity. Thus, the DS metric has met the first of several criteria for a valid metric; it has measured a new and distinct source of variation. In Chapter 7 we conduct the next level of validation. We want to establish in this next step that the DS metric will help us explain the observed variation in a criterion measure.

In passing, it is interesting to note the tenuous relationship between the unique operator count and the data structures metric. We see that η_1 appears to be inversely related to the DS metric. This reminds us of a book by Nicklaus Wirth entitled *Programs = Algorithms + Data Structures* that was popular in the 1970s. There are many ways to solve the same problem. We can, in essence, trade off data structures complexity for algorithmic complexity. This is most certainly the case with the use of pointers in the C programming environment. The use of pointers in these applications will certainly reduce the data structures complexity. There is an enormous cost to pay for this trade-off. The algorithmic complexity of a program will increase as a result of this design decision. We will see this in a concomitant increase in η_1 and η_3.

Let us return to the discrepancy reports for the PASS data and examine them further. PASS is a family of embedded real-time programs working together. Program synchronization (or lack thereof) is a significant source of errors made by the programmers. It would be very useful to identify measures of interprocess and intraprocess communication to be able to isolate these two sources of potential variation among program modules. To this end, a variety of candidate metrics were created. A subset of these measures were a measure in interprocess communication (SIGNALS) and intraprocess communication (SETS, RESETS, and CANCELS). These are simple enumeration of these HAL/S commands in the individual program modules.

Exhibit 12. PCA with Process Communication Metrics

Metric	Size	Control	Data Structures	Intraprocess	Interprocess
η_1	**0.65**	0.36	−0.25	0.13	0.10
η_2	**0.85**	0.36	−0.03	0.14	0.03
N_1	**0.91**	0.28	0.08	0.18	0.02
N_2	**0.91**	0.27	0.07	0.19	0.04
Exec	**0.90**	0.34	0.07	0.17	−0.01
LOC	**0.77**	0.37	0.05	0.30	−0.02
Nodes	0.47	**0.79**	0.00	0.15	−0.02
Edges	0.45	**0.80**	0.00	0.13	−0.02
Paths	0.39	**0.67**	0.02	−0.04	0.03
Cycles	0.11	**0.86**	0.03	0.06	0.07
Maxpath	0.35	**0.90**	0.00	0.17	0.06
Avepath	0.32	**0.90**	0.01	0.19	0.06
DS	0.05	0.03	**0.98**	0.02	0.02
Sets	0.25	0.16	0.05	**0.80**	−0.07
Resets	0.09	0.17	−0.01	**0.82**	−0.09
Signals	0.03	0.09	0.02	0.03	**0.96**
Cancels	0.21	−0.02	−0.03	**0.63**	0.27
% Variance	30.2	28.2	6.1	12.0	6.1

As was the case for the data structures metric, data was collected for these new program measures. The results of the PCA with these metrics and the established 13 metrics are shown in Exhibit 12. In this new case, we can identify two new sources of variation corresponding to the role that new metrics are playing in inter- and intraprocess communication.

Both the DS metric and the new process synchronization metrics represent steps in understanding the different sources of variation in program complexity. Some of this knowledge will prove useful and some will not. The driving force for discovery of new sources of variation is to identify those measurable program attributes that will allow us to improve our prediction of measures of software quality. That is, new measures must also vary in accordance with measures of software quality such as software faults. I can measure many distinct and different attributes of students in my class. Among these attributes, I could find, for example, a distinct source of variation in eye color, as measured by the wavelengths of light reflected from a student's iris. The knowledge gained from this measurement, however, would only be useful to me if it were related to a student's future performance in my class.

6.7 DOMAIN METRICS

One of the main problems encountered in working with raw metric data is that they are data. There is very little information content in raw metric data. Take, for example, the 12 raw metrics obtained from one particular build of the PASS system. A sample of data from 20 program modules is shown in Exhibit 13. It would be very difficult to impossible to draw any useful conclusions about, for example, module 6 in relation to module 9, or any other module for that matter. If we were measuring a system of 10,000 modules on 30 metrics, we would have even more of a problem.

We would like to convert the data shown in Exhibit 13 to information. The first step in this process is to understand each module in the context of the larger system. The last two rows of this table contain the means and standard deviations, respectively, for each metric for the entire software system. We can now look at module 6 and see that there are more than the average number of paths. For example, module 6 has 23,892 paths whereas the average module in this system has 7301 paths.

We can increase our understanding of the data represented in Exhibit 13 by converting the raw metric values to z-scores. The corresponding z-scores for each of the program modules are shown in Exhibit 14. Now our resolution on the data is beginning to improve. Module 6 from this new perspective is rather different from the majority of other program modules. With the possible exception of path complexity, module 6 is at least one standard deviation greater than the mean of each of 11 metrics. Module 9 in another module that is strikingly greater than average on most attributes. Module 7, on the other hand, has lots of negative values. It is typically less than average on all program attributes.

We discovered with the PCA of the 12 metrics listed in Exhibits 13 and 14 that there are only two distinct sources of variation. We would like to transform the 12 raw metric values to their corresponding equivalents in the two new metric domains. Fortunately, the PCA technique produces a set of coefficients that will send the 12 metric z-scores shown in Exhibit 14 into the two new metric domains. The transformation matrix for 12 metrics on the PASS data is shown in Exhibit 15.

The z-scores for the PASS sample data are shown in Exhibit 14. This is a 20×12 matrix. When it is post-multiplied by the 12×2 matrix of coefficients shown in Exhibit 15, the result is a 20×2 matrix of factor scores, which we will call domain scores for each of the 20 program modules. This product matrix of domain scores is shown in Exhibit 16, along with the observation that each domain score has a mean of 0 and a standard deviation of 1, just the same as the raw z-scores. We have now reduced the data of Exhibit 13 to information. The program module that exhibits the largest size attribute is module 3. The most complex module from a control perspective is module 8.

The size and control domain scores shown in Exhibit 16; both have a mean of 0 and a standard deviation of 1. We can therefore add them to create a new composite metric. This new metric sum is shown in the fourth column (Sum) of Exhibit 17. It is essentially a composite score of the program modules on size and control complexity. Exhibit 17 has also been sorted by this new sum. Now a new picture of the distribution of module

Exhibit 13. Raw Metric Values for 20 PASS Modules

Module	η_1	η_2	N_1	N_2	Exec	LOC	Nodes	Edges	Paths	Cycles	Maxpath	Avepath
1	45	282	1335	763	339	841	114	131	14652	13	168	136
2	14	13	43	18	11	22	8	9	4	0	7	6
3	47	259	2542	1154	559	1027	103	129	5001	4	143	129
4	3	5	4	5	1	399	14	10	4	0	10	10
5	34	117	867	371	212	248	78	103	23892	3	87	69
6	35	157	1040	484	226	475	129	168	13512	4	112	97
7	12	28	47	34	13	114	14	10	4	0	10	10
8	45	331	3493	1760	733	1451	405	531	3129	14	441	429
9	42	221	1365	667	377	740	235	310	50004	11	134	118
10	26	62	274	109	46	69	24	31	46	0	22	17
11	11	22	26	22	9	283	14	10	4	0	10	10
12	38	154	836	427	203	286	117	156	50001	7	109	87
13	24	48	289	145	86	92	51	68	16472	5	64	47
14	37	82	321	177	70	197	34	35	40	1	32	25
15	23	69	361	167	67	81	25	31	377	3	43	32
16	23	56	212	111	64	81	26	33	637	2	45	34
17	20	29	85	47	20	24	16	19	13	1	20	14
18	35	191	1189	569	311	431	174	244	2231	6	150	137
19	33	144	774	362	194	597	122	158	210	1	40	27
20	25	51	205	101	60	79	31	39	444	1	36	30
$\bar{x}$	16	50	300	154	70	138	34	44	7301	1	30	25
s	13	70	594	290	131	229	55	74	16668	3	47	43

Exhibit 14. z-Scores for Raw Metric Values

Module	η_1	η_2	N_1	N_2	Exec	LOC	Nodes	Edges	Paths	Cycles	Maxpath	Avepath
1	2.21	3.31	1.74	2.10	2.06	3.06	1.46	1.17	0.44	3.94	2.94	2.61
2	-0.12	-0.53	-0.43	-0.47	-0.45	-0.51	-0.48	-0.47	-0.44	-0.40	-0.50	-0.45
3	2.36	2.98	3.78	3.45	3.74	3.87	1.26	1.14	-0.14	0.94	2.40	2.45
4	-0.94	-0.65	-0.50	-0.52	-0.53	1.14	-0.37	-0.46	-0.44	-0.40	-0.43	-0.36
5	1.38	0.95	0.96	0.75	1.09	0.48	0.80	0.79	1.00	0.61	1.21	1.02
6	1.46	1.52	1.25	1.14	1.20	1.47	1.73	1.67	0.37	0.94	1.74	1.68
7	-0.27	-0.32	-0.43	-0.42	-0.43	-0.11	-0.37	-0.46	-0.44	-0.40	-0.43	-0.36
8	2.21	4.01	5.38	5.54	5.07	5.72	6.79	6.55	-0.25	4.28	8.76	9.50
9	1.98	2.44	1.79	1.77	2.35	2.62	3.67	3.58	2.56	3.28	2.21	2.19
10	0.78	0.17	-0.04	-0.16	-0.18	-0.30	-0.19	-0.17	-0.44	-0.40	-0.18	-0.18
11	-0.34	-0.41	-0.46	-0.46	-0.46	0.63	-0.37	-0.46	-0.44	-0.40	-0.43	-0.36
12	1.68	1.48	0.90	0.94	1.02	0.64	1.51	1.51	2.56	1.94	1.68	1.46
13	0.63	-0.03	-0.02	-0.03	0.12	-0.20	0.30	0.32	0.55	1.27	0.72	0.51
14	1.61	0.45	0.04	0.08	0.00	0.26	-0.01	-0.12	-0.44	-0.06	0.04	-0.01
15	0.56	0.27	0.10	0.04	-0.02	-0.25	-0.17	-0.17	-0.42	0.61	0.27	0.17
16	0.56	0.08	-0.15	-0.15	-0.04	-0.25	-0.15	-0.15	-0.40	0.27	0.31	0.19
17	0.33	-0.31	-0.36	-0.37	-0.38	-0.50	-0.34	-0.33	-0.44	-0.06	-0.22	-0.26
18	1.46	2.01	1.50	1.43	1.85	1.28	2.56	2.69	-0.30	1.61	2.55	2.62
19	1.31	1.34	0.80	0.72	0.95	2.00	1.60	1.53	-0.43	-0.06	0.21	0.04
20	0.71	0.01	-0.16	-0.18	-0.07	-0.26	-0.06	-0.07	-0.41	-0.06	0.12	0.12

Exhibit 15. Transformation Matrix for z-Scores

Metric	Size	Control
η_1	0.14	−0.03
η_2	0.22	−0.08
N_1	0.26	−0.13
N_2	0.26	−0.13
Exec	0.24	−0.10
LOC	0.20	−0.06
Nodes	−0.03	0.19
Edges	−0.04	0.20
Paths	−0.04	0.17
Cycles	−0.18	0.31
Maxpath	−0.10	0.26
Avepath	−0.11	0.27

Exhibit 16. Domain Scores for the PASS Data

Metric	Size	Control
1	1.74	2.06
2	−0.36	−0.40
3	3.78	0.17
4	−0.24	−0.37
5	0.76	0.78
6	1.08	1.24
7	−0.25	−0.38
8	3.25	6.07
9	1.42	2.92
10	0.13	−0.34
11	−0.16	−0.40
12	0.53	1.91
13	−0.34	0.92
14	0.44	−0.23
15	−0.01	0.12
16	−0.12	0.13
17	−0.30	−0.17
18	1.10	2.00
19	1.39	0.03
20	−0.05	−0.01

complexity clearly emerges. Module 8 is, by far, the most complex module of the 20 sample modules. If we have been very careful in our selection of metrics to include only those that are distinctly related to software faults, then the new domain scores represented by Exhibit 17 are particularly relevant. A large domain score on the control domain, such as is the case with module 8, indicates a real proclivity on the part of those writing module 8 to include control faults in that module.

The right-most of Exhibit 17 is very revealing. Imagine that the system of program modules represented by this table constitutes the entire system. Further imagine that we are going to have to ship this system sometime in the very near future. We would like to invest our test and inspection time wisely so that we can maximize our exposure to latent faults in the system. We would be wise to invest our time in proportion to the likelihood of

Exhibit 17. Sorted Domain Scores for the PASS Data

Metric	Size	Control	Sum
8	3.25	6.07	9.31
9	1.42	2.92	4.34
3	3.78	0.17	3.95
1	1.74	2.06	3.80
18	1.10	2.00	3.10
12	0.53	1.91	2.44
6	1.08	1.24	2.32
5	0.76	0.78	1.55
19	1.39	0.03	1.42
13	−0.34	0.92	0.58
14	0.44	−0.23	0.21
15	−0.01	0.12	0.12
16	−0.12	0.13	0.01
20	−0.05	−0.01	−0.06
10	0.13	−0.34	−0.21
17	−0.30	−0.17	−0.47
11	−0.16	−0.40	−0.56
4	−0.24	−0.37	−0.61
7	−0.25	−0.38	—0.63
2	−0.36	−0.40	−0.75

encountering faults in the code. The distribution of these faults in the code is not even. Control faults are more likely to be found in modules whose control domain scores are high. The right-most column of the table, (Sum) is our first cut at a fault surrogate. That is, it is a measure that varies in the same manner as software faults. There are other ways of creating surrogate fault measures, as we will now see.

6.8 A UNITARY MEASURE OF SOFTWARE COMPLEXITY

To simplify the structure of software complexity even further than the orthogonal domains produced by the principal component analysis, it would be useful if each of the program modules in a software system could be characterized by a single value representing some cumulative measure of complexity. The objective in the selection of such a linear function, g, is that it be related in some manner to software faults, either directly or inversely, such that $g(x) = ax + b$, where x is some unitary measure of program complexity. The more closely related x is to software faults, the more valuable the function g will be in the anticipation of software faults. Previous research has established that the fault index (FI) has properties that might be useful in this regard. The FI metric is a weighted sum of a set of uncorrelated attribute domain metrics.[4,5] This metric represents each raw metric in proportion to the amount of unique variation contributed by that metric.

The FI of the factored program modules can be represented as follows:

$$FI = \sum_j l_j d_{ji}$$

Exhibit 18. FI Values for the 20 PASS Metrics

Module	FI
1	19.03
2	-3.77
3	20.80
4	-3.02
5	7.77
6	11.62
7	-3.12
8	46.10
9	21.44
10	-0.93
11	-2.74
12	11.89
13	2.59
14	1.23
15	0.56
16	-0.02
17	-2.41
18	15.34
19	7.50
20	-0.29

where l_j is the eigenvalue associated with the jth factor and d_{ji} is the jth factor score of the ith program module on the jth domain. Each of the eigenvalues represents the relative contribution of its associated domain to the total variance explained by all of the domains. In essence then, the FI metric is a weighted sum of the individual domain metrics. In this context, the FI metric represents each raw complexity metric in proportion to the amount of unique variation contributed by that complexity metric.

The eigenvalues for the domain scores presented in Exhibit 17 are 5.29 and 4.77 for the size and control domains, respectively. If we weight each of the columns of Exhibit 17 by these two values, we will get a new vector of FI values for the 20 modules. These FI values are shown in Exhibit 18.

The role of the fault index in software development is best understood in terms of this classification process. Through the use of the FI metric, individual programs and program modules can be arranged and grouped by this single measure. Complex programs are known to require a disproportionate amount of development effort and are also known to contain a disproportionate number of faults. The FI metric provides a simple mechanism of aggregating the many similar complexity metrics into one single metric that is a linear compound of the variance components of the set of metrics used to describe a program or a set of programs.

FI is not necessarily intended to represent the complete abstract complexity of a program. In fact, in a typical application, there may be several complexity domains that are systematically excluded from the computation of FI. FI is a stand-in for aspects of software quality that we cannot directly measure (e.g., software faults). FI is simply a surrogate for software faults.

A careful distinction must be made between statistical relationship and causality. There is a direct relationship between complexity measures; more specifically, the relative complexity metric and measures of program quality (i.e., the number of faults). This in itself does not imply that program complexity will cause program faults. Further, it is clear that the act of simplifying the structure of a program will not automatically decrease the number of faults in that program or the number of changes that will need to be made to it. Simple or complex, bad code is bad code. All things being equal with regard to programmer ability, FI is a good predictor of program modules of poor quality. The modules of high complexity, on examination, are generally found to contain labyrinthine control structures and bushy logic. In this sense, there is reason to believe that the use of complexity metrics to guide the preparation of test cases should contribute to the enhancement of the testing process.

Software systems are designed to implement each of their functionalities in one or more code modules. In some cases there is a direct correspondence between a particular program module and a particular functionality. That is, if the program is expressing that functionality, it will execute exclusively in the module in question. In most cases, however, there will not be this distinct traceability of functionality to modules; rather, the functionality will be expressed in many different code modules.

6.9 SUMMARY

As programs have increased in length several orders of magnitude in the past three decades, the problems associated with measuring these programs have also increased several orders of magnitude. Furthermore, these systems experience a very large number of changes during their development and early deployment. Not all changes will have the same relative impact on the code in terms of its overall complexity. Some changes, by their very nature, will be innocuous, such as the introduction of comment statements. Other changes will make substantial changes to the basic architecture of a program module. Even the simplest measurements taken on each program module have a way of creating an enormous data management problem in the measurement of evolving systems. The key to the success of the measurement problem is to reduce the size of the problem with which we are working.

Some effort has been devoted to organizing the numerous metrics into various taxonomic categories in an attempt to understand the nature of the underlying complexity domains. These taxonomic structures, however, do not reflect the actual variation of the metrics when they are potentially applied to the development of measurement models. The technique we have developed is based on the variability of each metric in conjunction with other metrics in a set to show the structure of the complexity domains and ultimately represent this complexity with a single numerical value called the fault index (FI) using a statistical procedure known as principal component analysis (PCA).

The potential success of using complexity metrics is predicated on the ability of these metrics to describe all aspects of program variability. Problems have arisen in the past in the application of complexity metrics to predictive models for software development in that different program modules would have substantially different values of these metrics. In response to the need to compare programs one to another based on their complexity, we have developed a realistic methodology to determine the FI that will reflect the contribution of each program module to the total complexity of a software system. As a methodology, any relevant set of complexity metrics can be used to derive the FI measure. Typically, a working set of metrics would include metrics representing each of the complexity domains that we have determined to be directly related to our criterion measure — software faults.

The HALMET metric tool for the HAL/S language has been refined through three major revisions to generate a working set of software complexity metrics that serve to explain approximately 85 percent of the variation in the software faults in each program module as measured by Discrepancy Reports filed against that module. The driving force in the construction of this measurement tool is to construct suitable surrogate measures for software faults. These surrogate measures will vary in direct relation to the embedded software faults. While we would like to be able to measure software faults directly, these are known only to Nature. It is possible, however, to construct software measures that will vary directly with software faults. Orthogonal domain metrics and a single measure, FI, will be constructed to serve as such surrogates. If a change has been made to a system that results in a major increase in our fault surrogate, FI, then we will come to understand that this change will likely introduce a number of new faults proportional to the change.

There are many different aspects of a program that can be measured. Each of these attributes represents a different aspect of program complexity. Programs differ in the number of statements they contain. They differ in the control complexity arena; and they also differ in the data structures they use. There are literally hundreds of different complexity attributes that can be measured. From a software maintenance perspective, not all of these are of equal interest to us. The metrics we will choose to use will be selected because of their demonstrated relationship to faults.

References

1. Coulter, N.S., Software Science and Cognitive Psychology, *IEEE Transactions on Software Engineering*, 9(2), 166–171, 1983.

2. Munson, J.C. and Khoshgoftaar, T.M., The Dimensionality of Program Complexity, *Proceedings of the 11th Annual International Conference on Software Engineering*, IEEE Computer Society Press, Los Alamitos, CA, 1989, pp. 245–253.

3. Jackson, J.E., *A User's Guide to Principal Components*, John Wiley & Sons, New York, 1991.

4. Munson, J.C. and Khoshgoftaar, T.M., Applications of a Relative Complexity Metric for Software Project Management, *Journal of Systems and Software*, 12, 283–291, 1990.

5. Munson, J.C. and Khoshgoftaar, T.M., The Relative Software Complexity Metric: A Validation Study, *Proceedings of the Software Engineering 1990 Conference*, Cambridge University Press, Cambridge, U.K., 1990, pp. 89–102.

Chapter 7
Modeling with Metrics

7.1 INTRODUCTION

From the discussion in Chapter 5, it is clear that there are many different software attributes that we can measure. We can, for example, measure LOC, Exec, Nodes, etc. Knowledge of these specific attributes for a particular program module does us very little or no good. It is even more aggravated when we have these data on thousands of program modules. We easily come to the same conclusion as most people who have mindlessly measured code. So what? We have invested resources to acquire knowledge that we simply cannot put to good use.

For a moment, then, let us turn the question around. What is it that we really want to know about the programs that we are building? It would be relatively easy to construct such a list. We merely have to open just about any software engineering textbook and start writing. Following is a partial list of what we would like to know about our programs:

- Maintainability
- Reliability
- Availability
- Interoperability
- Portability
- Security

Unfortunately, it is very difficult to measure these things. In general, we will refer to these "ilities" as software quality attributes. The software attributes that lead to an understanding of software quality are the things that we most wish to measure. At the top of this list, perhaps, is the number of faults in each code module. If we were to know this, then we could set about to eliminate them one by one until we had perfect code. Software faults, however, are very elusive. They escape even the closest scrutiny. We can never know, with any degree of certainty, how many faults there are in a code module. We can only find them if we look very closely during software inspections or when the faults express themselves as failure events. This problem is exacerbated by the fact that the code base is probably changing over time. New faults are continually being added and some are being removed. In plain terms, we cannot measure the very thing that we wish to know. We can track with some precision how many faults we have removed from a system but we cannot know exactly how many we put there in the first place.

This is our dilemma. There are software attributes that we can measure; unfortunately, these attributes are not what we want to know. There are also software attributes that we cannot measure, but these are the very things that we must know. We can, however, learn from our past experiences in software development. We cannot know, for example, how many faults there are in our new DEF software system. We do have a pretty good idea how many faults there were in our legacy ABC system that is very similar to the DEF system that we are now developing. There is reason to believe that, all other software process issues being equal, the faults that were introduced by our software process in the development of the DEF system will be similar to those introduced into the ABC system during its development. If we have kept good records on the fault tracking system for the faults that were found during the development of the ABC system, we can develop a functional relationship between the number of faults found in each of the modules of the ABC system and certain measurable software attributes such as Exec and Nodes. This functional relationship is a model for the software faults of the ABC system.

If we assume that the new DEF system is similar to the ABC system in terms of software engineering methodology, programming language, and development team, then we can apply the model that we developed for the ABC system to the new DEF system. This will permit us to predict both the location and the quantity of faults in the new DEF system. In this case we can use our knowledge of things that we can measure but do not really want to know about the DEF system to predict the things that we cannot measure but really want to know.

Thus, there are really two different kinds of metrics. There are those that can be set by us to a particular value, or at least directly observed. For modeling purposes, we will call these independent variables. Then there are metrics whose values are directly affected by changes in the independent variables. These metrics we will call dependent variables or criterion variables. The "ilities" will always be our criterion measures.

In our investigations into modeling, we will first develop models that explore linear relationships between one or more independent models and a single criterion measure such as software faults. We will then study the particular case where the criterion measure has nominal values using a technique called discriminant analysis. Next we will investigate a family of models called canonical correlation, wherein we will have multiple, dependent variables. Finally, we will examine nonlinear relationships between our independent variables and a single dependent variable.

The predictive models that we develop in this chapter will allow us to map between the things that we can know and manipulate (i.e., the independent variables) and the things that we really want to know (i.e., the dependent variables). However, this measurement and modeling approach will work well if and only if we have good measurement data. If the data are weak, the predictive models that we develop will be equally weak. This is yet another example of the garbage-in and garbage-out problem.

One of the fundamental tenets of software measurement is that these measurements will disclose aspects of the quality of the system. In particular, we are interested in the use of metrics to determine the impact of change on the software quality of the system as the system changes over time. While we cannot know the numbers and locations of faults, we can build models based on observed relationships between faults and some other measurable software attributes. Software faults and other measures of software quality can be known only at the point the that software has finally been retired from service. Only then can it be said that all of the relevant faults have been isolated and removed from the software system. On the other hand, software complexity can be measured very early in the software life cycle. In some cases, these measures of software complexity can be extracted from design documents. Some of these measures are very good leading indicators of potential software faults.

7.2 SIMPLE LINEAR REGRESSION

Linear statistical modeling begins with a linear hypothesis. In the most simple case, there will have two variables. The most simple linear hypothesis will be that we wish to create a linear relationship between an independent variable (e.g., LOC) and a dependent variable such as faults. To formulate our hypothesis, we will postulate a linear relationship between faults, represented by the variable y, and lines of code, represented by the variable x. The model that we wish to create will be that of a straight line: $y = ax + b$. To build the model we will next need to collect some data. Note the order. First we will postulate the model and then we will get the data.

Modeling is a form of experimentation. We begin the experiment with a hypothesis. Next we identify and constrain external sources of variation that might contaminate our experiment. Now, a specific linear model will be chosen such as $y = ax + b$. Then we measure the system to get value pairs (x_i, y_i) for our variables. Finally, we attempt to fit the model to the data.

Once we have built the model (we will discuss that subject momentarily), we will then evaluate the quality of the model that we have developed. The data that we have used for this experiment are consumable. You may imagine that they will be totally destroyed by the model building process. They cannot be reused in any other experiment or model. They have validity only for the experiment for which they were collected. Linear modeling is not a tool for beating data into submission. It is part of the process of scientific inquiry.

All too frequently in the computer software literature we see models that have been developed to fit the data, and not the other way around as science would dictate. The problem with this approach is that we wind up building a science around measurement artifacts and other spurious aberrations in the data. If our model or our conjecture is not a good one, the disparity between the model and the actual data will contain information on where we went wrong. If we choose to ignore this very important data source, we will certainly build a science of software on a very weak or unstable foundation.

If we have the fortune of not being able to fit our predetermined model to the data, we will then analyze the outcome to understand what went wrong. This, in turn, will immediately lead to a new hypothesis, a new model, a new experiment, and a new set of problems. That is the process of scientific inquiry. The engine or motive force behind the scientific discovery process is the model that does not work too well. If we learn to listen to the data, they will certainly steer us in the right direction.

7.2.1 Examination of the Data

Above all, common sense should prevail in the modeling process. An understanding of the data that we are working with will reveal a great deal about what we will be able to learn from them. For the purposes of this discussion, we will use two variables: one dependent and one independent. This will simplify the discussion and permit us to demonstrate the modeling techniques in two-dimensional figures. We will call this technique "listening to the data." The data contain a message; they are trying to reveal something about the nature of the problem that we are studying. We must be attentive to what the data are trying to say. Altogether too often, data are used to confirm a pet hypothesis. We will have failed utterly if we use it in this manner. Sometimes, the messages in these data are very subtle. Some degree of statistical sophistication will be required to get the data to reveal their message. At other times, the message in the data will be quite obvious. We must learn to listen.

Let us begin our investigation with some hypothetical data that we have collected on our new Mnamana metric and software faults. We built a measurement tool to obtain metric data for a software system consisting of 24 program modules for the Mnamana metric. From our software quality assurance staff we also obtained fault data for these modules. The results of this measurement exercise are shown in Exhibit 1.

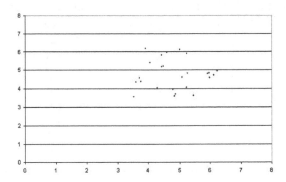

Exhibit 1. The Relationship between Mnamana and Faults

When we look at those data, we are filled with despair. There is no apparent relationship between these variables. When we examine the correlation coefficient between the data, we find that it is very low as well (at –0.004). Further, if we try to find a linear relationship, $y_i = \beta_0 + \beta_1 x_i$, between the data, we find that there are a very large number of lines that we could generate through this data, all of which would represent the data equally poorly. Our insistence on finding a model to fit this data will cause us to miss the obvious.

Let us find the *centroid*, $(\bar{x}, \bar{y})$, for this data. Now define a circle whose radius is ε around the centroid. This we will call the epsilon neighborhood of the centroid. It turns out that for relative small values, $\varepsilon < 2$, we can completely encapsulate all the data. This implies that there is a very strong relationship between the Mnamana metric and faults. It is a point relationship and not a linear one. There is not much variation in the software faults and there is not much variation in the Mnamana metric.

Now let us look at another example in which there is an apparent linear relationship between our independent measure of LOC and our dependent measure of faults. We have now measured another hypothetical software system with ten modules and obtained values for our independent and dependent variables as shown in Exhibit 2. Those data are also shown in an x-y plot in Exhibit 4. There is an apparent linear relationship between our two variables. The correlation coefficient for them is 0.88, which confirms our suspicion of a linear relationship. There are many straight lines that can be put through these data. The question at hand is what criterion measure to use to establish the best line.

First, let us address the criterion measure for quality of fit. Let y_i represent the observed value of the dependent variable and $\hat{y}_i$ the predicted value of the dependent variable from the model, $y_i = \beta_0 + \beta_1 x_i$. The difference between the predicted value and the observed value is called the

Exhibit 2. Measurements on Hypothetical Systems

Module	Faults	LOC
1	3	82
2	3	87
3	4	94
4	4	98
5	2	105
6	6	108
7	5	120
8	6	125
9	7	130
10	9	153
Mean	4.9	110.2

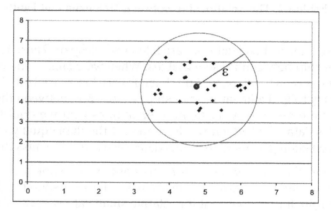

Exhibit 3. Epsilon Neighborhood about the Centroid

residual value, or error. Let $\varepsilon_i = y_i - \hat{y}_i$. Our first attempt at defining a criterion measure of model quality will be to let

$$q = \sum_i \varepsilon_i = \sum_i y_i - \hat{y}_i \qquad (1)$$

A good line will be one that minimizes q. This is a linear loss function; that is, q is linear in relation to y.

To return to the problem of fitting a line through the fault data shown in Exhibit 2, one possibility is to set the intercept to zero and pass the line through the centroid of the data. This line is shown superimposed on the data in Exhibit 4. Clearly, the two points that define this line are (0,0) and $(\bar{x}, \bar{y})$. Thus, the line will look like this:

$$y_i = b_1 x_i = \frac{\bar{y}}{\bar{x}} x_i \qquad (2)$$

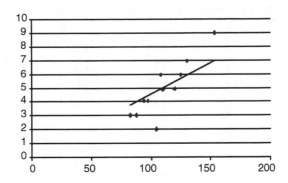

Exhibit 4. Plot of LOC and Faults for Hypothetical Data

where b_1 is our estimate for the parameter β_1. The residuals for this linear model are shown in Exhibit 5. Note that the sum of the residuals is zero. The sum of the residuals will always be zero by definition. Therefore, this sum is not a good indicator of the quality of the line that we have fit to the data. If, on the other hand, we compute the absolute value of the residuals, deviations, and add these deviations together, then we have a quality index that is different from zero. We can systematically investigate other models:

$$y_i = b_0 + b_1 x_i = b_0 + \frac{\bar{y}}{\bar{x}} x_i \tag{3}$$

where b_0 is not zero. In every one of these cases we will find that our quality index

$$q = \sum_i |y_i - \hat{y}_i| \tag{4}$$

is in every case greater than the quality index for the model where $b_0 = 0$.

Instead of defining a line with the two points $(0,0)$ and $(\bar{x}, \bar{y})$, we could also pick any other two points in the data and define a new line with those points. Using this fitting strategy, we could compute our quality index for each such pair of lines and pick the line that has the smallest value of q for all such lines. This will be a very time-consuming process, however, and we run a great risk of choosing a model that is heavily biased due to random artifacts in the data.

In a classical statistic sense, a technique called regression analysis is used to fit a straight line through the data. This technique is based, very classically, on a quadratic loss function, to wit:

$$q = \sum_i \varepsilon_i^2 = \sum_i (y_i - \hat{y}_i)^2 = \sum_i (y_i - \beta_0 - \beta_1 x_i)^2 \tag{5}$$

Exhibit 5. Measurements on Hypothetical Systems

Module	y_i	$\hat{y}_i$	$y_i - \hat{y}_i$	$|y_i - \hat{y}_i|$
1	3	3.65	−0.65	0.65
2	3	3.87	−0.87	0.87
3	4	4.18	−0.18	0.18
4	4	4.36	−0.36	0.36
5	2	4.67	−2.67	2.67
6	6	4.80	1.20	1.20
7	5	5.34	−0.34	0.34
8	6	5.56	0.44	0.44
9	7	5.78	1.22	1.22
10	9	6.80	2.20	2.20
Mean	4.9	4.9	0.00	1.01

In this circumstance, we select estimates b_0 and b_1 for our parameters β_0 and β_1 that will minimize the squared error term q. To do this we will first differentiate q with respect to β_0 and then with respect to β_1.

$$\frac{\delta q}{\delta \beta_0} = -2\sum_i (y_i - \beta_0 - \beta_1 x_i) \tag{6}$$

$$\frac{\delta q}{\delta \beta_1} = -2\sum_i x_i(y_i - \beta_0 - \beta_1 x_i) \tag{7}$$

Now, if we substitute our estimates b_0, b_1 for our parameters β_0, β_1 and set the differentials to zero, we have two equations in two unknowns, to wit:

$$-2\sum_i (y_i - b_0 - b_1 x_i) = 0 \tag{8}$$

$$-2\sum_i x_i(y_i - b_0 - b_1 x_i) = 0 \tag{9}$$

Solving first for b_1, we find that

$$b_1 = \frac{Cov(x,y)}{Var(x)} = \frac{\sum_i (x_i - \bar{x})(y_i - \bar{y})}{\sum_i (x_i - \bar{x})^2} \tag{10}$$

and that

$$b_0 = \bar{y} - b_1\bar{x} \tag{11}$$

There are still other alternatives for our loss function. We could also consider a host of loss functions in polynomials of ε. The choice of the quadratic loss function is simply one of inertia. There is a wealth of historical effort and energy that has been invested in this area of least squares linear fit of data. In addition, this is not a text in statistics. Suffice it to say that we will use a quadratic loss function, not because it is necessarily the

Exhibit 6. Slope Calculation Data

Module	y_i	x_i	$(x_i - \bar{x})^2$	$(x_i - \bar{x})(y_i - \bar{y})$
1	3	82	795.2	53.6
2	3	87	538.2	44.1
3	4	94	262.4	14.6
4	4	98	148.8	11.0
5	2	105	27.0	15.1
6	6	108	4.8	−2.4
7	5	120	96.0	1.0
8	6	125	219.0	16.3
9	7	130	392.0	41.6
10	9	153	1831.8	175.5
Sum	49	1102	4315.6	370.2

best for our modeling concerns in software engineering. We will do so strictly out of convenience at this point.

We will now revisit the data shown in Exhibit 2 and recompute a new line through this data using the least squares fit technique. The requisite calculations for our estimator of the slope, b_1, of the regression line are shown in Exhibit 6. We will compute b_1 as follows:

$$b_1 = \frac{\sum_i (x_i - \bar{x})(y_i - \bar{y})}{\sum_i (x_i - \bar{x})^2} = \frac{370.2}{4315.6} = 0.086 \tag{12}$$

Next we will find the intercept for the line:

$$b_0 = \bar{y} - b_1\bar{x} = 4.9 - 0.086 * 110.2 = -4.55 \tag{13}$$

Thus, our final least squares model for predicting faults from lines of code is:

$$y = 0.086 * x - 4.55 \tag{14}$$

To compare the new least squares fit with the first model we developed, we will need to compute the residuals for each model. This comparison is shown in Exhibit 7. Using the least squares criterion for model evaluation, Model 2 is clearly better than Model 1 in that the sum of the squared residuals for Model 2 is 9.14 as opposed to 16.51 for Model 1. Both models would have been considerably better off without module 5 in them. This residual value is very large for both modules. Module 5 is an outlier. There is a great temptation, at this point, to toss out module 5 altogether. It appears to be corrupting our model. Actually, the contrary is true. It is perhaps our most important data point. There is real information in this datum. We do not know what it is but we should certainly take the time to find out.

We must investigate four very important issues before we take our new model seriously and use it for the evaluation of all future code develop-

Exhibit 7. Residual Analysis of the Two Models

Module	y_i	Model 1 $y_i - \hat{y}_i$	Model 1 $(y_i - \hat{y}_i)^2$	Model 2 $y_i - \hat{y}_i$	Model 2 $(y_i - \hat{y}_i)^2$
1	3	−0.65	0.42	0.52	0.27
2	3	−0.87	0.75	0.09	0.01
3	4	−0.18	0.03	0.49	0.24
4	4	−0.36	0.13	0.15	0.02
5	2	−2.67	7.12	−2.45	6.02
6	6	1.20	1.43	1.29	1.66
7	5	−0.34	0.11	−0.74	0.55
8	6	0.44	0.20	−0.17	0.03
9	7	1.22	1.49	0.40	0.16
10	9	2.20	4.83	0.43	0.18
Sum	49	0.0	16.51	0.0	9.14

ment projects. First, we need to know how well the line we have chosen fits the data. Second, we need to know whether the line we have found is really better than any other line obtained by chance. Third, and most important, we will must develop an estimate for the predictive validity of this model. It is clear that we can plug a value for lines of code into this model and get out a value for the anticipated number of faults in the model, but we really do not know at this point that what we have done is meaningful. Finally, we need to establish that we have found the right model for our data. It is quite possible that we could fit a linear model to data that are intrinsically non-linear. What is worse is that we could have fit a model to data that were severely corrupted with measurement error. Just because we developed a model does not mean that our modeling task is over. Quite the contrary, it has just now begun.

In Chapter 2 we discussed the conduct of scientific inquiry. It is an iterative process. We will formulate a hypothesis about the nature of the world. We will conduct an experiment to gather data to explore our hypothesis. From this data we will build a model. We will apply the model to the data to see what went wrong. In the case of regression modeling, the residuals will disclose our inadequacies. We must learn to listen to what these residual values are telling us. They will reveal to us our next hypothesis in the conduct of our inquiry. The bottom line is that the model is not the end of the process; it is the beginning of the next cycle of the process of scientific inquiry. No model in the history of science has ever been capable of perfect prediction. That is not our goal. What is really of interest to us is why the model really did not work. All of this information is in the residuals. We must learn how to tease it out. The model is not our objective; the residuals are. That is where the gold is.

7.2.2 The Regression ANOVA

The least squares regression model that we just developed

$$y = 0.086 * x - 4.55 \tag{15}$$

is of value to us if it has credibility. We would like to be able to make some assertions about the quality of prediction of this model. That is, is the model that we developed better than one that we would have developed by chance? To answer this question we will use a statistical procedure called analysis of variance. Observe that:

$$y_i - \hat{y}_i = y_i - \bar{y} + \bar{y} - \hat{y}_i = (y_i - \bar{y}) - (\hat{y}_i - \bar{y}) \tag{16}$$

We now square both sides of this equation such that:

$$(y_i - \hat{y}_i)^2 = [(y_i - \bar{y}) - (y_i - \bar{y})]^2 \tag{17}$$

Now, if we add the residual squares we obtain:

$$\sum_i (y_i - \hat{y}_i)^2 = \sum_i [(y_i - \bar{y}) - (\hat{y}_i - \bar{y})]^2 \tag{18}$$

Now we expand the right-hand side. The cross product terms will drop out because they always do (see Appendix 1), and we obtain:

$$\sum_i (y_i - \hat{y}_i)^2 = \sum_i (y_i - \bar{y})^2 - \sum_i (\hat{y}_i - \bar{y})^2 \tag{19}$$

which can be rewritten as:

$$\sum_i (y_i - \bar{y})^2 = \sum_i (y_i - \hat{y}_i)^2 + \sum_i (\hat{y}_i - \bar{y})^2 \tag{20}$$

The left-hand side of this equation is the sum of squares about the mean of the observed data. This is the variance term for the variance in the *y*s. The first term on the right-hand side is the sum of squares error. It is the residual or error variance. The second term on the right-hand side of the equation is the sum of squares due to regression. This is the variance term for the predicted data.

Each of the sums of squares has an associated number called degrees of freedom. Let us observe that the term $\bar{y}$ is a constant. We know its value. If we look at the deviation scores $d_i = y_i - \bar{y}$, we know that their sum must be zero, by definition. Now if we examine these terms one at a time from y_1 to y_{n-1}, we simply cannot predict what any of these values might be. However, when we know all of the values for y_1 to y_{n-1}, then we will automatically know the final one, y_n. There will be no new information in the value of y_n. While the first 1 through $n-1$ values of *y* are free to vary, the last one, y_n, will be determined precisely by the other $n-1$ values. Therefore, the sum of the deviation scores squared has $n-1$ degrees of freedom.

In that

$$\sum_i (\hat{y}_i - \bar{y})^2 = b_1^2 \sum_i (x_i - \bar{x})^2 \tag{21}$$

147

Exhibit 8. The Regression ANOVA

Source	Sum of Squares	Degrees of Freedom	Mean Square	F-Ratio
Due to regression	$SS_R = \sum_i (\hat{y}_i - \bar{y})^2$	1	$MS_R = SS_R / 1$	$F = MS_R / MS_E$
Residual	$SS_E = \sum_i (y_i - \hat{y}_i)^2$	$n-2$	$MS_E = SS_E / (n-2)$	
Total	$SS_{TOT} = \sum_i (y_i - \bar{y})^2$	$n-1$		

Exhibit 9. Regression ANOVA for Sample Data

Source	Sum of Squares	Degrees of Freedom	Mean Square	F-Ratio
Due to regression	31.76	1	31.76	$F = 27.80$
				$p < 0.05$
Residual	9.14	8	1.14	
Total	40.90	9		

it is a single function of y and therefore has but one degree of freedom. Hence, by subtraction we determine that the sum of squares about regression (error) has $n - 2$ degrees of freedom.

We can now construct the Analysis of Variance (ANOVA) table for the regression model. This is shown in Exhibit 8. The Mean Square column of this table is derived by dividing the sums of squares residual and regression by their respective degrees of freedom. The F statistic in the final column is the ratio of the mean squares due to regression to the mean square error term. This F statistic has one degree of freedom in the numerator and $n - 2$ degrees of freedom in the denominator.

Let us now take our sample data from Exhibit 2 and perform the regression analysis of variance for this data. The results of this analysis are shown in Exhibit 9. We would now like to ascertain whether our new model is different from one that Nature would have derived by chance alone. As per Chapter 2, we will have determined long before we collected data for this experiment what risk we were willing to take about this conjecture. Let us assume that it was one chance in 20. Then we would like to know at the 95 percent confidence level whether the observed F statistic is greater than $F(0.95;1,8) = 5.32$. Our calculated F at 27.80 is certainly much greater than this value. In that we decided a prior to set our Type I error to 5 percent it would be at once gauche and naive to report that our F statistic was also significant at the 0.5 percent level as well. We are only concerned that our initial experimental criterion level of 5 percent was met.

Exhibit 10. Sample Data from Four Experiments

Case 1		Case 2		Case 3		Case 4	
x	y	x	y	x	y	x	y
10	8.04	10	9.14	10	7.46	8	6.58
8	6.95	8	8.14	8	6.77	8	5.76
13	7.58	13	8.74	13	12.74	8	7.71
9	8.81	9	8.77	9	7.11	8	8.84
11	8.33	11	9.26	11	7.81	8	8.47
14	9.96	14	8.1	14	8.84	8	7.04
6	7.24	6	6.13	6	6.08	8	5.25
4	4.26	4	3.1	4	5.39	19	12.5
12	10.84	12	9.13	12	8.15	8	5.56
7	4.82	7	7.26	7	6.42	8	7.91
5	5.68	5	4.74	5	5.73	8	6.89

Exhibit 11. Regression ANOVA for Four Experiments

Case	Source	Sum of Squares	Degrees of Freedom	Mean Square	F-Ratio
1	Regression	27.5	1	27.5	$F = 27.5$
	Residual	13.8	9	1.5	
	Total	41.3	10		
2	Regression	27.5	1	27.5	$F = 27.5$
	Residual	13.8	9	1.5	
	Total	41.3	10		
3	Regression	27.5	1	27.5	$F = 27.5$
	Residual	13.8	9	1.5	
	Total	41.3	10		
4	Regression	27.5	1	27.5	$F = 27.5$
	Residual	13.8	9	1.5	
	Total	41.3	10		

We now know that our regression line was satisfactory. The next question is how well did the model perform. We can compute the coefficient of determination as $R^2 = SS_R / SS_{TOT}$. This will give us the proportion of variation of y explained by the regression equation. Clearly, if the residual sum of squares, or error sum of squares, is zero, then $R^2 = 1.0$. In the example above, $R^2 = 31.76 / 40.90 = 0.78$. This says that we are able to explain about 78 percent of the variation in y with a concomitant variation in our independent variable x.

We must be very careful about what we think that we have learned from the regression ANOVA. Consider the data presented in Exhibit 10 from Tufte.[1] Here are data from four successive hypothetical experiments. When we compute the least squares regression line for each of these cases, we find that $y = 0.5x + 3$. The models are identical. Furthermore, when we perform the analysis of variance for each of these cases, we find that the results of these analyses are all identical. They all account for exactly the same amount of variation in the dependent variable. Yet, the data are not identical (see Exhibit 10). They are very different from case to case.

Exhibit 12. Residual Values and Independent Variable

	Case 1		Case 2		Case 3		Case 4
x	$y_i - \hat{y}_i$	x	$y_i - \hat{y}_i$	x	$y_i - \hat{y}_i$	x	$y_i - \hat{y}_i$
4.00	−0.74	4.00	−1.90	4.00	0.39	19.00	0.00
5.00	0.18	5.00	−0.76	5.00	0.23	8.00	−0.11
6.00	1.24	6.00	0.13	6.00	0.08	8.00	−1.75
7.00	−1.68	7.00	0.76	7.00	−0.08	8.00	0.91
8.00	−0.05	8.00	1.14	8.00	−0.23	8.00	−1.24
9.00	1.31	9.00	1.27	9.00	−0.39	8.00	1.84
10.00	0.04	10.00	1.14	10.00	−0.54	8.00	−0.42
11.00	−0.17	11.00	0.76	11.00	−0.69	8.00	1.47
12.00	1.84	12.00	0.13	12.00	−0.85	8.00	−1.44
13.00	−1.92	13.00	−0.76	13.00	3.24	8.00	0.71
14.00	−0.04	14.00	−1.90	14.00	−1.16	8.00	0.04

There must be something that we have missed in our model analysis. Indeed there is. Perhaps the most important step in modeling is a detailed examination of the residuals. As amazing as it might seem, we should be more interested in the deviations from our predictions than in our successful predictions.

7.2.3 Residual Analysis

In the great scheme of things, if we were to create a model where all the values of the dependent variable had fallen on the regression line, the residuals would all have been zero. Given that there is some error introduced by the observation process alone, there will be no functional relationship between the errors and our dependent variable. That is, ε and x will be unrelated. Now look at the residuals for the data on the four hypothetical experiments shown in Exhibit 10.

The residuals for the four cases are shown in Exhibit 12. If the εs are unrelated to the xs, then there should be no particular pattern in the residuals. We can explore this conjecture visually by plotting the residuals against the independent variable x. These plots are shown in Exhibits 13 through 16.

The first observation that we can make about the residual data shown in Exhibits 13 through 16 is that they are fantastically different. This is particularly astonishing in that everything that we have done in model construction and ANOVA seems to suggest that these data are very similar. Obviously, there is much more to the modeling process than just building the model and evaluating it with the ANOVA. That is only the first step. The residual analysis is where the model building fun really begins. Let us begin this process with Exhibit 13 for Case 1.

If the residuals were truly randomly distributed with respect to the independent variable, then there would be a random distribution of this data. There would be no clear pattern in these data. That is certainly not the

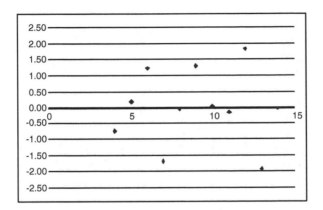

Exhibit 13. Residual Values for Case 1

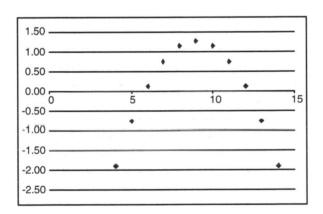

Exhibit 14. Residual Values for Case 2

case for Exhibits 14 through 16. The data in these figures are anything but random. In Exhibit 13, however, there is no clear relationship between the residuals and the independent variable. The correlation coefficient between them is essentially zero. There is an apparent tendency for the residuals to grow larger, as does the independent variable. However, if we compute the correlation coefficient of $|\varepsilon|$ with x, it is 0.08, which is not significantly greater than zero. That is, the 95 percent confidence intervals for this correlation include the value zero. This will lead us to discard the conjecture that the residuals are becoming larger as x becomes larger.

If, on the other hand, we compute the correlation coefficient between ε and y, we find that there is a significant correlation between these variables at 0.58, indicating a linear relationship between the two. We are deeply concerned about these kinds of relationships because they are leading indica-

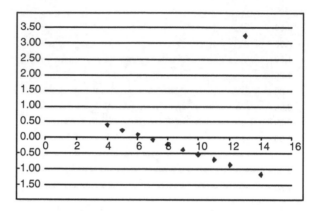

Exhibit 15. Residual Values for Case 3

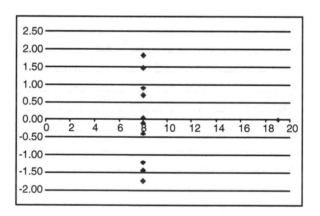

Exhibit 16. Residual Values for Case 4

tors of a flawed measurement process. If the residuals grow with respect to either the dependent variable or an independent variable, then it is highly likely that errors are creeping in because of our measurement tool. Let us suppose, for example, that the algorithm that we use to measure the executable statement count underreports these values by 5 to 10 percent. Then the measurements taken on larger program modules will have greater error.

There are a host of different techniques that we can apply to determine whether there are trends in the residuals, either with respect to the dependent variable or the independent variable. There are nonparametric procedures of sign tests and run tests. Autocorrelation is also a very useful technique for exploring trends in residuals. In every case, we are trying to eliminate the possibility that we have introduced systematic trends in these residuals, either by the formulation of the wrong hypothesis or by measurement error.

The residuals shown in Exhibit 14 for Case 2 show a very clear trend. It is clear that these residuals are nonlinear with respect to x, and that a second-order polynomial model would probably fit these data much better. We may have had the wrong hypothesis in mind when we developed the experiment. What we *cannot* do is rerun this data through another model. We used these data once and now the juice is out of them. We really need to do some soul searching about the data themselves. There are three points in these data that are particularly relevant: the maximum value and the two minima. We need to extract these points and study very carefully the circumstance that created them. If, after close scrutiny, we can see a distinct reason for why there is a quadratic relationship between the dependent and independent variable, then we will reformulate a new quadratic hypothesis, collect new data from a new experiment, and then fit a new model. The worst thing that we could do is to revisit this data with a new model and then invent an hypothesis to go with the new model. That methodology will fall well outside the realm of valid scientific investigation.

The real danger of fitting a new model to used data is that the quadratic trend that we observed in the data may be a measurement artifact. We could imagine, for example, that we were using a thermocouple in this experiment that took a while to warm up; hence the rising slope of the first residual data points. Then, after our thermocouple got warm, it underwent some physical change that caused its resistance to drop over time. This is an artifact of the measurement process. The underlying problem that we are investigating might, in fact, be a simple linear relationship. If we fit a nonlinear model to this data, we will be learning about our measurement tools and not about the very thing that we wish to model. We will only learn about the true cause of this trend in the residuals if we do the necessary forensic investigation on the data themselves.

The residuals for Case 3 are shown in Exhibit 15. Here is a very disturbing trend. This pattern was created by the single point that falls way off the line of the other points, the outlier. If it were not for this outlier, we would have a pretty good model. We find that if we remove this point (13,12.74) from the original data set and recompute the regression line, we will have a perfect line. The residuals all become zero. It is very tempting to remove this offending point. After all, what is one point? Then we would have a perfect experimental outcome.

We simply cannot remove data points because they disturb the aesthetics of our model and our experiment. Sometimes, these outliers are very poignant. We might well be observing a very important but also very tenuous phenomenon in our data. Because of our limited sampling, we only saw one instance of this phenomenon that may contain more information than all of the other points put together. To cast this point out summarily would be a crime against science. Our outlier is perhaps the most important point of the lot. Something either went heroically wrong in our observation/measurement process or something very important happened once and only once. Again, we need to do a thorough forensic analysis on the point (13,12.74) to try to discover why it was an outlier. If in the process of this investigation we were to discover that we had simply made a big mistake in our observation process and had evidence to support that conclusion, then and only then could we remove this point from the set of legitimate observations.

Finally, there is Case 4 shown in Exhibit 16. Except in the case of our one outlier, there is a perfect nonrelationship between x and y. With the exception of the outlier, y varies while x is constant. These residual data suggest that there is almost no predictive capability in the model. It is time to formulate a new hypothesis. Again, it will be well worth our while to see just exactly why x has the value of 19 once when all of the other observations were 8. We can only analyze this if we have preserved the circumstances that surrounded the original measurement during the experiment.

Let us remember that the regression ANOVA and the linear regression models for each of these cases were identical. Only on the examination of the residuals did we really begin to understand what each of these experimental outcomes really was. Essentially, the residuals were the experimental outcome.

7.2.4 Multiple Linear Regression

Unfortunately, the world we live in is very complicated. Software faults, for example, are not evenly distributed in source code. If they were, we would only need simple univariate linear regression between our independent variable of, say, lines of code and our dependent variable of software faults. People inject these faults into code for a variety of different reasons. Sometimes, developers make errors on predicate clauses. Sometimes, they make errors on the declaration or use of data structures. Errors are made for a variety of reasons. Therefore, we will need to measure a variety of different program attributes to get a reasonable handle on the faults themselves. We will require much more sophisticated models to cope with the simultaneous variation in each of these attributes. To this end we will employ a more general first-order linear model in multiple independent variables as follows:

$$y = \beta_0 + \beta_1 x_1 + \beta_2 x_2 + \ldots + \beta_p x_p + \varepsilon \tag{22}$$

The least squares estimates for the parameters of this equation are obtained from:

$$\mathbf{b} = (\mathbf{X}^T \mathbf{X})^{-1} \mathbf{X}^T \mathbf{Y} \tag{23}$$

Exhibit 17. ANOVA for Multiple Regression

Source	Sum of Squares	Degrees of Freedom	Mean Square	F-Ratio
Due to regression	SS_R	p	$MS_R = \dfrac{SS_R}{p}$	$F_c = MS_R \,/\, MS_E$
Residual	SS_E	$n - p - 1$	$MS_E = \dfrac{SS_E}{n - p - 1}$	
Total	SS_{TOT}	$n - 1$		

where $\mathbf{X}$ is an $n \times (p + 1)$ matrix of n observations on each of the p independent variables and $\mathbf{X}^T$ is its transpose. The first column of $\mathbf{X}$ is a vector of n ones and $\mathbf{Y}$ is a vector of n observations on the dependent variable. The vector, $\mathbf{b}$, has $(p + 1)$ elements and will contain the estimates for the parameters $\beta_0, \beta_1, \beta_2, \ldots, \beta_p$.

The sums of squares for the multiple linear regression model are:

$$SS_R = \mathbf{b}^T \mathbf{X}^T \mathbf{Y} - \left(\frac{1}{n}\right) \mathbf{Y}^T \mathbf{U} \mathbf{U}^T \mathbf{Y} \tag{24}$$

$$SS_E = \mathbf{e}^T \mathbf{e} = (\mathbf{Y} - \mathbf{Xb})^T (\mathbf{Y} = \mathbf{Xb}) = \mathbf{Y}^T \mathbf{Y} - \mathbf{b}^T \mathbf{X}^T \mathbf{Y} \tag{25}$$

$$SS_{TOT} = \mathbf{Y}^T \mathbf{Y} - \left(\frac{1}{n}\right) \mathbf{Y}^T \mathbf{U} \mathbf{U}^T \mathbf{Y} \tag{26}$$

where

$$\mathbf{e} = \mathbf{Y} - \hat{\mathbf{Y}} = \mathbf{Y} - \mathbf{Xb} \tag{27}$$

and $\mathbf{U}$ is an $n \times 1$ element vector containing all 1s. As was the case for simple linear regression, the SS_{TOT} has $n{-}1$ degrees of freedom. There are now p parameters to be estimated in this new model. That means that the sum of squares due to regression, SS_R, will have p of freedom. By subtraction, this means that the sum of squares error, SS_E, will have $n - p - 1$ degrees of freedom. The ANOVA for the multiple linear regression is shown in Exhibit 17.

In the simplest case of hypothesis testing, either the regression equation explains a significant amount of variation in the dependent variable or it does not. Hence, we will choose between the two alternate hypotheses as follows:

$$H_0 \colon \beta_0 = \beta_1 = \cdots = \beta_{p-1} = 0$$

$$H_1 \colon \text{not all } \beta_j = 0, \ k = 1, \ldots, p - 1 \tag{28}$$

depending on the computed value of the F statistics, F_c. Given that we have determined α to be 0.05 as before, then we will accept:

$$H_0 \text{ if } F_c \leq F(0.95; \, p, n - p - 1) \tag{29}$$

Otherwise,

$$H_1 \text{ if } F_c > F(0.95; \, p, n - p - 1) \tag{30}$$

Again, just because we have rejected the null hypothesis does not mean that we have produced a useful regression model. Its utility must be measured in terms of its ability to predict the future. However, we can evaluate the quality of the fit of the model with the coefficient of multiple determination that we discussed earlier as $R^2 = SS_R / SS_{TOT}$.

Now that we know how, we can easily build very complex regression models with multiple independent variables. For small data sets, we can very rapidly reach a point of diminishing returns. Observe that F_c has p degrees of freedom in the numerator and $n - p - 1$ degrees of freedom in the denominator. As we add terms to the regression equation, the degrees of freedom numerator rises and the degrees of freedom denominator falls. The critical value of the F statistic begins to fall as the numerator for F_c rises. More is not necessarily better.

We will now begin to explore our new modeling knowledge with two random samples of data from program modules drawn from the Space Shuttle PASS. The first sample will consist of data from 100 program modules. The second sample, the validation sample, will consist of data from 50 program modules. This second data set will be used to validate the models that we will create using the first data set. It is called a hold-back or confirmatory data set. The problem with predictive models is that they predict the past. They have been developed from data we collected in the past. We do not know how well they will predict new data that is not part of the original data set used to develop the model.

Regression models were developed for the original 100 observations. New models were created that systematically added each of the metrics. Thirteen such models were developed. These are shown in Exhibit 18. The first column of this table is the constant term. The first model in this table is the simple linear regression of η_1 on the dependent variable that was DR-Count or the count of the number of Discrepancy Reports that were filed for each program module. This table shows 13 of 8191 of all of the possible combinations of models built from these 13 metrics. It is quite possible that the best model is not shown here. In the next section we will look at techniques to help us find the best model.

The regression ANOVA for each of the 13 regression models is shown in Exhibit 19. Here we can see that the regression degrees of freedom are

Exhibit 18. Regression Models for the 13 Dependent Variables

Cons	η_1	η_2	N_1	N_2	Exec	LOC	Nodes	Edges	Paths	Cycles Paths	Max Paths	Ave Paths	DS
-0.841	0.156												
-0.346	0.062	0.018											
0.450	0.018	-0.020	0.007										
0.451	0.017	-0.017	0.008	-0.002									
0.342	0.045	-0.043	-0.004	0.014	0.029								
-0.178	0.028	-0.040	-0.005	0.014	0.015	0.012							
-0.152	0.025	-0.040	-0.004	0.014	0.013	0.012	0.003						
-0.020	0.040	-0.038	-0.001	0.011	0.001	0.015	-0.150	0.107					
-0.004	0.040	-0.039	-0.001	0.011	0.001	0.015	-0.154	0.110					
0.067	0.078	-0.059	-0.009	0.021	0.021	0.016	-0.346	0.264	0.000	-0.399			
0.143	0.076	-0.057	-0.010	0.022	0.023	0.015	-0.287	0.229	0.000	-0.169	-0.029		
0.132	0.078	-0.058	-0.009	0.022	0.022	0.015	-0.284	0.226	0.000	-0.171	-0.041	0.014	
0.100	0.074	-0.054	-0.008	0.019	0.018	0.014	-0.298	0.239	0.000	-0.194	-0.046	0.017	0.009

Exhibit 19. Regression ANOVAs for 13 Models

Model	Source	Sum of Squares	d.f.	Mean Square	F_c	$F_{(0.95;n,d)}$
1	Regression	314.23	1	314.23	18.74	3.96
	Residual	1643.48	98	16.77		
2	Regression	517.74	2	258.87	17.44	3.11
	Residual	1439.97	97	14.85		
3	Regression	1015.92	3	338.64	34.52	2.72
	Residual	941.79	96	9.81		
4	Regression	1016.39	4	254.10	25.64	2.49
	Residual	941.32	95	9.91		
5	Regression	1060.01	5	212.00	22.10	2.33
	Residual	897.70	94	9.55		
6	Regression	1492.06	6	248.68	49.67	2.22
	Residual	465.65	93	5.01		
7	Regression	1493.32	7	213.33	42.26	2.13
	Residual	464.39	92	5.05		
8	Regression	1507.92	8	188.49	38.14	2.06
	Residual	449.79	91	4.94		
9	Regression	1508.14	9	167.57	33.55	2.00
	Residual	449.56	90	4.10		
10	Regression	1585.34	10	158.53	37.89	1.95
	Residual	372.37	89	4.18		
11	Regression	1594.12	11	144.92	35.08	1.91
	Residual	363.59	88	4.13		
12	Regression	1594.25	12	132.85	31.80	1.87
	Residual	363.46	87	4.18		
13	Regression	1604.87	13	123.451	30.09	1.83
	Residual	352.85	86	4.10		

increasing from 1 to 13. At the same time that the degrees of freedom due to regression (numerator) are increasing, the degrees of freedom residual (denominator) are declining. The calculated F statistic, F_c, rises fairly steadily to the sixth model and then declines. The criterion F statistic for $\alpha < 0.05$ is shown in the last column. It falls steadily as the degree of freedom numerator increases and degrees of freedom denominator declines.

Now let us turn our attention to the performance of the subset of regression models that we have evaluated. First, we will assess the quality of fit of each of the models. This is given to us by the R^2 term in Exhibit 20. It would appear that R^2 is a monotonically increasing function of the number of terms in the model. It improves to the point that with all 13 metrics in the model we appear to be able to account for about 82 percent of the variation in the program module DR-Count.

Another measure of the fit of the regression model is the mean square error term calculated as:

$$MSE_{Fit} = \frac{1}{n} \sum_{i=1}^{n} (y_i - \hat{y}_i)^2 \tag{31}$$

Exhibit 20. Regression Model Performance

Model	R^2	MSE_{Fit}	MSE_{Pred}
1	0.16	16.28	39.58
2	0.26	14.28	34.85
3	0.52	9.47	44.66
4	0.52	9.36	44.38
5	0.54	8.95	38.40
6	0.76	4.71	40.51
7	0.76	4.77	41.72
8	0.77	4.55	50.80
9	0.77	4.57	51.23
10	0.81	3.74	47.19
11	0.81	3.63	47.76
12	0.81	3.72	49.48
13	0.82	3.54	52.29

where n in this case is 100. We can clearly see that there is a point of diminishing returns at model 6. That is, MSE_{Fit} declines rapidly and then stabilizes at about model 6. Even so, these are relatively small values for MSE_{Fit}. The models that we have developed fit the data fairly well.

7.2.5 Model Predictive Validity

The main problem with our predictive models is that they predict past events; that is, they are derived from events that have already taken place. If our objective is to understand functional relationships among independent variables and a dependent variable as they have existed, these models will do very well. The reason that most scientists develop predictive models is that they want to be able to predict future events. Predicting the past and predicting the future are two very different things. If we wish to use a model for future prediction, then we must attempt to validate its ability to do so.

Now let us turn our attention to the last column in Exhibit 20. This last column also has in it the mean square error terms but this time they are derived from the hold-back data set. That is, the model developed with the first 100 observations was then applied to the 50 observations. The means square error predictive term is calculated as:

$$MSE_{Pred} = \frac{1}{m} \sum_{i=1}^{n} \left(y_i' - \hat{y}_i \right)^2 \tag{32}$$

where m = 50, y_i' is the DR-Count value from the hold-back data set, and is the predicted y_i' from each of the models. Both the MSE_{Fit} and the MSE_{Pred} values for the 13 models are shown in Exhibit 21. We can see that there is a real disparity in the residual values for these two terms. The predicted values are much larger than those obtained by the model.

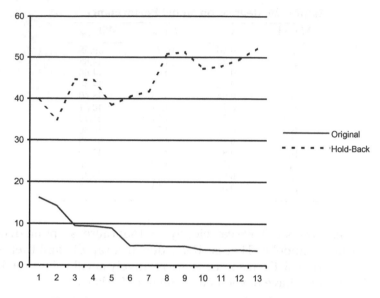

Exhibit 21. The Original and Predicted MSE Values

The moral of this story is that a good model fit does not mean that the model is of value for future prediction. With the kind of MSE_{Pred} values that we have seen from these 13 models, the derived models were of very limited value. They fit the data well but they failed utterly to give us a quality future predictive ability. It is clear that if the model were to yield the best possible future prediction, then $MSE_{Fit} = MSE_{Pred}$. To the extent that $MSE_{Pred} > MSE_{Fit}$, then the predictive validity of the model is not good.

In Exhibit 21, we had the fortune to have enough data that we could generate a hold-back data set to validate each of the models. Sometimes, the data are much too costly and too sparse. We are obliged to use every last datum in constructing the model. This does not preclude our assessment of the predictive validity of the model. In this case we can use the PRESS statistic to give an assessment of the future prediction potential for a model. To compute the PRESS statistic, we will select and remove one data point from an initial set of n data points and construct our predictive model from the remaining $n - 1$ observations. We then compute the residual value of the one point that was held back from the model. Let $y_{(1)}$ represent the y value of the data point held back from the first model. Then, $y_{(1)} - \hat{y}_{(1)}$ will represent the residual value of this dependent variable value when the first model is applied to the first hold-back data point.

The PRESS statistic, then, is computed as follows:

$$PRESS = \sum_{i=1}^{n} \left(y_{(i)} - \hat{y}_{(i)} \right)^2 \tag{33}$$

A good model with good future predictive potential will have a small value of the PRESS statistic.

7.2.6 Selecting the Best Regression Model

As mentioned in passing in the previous section, with 13 dependent variables it is possible to construct 8191 models of all possible combinations of variables in the models. Some of these models will be better than other models in terms of their quality of fit. We could evaluate each of these models with any one of several criteria. For example, one such criterion would be to select the model with the best R^2. Our experience with the Space Shuttle data example should make us a little shy about this sole criterion. Of the 13 models that we built for that example, the one with the highest R^2 had the worst MSE_{Pred}. Another alternative would be to select the model with the highest calculated F_c statistic.

There are several methodologies available that will short-circuit this grueling process for us. They are iterative processes that build successively better models for us. They are the step-wise model building techniques. There are procedures for the forward step-wise process wherein we will start with a single independent variable and then add new variables until a maximum value of a criterion measure is met. There are also backward elimination step-wise procedures that start with all dependent variables in the model and systematically remove those independent variables that do not contribute significantly to the model. These procedures are well beyond the scope of this text. They are commonly available in most statistical software packages.

7.2.7 Regression with Dummy Variates

Consider the data in Exhibit 2 with a special focus on the sources of variation in the dependent variable, faults. There may very well be sources of variation in these data that are not related to the independent variable, LOC. It turns out that the program modules in this example were written by two different people. The data are reproduced in Exhibit 22, this time with the developers that wrote each module. We can see in this exhibit, for example, that Mary wrote modules 1, 2, 3, 4, and 6. The remainder were written by Betty. Just looking at the data, it would appear that Betty had more faults reported than Mary. This might be due to the fact that Betty was responsible for more complex code. It might be due to the fact that Betty was more diligent in reporting her faults. The main point here is that we do not have enough information to know just why they may be different in regard to the number of faults that have been reported in their code. We would, however, like to control for the constant differences between them, if any.

Exhibit 22. Sample Data by Developer

Module	Faults	LOC	Mary	Betty
1	3	82	1	0
2	3	87	1	0
3	4	94	1	0
4	4	98	1	0
5	2	105	0	1
6	6	108	1	0
7	5	120	0	1
8	6	125	0	1
9	7	130	0	1
10	9	153	0	1

Exhibit 23. Regression Model with Dummy Variate

Constant	LOC	Mary	R^2
−4.55	0.09		0.78
−11.53	0.14	2.69	0.94

To initiate this control for the constant effect of the developer, we will create a new independent variable that has discrete values. This new variable will have the value of 1 if Mary wrote the code and a value of 0 if Betty wrote the code. This new variable is called a dummy variable. It has the discrete values of 1 or 0. When we build a new regression model with this dummy variate in it, the model coefficient for this independent variable will, in fact, represent the constant difference in faults in the modules that Mary has written.

The regression model for this data is shown in Exhibit 23. The regression coefficient for Mary is 2.69. This is the constant difference between the faults in Mary's code and Betty's code. On average, the modules written by Mary have roughly two and one half more faults in them than Betty's code. That is an interesting fact in and of itself. Looking further into the table we see a notable increase in R^2 as well. The second model fits the data much better.

We now turn our attention to the regression ANOVAs for the two models (Exhibit 24). The calculated F statistic (F_c) for the model with the dummy variate is much higher than the F statistic for the initial model. Clearly, we have identified and controlled an extraneous source of variation in the dependent variable that is affecting our model. By introducing the dummy variate to control for the constant difference between the fault reporting observed between Mary and Betty, we have greatly improved our understanding of the relationship between LOC and faults.

We cannot incorporate a dummy variate for both Betty and Mary in the same model because they are linearly dependent. The sum of the variable

Exhibit 24. Regression ANOVA for Two Models

Source	Sum of Squares	d.f.	Mean Square	F_c	$F_{(0.95;n,d)}$
Regression	31.75	1	31.76	27.79	5.32
Residual	9.14	8	1.14		
Regression	38.57	2	19.29	58.04	4.74
Residual	2.33	7	0.33		

values for Betty and Mary will always be 1. A basic assumption in linear modeling is that the data vectors representing the independent variables will have no linear dependencies.

In a more general sense, if we wish to represent the constant differences among a group of m members, we will use $m-1$ dummy variates to do this. That is, if we had a team of six programmers and we wanted to control for constant differences for members of this team, we would create a model with five dummy variates in it. If we suspected that there is a constant difference between male and female developers, for example, we could create a male (or female) dummy variate. The coefficient of this variable in the regression equation would represent the constant difference between males and females. In this manner we are able to identify and control for a source of variance that would otherwise contribute noise to the regression model. The downside of the use of dummy variates is that they tend to represent a large contribution to the numerator degrees of freedom in the regression ANOVA.

7.3 NONLINEAR MODELS

The nonlinear modeling process begins with a nonlinear hypothesis. There are essentially two types of nonlinear models that are used for software measurement data. First, are the polynomial models of the form:

$$y = \beta_0 + \beta_1 x + \beta_2 x^2 \tag{34}$$

These models can grow quite complex when we have multiple independent variables. A model can be linear in a subset of independent variables and nonlinear in the rest. An alternate nonlinear model can take the form:

$$y = \beta_0 + \beta_1 x^\alpha \tag{35}$$

where α is a parameter of the model.

Nonlinear models of the second type have little place or value in our work in software measurement. They are of no utility because we cannot formulate a reasonable prior hypothesis that looks like this: Faults = 0.04 * LOC[1.62]. We commonly see these models employed by researchers who are ignorantly beating their data with a big statistical stick. They are trying to find a model to fit the data. Finding a model that fits the data and one that provides good future predictive capability are two very different things. The activity of fitting a model to the data is an unfortunate result of the common availability of very sophisticated and inexpensive statistical analysis tools. An excellent set of mechanic's tools will not make a novice a good mechanic. Arming a common foot soldier with a tank will not make him an effective warfighter; it will just make him dangerous. W. Edwards Deming is on record as having allowed that nobody should be allowed access to raw data without a substantial background in statistics. We firmly believe that the use of statistical packages should be restricted to those individuals with a fair level of training in statistical analysis.

Polynomial models do have some practical validity. We can easily imagine circumstances when they are very representative of a reality that we have personally experienced. Consider the relationship between the feeling of euphoria and beer consumption. Just about every college freshman has conducted an ad hoc experiment on this relationship. When said college freshman attends his first keg party, he notices that his feeling of euphoria rises with every glass of beer consumed, up to a point. Then the incremental increase euphoria begins to drop. At some point in the consumption process, the euphoria value will have peaked and will start decreasing. The final glass of beer consumed will make our freshman regret the day he was born. This phenomenon clearly warrants a nonlinear hypothesis. We can go straight there. For those of us who have had the experience, there will be no need to conduct this experiment twice, first with a linear model and then with the obvious nonlinear second-order polynomial model.

Sometimes, nonlinear relationships with independent variables are not initially apparent. When we plot the residuals against each of the independent variables, we do expect that these values will be randomly distributed about each of the independent variables. If we see evidence of second- or third-order effects in the residuals (see Exhibit 14), then we will carefully examine the data and the measurement processes to try and determine the source of nonlinearity. Again, if we are satisfied that we have truly observed a nonlinear relationship between the dependent variable and one or more of the independent variables, we must formulate a new hypothesis to reflect this nonlinearity, design a new experiment, collect new data, and fit our new nonlinear model to the new data.

Sometimes, the data we work with are of great magnitude. Tiny relative fluctuations in these data will dominate more subtle phenomena that we are also modeling. In this case, it might be genuinely useful to transform the raw data. A common transformation is the logarithmic transformation. This transformation is commonly used for measuring the relative strengths of earthquakes on the logarithmic Richter scale. If we wish to perform a suitable transformation on our data, then our experimental hypothesis must reflect this transformation. If, for example, we were to model the linear relationship of the frequency of canary chirps and local earthquakes measured on the Richter scale, then we are really modeling the exponential relationship between chirps and the absolute energy of earthquakes. Stated another way, the models that we build that employ data transformations must make sense in terms of the inverse mapping of the transformed data.

7.4 PROBLEMS ASSOCIATED WITH MULTICOLLINEARITY

The basic regression models are based on the assumption that the independent variables of the analysis are neither linear compounds of each other nor share an element of common variance. Two variables sharing a common element of variance are said to be *collinear*. Unfortunately, we know this is not the case with software metrics as independent variables. As we have seen in Chapter 6, the correlation coefficients among our independent variables are very large, indicating a high degree of collinearity. In fact, we saw with our 13 metrics on the PASS data that there were only three distinct sources of variation, not 13.

There are several problems that a high degree of multicollinearity can cause in the modeling process. The main problem is that the regression coefficients formed by the model are really not representative of the relative contribution of a particular independent variable to the variation in the dependent variable. That is, the effect of a particular independent variable, say LOC, has on our dependent variable, Faults, is dependent on whether Exec is already in the model. We know that LOC and Exec are highly correlated. They are measuring essentially the same phenomenon of program size. Thus, if we were to build a model with LOC as a predictor of faults and then add Exec to this model, the regression coefficient would reflect only a marginal or partial effect that Exec contributes to the model.

Quite simply, multicollinearity among the independent variables undermines our ability to use the regression model coefficients in any meaningful way. With a given set of highly correlated independent variables, a model built from them will be capricious. We will benefit little in understanding the particular contribution of each independent variable to the observed variation in the independent variable. However, this is the very reason that we are modeling in the first place.

As we saw in Chapter 6, principal component analysis (PCA) can be used to detect and eliminate this collinearity in the software complexity metrics. When confronted with a large number of variables known to be highly correlated, it may be desirable to represent the set by some small number of variables that convey all or most of the information in the original set. The principal components are constructed so that they represent transformed domain scores on dimensions that are orthogonal.

Exhibit 25. Regression Equation for Domain Scores

Constant	Size	Control	DS	R^2
2.23	2.32	1.81	1.47	0.55

Exhibit 26. Regression ANOVA for Domain Scores

Source	Sum of Squares	d.f.	Mean Square	F_c	$F_{(0.95;n,d)}$
Regression	1071.91	3	357.31	38.72	2.72
Residual	885.80	96	9.23		

We will now apply PCA to our sample of 100 data modules from the PASS system so that we can eliminate the problem of multicollinearity in this data and build a better model. When we do this we get three factors or principal components, as per our analysis of the complete PASS data set in Chapter 6. In this reduced subset of program modules, the new factors or principal components account for approximately 90 percent of the variance in the original set of 13 raw measures. We will use the factors scores or domain scores to build our regression model, with the DR-Count as the dependent variable. The resulting model is shown in Exhibit 25. In this exhibit, the factors have been labeled as Size, Control, and DS, just as they were in Chapter 6 for the complete set of data. We can see that these new domain metrics account for approximately 55 percent of the variation in the dependent variable DR-Count.

The regression model presented in Exhibit 25 is very different from the models derived from these data and shown in Exhibit 18. This time, we can interpret the model coefficients directly. Remember, first of all, that the domain scores from the Size, Control, and Data Structures domains are z-scores. That is, they all have a mean of zero and a standard deviation of one. Thus, the coefficients shown in Exhibit 25 are on the same scale. They show the relative contribution of each of the new orthogonal independent variables to the variation observed in the DR-Count. The relative contribution of Size at 2.32 exceeds that of Control at 1.81, which in turn exceeds that of Data Structures at 1.47. The relative contribution of Data Structures to this model is somewhat surprising in that there is but one variable in this principal component from the original set of 13.

The regression ANOVA for the orthogonal domain scores model is shown in Exhibit 26. Remember that, in effect, all 13 variables of the original data set are present in this model in a transformed form. Instead of 13 degrees of freedom numerator, we now have 3. The calculated F statistic is greater than all but two of the models from the original analysis shown in Exhibit 18.

Exhibit 27. Comparison of Domain Score Model with Raw Score Models

Model	R^2	MSE_{Fit}	MSE_{Pred}
1	0.16	16.28	39.58
2	0.26	14.28	34.85
3	0.52	9.47	44.66
4	0.52	9.36	44.38
5	0.54	8.95	38.40
Domain	0.55	8.85	34.03

Now it really gets interesting. The 13 metrics from the hold-back data set of 50 observations that we used earlier will now be converted to z-scores by dividing by each of the raw metric values by the means and standard deviations of the metrics from the original data set of 100 observations. We will now multiply this new 50×13 matrix of z-scores by the transformation matrix generated by the original PCA to produce the original 100 domain scores to create a new 50×3 matrix of domain scores for the hold-back data set. We will now plug these data back into the model developed earlier and shown in Exhibit 25. This will give us a vector of 50 observations of predicted DR-Counts for the hold-back data set. We can then compute the associated residuals and then the MSE_{Pred} for the 50 hold-back residuals. This value is shown in last row of Exhibit 26.

The MSE_{Pred} value for our new orthogonal model is better than any of the 13 models developed using the original raw data. The first five models are repeated in Exhibit 27 for comparison because these were the models that had the best predictive value based on the MSE_{Pred} criterion.

When we model with the orthogonal metric set, we achieve several objectives. First, we eliminate the problem of multicollinearity. This means that we are able to make a direct interpretation of the effect of each of the orthogonal domains on the dependent variable. But most important of all, we have eliminated sources of noise due to multicollinearity so that our model has better predictive validity. All of this, despite the fact that the new set of three orthogonal variables represents only 90 percent of variation in the original model.

7.5 REGRESSION AS A METRIC VALIDATION TOOL

Regression analysis will be one of our primary tools in the validation of new software metrics. One of the primary criteria for the use of a new metric in our metric suite will be that it identifies a unique source of variation in one or more criterion measures. If, for example, our criterion measure is software faults, then a new metric under consideration will contribute significantly to the regression ANOVA. We will notice this improvement in one of two ways: (1) the adjusted R-square statistic will increase, and (2) the regression F statistic will increase.

Sometimes, the effect of a new metric will be very difficult to isolate in a regression model with raw metrics because of the problems with multicollinearity. We noted that the use of the orthogonal domain metrics in the metric validation process would eliminate this problem. In this case we would first perform the PCA on the raw metrics, including the new metric that we wish to validate. The resulting factor scores (domain metrics) would then be used as the independent variables in a regression analysis with the fault measure as a dependent variable.

Whether our regression analysis is performed on the raw metrics or the domain metrics, we will not consider using any metric in our working metric set that does not enhance our understanding of the criterion variable(s). In the context of regression analysis, we will see this enhancement by our ability to explain ever-increasing amounts of the variation in the dependent variable(s).

7.6 CANONICAL CORRELATION

Software development is a very complex process. It is clear that there are multiple software attributes for source code. This is a multivariate problem. Unfortunately, the world of software quality attributes is also multivariate. We are interested in more than just software faults; we need to worry about all of the "ilities" simultaneously. It might well be that actions taken to reduce the rate at which faults are introduced may have an adverse effect on the maintainability of the software. We need a modeling process, then, that will allow us to map multiple independent variables onto a set of multiple dependent variables. We will use a procedure called *canonical correlation* for this modeling process.

We will use the data drawn from the Primary Avionics Software System (PASS) of the Space Shuttle to study the various aspects of canonical correlation. Nineteen software metrics were collected using a measurement tool called HALMET written specifically for the HAL/S language. In addition to the 19 software metrics, four quality metrics — Q_1, Q_2, Q_3, and Q_4 — were collected. These metrics relate to the number of faults and change requests that have been made to each of the program modules.

The correlation coefficients for the four quality metrics and the 19 complexity metrics are shown in Exhibit 28. When each of the 19 metrics is correlated with each of the quality metrics, the correlation coefficients are reasonably large. The problem with the data is that there is little or no information here. There are a lot of numbers but no global picture of the relationship among the quality metrics and the complexity metrics. We will need multivariate statistical techniques to extract these relationships.

Exhibit 28. Correlation Coefficients of Quality Metrics with Complexity Metrics

	Q_1	Q_2	Q_3	Q_4
η_1	0.48	0.15	0.45	0.39
η_2	0.64	0.43	0.68	0.48
N_1	0.54	0.47	0.58	0.28
N_2	0.59	0.45	0.60	0.40
Stmt	0.57	0.51	0.63	0.28
LOC	0.76	0.41	0.73	0.60
Comm	0.74	0.50	0.73	0.54
Nodes	0.55	0.31	0.56	0.31
Edges	0.51	0.31	0.54	0.26
Paths	0.36	0.28	0.44	0.11
Cycle	0.24	0.10	0.22	0.13
MaxP	0.46	0.27	0.46	0.25
AveP	0.44	0.25	0.45	0.24
Sets	0.29	0.19	0.19	0.25
Reset	0.41	0.21	0.30	0.38
Can	0.36	0.14	0.25	0.36
SetA	0.28	0.18	0.21	0.21
ResA	0.35	0.11	0.25	0.34
CanA	0.42	0.09	0.28	0.41

Exhibit 29. Correlation Coefficients of Quality Metrics

	Q_1	Q_2	Q_3
Q_2	0.32		
Q_3	0.75	0.47	
Q_4	0.66	0.11	0.51

Unfortunately, the software development process is not intrinsically univariate in nature. It is clear that the independent variables are highly correlated one with another. A similar pattern emerges for the quality metrics, as is shown in Exhibit 29. There is a strong interrelationship among the metrics.

The general notion of linear regression is to select from a set of independent variables a subset of these variables that will explain the most amount of variance in a dependent variable. Coefficients for the independent variables are produced by a least squares fit of these variables to sample data. The key to model development is to choose the subset of independent variables in such a manner as to not introduce more variance (or noise) in the model than might be contributed by introducing into the model a new independent variable.

The canonical correlation model is multivariate in both the dependent variables and the independent variables. These models permit the formulation of correlations between two *sets* of variables. They have the general form:

169

$$b_1y_1 + b_2y_2 + \ldots + b_py_p = a_1x_1 + a_2x_2 + \ldots + a_mx_m \tag{36}$$

where p is the number of criterion variables and m is the number of independent variables (metrics). An example of two such variable sets might be drawn from the relationship between aspects of software quality and code complexity. We know that there are significant correlations among the variables in each of these sets. Several separate multiple regression models would use the information provided by the quality metrics interrelationships, but would still fail to use the information provided by the code metrics interrelationships. Canonical correlation analysis, on the other hand, will provide information on the simultaneous relationship between two distinct sets of measures. This is particularly true when the variable sets are highly correlated, as is the case with quality and code metrics.

Canonical correlation reveals the complex relationships between two distinct metric sets by isolating pairs of linear combinations of these metrics.[2] Let $\mathbf{X} = X_1, X_2, \cdots, X_m$ and $\mathbf{Y} = Y_1, Y_2, \cdots, Y_p$ represent, respectively, the m-dimensional vector of code metrics, and the p-dimensional vector of quality metrics. Let $\boldsymbol{\mu}_x$ and $\boldsymbol{\mu}_y$ represent the mean vectors for the code and quality metrics, respectively. Then the relationships between the two sets of metrics can be expressed in terms of the covariance within the code set:

$$\sum_{xx} E\left[(\mathbf{X} - \boldsymbol{\mu}_x)(\mathbf{X} - \boldsymbol{\mu}_x)^T\right] \tag{37}$$

the covariance within the quality set:

$$\sum_{yy} E\left[(\mathbf{Y} - \boldsymbol{\mu}_y)(\mathbf{Y} - \boldsymbol{\mu}_y)^T\right] \tag{38}$$

and the covariance between the sets:

$$\sum_{xy} E\left[(\mathbf{X} - \boldsymbol{\mu}_x)(\mathbf{Y} - \boldsymbol{\mu}_y)^T\right] \tag{39}$$

The first step in canonical correlation analysis is to find a linear combination of quality metrics that maximally correlates with a linear combination of the code metrics. This will proceed in a fashion very similar to principal components analysis. The next step is to find the maximally correlated pair of linear combinations among all pairs that are uncorrelated with the first pair. This process continues until, at most, $M = \min(m, p)$ uncorrelated pairs are isolated. The pairs and their correlations are called canonical variates and canonical correlations. In addition to the canonical correlations, a number of derived quantities are important in interpreting the results of a canonical correlation analysis. Canonical weights are comparable to regression weights. They are the coefficients in the linear combinations that define the canonical variates. The ith canonical variate representing the Xs is given by:

Exhibit 30. Canonical Correlation Analysis

Canonical Variate	Canonical Correlation	Standard Error	Eigenvalue	Proportion	Cumulative
1	0.896	0.007	4.10	0.78	0.78
2	0.693	0.018	0.93	0.17	0.96
3	0.342	0.032	0.13	0.02	0.98
4	0.264	0.033	0.07	0.01	1.00

$$V_{x,i} = \mathbf{a}_{i,1}\mathbf{x} = a_{i,1}x_1 + a_{i,2}x_2 + \cdots + a_{i,m}x_m \tag{40}$$

and the ith canonical variate representing the Ys is given by:

$$V_{y,i} = \mathbf{b}_{i,1}\mathbf{y} = b_{i,1}y_1 + b_{i,2}y_2 + \cdots + b_{i,p}x_p \tag{41}$$

where the vectors $\mathbf{a}_i$ and $\mathbf{b}_i$ give the canonical weights for the code and quality metrics, respectively. The magnitude of a weight, $a_{i,j}$ (or $b_{i,j}$), indicates the importance of variable X_j (respectively Y_j) with regard to Y (respectively X) in obtaining the canonical correlation of the ith canonical variate.

Because a canonical variate is not directly observable, it is best understood in terms of those variables that are related to it. Canonical loadings are comparable to the factor loadings in principal components analysis. They give the correlations of the raw variable scores with the canonical variate scores. The canonical loadings for the ith canonical variate are given by two vectors: one for the code metrics and one for the design metrics. These vectors are, respectively, $\mathbf{r}_{x,i} = \mathbf{R}_{xx}\mathbf{a}_i$ and $\mathbf{r}_{y,i} = \mathbf{R}_{yy}\mathbf{b}_i$, where $\mathbf{R}_{xx}$ and $\mathbf{R}_{yy}$ are the within-set correlation matrices for the independent and dependent variables, respectively. The canonical loadings obtained in this analysis correspond directly with the factor loadings obtained in principal components analysis.

The canonical correlation technique was performed on the PASS software metrics shown above. The canonical correlation analysis for these data is shown in Exhibit 30. In this case there were exactly four canonical variates. The first two canonical variates account for most of the total variation. Canonical Variate 1 accounts for 78 percent of the variance and Canonical Variate 2 accounts for 1 percent of the variance. Canonical Variates 3 and 4 contribute little to our understanding of the simultaneous variation of code and quality metrics. The first two variates account for approximately 96 percent of the total variance. The canonical correlation of the set of quality and code metrics with the first canonical variate is 0.896. The canonical correlation of these metrics with the second variate is less, at 0.693. In both cases, these correlations are significant ($p < 0.05$).

**Exhibit 31. Canonical Structure of
Code and Quality Metrics**

	Canonical Variate 1	Canonical Variate 2
Code Metrics		
η_1	0.55	0.05
η_2	0.77	0.32
N_1	0.61	0.51
N_2	0.70	0.37
Exec	0.64	0.59
LOC	0.90	0.21
Com	0.87	0.35
Nodes	0.60	0.37
Edges	0.55	0.40
Paths	0.38	0.47
Cycle	0.25	0.11
MaxP	0.49	0.32
AveP	0.47	0.31
Sets	0.35	−0.01
Reset	0.49	−0.06
Can	0.44	−0.13
SetA	0.32	0.06
ResA	0.42	−0.11
CanA	0.49	−0.18
Quality Metrics		
Q_1	0.92	0.11
Q_2	0.44	0.62
Q_3	0.83	0.41
Q_4	0.85	−0.50

Exhibit 31 reveals the canonical structure of the code and quality metrics. The numbers in the columns reveal the relative strength of the relationship of each of the code and quality metrics with Canonical Variates 1 and 2. We can see, for example, that the metrics η_2, LOC, Com, and Q_1 are all strongly related to Canonical Variate 1. On the other hand, Canonical Variate 2 is more closely associated with *Paths* and Q_2.

The basic notion of canonical program complexity is that each raw complexity metric will have an appropriate canonical weight assigned by the analysis. These weights will be used to send the multivariate complexity metrics onto a single canonical variate of canonical complexity. Consider now a scenario where we have chosen to form canonical variates for a set of quality metrics in relation to a set of source code metrics. For each canonical variable there will be two vectors, **w**, of these weights. Let $\mathbf{w}^c$ represent the set of weights for the code metrics and $\mathbf{w}^q$ the weights for the quality metrics. These weights will send the set of raw standardized complexity metrics onto a single value canonical complexity, γ. When the matrix **z** of standardized metric values is multiplied by the vector of weights for the code metrics, there will be a canonical complexity vector for the code metrics as follows:

$$\gamma^c = \mathbf{w}^c \mathbf{z} \qquad (42)$$

Similarly, there is a corresponding canonical complexity metric value γ^q for the quality metrics.

In an alternate scenario, we might wish to construct canonical complexity metrics from a domain of source code metrics compared with a domain of software design metrics. This is an example of a mapping from two metric sets within the product metric domain. The canonical complexity will be that value that maximizes the relationship between the complexity domain and the quality domains. The canonical complexity of a program would then represent the complexity of the associated source code in relation to measures of software design.

References

1. Tufte, E.R., The Visual Display of Quantitative Information, Graphics Press, Cheshire, CT, 1983.
2. Dillion, W. and Goldstein, M., *Multivariate Analysis: Methods and Applications*, John Wiley & Sons, New York, 1984.

Chapter 8
Measuring Software Evolution

8.1 INTRODUCTION

As software systems change over time, it is very difficult to understand and measure the effect of the changes. We would like to be able to describe, numerically, the way that each system increment, or build, is different from its successor and its predecessor. This is a very complex problem in that most modern software systems consist of thousands of program modules, on each of which there may be as many as 20 to 30 distinct metrics collected. For any one build, there may be tens of thousands of metrics collected on a typical large system. Knowing what to measure, how to measure, and when to measure will be a key step in understanding the software evolution process.

We accept the fact that our children develop and change on a daily basis. We measure their height and weight to track their development as they grow. Software systems grow and mature in just the same way. We would not measure a child at birth and think that we know what there is to know about that child. Measurement is an ongoing process. We must, therefore, come to understand that our software systems change rapidly over time. Whenever they are changed, they must be remeasured. To understand what a software system is today, we must have current measurement data on the system, together with data on its evolution. We know that faults are removed over time. Modules that have not changed very much are likely to have had most of their faults removed. Modules that have changed a lot are very likely to have had new faults introduced into them. Hence, understanding change activity is vital to our understanding of where the problems in the system might be.

8.2 MEASURING EVOLVING SOFTWARE

Software systems change dramatically as they go through their various stages of development. From the first build of each such system to the last build, the differences may be so great as to obscure the fact that it is still the same system. Developers commonly make this mistake when they talk about the system they are developing. It might be referred to as the "file

175

management system" or whatever name seems to describe the software. This seems to imply that there is but one file management system. The fact that is obscured when we talk about the file management system is that today's build of the file management system is probably vastly different in composition and functionality from the original first-born file management system of the first system build. We would like to be able to quantify the differences in the system from its first build, through all builds, to the current one. Then and only then will it be possible to know how these systems have changed.

8.2.1 Baselining the System

The measurement of an evolving software system through the shifting sands of time is not an easy task. Perhaps one of the most difficult issues relates to the establishment of a baseline against which the evolving systems can be compared. This problem is very similar to that encountered by the surveying profession. If we were to buy a piece of property, there are certain physical attributes that we would like to know about that property. First, we might wish to know the total area of the property. Next, we might want to establish the physical shape, the physical elevation, and the physical topology of the property. We can establish the area and the shape of the property with a transit and a measuring tape at the site. To answer the questions as to the location or the elevation of the property, we cannot make these determinations from the site alone. We will have to seek out a benchmark. The benchmark is a survey marker that represents a point in a larger standard grid wherein each point is clearly related to every other point in the grid, both in terms of distance and elevation. This benchmark may be some distance from the property. To measure the topology of the property, we must first establish a fixed point or baseline on the property. The distance and the elevation of every other point on the property can then be established in relation to the fixed baseline. Interestingly enough, we can pick any other point on the property, establish a new baseline, and get exactly the same topology for the property. The property does not change; only our perspective changes.

The software measurement process is very much the same as the survey process. We wish to understand the individual elements of the whole system in relation to each other. We also wish to understand just how a system has evolved over time. It is very difficult to use raw complexity metrics for either of these purposes. The dilemma confronted by those who wish to use measurement of evolving software systems can be seen in Exhibit 1. In this exhibit there are two program modules: A and B. We have two measurements on each of these two modules; lines of code (LOC) and unique operator count, η_1. Measurements have been taken at build 1 and build 2. First, let us look at the two modules A and B at build 1. It is not clear whether module A is more complex than B. Now look at how the system

Exhibit 1. Build Comparisons

Module	Build 1		Build 2	
	A	B	A	B
LOC	200	250	210	230
η_1	20	15	19	18

containing modules A and B has changed from build 1 to build 2. It is very difficult to establish whether or not the system is more complex at build 2 than at build 1. Clearly, the total number of lines of code has dropped by ten from build 1 to build 2. However, the unique operator count has risen from 35 to 37.

The whole notion of establishing a baseline system will allow us to begin to answer the questions raised in the dilemma created by the data represented in Exhibit 1. The first thing we must do is identify common sources of variation among the metrics. We will use principal components analysis (PCA) to create a set of orthogonal measures for the software modules, all of which will be defined on the same scale. From these common domain metrics, we then will reduce the measurement problem to a single fault surrogate measure for each of the program modules. This will reduce the dimensionality of the complexity problem to one single measure for each program.

When a number of successive system builds are to be measured, we will choose one of the systems as a baseline system. All others will be measured in relation to the chosen system. This is exactly analogous to the selection of an arbitrary point or a piece of property to begin a topological survey. Sometimes it will be useful to select the initial system build for this baseline. If we select this system, then the measurements on all other systems will be taken in relation to the initial system configuration.

8.2.2 System Evolution

A complete software system generally consists of a large number of program modules. Each of these modules is a potential candidate for modification as the system evolves during development and maintenance. As each program module is changed, the total system must be reconfigured to incorporate the changed module. We refer to this reconfiguration as a *build*. For the effect of any change to be felt, it must physically be incorporated into a build.

As program modules change from one build to another, the attributes of the changed program modules change. This means that there are measurable changes in modules from one build to the next. Each build is numerically and measurably different from its predecessor with respect to a particular set of metrics. Thus, there is no such thing as measuring a software system but once. Many software developers who profess to be deeply committed to measurement are still tempted to represent a system by a set of measurements taken at one point in a system's evolution. The truth is that measurement is a process. Whenever changes are made to a system, those system elements that have changed must be remeasured.

To describe the complexity of a system at each build, it will be necessary to know what the version of each of the modules was in the program that failed. Each of the program modules is a separate entity. Each will evolve at its own rate. Consider a software system composed of n modules as follows: $m_1, m_2, m_3, \ldots, m_n$. Each build of the system will unify a set of these modules. Not all the builds will contain precisely the same modules. Clearly, there will be different versions of some of the modules in successive system builds.

We can represent the build configuration in a nomenclature that will permit us to describe the measurement process more precisely by recording module version numbers as vector elements in the following manner: $\mathbf{v}^i = <v_1^i, v_2^i, v_3^i, \cdots v_m^i>$. This build index vector will allow us to preserve the precise structure of each for posterity. Thus, v_i^n in the vector $\mathbf{v}^n$ would represent the version number of the ith module that went to the nth build of the system. The cardinality of the set of elements in the vector $\mathbf{v}^n$ is determined by the number of program modules that have been created up to and including the nth build. In this case, the cardinality of the complete set of modules is represented by the index value m. This is also the number of modules in the set of all modules that have ever entered any build.

Program modules are similar to stars in a galaxy. Some of these stars (modules) have a relatively short life span. Other stars burn for a very long time. Thus, there is a constant flux of the stars in the galaxy. In a typical software build environment, there is a constant flux of modules going in and out of the build.

Exhibit 2 shows the evolution of a hypothetical software system consisting of a set of ten program modules. In this example, we can see that build 1 has six modules in it and the build index vector would look like this: $\mathbf{v}^1 = <1,2,1,2,1,1>$. This build index vector has six elements because that is the number of modules that have been sent to the build to date. On build 2 we can see that the first four modules have gone through a number of revisions and have probably changed quite a bit. Modules 5 and 6 on this build have not changed at all. The entire code churn has happened in the first four modules on this build. On build 3, a new module (module 7) enters the build. Module 6 is pulled from this build. This event is represented by a zero for the version number of module 6 on build 3. The build index vector for this build looks like this: $\mathbf{v}^3 = <6,4,6,4,1,0,1>$. It now has seven elements in it. In fact, as this system evolves, it will grow in total modules. The build index vector will also grow in size.

Exhibit 2. Hypothetical Build Example

Module	Build				
	1	2	3	4	5
1	1	5	6	8	7
2	2	3	4	0	0
3	1	3	6	7	8
4	2	3	4	5	5
5	1	1	1	1	1
6	1	1	0	2	2
7			1	2	4
8				2	3
9				2	3
10					1

On build 4, module 6 returns to the build as a new version. Module 2 has vanished from the build and will remain gone, its services no longer required. Finally, on build 5, the system has reached its maximum size of nine program modules. The build index vector for build 5 looks like this: $v^5 = \, <7,0,8,5,1,2,4,3,3,1>$. It has ten elements. Although module 2 has vanished from this and subsequent builds, it has a historical presence in the current build. That is, if we wish to compare build 5 with build 3, the module 2 will be present on build 3.

A natural way to capture the intermediate versions of the software is to have the system development occur under a configuration management system. For a system running under configuration management, all versions of all modules can be reconstructed from the time the program was placed under configuration control.

Management of the configuration of each of the program modules is one aspect of the software management process. Another vital piece is the build index vector; it is the only record of the module version that went to each build. This build index vector must be maintained in some type of build management database. There are many sad stories in the software maintenance community about software systems that have been delivered to a customer without such a record. It is almost impossible to interpret trouble reports from customers if the structure of the build that the customer is using is not known.

A natural way to capture the intermediate measurements for each build would be to incorporate the measurement tools within the configuration management system. Just as code deltas are maintained for each program module, so should deltas for the code attributes also be kept by the configuration management system.

The prime objective of this discussion is to demonstrate the measurement process for measuring successive stages of an evolving software system. Thus, we will be able to assess the precise effect of the change from

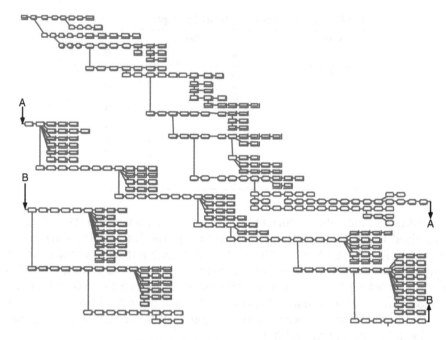

Exhibit 3. Spider Chart for PASS

the build represented by v^i to v^{i+1} or even v^i to v^{i+k} or v^{i-k}. These data will serve to structure the regression test activity between builds. Those modules that have the greatest change in complexity from one build to the next should receive the majority of test effort in the regression test activity.

The actual evolution of a large software system can be very complicated. Exhibit 3 presents a chart of the evolution of the many builds of the Space Shuttle PASS from Operational Increment 8 through Operational Increment 22. Each box, or lozenge, on this chart represents a different build of the system. This evolutionary chart is known internally as a spider chart. The leaf nodes of this graph are all rectangular except for the most recent build. These are the software systems that actually flew on space shuttle missions.

One of the most important observations that can be drawn from Exhibit 3 is that not all of the builds are direct antecedents of the most current build. In fact, only a rather small subset of the total set of system builds can have this property. When we wish to measure a build in relation to its antecedent builds, we can only use those builds that are on the antecedent path to the build in question. The same principle is true for the collection of fault data. The total number of faults across all builds would be a misleading quality metric for understanding the most recent build. Some of these fault data clearly relate to code segments that are not included in the module set on the antecedent path for this most recent build. The spider chart, then, is a most valuable tool in that it permits us to identify the antecedent path for any program module.

In the close inspection of the spider chart for PASS we can observe that there is a *main sequence* of builds that goes from the top left of the chart to the bottom right (with the two discontinuities at points A and B). There are exactly 102 builds on this main sequence. At various intervals along this main sequence, a branch was pulled and a short evolutionary tree was built. There are 252 builds in these sub-trees off the main sequence, for a total of 354 total builds in the evolutionary sequence represented in this spider chart.

This type of build evolution represents yet another incremental problem in software measurement. Many different modules can be created and added on each of the sub-trees. If these new modules are never integrated into any of the builds on the main sequence, then they have no measurement consequence for the current system. The current system, of course, is always the last node on the main sequence. This is a particular problem for fault reporting systems. In a typical fault reporting system, all fault and failure reports are kept in a common reporting system. If we are interested in the total faults that have been reported for our current system, we must carefully sort all of those faults recorded against program modules that are *currently* on the main sequence. If a fault has been reported against a module that was on the main sequence but is no longer part of the build, then this fault must not be included in the total count. Similarly, any faults reported against modules that were developed on branches must also be removed from the current count. In essence, we are interested only in the direct antecedents of the modules in the current build.

When evaluating the precise nature of any changes that occur to the system between any two builds *i* and *j*, we are interested in three sets of modules. The first set, $M_c^{i,j}$, is the set of modules present in both builds of the system. These modules may have changed since the earlier version but were not removed. The second set, $M_a^{i,j}$, is the set of modules that were in the early build, *i*, and were removed prior to the later build, *j*. The final set, $M_b^{i,j}$, is the set of modules that has been added to the system since the earlier build.

As an example, let build *i* consist of the following set of modules:

$$M^i = \left\{ m_1, m_2, m_3, m_4, m_5 \right\}$$

Between build *i* and *j* module m_3 was removed, giving:

$$M^j = M^i \cup M_b^{i,j} - M_a^{i,j}$$

$$= \{ m_1, m_2, m_3, m_4, m_5 \} \cup \{ \ \} - \{ m_3 \}$$

$$= \{ m_1, m_2, m_4, m_5 \}$$

Then between builds j and k two new modules, m_7 and m_8, are added and module m_2 is deleted, giving:

$$M^k = M^j \cup M_b^{j,k} - M_a^{j,k}$$

$$= \{ m_1, m_2, m_4, m_5 \} \cup \{ m_7, m_8 \} - \{ m_2 \}$$

$$= \{ m_1, m_4, m_5, m_7, m_8 \}$$

8.2.3 Establishing a Software Measurement Baseline

For measurement purposes, it will be necessary to standardize all original or raw metrics so that they are on the same relative scale. For the ith module m_i^j on the ith build of the system, there will be a data vector $\mathbf{x}_i^j = <x_{i1}^j, x_{i2}^j, \ldots, x_{ik}^j>$ of k raw complexity metrics for that module. We can standardize each of the raw metrics by subtracting the mean $\bar{x}_1^j$ of the metric #1 over all modules in the ith build and dividing by its standard deviation δ_1^j such that

$$z_{1i}^j = \frac{x_{1i}^j - \bar{x}_1^j}{\delta_1^j}$$

represents the standardized value of the first raw metric for the ith module on the ith build. The problem with this method of standardizing is that it will erase the effect of trends in the data. For example, let us assume that we were taking measurements on LOC and that the system we were measuring grew in this measure over successive builds. If we were to standardize each build of the system by its own mean LOC and its own standard deviation, the mean of this system would always be zero. Thus, we will standardize the raw metrics using a baseline system such that the standardized metric vector for the ith module m_i^j on the ith build would be:

$$\mathbf{w}_i^j = \frac{\mathbf{x}_i^j - \bar{\mathbf{x}}_i^B}{\delta_i^B}$$

where $\bar{\mathbf{x}}_i^B$ is a vector containing the means of the raw metrics for the baseline system and δ_i^B is a vector of standard deviations of these raw metrics. Thus, for each system, we can build an $m \times k$ data matrix, $\mathbf{W}^j$, that contains the standardized metric values relative to the baseline system on build B.

A simple example will serve to identify some of the problems surrounding the measurement of an evolving software system. The purpose of this

Exhibit 4. Hypothetical Software System

Module	Exec	N_1	η_1	N_2	η_2	Nodes	Edges
1	100	303	34	92	20	15	12
2	158	352	42	104	18	23	18
3	99	208	32	88	27	20	15
4	30	35	21	26	8	5	4
5	64	45	14	14	5	24	20
6	85	157	19	20	12	19	14
7	198	268	32	105	15	32	20
8	154	360	15	105	30	15	13
9	96	185	22	35	11	25	15
10	74	56	9	44	13	13	10
$\bar{x}$	105.8	196.9	24	63.3	15.9	19.1	14.1
δ	50.2	123.8	10.5	38.6	8.0	7.5	4.8

exercise is to demonstrate the steps that we have employed to solve the measurement of software evolution. It is a contrived example whose purpose is strictly pedagogical. It is much easier to show all of the data and all of the resulting analysis for a problem of this scale than it is for a real problem. For the real problem, data will be drawn from our investigations of the evolution of the Space Shuttle PASS. The data from PASS would be almost unintelligible without this example in the small.

Let us assume that our hypothetical software system has ten modules and we are collecting measurements on seven program attributes. If we apply our measurement tool to this system, we will get data represented by Exhibit 4. Each row in this exhibit represents the measurements derived from one program module.

The means and standard deviations for each of the metrics are shown in the last two rows of this exhibit. These data are part of the baseline transformation data. We will use them to transform the raw data for this build and other builds from the raw data to z-scores. Observe that each metric has a different mean and standard deviation. Thus, each metric represents a value drawn from a different population. Very simply, what this means is that we cannot add values of any two of these metrics. It is meaningless to add N_1 and N_2 and learn anything meaningful from the sum. Maurice Halstead, as you will remember, suggested that we could create a derived metric, program vocabulary, in the following manner: $\eta = \eta_1 + \eta_2$. The mean of the distribution of η_1 is 24 and its standard deviation is 10.5. The mean of η_2 is 15.9 and its standard deviation is 7.5. The sum of any of the two metrics for any program module is disinformation. We can solve the problem of dissimilar distributions of these metrics by transforming them into z-scores. The transformation of these metrics is shown in Exhibit 5.

Whereas Exhibit 4 containing the raw metric values has *data* in it, Exhibit 5 has *information* in it. Let us look, in particular, at modules 2 and 3. For module 2, the values of η_1 and η_2 are 42 and 18, respectively. For mod-

Exhibit 5. z-Scores for the Hypothetical System

Module	Exec	N_1	η_1	N_2	η_2	Nodes	Edges
1	−0.12	0.86	0.95	0.74	0.51	−0.54	−0.43
2	1.04	1.25	1.71	1.05	0.26	0.52	0.81
3	−0.14	0.09	0.76	0.64	1.39	0.12	0.19
4	−1.51	−1.31	−0.29	−0.97	−0.99	−1.87	−2.09
5	−0.83	−1.23	−0.95	−1.28	−1.37	0.65	1.22
6	−0.41	−0.32	−0.48	−1.12	−0.49	−0.01	−0.02
7	1.84	0.57	0.76	1.08	−0.11	1.71	1.22
8	0.96	1.32	−0.86	1.08	1.77	−0.54	−0.23
9	−0.20	−0.10	−0.19	−0.73	−0.61	0.78	0.19
10	−0.63	−1.14	−1.43	−0.50	−0.36	−0.81	−0.85

ule 3, the corresponding values are 32 and 27. From these two comparisons, it is clear that module 2 has more unique operators than does module 3. Similarly, module 2 has quite a few more unique operands than does Module 3. We really do not know what this means. We have data that we really cannot use. It is no wonder that so many people who have "tried metrics and they didn't work" have come to this conclusion.

Now let us look at the same data from modules 2 and 3 from a different perspective. Exhibit 5 contains the z-scores for the same data. All of the data in Exhibit 5 have the same mean (0) and the same standard deviation (1). Now, if we look at η_1 and η_2 from this table for module 2, we see that the number of unique operators η_1 for this module is 1.71. This is almost two standard deviations above the mean for all program modules. There must be some serious computation complexity in this module. When we look at η_2 for this module, we see that the number of unique operands is 0.26, which is very close to the average of all modules. If we look at module 3 from the same perspective, we see that the values for η_1 and η_2 are 0.76 and 1.39, almost the reverse of module 2. Module 2 is clearly richer in its potential data complexity, as represented by the number of distinct operands, than is module 3. Module 3 is clearly more computationally complex than module 2 in that the number of distinct operators is much greater.

The raw data have been converted into information that we can analyze and begin to draw some preliminary conclusions about what is going on in each of the modules. Let us delve further into this process of extracting information from the data. To do this we will perform a principal components analysis (PCA, with a varimax rotation) on the raw data matrix. The factor pattern for this PCA is shown in Exhibit 6.

The PCA technique has revealed two distinct sources of variation in the original data. We can clearly see that the metrics Exec, N_1, η_1, N_2, and η_2, are associated with the first domain (principal component). The metrics Nodes and Edges are clearly and unambiguously associated with Domain 2. The metrics associated with Domain 1 are all measuring essentially the

Exhibit 6. The Principal Components of the Hypothetical System

Metric	Domain 1 Size	Domain 2 Control
Exec	0.73	0.59
N_1	0.92	0.25
η_1	0.62	0.32
N_2	0.96	0.17
η_2	0.89	−0.17
Nodes	0.10	0.98
Edges	0.13	0.95
Eigenvalues	3.5	2.5
Percent variation	60	25

same thing, program size. The metrics associated with Domain 2, the Control domain, are both attributes of the control flowgraph structure of a program module. They are clearly identifying a different source of variance from the size metrics. This is not a matter of speculation: PCA has revealed this fact to us.

The eigenvalues for each of the size and control domains are 3.5 and 2.5, respectively. Together, these two principal components then account for a total of 85 percent of the variation in the original problem space.

Now let us return briefly to Halstead's metric $\eta = \eta_1 + \eta_2$ of program vocabulary. As pointed out earlier, the raw metric values η_1 and η_2 simply cannot be added together because we feel like creating a new metric called vocabulary. The values for each metric on each module are drawn from a different distribution. We will learn nothing from their combination. Again, this is not a matter of speculation. Let us augment the original data matrix containing the raw metric values with a column representing the new vocabulary metric. When we perform the PCA, we get the result shown in Exhibit 7.

Voila! We have transformed two measures of size complexity to yet another measure of size complexity. We have learned nothing new with this new metric. The metric primitives contain all of the juice. We just do not get three oranges if we add two oranges together.

Returning to the problem of measuring software evolution, we have a real problem in the volume of data that we are trying to manage with just ten modules and seven metric values. A much more realistic problem would be a system with 5000 modules and 20 metric primitives. We desperately want some mechanism to reduce the size of the problem with which we are working.

A by-product of the original PCA of the ten program modules and the seven metric primitives is a transformation matrix **T** that will map the ten z-scores of the raw metrics into the reduced space represented by the two

Exhibit 7. Revised PCA

Metric	Domain 1 Size	Domain 2 Control
Exec	0.687	0.608
N_1	0.904	0.267
η_1	0.692	0.302
N_2	0.945	0.181
η_2	0.872	-0.151
Nodes	0.092	0.981
Edges	0.117	0.955
η	0.944	0.131

Exhibit 8. Transformation Matrix

Size	Control
0.155	0.171
0.268	-0.017
0.159	0.062
0.293	-0.064
0.32	-0.215
-0.111	0.453
-0.098	0.435

Exhibit 9. Factor Scores

Module	Size	Control
1	0.85	-0.57
2	1.03	0.72
3	0.72	-0.18
4	-0.82	-1.73
5	-1.61	1.02
6	-0.71	0.07
7	0.53	1.61
8	1.33	-0.71
9	-0.60	0.57
10	-0.72	-0.80

principal components of size and control. Let **Z** represent the matrix of z-scores shown in the exhibit above for the original data shown in Exhibit 5. We can obtain new domain metrics, **D**, using the transformation matrix **T** as follows: **D = ZT**, where **Z** is a 10×7 matrix of z-scores, **T** is a 7×2 matrix of transformation coefficients, and **D** is a 10×2 matrix of domain scores. The matrix **T** for this solution is shown in Exhibit 8.

The domain metrics (transformed z-scores or factor scores) formed by the product are shown in Exhibit 9.

For each module, there are now two metrics: size and control. These new metrics represent the underlying domains or sources of variation uncovered by principal component analysis. They also have the interesting property that they are uncorrelated. Each of the new metrics represents a distinct source of variation. There is no overlap. We have reduced the dimensionality of the problem from seven metrics to two new metrics that account for approximately 86 percent of the variation seen in the original seven metrics.

By inspection of Exhibit 9 we can see that module 8 has the highest size complexity of all modules. It is clearly not the largest in terms of Exec but it is larger in terms of the cumulative size attributes. We can also see that the greatest control complexity occurs in module 7. We are now in a very good position to understand the differences among the program modules based on the attributes we are measuring. When we have a clear indication of what we are measuring, as revealed in the PCA, we also have a good clear view of what we are not measuring. For example, we know that program modules differ with regard to their coupling complexity (their relationships with other program modules) or their data structures complexity. However, we are not measuring these attributes.

At this stage we might wish to simplify the problem further. We can further reduce the complexity dimensionality by forming a linear combination of the domain metrics. At the outset we could simply add them together for each module: $y_i = d_{1,i} + d_{2,i}$. We can do this because d_1 and d_2 have the same distribution. These values are both drawn from a population with a mean of 0 and a standard deviation of 1. The new variable, y, created through this synthesis should meet the criterion that it be related to software faults, as we have seen in Chapters 4 and 7. If we were to model this behavior, we could discover that y would do a reasonable job. We could, of course, regress our two domain metrics on actual fault data from our historical fault database and this would yield a new metric, $y_i = ad_{1,i} + bd_{2,i}$. We have found that a fault index (FI) derived from the eigenvalues does a reasonably good job as a fault surrogate. This FI, represented by y, is defined by $y_i = \lambda_1 d_{1,i} + \lambda_2 d_{2,i}$, where λ_1 and λ_2 are the eigenvalues associated with each of the two domains or principal components.

The main problem with the FI metric is that its mean value will be 0. This means that half of the metric values will be negative. We would like to adjust FI so that has a distribution that is more socially acceptable. To do this we will choose to center the distribution about 100 with a standard deviation of 10 as follows: $\rho_i = 10 \times (\lambda_1 d_{1,i} + \lambda_2 d_{2,i}) + 100$. There is no magic in this transformation. It is the same distribution as IQ scores. People are comfortable with it. The FI values for the system of ten modules currently under investigation is shown in Exhibit 10.

The values in this Exhibit 10 represent the fault potential of each module. This is not an act of faith. We have found this to be valid in many different studies. If we are very careful in selecting a working set of metrics (see Chapter 7), we can *make* FI account for more than 95 percent of the total variation observed in historical fault data. In the specific case of the

Exhibit 10. The Fault Index

Module	Fault Index ρ
1	115
2	154
3	121
4	28
5	69
6	77
7	159
8	129
9	93
10	54
Total	1000

Space Shuttle PASS, the correlation between the FI metric and the DR Count from the historical database was 0.92. Very simply stated, the FI metric accounted for more than 80 percent of the variation in the DR, or fault data. With the two metric domains of size and control of this contrived example, it is not likely that the FI represented in Exhibit 10 would account for more than 65 percent of the variation in corresponding fault data. From a scientific standpoint, 65 percent is a lot better than no information or simple speculation.

The sum of the FIs for all for all modules is, of course, 1000. This is not surprising. The mean was set to 100 and there are ten modules. We would look for problems in our calculations had this sum not been 1000.

From the standpoint of the data in Exhibit 10, if we were looking for problems in the code, we would certainly focus our efforts on module 7, because it has the highest FI value. If we have a fixed amount of inspection time (and we always do), then it would behoove us to invest this time wisely. Modules 1, 2, 3, 7, and 8 would certainly command our attention. If and only if we had surplus resources would we spend time with modules 4 and 10. This is a case of the classical trade-off between fairness and optimality. The optimal solution would focus all review efforts on the most complex systems. These are the ones where the majority of faults will probably be found. It takes just one fault in the right place to bring any system to its knees, however. The fair solution requires that we invest inspection resources in proportion to the FI. The fair solution for apportioning our inspection (test) resources is shown in Exhibit 11 in terms of percentage of effort.

The whole purpose of the reduction in dimensionality of the measurement problem is to convert the measurement data to usable information. Exhibit 11 is a good example of the utility achieved in the simplification of the measurement problem. It would have been very difficult to arrive at any meaningful conclusion about our software system based on the data shown in the original raw metric data in Exhibit 4.

Exhibit 11. Optimal Resource Allocation

Module	Percentage Effort
7	16
2	15
8	13
3	12
1	12
9	9
6	8
5	7
10	5
4	3

In summary, then, the measurement baseline will consist of three arrays. First is the array of means $\bar{x}$ for the baseline metric data. Next is the vector of standard deviations **s** for each of the metrics on the baseline system. Finally, there is the transformation matrix **T** that will map the z-scores of the metrics to orthogonal domain scores.

8.2.4 Measuring Changes to the System

As has been noted, a significant problem in the measurement of evolving software systems is that software modules come and go. This is not a problem when it comes to the computation of the individual module domain metrics and the computation of the module fault index. It is, however, a problem when we are looking at the average system metrics. For example, if the initial build of a system contained m program modules and the next system contains $m+1$ modules, there is some ambiguity in calculating the average FI of the new system. We can understand this problem a little better if we consider a program module that was simply split into two modules from the first to the second build. This being the case, the FI of each of the two new modules will be less than the FI of the parent module. Thus, if we were to compute the average FI of the new system with the value of $m+1$ as the normalizing value, then the apparent complexity of the new system will have been reduced. However, because of the coupling complexity introduced between the two new modules, the net system complexity will have increased. To this end, the normalizing value for the computation of all averages will be the cardinality of the set of modules in the baseline system.

By definition, the average FI of the baseline *system* at build B will be:

$$\rho^B = \frac{1}{N^B} \sum_i \rho_{v_i^B} = 100$$

where N^1 is the cardinality of the set of program modules on the first build of the system. As the system progresses through a series of builds, system complexity will tend to rise. Thus, the system FI of the kth version of a system can be represented by a function of module FI as follows:

Exhibit 12. Build 2 Raw Metric Data

Module	Exec	N_1	η_1	N_2	η_2	Nodes	Edges
1	100	303	34	92	20	15	12
2	158	352	41	104	18	23	18
3	99	208	32	88	25	20	15
4	45	36	22	24	10	6	5
5	64	45	14	14	5	24	20
6	85	157	19	20	12	19	14
7	179	205	32	95	15	32	20
8	154	360	15	105	30	15	13
9	96	185	22	35	11	25	15
10	74	56	9	44	13	13	10
11	11	50	32	16	26	15	10

Exhibit 13. z-Scores for Build 2 Scaled by Build 1 Baseline

Module	Exec	N_1	η_1	N_2	η_2	Nodes	Edges
1	−0.12	0.86	0.95	0.74	0.51	−0.54	−0.43
2	1.04	1.25	1.62	1.05	0.26	0.52	0.81
3	−0.14	0.09	0.76	0.64	1.14	0.12	0.19
4	−1.21	−1.30	−0.19	−1.02	−0.74	−1.74	−1.88
5	−0.83	−1.23	−0.95	−1.28	−1.37	0.65	1.22
6	−0.41	−0.32	−0.48	−1.12	−0.49	−0.01	−0.02
7	1.46	0.07	0.76	0.82	−0.11	1.71	1.22
8	0.96	1.32	−0.86	1.08	1.77	−0.54	−0.23
9	−0.20	−0.10	−0.19	−0.73	−0.61	0.78	0.19
10	−0.63	−1.14	−1.43	−0.50	−0.36	−0.81	−0.85
11	−1.11	−1.33	−0.76	−0.97	−0.11	−1.21	−1.26
Mean	−0.11	−0.17	−0.07	−0.12	−0.01	−0.10	−0.10

$$\rho^k = \frac{1}{N^k} \sum_i \rho_i^{v_i^k}$$

where v_i^k represents an element from the configuration vector $\mathbf{v}^k$ described earlier.

Let us now assume that the example system of ten program modules has been modified somewhat and new functionality has been added to the system. There are now 11 modules in the system as represented in Exhibit 12.

In addition to the changes represented by adding a new module to this system, there have been changes to modules 4 and 7 as well. It is not clear exactly how the existing modules 4 and 7 have changed with regard to the whole system. We now want answers to two questions. First, what is the nature of the changes to modules 4 and 7? Second, what is the effect of adding the new module 11 to the system? To take the first step in answering these questions, we will convert the metrics in Exhibit 12 to z-scores using the baseline means and standard deviations. This will yield the results displayed in Exhibit 13.

The general characteristics of the new module 11 can be seen from the last row in this Exhibit 13. In relation to the modules that were present on

Exhibit 14. A Comparison of Build 2 to Build 1

Module	Build 1 Size	Build 1 Control	Build 2 Size	Build 2 Control	Build 2–Build 1 Size	Build 2–Build 1 Control
1	0.85	−0.57	0.85	−0.57	0	0
2	1.03	0.72	1.03	0.72	0	0
3	0.72	−0.18	0.72	−0.15	0	0
4	−0.82	−1.73	−0.72	−1.58	0.09	0.16
5	−1.61	1.02	−1.61	1.02	0	0
6	−0.71	0.07	−0.71	0.07	0	0
7	0.53	1.61	0.26	1.57	−0.27	−0.04
8	1.33	−0.71	1.33	−0.71	0	0
9	−0.60	0.57	−0.60	0.57	0	0
10	−0.72	−0.80	−0.72	−0.80	0	0
11	—	—	−0.71	−1.22	−0.71	−1.22
Mean	0	0	**−0.09**	**−0.10**		

the first build, this module is a very simple one. The most complex characteristic of this module is that the number of unique operands, η_2, seems inordinately high in terms of the overall magnitude of the other metrics. It is interesting to note that the mean of these z-scores is no longer zero. This is because there has been a new module added to the system that is lower overall in the attributes being measured. In addition, it is clear that modules 4 and 7 have changed as well.

Once the z-scores for build 2 of the hypothetical system have been established, the transformation matrix T, which was also part of the baseline for build 1, can now be applied to these new z-scores. The result of this matrix multiplication is shown in Exhibit 14 for both builds 1 and 2. The two columns for build 2 are the new metric domain scores. As with the baselined z-scores, the mean of the domain scores is no longer zero because of the departures of the new module from the mean and also because of the changes that have occurred in modules 4 and 7.

The final two columns of Exhibit 14 are perhaps the most informative with regard to the precise manner in which the software has changed from build 1 to build 2. Modules 4 and 7 have changed. There has been an increase in both the size and control complexity on module 4 although this is not immediately apparent by looking at the signs of the differences. There has been a decrease in both the size and control complexity on module 7. Further, there is the addition of a new module altogether, Module 11.

Ultimately, we are interested in what has happened to the system as a whole between builds 1 and 2. This can best be seen in terms of the FI metric. Exhibit 15 displays the new FI values for build 2. The total system FI has now increased to 1039 from the beginning value of 1000. Modules 4 and 7 have changed in complexity and the overall net system complexity has increased. The last two columns in Exhibit 15 represent the difference between the FI values on the two incremental builds. The column labeled

Exhibit 15. FI Build Deltas

Module	Fault Index ρ	Build Difference	Absolute Build Difference
1	115	0	0
2	154	0	0
3	121	0	0
4	35	7	7
5	69	0	0
6	77	0	0
7	148	−10	10
8	129	0	0
9	93	0	0
10	55	0	0
11	44	44	44
Total	1039	41	61

Build Difference shows the increase (or decrease) in FI for each module build 1 to build 2. Module 4 has increased in net FI by 7, and module 7 has decreased in net FI by 10. The net system increase is 41.

The last column in Exhibit 15 represents the difference in absolute value between build 1 and 2 for each module. This represents the net change in FI (up or down) between the two builds. From this perspective the net change in the system between the two builds has increased by 61.

FI is a fault surrogate. The FI on the first build represents the fault potential or the fault burden of each module on this initial build. Changes to the system will possibly introduce new faults to the system. As we will see, faults introduced into the code over time will vary directly with the changes to FI.

8.2.5 Evaluating Changes across Builds: An Example from PASS

We will now examine the application of this methodology to the evolution of the Space Shuttle Primary Avionics Software System (PASS). For the PASS data, we can transform the 20 raw attribute measures for each of the 765 program modules into four orthogonal domain metrics. This transformation from correlated metric z-scores to uncorrelated metric domain scores (factor scores) is achieved through the multiplication of the standardized metrics by a transformation matrix produced by the principal components analysis. The transformation matrix for this specific example is shown in Exhibit 16. This is a 20×4 matrix that will transform the standardized metrics on each of the 765 modules to form uncorrelated domain metrics for each of the modules. While this reduction in the number of metrics has simplified the problem somewhat, we really would like to represent each program with a single metric that would serve as a measure of module complexity, simultaneously representing all four orthogonal domains of complexity.

Exhibit 16. The PASS Baseline Transformation Matrix

	D1 Control	D2 Size	D3 Semaphore	D4 Temporal
η_1	−0.019	0.103	0.032	−0.055
η_2	−0.064	0.183	−0.014	−0.029
N_1	−0.101	0.228	−0.051	−0.036
N_2	−0.104	0.223	−0.042	−0.009
Stmt	−0.077	0.217	−0.057	−0.040
LOC	−0.050	0.141	0.013	0.062
Comm	−0.071	0.173	−0.019	0.013
Nodes	0.188	−0.027	−0.004	−0.003
Edges	0.198	−0.031	−0.015	−0.009
Paths	0.167	−0.012	−0.054	−0.032
Cycle	0.296	−0.145	−0.033	0.023
MaxP	0.263	−0.095	−0.004	0.020
AveP	0.268	−0.104	−0.000	0.026
DataStr	−0.009	0.142	−0.060	−0.069
Sets	−0.031	−0.041	0.303	0.000
Reset	−0.006	−0.090	0.346	−0.012
Can	0.007	−0.055	−0.063	0.546
SetA	−0.030	−0.034	0.320	−0.093
ResA	−0.044	−0.055	0.364	−0.108
CanA	0.008	−0.056	−0.074	0.554

Exhibit 17. Average FI across Sequential Builds

The change in the overall FI of the PASS system over time is represented pictorially in Exhibit 17. This is an example of the FI of the most recent 20 software builds for the Space Shuttle PASS. For this presentation, the baseline system is represented by the system 0 on the *x*-axis of this graph. All other systems are measured relative to this one.

One pattern that becomes obvious from Exhibit 17 is that the complexity of a system continues to rise over the life of the software system. This is particularly interesting in a mature system such as PASS. This system has evolved through hundreds of builds (see also Exhibit 3). It is still increasing in complexity. If we were to move the baseline system back another ten builds in time, the general upward trend of the complexity of

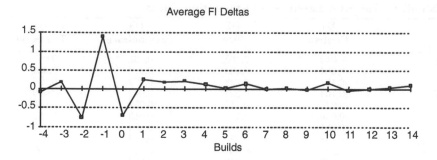

Exhibit 18. Deltas in FI across Sequential Builds

the system would be sustained. The particular baseline for this exhibit was selected because of the change activity that we had observed before and after this baseline build. There were substantial changes made in PASS prior to the build labeled as build 0 on the x-axis of this figure. This activity is evidenced by the substantial variation in ρ around build 0 as seen in Exhibit 18.

The general upward trends in system complexity as shown in Exhibit 17 can be eliminated by computing the differences, or deltas, in complexity from one build to the next. These deltas, then, show the relative magnitude of the changes that have occurred at each build. They provide an excellent view of the impact on the total system of the incremental changes between builds. The deltas for FI are shown in Exhibit 18 for the same builds represented in Exhibit 17.

The average FI gives a real good indication of the global nature of the evolution of a system. In Exhibit 17, we can see that the baseline system has been labeled as build 0 on the x-axis. By definition, it has an average FI of 50. What is interesting are the fluctuations in the curve about this point. We can see the builds –4, –3, and –2 are relatively stable and have an average FI value of about 49.25, somewhat less than build 0. A very interesting event occurs at build –1. A unilateral decision was made to overhaul the system and *simplify* the code after build –2. This resulted in the new build at build –1. Indeed, we can see that the goal was achieved in that the average FI on build –1 is 48.5. However, between build –1 and build 0 it was discovered that the new changes created heroic problems. These problems were resolved on build 0. Now the system complexity has risen much higher than it was before the great leap forward. Eventually, the process oscillation damps out and the curve resumes essentially where it would have been if Nature had been allowed to take its course.

The system evolution event represented by Exhibit 17 is very typical of software development efforts in the absence of a mechanism to measure evolution. Heroic changes are made to happen on software systems typically by program managers. This effort is always made to "clean up the code." By our definition, the code will be "cleaned up" if there has been a sustainable net decline in the average FI for the system. What very often happens, however, is that the system is no better (and sometimes much worse) off after the simplification effort. The average FI values shown in the Exhibit 17 clearly show this phenomenon.

Exhibit 18 gives a clear indication of exactly what happened during the great leap forward. Between builds –2 and –1, a substantial amount of code was dumped and the average FI delta went down. Immediately after the great leap forward, the consequences of the change were felt and problems were fixed. New code is added between builds –1 and build 0 to rectify the problems found. This oscillation continues for awhile and eventually the system reaches its steady-state evolution process again. If we are watching and measuring, we can discover that there was extreme code churn in this process and probably no net benefit in the system overhaul.

As changes are made to individual software modules in an evolving software system, the complexity of the system will tend to grow. This will lead to problems in the maintainability of the code. As the system becomes more complex, it will be more difficult to maintain. The increase in complexity will also result in the introduction of new faults into the system in direct proportion to the increase in the complexity of the code. The measurement methodology introduced in this study will permit direct measurement of the complexity measurements that are likely to be related to software faults. From a maintenance perspective, an increase in program complexity from one build to another will create a concomitant increase in the cost of maintaining the program. From a software test perspective, the rate of fault injection by changes from one build to the next will be directly proportional to the change in the system complexity. This, in turn, will create the need for increased test efforts directly proportional to the net change in program complexity.

8.2.6 Examining the Specific Changes in the Evolution of PASS

The Space Shuttle PASS is of great interest in the study of software evolution for a number of reasons. Primary among these reasons is that the system was developed by a systems group that was for many years the only viable candidate for a Level 5 development organization on the Software Engineering Institute Capability Maturity Model. A tremendous historical database exists for this software system across its many distinct builds. Furthermore, the development group has maintained accurate measurement data over the life of this system. It represents an optimal opportunity for the study of software evolution.

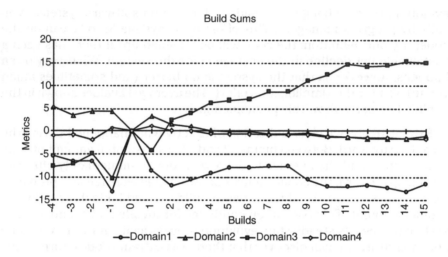

Exhibit 19. Baselined Domain Metrics Across Builds

Now we would like to present an example of specific attribute measurements across software builds. To this end, we will examine the last 20 system builds baselined on the fifth one of this series. There is a very good reason for examining these particular systems. There were some major changes occurring at the fifth build, as can well be seen in Exhibit 19. For each of the 20 system builds represented in this exhibit, the four domain metrics were computed for each program module. System totals were then computed for the domain metrics for all modules of each of the systems. These four total domain values were then plotted for each system.

The domain metrics of all of the systems were computed with build 0 as a baseline system. In that the domain metrics have a mean of zero and a standard deviation of one for the baseline system, we can see from Exhibit 18 that all four domain metric lines cross at the x-axis for this system. In that all other systems are baselined relative to build 0, the domain metrics show changes in the complexity on each of the domains relative to build 0.

Some very interesting patterns emerge from Exhibit 19. We can see that in the series of builds from build 0, there is a general upward trend in the source of complexity represented by Domain 3, semaphore complexity. Alternatively, there has been a substantial decline in the source of complexity represented by Domain 1. Domain 1, it will be remembered from the earlier discussion, is a Control complexity domain. We can see that the control complexity of recent systems has been in the direction of simplification of the program modules.

One clear way to reduce control complexity is to reduce the size of each program module. The best way to reduce the size of program modules is to

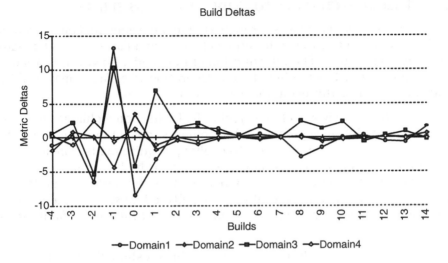

Exhibit 20. Deltas in Domain Metrics across Builds

break big modules into two or more smaller modules. This fragmentation, however, simply shifts complexity from one domain, Control, to another, Semaphore, to cope with the increasing coupling complexity among the modules.

Recent builds of the software have resulted in some substantial functional changes in the real-time control complexity of the modules. The activity in and around build 0 shows material changes in the software in the systems immediately before and immediately after this build. There were substantial changes being made to PASS during this time. This system change activity may also be seen from a more global perspective in Exhibit 3.

Just as was the case for the analysis of the system FI, it is possible to compute the incremental changes, or deltas, in each of the domain metrics for each of the builds. This will effectively eliminate the trends in the metrics and permit a distinct focus on the precise nature of each of the changes to each of the builds. The deltas for the domain metrics are shown in Exhibit 20. From this new focus, some interesting observations can be made. We can see, for example, a relatively large fluctuation in the Control complexity domain on builds −2, −1, 0, and 1. This oscillation in the control domain metrics is typical of attempts to introduce major changes in a system. First, there is the simplification attempt, build −2; then there is the rebound, build −1, indicating that some desirable features have been removed, followed by yet another reduction in control complexity, and finally a gradual dampening in the oscillation. A very similar pattern is revealed in Domain 3 over builds −2 through 2.

8.3 MEASURING CHANGES TO MODULES ACROSS BUILDS

As a software system evolves through a number of sequential builds, faults will be identified and the code will be changed in an attempt to eliminate the identified faults. The introduction of new code, however, is a fault-prone process just as the initial code generation was. Faults may well be introduced during this evolutionary process.

Code does not always change just to fix faults. Some changes to code during its evolution represent enhancements, design modifications, or changes in the code in response to evolving requirements. These incremental code enhancements may also result in the introduction of still more faults. Thus, as a system progresses through a series of builds, the FI of each program module that has been altered must also change. The rate of change in FI will serve as a good index of the rate of fault introduction.

Once the rate of fault introduction has been established, it becomes possible to estimate the number of faults remaining in the system at any point during the development. Because we use changes in FI as a measure of the fault introduction rate, it becomes possible to estimate the number of residual faults at the module level, in which a module is taken to be a procedure, function, or method. This information is useful to software development managers wishing to estimate the resources required to remove the remaining faults — not only can the number of remaining faults be estimated, but it is possible to direct fault detection and removal resources at those portions of the software estimated to have the highest concentrations of residual faults. However, this is only half of the picture. Once the software is operating in the field, we would like to establish its reliability. The estimated number of residual faults, a static measure, must be transformed into an estimate of the system's dynamic behavior.

The general notion of software test is that rate of fault removal will generally exceed the rate of fault introduction. In most cases, this is probably true. Some changes are rather more heroic than others. During these more substantive change cycles, it is quite possible that the actual number of faults in the system will increase. We would be very mistaken, then, to assume that software test will monotonically reduce the number of faults in a system. This will only be the case if the software development process is sufficiently good as to ensure that more faults are being removed than are being introduced at each code change. The rate of fault removal is relatively easy to measure. The rate of fault introduction is much more tenuous. This fault introduction process is directly related to two measures that we can take on code as it evolves: code change and code churn.

8.3.1 Measures of Code Module Evolution

With a suitable baseline in place, it is possible to measure software evolution across a full spectrum of software metrics. We can do this first by comparing average metric values for the different builds. Second, we can measure the increase or decrease in system complexity as measured by the code delta, or we can measure the total amount of change the system has undergone between builds, code churn.

To establish the complexity of a system across builds in the face of changing modules and changing sets of modules is in itself a very complex problem. In terms of the example above, the FI of the system $R^{B,i}$ at build i, the early build, is given by:

$$R^{B,i} = \sum_{m_c \in M^i} \rho_c^{B,i}$$

where $\rho_c^{B,i}$ is the FI of module m_c on this build baselined by build B. Similarly, the FI of the system $R^{B,j}$ at build j, the latter build is given by:

$$R^{B,j} = \sum_{m_c \in M^j} \rho_c^{B,j}$$

The latter system build is said to be more complex if $R^{B,j} > R^{B,i}$.

Regardless of which metric is chosen, the goal is the same. We wish to assess how the system has changed over time with respect to that particular measurement. The concept of a code delta provides this information. A code delta is, as the name implies, the difference between two builds as to the FI metric.

The change in the FI in a single module between two builds can be measured in one of two distinct ways. First, we can simply compute the difference in the module FI between build i and build j. This value is the *code delta* for the module m_a, or $\delta_a^{i,j} = |\rho_a^{B,j}| - |\rho_a^{B,i}|$. The absolute value of the code delta is a measure of *code churn*. In the case of code churn, what is important is that the absolute measure of the nature of that code has been modified. From the standpoint of fault introduction, removing a lot of code is probably as catastrophic as adding a lot of code. The new measure of code churn, χ, for module m_a is simply $\chi_a^{i,j} = |\delta_a^{i,j}| = |\rho_a^{B,j} - \rho_a^{B,i}|$.

It is now possible to compute the total change activity for the aggregate system across all of the program modules. The total net fault change (NFC) of the system is the sum of the code delta's for a system between two builds i and j is given by

$$\Delta^{i,j} = \sum_{m_c \in M^i} \delta_c^{i,j} - \sum_{m_a \in M_a^{i,j}} \rho_a^{B,i} + \sum_{m_b \in M_b^{i,j}} \rho_a^{B,j}$$

With a suitable baseline in place, and the module sets defined above, it is now possible to measure software evolution across a full spectrum of software metrics. We can do this first by comparing average metric values for the different builds. Second, the increase or decrease in system complexity can be measured by a selected metric, code delta, or by the total amount of change the system has undergone between builds, code churn.

A limitation of measuring code deltas is that it does not give a good, clear indication of how much change the system has undergone. If, between builds, several software modules are removed and replaced by modules of roughly equivalent complexity, the code delta for the system will be close to zero. The overall complexity of the system, based on the metric used to compute deltas, will not have changed much. However, the reliability of the system could have been severely affected by the process of replacing old modules with new ones. What we need is a measure to accompany the NFC that indicates how much change has occurred. Net code churn (NCC) is a measurement, calculated in a similar manner to code delta, that provides this information. The net code churn of the same system over the same builds is:

$$\nabla^{i,j} = \sum_{m_c \in M_c} \chi_c^{i,j} + \sum_{m_a \in M_a^{i,j}} \rho_a^{B,i} + \sum_{m_b \in M_b^{i,j}} \rho_b^{B,j}$$

When several modules are replaced between builds by modules of roughly the same complexity, code delta will be approximately zero but code churn will be equal to the sum of the value of ρ for all of the modules, both inserted and deleted. Both the NFC and NCC for a particular metric are needed to assess the evolution of a system.

8.3.2 Obtaining Average Build Values

By definition, the average FI, $\overline{\rho}$, of the baseline *system* will be:

$$\overline{\rho}^B = \frac{1}{N^B} \sum_{i=1}^{N^B} \rho_i^B = 50$$

where N^B is the cardinality of the set of modules on build B, the baseline build. FI for the baseline build is calculated from standardized values using the mean and standard deviation from the baseline metrics. Again, the FIs are scaled to have a mean of 50 and a standard deviation of 10. For that reason, the average FI for the baseline system will always be a fixed point. Subsequent builds are standardized using the means and standard deviations of the metrics gathered from the baseline system to allow comparisons. The average FI for subsequent builds is given by:

$$\overline{\rho}^k = \frac{1}{N^k} \sum_{i=1}^{N^k} \rho_i^{B,k}$$

where N^k is the cardinality of the set of program modules in the kth build and $\rho_i^{B,k}$ is the baselined FI for the ith module of that set.

The total FI, R^0, of a system on its initial build is simply the sum of all module FI values of the initial system:

$$R^0 = \sum_{i=1}^{N} \rho_i^0$$

In that FI functions as a fault surrogate the fault potential, r_i^0, of a particular module i is directly proportional to its value of the FI fault surrogate. Thus,

$$r_i^0 = \rho_i^0 \Big/ R^0$$

To derive a preliminary estimate for the actual number of faults per module, we can make judicious use of historical data. From previous software development projects it is possible to develop a proportionality constant, say k, that will allow the total system FI to map to a specific system fault count as follows: $F^0 = kR^0$ or $R^0 = F^0/k$, where F^0 is the total number of faults that have been discovered to have been present in the first build of the system. Clearly, F^0 is an estimate for the initial fault count in that the true value is probably not knowable. We can only estimate F^0 if we have valid historical fault data for our software process to have a reasonably accurate estimate for the proportionality constant k. Substituting for R in the above equation, we find that:

$$r_i^0 = k\rho_i^0 \Big/ F^0$$

Our best estimate, then, for the number of faults in module i in the initial configuration of the system is:

$$g_i^0 = r_i^0 F^0$$

After an interval of testing, a number of faults will be found and fixes made to the code to remedy the faults. Let F^j be the total number of faults found in the total system up to and including the jth build of the software. In a particular module I, there will be f_i^1 faults found in the first build that are attributable to this module. The estimated number of faults remaining in module i will then be:

$$g_i^1 = g_i^0 - f_i^1$$

assuming that we have only fixed faults in the code and not added any new ones.

Our ability to locate the remaining faults in a system will relate directly to our exposure to these faults. If, for example, at the jth build of a system there are g_i^j remaining faults in module i, we cannot expect to identify any of these faults unless some test activity is allocated to exercising module i, or that there is an external code review process that will also serve to identify faults.

8.3.3 Software Evolution and the Fault Introduction Process

Initially, our best estimate for the number of faults in module i in the initial configuration of the system is:

$$g_i^0 = r_i^0 F^0$$

As the ith module was tested during the test activity of the first build, the number of faults found and fixed in this process was denoted by f_i^1. However, in the process of fixing this fault, the source code will change. In all likelihood, so too will the FI of this module. Over a sequence of builds, the complexity of this module may change substantially. Let

$$\Delta_i^{0,j} = \sum_{k=1}^{j} \Delta_i^{k-1,k} \text{ and } \nabla_i^{0,j} = \sum_{k=1}^{j} \nabla_i^{k-1,k}$$

represent the module level NFC and NCC in FI to the ith module over the first j builds. Then the system level NFC and NCC in FI over these j builds will be:

$$\Delta^{0,j} = \sum_{i=1}^{N_j} \Delta_i^{0,j} \text{ and } \nabla^{0,j} = \sum_{i=1}^{N_j} \nabla_i^{0,j}$$

where N_j is the cardinality of the set of all modules that were in existence over these j builds. The complexity of the ith module will have changed over this sequence of builds. Its new cumulative FI will be $\rho_i + \Delta_i^{0,j}$. The system complexity R will also have changed. Its new cumulative FI will be $R^0 + \Delta^{0,j}$. Some changes may increase the FI of this module and others may decrease it. A much better measure of the cumulative change to the system will be $\rho_i + \nabla_i^{0,j}$.

On the initial build of the system, the initial burden of faults in a module was proportional to the FI of the module. As the build cycle continues, the rate of fault introduction is most closely associated with the code churn. Thus, the proportion of faults in the ith module will have changed over the sequence of j builds, related to its initial FI and its subsequent code churn. Its new value will be:

$$r_i^j = (\rho_i^0 + \nabla_i^{0,j}) \Big/ (R^0 + \nabla^{0,j})$$

We now observe that our estimate of the number of faults in the system has changed. On the jth build there will no longer be F^0 faults in the system. New faults will have been introduced as the code has evolved.

In all likelihood, the initial software development process and subsequent evolution processes will be materially different. This means that there will be a different proportionality constant, say k', representing the rate of fault introduction for the evolving system. For the total system, then, there will have been $F^j = kR^0 + k'\Delta^{0,j}$ faults introduced into the system from the initial build through the jth build. Each module will have had $h_i^j = r_i^j F^j$ faults introduced into it, either from the initial build or on subsequent builds. Thus, our revised estimate of the number of faults remaining in module i on build j will be:

$$g_i^j = h_i^j - f_i^j$$

The rate of fault introduction is directly related to the change activity that a module will receive from one build to the next. At the system level, we can see that the expected number of introduced faults from build j to build $j+1$ will be:

$$F^{j+1} - F^j = kR^0 + k'\nabla^{0,j+1} - kR^0 + k'\nabla^{0,j}$$

$$= k'(\nabla^{0,j+1} - \nabla^{0,j})$$

$$= k'\nabla^{j,j+1}$$

At the module level, the rate of fault introduction will again be proportional to the level of change activity. Hence, the expected number of introduced faults between build j to build $j+1$ on module i will be simply $h_i^{j+1} - h_i^j$.

The two proportionality constants k and k' are the ultimate criterion measures of the software development process and software maintenance processes. Each process has an associated fault introduction proportionality constant. If we institute a new software development process and observe a significant downward change in the constant k, then the change would have been a good one. Very frequently, however, software processes are changed because development fads change and not because a criterion measure has indicated that a new process is superior to a previous one. We will consider that an advance in software development process has occurred if either k or k' has diminished for that new process.

8.3.4 The Cassini System: A Case Study

To estimate rates of fault introduction, we now turn our attention to a complete software system on which every version of every module has been archived, together with the faults that have been recorded against the system as it evolved.[2-4] On the first build of the Cassini system there were approximately 96K source lines of code in approximately 750 program modules. On the last build there were approximately 110K lines of source code in approximately 800 program modules. As the system progressed from the first to the last build, there were a total of 45,200 different versions of these modules. On the average, then, each module progressed through an average of 56 evolutionary steps or versions. For the purposes of this study, the Ada program module is a procedure or function. It is the smallest unit of the Ada language structure that can be measured. A number of modules present in the first build of the system were removed on subsequent builds. Similarly, a number of modules were added.

The Cassini Command and Data Subsytem (CDS) does not represent an extraordinary software system. It is quite typical of the amount of change activity that will occur in the development of a system on the order of 100 KLOC (thousand lines of code). It is a nontrivial measurement problem to track the system as it evolves. Again, there are two different sets of measurement activities that must occur at once. We are interested in both the changes in the source code and the fault reports that are being filed against each module.

To determine the efficiency of a test activity, it is necessary to have a system in which structural changes between one increment and its predecessor can be measured, together with the execution profile observed during test. Because we were unable to accomplish this for the Cassini CDS flight software, we studied the real-time software for a commercial embedded system. This will be discussed in Chapter 11.

In measuring the evolution of the system to talk about rates of fault introduction and removal, we measure in units proportional to the way the system changes over time. Changes to the system are visible at the module level, and we attempt to measure at that level of granularity. Because the measurements of system structure are collected at the module level (by module, we mean procedures and functions), information about faults must also be collected at the same granularity.

A fault, for the purposes of this particular investigation, is a structural imperfection in a software system that may lead to the system eventually failing. That is, it is a physical characteristic of the system of which the type and extent can be measured using the same ideas used to measure the properties of more traditional physical systems. Faults are introduced into a system by people making errors in their tasks. These errors can be errors of commission or errors of omission.

To count faults, there must be a well-defined method of identification that is repeatable, consistent, and identifies faults at the same level of granularity as our structural measurements. In analyzing the flight software for the Cassini Orbiter Command and Data Subsystem project at the Jet Propulsion Laboratory (JPL), the fault data and the source code change data were available from two different systems. The problem reporting information was obtained from the JPL institutional problem reporting system. For the Cassini system, failures were recorded starting at subsystem-level integration, and continuing through spacecraft integration and test. Failure reports typically contain descriptions of the failure at varying levels of detail, as well as descriptions of what was done to correct the fault(s) that caused the failure. Detailed information regarding the underlying faults (e.g., where were the code changes made in each affected module) is generally unavailable from the problem reporting system.

The entire source code evolution could be obtained directly from the Software Configuration Control System (SCCS) files for all versions of the flight software. The way in which SCCS was used in this development effort makes it possible to track changes to the system at a module level, in that each SCCS file stores the baseline version of that file (which may contain one or more modules) as well as the changes required to produce each subsequent increment (SCCS delta) of that file. When a module was created, or changed in response to a failure report or engineering change request, the file in which the module is contained was checked into SCCS as a new delta. This allowed us to track changes to the system at the module level as it evolved over time. For approximately 10 percent of the failure reports, we were able to identify the source file increment in which the fault(s) associated with a particular failure report were repaired. This information was available either in the comments inserted by the developer into the SCCS file as part of the check-in process, or as part of the set of comments at the beginning of a module that tracks its development history.

Using the information described above, we then set about to identify faults as per our working definition. For each problem report, the SCCS files were searched to identify all modules and the version(s) of each module for which the software was changed in response to the problem report. For each version of each module so identified, the assumption was made that all differences between the version in which repairs are implemented and the previous version are due solely to fault repair. This is not necessarily a valid assumption in that developers may also be making functional enhancements to the system in the same version that fault repairs are being made. Careful analysis of failure reports for which there was sufficiently detailed descriptive information served to separate areas of fault repair from other changes. A differential comparator (e.g., UNIX `diff`) was then used to obtain the differences between the versions in which the fault(s) were repaired and the immediately preceding version.

After completing the last step, the process of identifying and counting the faults began. The results of the differential comparison cannot simply be counted up to give a total number of faults. So that the faults could be reliably tallied, we developed a taxonomy for identifying and counting faults.[4] This taxonomy differs from others in that it does not seek to identify the root cause of the fault. Rather, it is based on the types of changes made to the software to repair the faults associated with failure reports. In other words, it constitutes an operational definition of a fault. We found that this taxonomy allowed us to identify faults in the software used in the study in a consistent manner at the appropriate level of granularity.

There was still substantial variability in the granularity of the definition of a fault. This was the primary motivation for the new definition for software faults shown in Chapter 5. Some of the faults in this study involved relatively little change in the code base. Other faults changed the code base materially. This granularity of measurement was simply not reflected in the taxonomy that we had developed for fault enumeration.

8.3.4.1 The Relationship between Faults and Code Changes. Having established a theoretical relationship between software faults and code changes, it is now of interest to validate this model empirically. This measurement occurred on two simultaneous fronts. First, all versions of all the source code modules were measured. From these measurements, code churn and code deltas were obtained for every version of every module. The failure reports were sampled to lead to specific faults in the code. These faults were classified manually according to the above taxonomy and on a case-by-case basis. Then we were able to build a regression model relating the code measures to the code faults.

The Ada source code modules for all versions of each of these modules were systematically reconstructed from the SCCS code deltas. Each of these module versions was then measured by the UX-Metric analysis tool for Ada. Not all metrics provided by this tool were used in this study. Only a subset of these actually provide distinct sources of variation. The specific metrics used in this study are shown in Exhibit 21.

To establish a baseline system, all of the metric data for the module versions that were members of the first build of CDS were then analyzed by our PCA-FI tool. This tool is designed to compute FI values, either from a baseline system or from a system being compared to the baseline system. In that the first build of the Cassini CDS system was selected to be the baseline system, the PCA-FI tool performed a principal components analysis on this data with an orthogonal varimax rotation. The objective of this phase of the analysis is to use the principal components technique to reduce the dimensionality of the metric set.

Exhibit 21. Software Metric Definitions

Metrics	Definition
η_1	Count of unique operators
η_2	Count of unique operands
N_1	Count of total operators
N_2	Count of total operands
P/R	Purity ratio: ratio of Halstead's $\hat{N}$ to total program vocabulary
V(g)	McCabe's cyclomatic complexity
Depth	Maximum nesting level of program blocks
AveDepth	Average nesting level of program blocks
LOC	Number of lines of code
Blk	Number of blank lines
Cmt	Count of comments
CmtWds	Total words used in all comments
Stmts	Count of executable statements
LSS	Number of logical source statements
PSS	Number of physical source statements
NonEx	Number of nonexecutable statements
AveSpan	Average number of lines of code between references to each variable
Vl	Average variable name length

Exhibit 22. Principal Components of Software Metrics

Metric	Size	Structure	Style	Nesting
Stmts	0.968	0.022	−0.079	0.021
LSS	0.961	0.025	−0.080	0.004
N_2	0.926	0.016	0.086	0.086
N_1	0.934	0.016	0.074	0.077
η_2	0.884	0.012	−0.244	0.043
AveSpan	0.852	0.032	0.031	−0.082
V(g)	0.843	0.032	−0.094	−0.114
η_1	0.635	−0.055	−0.522	−0.136
Depth	0.617	−0.022	−0.337	−0.379
LOC	−0.027	0.979	0.136	0.015
Cmt	−0.046	0.970	0.108	0.004
PSS	−0.043	0.961	0.149	0.019
CmtWds	0.033	0.931	0.058	−0.010
NonEx	−0.053	0.928	0.076	−0.009
Blk	0.263	0.898	0.048	0.005
P/R	−0.148	−0.198	**−0.878**	0.052
Vl	0.372	−0.232	**−0.752**	0.010
AveDepth	−0.000	−0.009	0.041	**−0.938**
% Variance	37.956	30.315	10.454	6.009

As can been seen in Exhibit 22, there are four principal components for the 18 metrics shown in Exhibit 20. For convenience, we have chosen to name these principal components as size, structure, style, and nesting. From the last row in Exhibit 22 we can see that the new reduced set of orthogonal components of the original 18 metrics account for approximately 85 percent of the variation in the original metric set.

8.3.4.2 Estimation of the Proportionality Constant: An Example from Cassini.
As is fairly typical in the principal components analysis of metric data, the size domain dominates the analysis. It alone accounts for approximately 38

Exhibit 23. Baseline Transformation Data for the Cassini Data

Metric	$\bar{x}^B$	s^B	Domain 1	Domain 2	Domain 3	Domain 4
Stmts	11.37	7.79	0.10	−0.02	0.26	0.05
LSS	25.18	27.08	0.13	0.00	0.04	−0.09
N_2	79.59	129.08	0.13	0.02	−0.17	−0.08
N_1	68.24	115.72	0.13	0.02	−0.17	−0.09
η_2	1.32	0.54	0.00	−0.07	0.54	−0.16
AveSpan	4.77	6.19	0.12	0.01	−0.03	0.07
$V(g)$	1.48	1.58	0.10	−0.01	0.17	0.30
η_1	0.00	0.05	0.01	0.00	0.06	0.88
Depth	162.05	515.83	−0.01	0.17	0.07	−0.02
LOC	19.05	30.14	0.03	0.16	0.07	−0.02
Cmt	34.19	124.24	−0.01	0.17	0.09	−0.01
PSS	139.27	452.48	0.00	0.16	0.10	0.00
CmtWds	16.61	20.44	0.14	0.01	−0.07	−0.05
NonEx	17.52	23.50	0.14	0.01	−0.07	−0.04
Blk	108.80	372.11	−0.01	0.17	0.06	−0.02
P/R	7.36	22.84	−0.01	0.16	0.10	0.00
Vl	5.75	8.26	0.12	0.02	−0.11	0.06
AveDepth	9.00	4.40	0.07	−0.06	0.40	−0.11
Eigenvalues			6.832	5.457	1.882	1.082

percent of the total variation in the original metric set. Not surprisingly, this domain contains the metrics of total statement count (*Stmts*), logical source statements (LSS), and the Halstead lexical metric primitives of operator and operand count, but it also contains cyclomatic complexity ($V(g)$). The structure domain contains those metrics relating to the physical structure of the program, such as nonexecutable statements (*NonEx*) and the program block count (*Blk*). The style domain contains measures of attribute that are directly under a programmer's control, such as variable length (*Vl*) and purity ratio (*P/R*). The nesting domain consists of the single metric that is a measure of the average depth of nesting of program modules (*AveDepth*).

To transform the raw metrics for each module version into their corresponding FI values, the means and the standard deviations must be computed. These are shown in Exhibit 23. These values will be used to transform all raw metric values for all versions of all modules to their baselined z-score values. The last four columns in Exhibit 23 contain the actual transformation matrix that will map the metric z-score values onto their orthogonal equivalents to obtain the orthogonal domain metric values used in the computation of FI. Finally, the eigenvalues for the four domains are presented in the last row of Exhibit 23.

Exhibit 23, then, contains all of the essential information needed to obtain baselined FI values for any version of any module relative to the baseline build. As an aside, it is not necessary that the baseline build be the initial build. As a typical system progresses through hundreds of builds in the course of its life, it is well worth reestablishing a baseline closer to the current system. In any event, this baseline data is saved by the PCA-FI tool

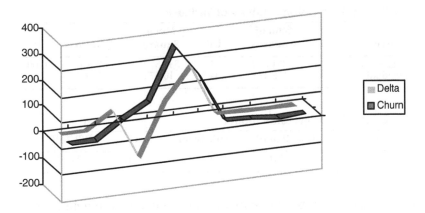

Exhibit 24. Code Churn and Code Deltas across all Builds

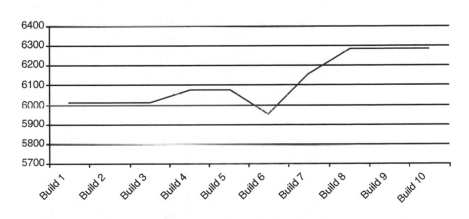

Exhibit 25. FI across all Builds

for use in later computation of metric values. Whenever the tool is invoked referencing the baseline data, it will automatically use this data to transform the raw metric values given to it.

Exhibits 24 and 25 clearly show the evolution of the code across the ten builds of the system. By looking at the code deltas we can see that there was substantial change on build 4 to simplify the system. The total code delta went down. As we saw on the Space Shuttle PASS, this was immediately followed by a substantial upward swing in the code delta. Maximum change activity occurred between builds 3 and 7, as evidenced by the code churn values. The plot of system FI values in Exhibit 25 shows the typical net upward trend in total system complexity from the first build to the last.

Exhibit 26. Regression Analysis of Variance

Source	Sum of Squares	DF	Mean Square	F Ratio	P
Regression	331.879	1	331.879	62.996	0.00
Residual	179.121	34	10.673	5.268	

Exhibit 27. Regression Model

Effect	Coefficient	Std. Error	t	P(2-Tail)
Churn	0.576	0.073	7.937	0.000

In relating the number of faults introduced in an increment to measures of a module's structural change, we had only a small number of observations with which to work. Problem reports could not be consistently traced back to source code. The net result was that of the more than 100 faults that were initially identified, there were only 35 observations in which a fault could be associated with a particular increment of a module, and with that increment's measures of code delta and code churn.

For each of the 35 modules for which there was viable fault data, there were three data points. First, we had the number of introduced faults for that module that were the direct result of changes that had occurred on that module between the current version that contained the faults and the previous version that did not. Second, we had code delta values for each of these modules from the current to the previous version. Finally, we had code churn values derived from the code deltas.

Linear regression models were formulated for code churn and code deltas with code faults as the dependent variable in both cases. Both models were built without constant terms in that we surmise that if no changes were made to a module, then no new faults could be introduced. The results of the regression between faults and code deltas were not at all surprising. The squared multiple R for this model was 0.001, about as close to zero as you can get. This result is directly attributable to the nonlinearity of the data. Change comes in two flavors: change can increase the complexity of a module or change can decrease the complexity of a model. Faults, on the other hand, are not related to the direction of the change but to its intensity. Removing masses of code from a module is just as likely to introduce faults as adding code to it.

The regression model between code churn and faults is dramatically different. The regression ANOVA for this model is shown in Exhibit 26. Whereas code deltas do not show a linear relationship with faults, code churn certainly does. The actual regression model is given in Exhibit 27. The regressions statistics are summarized in Exhibit 28. Of particular inter-

Exhibit 28. Regression Statistics

N	Multiple R	Squared Multiple R	Standard Error of Estimate
35	0.806	0.649	2.296

est in Exhibit 28 is the Squared Multiple R term. This has a value of 0.649. This means, roughly, that the regression model will account for more than 65 percent of the variation in the faults of the observed modules based on the values of code churn.

The regression coefficient shown in Exhibit 27 is, in fact, the estimate of the proportionality constant k'. This is the relative rate of fault introduction as a function of code churn.

8.4 SUMMARY

The central theme of this chapter has been to focus on the problem of measuring and understanding evolving software systems. Clearly, as systems change over time, the numerical characteristics of their many measurable attributes will change as well. We have chosen to address two central problems in the measurement of systems as they evolve. First, there is the problem of establishing a measurement baseline. A single system in a chain of evolving systems will be chosen as a baseline system against which all others will be measured. Second, we have identified a mechanism wherein the precise manner in which they differ from each other can be measured. With this methodology, we can determine the changes that have occurred in evolving systems and the relative degree of this change.

Change can be measured in a variety of different ways. We can, with limited success, choose to try to use raw complexity metrics to measure change among systems. Alternatively, we see from this chapter that a far better method for measuring programs is to form orthogonal domain metrics for each system. These orthogonal metrics measure the distinct sources of variation in the suite of raw complexity metrics. This permits the direct comparison of each system build with its predecessor and successor builds. Finally, we have shown that it is possible to characterize each module of each system with a single measure of system complexity, the fault index (FI). This concept of system complexity from a software quality perspective permits a more global understanding of how systems evolve over time.

There are two distinct aspects of this measurement process. First, there are the static measures of fault liability. In this regard, we have developed a measure of the overall burden of a program module, the fault index, and also measures of new fault potential in the fault delta and the NFC. Second, we have developed a measure of test profiles to show the activity of test functionalities in individual program modules.

There is a distinct and a strong relationship between software faults and measurable software attributes. This is in itself not a new result or observation. The most interesting result of this current endeavor is that we also found a strong association between the fault introduction process over the evolutionary history of a software system and the degree of change taking place in each of the program modules. We also found that the direction of the change had an effect on the number of faults introduced. Some changes will have the potential of introducing very few faults, while others may have a serious impact on the number of latent faults. Different numbers of faults can be introduced, depending on whether code is being added to or removed from the system.

For the measurement process to be meaningful, the fault data must be very carefully collected and managed. In our continuing investigations of software evolution, the data was extracted *ex post facto* as a very labor-intensive effort. Because fault data cannot be collected with the same degree of automation as much of the data on software metrics being gathered by development organizations, material changes in the software development and software maintenance processes must be made to capture this fault data. Among other things, a well-defined fault standard and fault taxonomy must be developed and maintained as part of the software development process. Further, all designers and coders should be thoroughly trained in its use. A viable standard is one that can be used to classify any fault unambiguously. A viable fault recording process is one in which any one person will classify a fault exactly the same as any other person.

The whole notion of measuring the fault introduction process is its ultimate value as a measure of software process. The software engineering literature is replete with examples of how software process improvement can be achieved through the use of some new software development technique. What is almost absent from the same literature is a controlled study to validate the fact that the new process is meaningful. The techniques developed in this study can be implemented in a development organization to provide a consistent method of measuring fault content and structural evolution across multiple projects over time. The initial estimates of fault introduction rates can serve as a baseline against which future projects can be compared to determine whether progress is being made in reducing the fault introduction rate, and to identify those development techniques that seem to provide the greatest reduction.

A constant theme of this chapter has been on the act of measurement. Faults were measured. Software source code was measured. Measurement is the foundation of science and engineering. Today's software systems are simply too large to be hand-crafted as they were in the past. They must now be engineered. Every aspect of the evolving system must be carefully designed and tested based on sound engineering principles. These engineering principles have, as their foundation, sound measurement principles.

References

1. Munson, J.C., Software Faults, Software Failures, and Software Reliability Modeling, *Information and Software Technology*, December 1996.

2. Nikora, A.P., Software System Defect Content Prediction from Development Process and Product Characteristics, Doctoral dissertation, Department of Computer Science, University of Southern California, Los Angeles, May 1998.

3. Nikora, A.P. and Munson, J.C., Software Evolution and the Fault Process, Proceedings of the 23rd Annual Software Engineering Workshop, NASA/Goddard Space Flight Center (GSFC) Software Engineering Laboratory (SEL), Greenbelt, MD, 1998.

4. Nikora, A.P. and Munson, J.C., Determining Fault Insertion Rates for Evolving Software Systems, Proceedings of the 1998 IEEE International Symposium of Software Reliability Engineering, Paderborn, Germany, November 1998, IEEE Computer Society Press.

Chapter 9
Software Specification and Design

9.1 INTRODUCTION

In Chapter 10 we will discuss how to measure a software system that is running. To facilitate this discussion it will be necessary to understand just what we are measuring. In the final analysis, a typical computer program is nothing more than a poorly designed set of machine-level instructions. The typical instruction repertoire on a typical computer is crafted by hardware engineers who have little understanding of or interest in what a programmer will need to perform his or her work most efficiently. We will learn very little if we just monitor these instructions as they execute. We will, in fact, be overwhelmed with data. It is appropriate, then, to take the time to understand just what is going on when the machine instructions are executing.

Each software system begins with a set of requirements. These requirements are either explicit and well defined, or they are implicit and not so well defined. In either case, the requirements will specify *what* the software system will do. These requirements will delineate a set of *operations* that a user will perform in interacting with the system. The user can be a person, a hardware system, or another software system.

Once we have defined what the system will do, we next will turn our attention to *how* the operations will be accomplished on our computer system. The design of a system will articulate a set of *functionalities* that describe how each operation will be implemented in the new software system. Again, under the best of circumstances, the functionalities will be completely and unambiguously defined. In the worst of circumstances, but far more typical, the functionalities will reside only in the heads of key software developers.

Ultimately, the structure of the system will resolve into a set of program modules. Each of the modules will implement one or more of the functionalities. At the design stage, these modules can be specified with some level

215

of precision in the low-level design. More typically, the modular structure will simply emerge in source code as developers struggle to implement their ad hoc design.

For measurement purposes, we will need a bit more definition on the software development process. To that end, we will now specify each of the activities in the software specification process a little more precisely.

9.2 SOFTWARE OPERATIONAL REQUIREMENTS SPECIFICATION

The first step in the software specification process will be the definition of our system at the operational level. This is the user's view of the system. With our software skills, we can create virtually any reality we wish. However, we must first specify the reality that we want. The most difficult aspect of software development is that we can operate virtually without constraint in the reality that we can fabricate for a user. Before we can begin the operational specification process, we must first define this reality. This virtual system we will call the *operational* metaphor.

9.2.1 Operational System Overview

We will begin our operational specification with the operational system overview. This is a simple *précis* of the system. It is a concise statement of the basic operation of the system from the user's perspective. It gives the customer, the designer, and the developer an overview of the operation of the system. This is the kind of thing that would be printed on the cover of a CD-ROM containing the software. We will be able to read this description and know what the system will do for us.

The term "user" or "client" does not always imply the existence of a human being in this process. For embedded systems, the client is the hardware that is being driven by the software. In other circumstances, the user or client could be one or more independent software systems.

The operational system overview will also embody nonoperational requirements that need to be formalized to ensure that the software meets the user's needs. These can be broken down into a taxonomy as follows:

- Quality requirements
  - Reliability
  - Maintainability
  - Availability
- Performance requirements
- Compatibility requirements
  - Hardware
  - Software
  - Network protocol

9.2.2 Operational System Metaphor

The next step in the specification process is to construct the operational system metaphor. Again, we can create virtually any reality that we wish with our modern software technology. We are going to build an imaginary castle in the sky for our user. The precise description of this castle is the operational system metaphor. It will define very precisely the user's overview of the system operation. It answers the question of *what* the system does. It should provide the system user with a complete description of the abstract model that will interact with the user.

If, for example, our task is to construct a calculator for a user to deploy on his or her desktop, we must work to define the precise metaphor for the calculator. One calculator that we could build would work in the command mode and would behave in a similar fashion to the traditional UNIX dc calculator. We would then define for the user how many decimal places the calculator would maintain for calculations, what operations were permissible, how the data would be entered, and how the data would be displayed. In essence, we would write a simple user's manual that would describe our calculator metaphor so that the user could operate it correctly within the framework of the command line calculator.

The complete and accurate specification of the operational metaphor is vital to the next step, which is to identify the set of operations that the user can perform on the hypothetical calculator that our metaphor describes. A sample metaphor of our hypothetical calc command line calculator might look something like this:

> calc is an integer arithmetic calculator. It will be initiated from a UNIX command line by typing the name calc with no arguments. It operates on decimal integers. Accuracy is limited to ten digits. The overall structure of calc is a stacking (reverse Polish) calculator.
>
> calc will prompt the user with a ">" symbol. At the prompt, the user can type any one of the operations listed in Exhibit 1, followed by a carriage return keystroke. The description of each of the permitted operations is shown in the second column of Exhibit 1.

9.2.3 Operations

At this level we will specify very precisely the operations that can be performed on our operational metaphor. These are a set a mutually exclusive activities or operations that the user can execute. A list of operations for our hypothetical calc software is shown in Exhibit 1. Each operation can also have nonoperational attributes in its description. We might wish, for example, that all operations be executed in less than one second on a real-time clock.

Exhibit 1. Operations for Hypothetical Software

Operation	Description
<enter number>	The value of the number is pushed on the stack. A number is an unbroken string of the digits 0 through 9. It can be preceded by an underscore (_) to input a negative number.
+	The top two values on the stack are popped, added, and their sum pushed back on the stack.
−	The top two values on the stack are popped, the first number is subtracted from the second, and the difference is pushed back on the stack.
*	The top two values on the stack are popped, multiplied, and the least significant ten digits of the product is pushed back on the stack.
%	The top two values on the stack are popped, the first number is divisor, and the second number is the dividend. The remainder is pushed onto the stack followed by the quotient.
d	The top value on the stack is duplicated.
p	The top value on the stack is printed. The top value remains unchanged. p interprets the top of the stack as an ASCII string, removes it, and prints it.
f	All values on the stack are printed.
q	Exits the program. If executing a string, the recursion level is popped by two. If q is capitalized, the top value on the stack is popped and the string execution level is popped by that value.
c	All values on the stack are popped.

Each operation is distinct. We cannot combine them. The user will be constrained to doing one at a time in serial order. Essentially, we are going to insist that each operation be entered, followed by a carriage return. It should be obvious that there are no implementation details considered in the set of operations. These operations are strictly what the user will do to interact with our `calc` software.

9.3 SOFTWARE FUNCTIONAL REQUIREMENTS SPECIFICATION

The system functional requirements will specify the design of the system that we will develop to implement the operational metaphor. In the functional requirements we will contrive a functional metaphor that will make our software system appear to operate in the manner articulated in the operational specification. It will contain the high-level design of an intermediate system to implement the operational specifications.

9.3.1 Functional System Overview

Just as was the case with the operational system overview, we will need to create a statement of purpose for the system designers. That is the role of the functional system overview. This document will set certain design parameters and take the first step in the restriction of the degrees of freedom in the design process. In the case of the `calc` system, we could start this constraint development process by insisting that the underlying engine for our calculator be a decimal machine. That is, we will keep all the stack contents for our calculator in either packed decimal internal representation or as a string of decimal digits. This will immediately eliminate the design alternative of using binary arithmetic to represent our numbers internally at the functional level.

As we get further into the specification of the system, we are systematically constraining the problem and eliminating degrees of design freedom at every step. Ultimately, when the time comes to code the system, a programmer will literally have zero degrees of design freedom. Programmers should be automatons: slaves to the design documents.

Just as was the case with the operational requirements, there will certainly be nonfunctional requirements placed on the evolving design. These nonfunctional requirements might well include such items as operating system compatibility, protocol compatibility, and hardware compatibility.

9.3.2 Functional System Metaphor

The functional system metaphor will provide a system-level description of *how* the system will be implemented. In our `calc` example, we could implement the operational metaphor in any number of ways. We have several choices as to the nature of the arithmetic that we will use on the target machine. We could represent the contents of the stack as binary numbers, as character strings, as decimal strings, as packed decimal or even as floating point numbers. The stack could be represented in a variety of different data structures, such as an array or as a linked list. Even for this simple `calc` machine there are an astonishing number of degrees of freedom in how we are going to really implement the operational metaphor.

We will now turn our attention to describing the virtual machine (the system metaphor) that we will use to implement the operations. The framework for this machine is shown in Exhibit 2. We can see from this exhibit that there is a basic decimal arithmetic engine that runs the show. Data arrive from the user in an input string buffer. These data are then converted by the engine to a token representing each of the distinct inputs from the user. For example, if we find the string "+426" in the input string buffer, then this will be converted to a decimal number token. Results to be displayed to the user will be converted to an ASCII string and placed in the output string buffer. All arithmetic operators will be applied to the top two operands on the operand stack and the results will be pushed onto this stack. All arithmetic will be performed in decimal and the results of the arithmetic operations will be signed decimal numbers. All decimal numbers will include a sign in the leftmost position followed by ten decimal digits. Only the ten least significant digits of any calculation will be pushed back onto the decimal number stack.

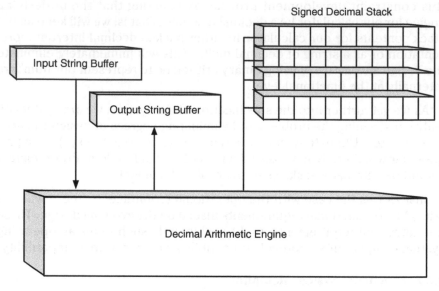

Exhibit 2. Hypothetical Decimal Machine

This decimal machine metaphor is really a trivial example. Necessarily, it would be of limited utility in the real world. It does serve our purpose to convey the essence of the notion of what a functional metaphor should embody. The important thing to note is that the functional metaphor solves the problem of how we are going to implement the user operations. It has constrained the problem from the standpoint of design. There is no doubt as to how the numbers are to be represented in the virtual machine and how arithmetic is to be performed.

9.3.3 Functionalities

The word "functionality" is used to convey the sense of the functional description of the things that the virtual machine described in the functional metaphor will do. Functionalities are in no way to be construed as software functions or subroutine. Functionalities are the operational properties of the functional system metaphor.

A subset of the functionalities for the virtual decimal machine are shown in Exhibit 3. The functionalities listed are certainly not exhaustive. Even in this most trivial of examples it will take a lot of space to represent all of the functionalities. This is because of the degree of specificity of the functionality. It is clearly an issue of granularity of description. We could, for example, define the functionality: add two decimal numbers. Adding decimal numbers, however, is not an easy thing to do. This functionality must be decomposed into its constituent parts. We must have a functionality to

Exhibit 3. Functionalities from Hypothetical Software

Functionality	Description
get	Accept a string from the user input line.
put	Print the string in the output buffer to the user's display.
analyze input buffer	Convert the input buffer contents to a token.
pop stack	Load the contents of the top of the stack into the analysis engine.
copy stack entries	The top two values on the stack are popped, the first number is the divisor, and the second number is the dividend. The remainder is pushed onto the stack followed by the quotient.
set stack pointer down	Move the top-of-stack pointer to the next entry.
exit	Exit the program.
translate number token	The contents of the ASCII string number token are translated to decimal.
translate decimal value	A decimal number is translated to an ASCII string.
add decimal digit	Two decimal digits from the signed decimal stack are added with a carry digit and the carry digit is updated from the sum.
•	•
•	•
•	•

check signs. If the signs are different, then we will need to compute the difference and not the sum. We must have a functionality to add decimal digits; we must have a functionality to iterate our digit adder; etc.

Getting the granularity of definition of a functionality right is not always easy. Perhaps the best way to do this is to start at the highest level, such as: add two decimal numbers, and then decompose this functionality into the next level of specificity until all possible ambiguities have been removed. Again, the purpose of the high-level design is to constrain the solution space for the functional metaphor. We will have achieved the proper level of granularity of specification when all possible solution alternatives have been eliminated, save the one we wish to occur. We do not want programmers performing the design function. If we permit this to occur, they will simply tuck functional specifications into their code where they will reside implicitly. We want the entire functionality of our software to be articulated in the design specification and not in the code. This is a particularly vital consideration if the target language for our calc system will be write-only code such as C or C++.

9.4 SOFTWARE MODULE REQUIREMENTS SPECIFICATION

The module requirements specification is the low-level design specification for the system. At this level, we will be concerned for the first time with implementing the system in a programming language metaphor. Each programming language creates a different metaphor. There is, for example, a C++ machine. This particular language metaphor is created through a very large library of runtime support services. There is a distinctly different metaphor created by the Java runtime environment. We will not concern ourselves with this low-level implementation detail until we actually begin to map our high-level design metaphor onto a particular language runtime environment. The module requirements specification is simply a low-level partition of the system functionality. The three central issues that emerge from the module description will be (1) the structure of the system, (2) the precise specification of data structures, and (3) the data flow from one module to another. There must be, however, a one-to-one mapping between module specifications and code modules. Each module specification will result in exactly one code module. There will be no code modules that do not have design module specifications.

One thing that will become central to our thinking in the module specification is that there must be a well-defined grammar that controls this specification. Our first automatic system measurements will occur at this level. Essentially all of the control flow metrics can be obtained from the design module specifications. All of the pertinent data structures information can be obtained here as well.

It is our expectation that there will be no comment statements in the source code for the program we have specified. All program documentation will be kept outside the source code module. Each source code module will have its own design documentation. All of the pertinent information about the module will be held in the design documentation. If there is a fault in the design, then the design must be modified followed by the associated code modules. The only circumstance under which a code module should ever be modified without modification of its design specification is in the case where the code module does not accurately reflect the design module.

9.4.1 Module Specifications

In our evolving specification scheme there will be a separate specification for each program module. The structure of this specification is outlined in Exhibit 4. In the interest of brevity we will not attempt to build module descriptions for the hypothetical `calc` system. The most important thing to be established at this point is that there are certain elements of module description that must be specified very precisely at this point.

The Module Header Section will articulate the data binding between this module and those that will call it. The Call Section of our module specification shows the control flow binding between this module and those it will call and will be called by it. We will use this section to derive our Fan-In and Fan-Out metrics. The Algorithm Section will be used to derive the module control flow metrics discussed in Chapter 5. The Data Definition Section will show us the scope of each variable. In addition, this section will allow

Exhibit 4. Elements of Module Specification

```
Module_Header_Section      <Module_Name> with
                               <Parameters> In/Out
                               <Parameters> In
                               <Parameters> Out
Call_Section               Called Modules   <Module Name List>|<Empty>
                           Calling Modules  <Module Name List>|<Empty>
Description_Section         Comprehensive description of the functionality
                               of the module including:
                               Start state
                               End state
                               Data transformations
                               Brief description of the relationship with
                               this module to called and calling modules
Algorithm_Section           Pseudo-code description of the algorithm for
                               this module
Data_Definition_Section     Variables:
                               Parameter List
                                   Incoming
                                       <Variable Names>
                                   Outgoing
                                       <Variable Names>
                                   Local
                                       <Variable Names>
                               Constants
                                   <Constant List>
                               Variable Declarations
                               Variable Name ::= <Type>; <Scale>;
                                   <Precision>; <Range>;
                                   <Parameter>|<Local>
```

us to specify the precise nature of each data variable and the range of data that it may contain.

9.4.2 Module Call Graph Structure

Once we have built the module specification for each module we can clearly model the interaction of each module with its immediate neighbors. We will know exactly which module calls another module and those modules that call it. The existence of this call graph structure will serve to eliminate one of the most trying software maintenance problems. That is, when the functionality of a module is changed, then any module that invokes the change module will be impacted by the change. The module call graph structure is a graphical image of the system showing the call-return binding of the program modules. Each module, represented by a node in the graph, will be connected to each called module by an arc in the graph. From this graph, the relationship among calling modules can be easily observed.

9.5 A FORMAL DESCRIPTION OF PROGRAM OPERATION

To assist in the subsequent discussion of program specification, it will be useful to make this description somewhat more precise by introducing some notation conveniences. Assume that a software system S was designed to implement a specific set of mutually exclusive functionalities F. Thus, if the system is executing a function $f \in F$, it cannot be expressing elements of any other functionality in F. Each of these functions in F was designed to implement a set of software specifications based on a user's requirements. From a user's perspective, this software system will implement a specific set of operations, O. This mapping from the set of user-perceived operations O to a set of specific program functionalities F is one of the major tasks in the software specification process.

A pilot astronaut on the Space Shuttle is not aware of the functionality of the Primary Avionics Software System (PASS) that governs the complete operation of the shuttle. A metaphor has been carefully constructed by system designers that permits the pilot to control the shuttle as if it were a standard airplane. The pilot, for example, has a control stick that controls two user-perceived operations: roll and pitch. These operations are implemented in software functions that monitor, for example, the change in resistance in x- and y-coordinate rheostats in the base of the control stick. The pilot *operates* the spacecraft. The software *functions* monitor the change in resistance in the rheostats.

Each operation that a system may perform for a user can be thought of as having been implemented in a set of business requirements. There may be a one-to-one mapping between the user's notion of an operation and a program function. In most cases, however, there will be several discrete

Exhibit 5. Example of the IMPLEMENTS Relation

$O \times F$	f_1	f_2	f_3	f_4
o_1	T	T		
o_2		T	T	T

Exhibit 6. Example of the p' Relation

$p'(o,f)$	f_1	f_2	f_3	f_4
o_1	0.2	0.8	0	0
o_2	0	0.4	0.4	0.2

functions that must be executed to express the user's concept of an operation. For each operation o that the system may perform, the range of functionalities f must be well known. It is possible, then, to define a relation *IMPLEMENTS* over $O \times F$ such that *IMPLEMENTS*(o,f) is true if functionality f is used in the specification of an operation, o. Within each operation, one or more of the system's functionalities will be expressed. For a given operation o, these expressed functionalities are those with the property:

$$F^{(o)} = \left\{ f : F | \forall IMPLEMENTS(o,f) \right\}$$

For each operation $o \in O$, there is a relation p' over $O \times F$ such that $p'(o,f)$ is the proportion of activity assigned to functionality f by operation o. An example of the *IMPLEMENTS* relation for two operations implemented in four specified functions is shown in Exhibit 5. In this exhibit, we can see that functions f_1 and f_2 are used to implement the operation o_1. We can also see that functionality f_2 is a functional part of both operations.

Exhibit 6 provides an example of the p' relation. These numbers represent the proportion of time each of the functions will execute under each of the operations. In operation o_1 functionality f_1 may or may not execute. The functionality f_2, on the other is hand, is quite likely to execute on operation o_1.

The software design process is basically a matter of assigning functionalities in F to specific program modules $m \in M$, the set of program modules. The design process can be thought of as the process of defining a set of relations, ASSIGNS over $F \times M$ such that ASSIGNS(f, m) is true if functionality f is expressed in module m. For a given software system S, let M denote the set of all program modules for that system. For each functionality $f \in F$, there is a relation p over $F \times M$ such that $p(f,m)$ is the proportion of execution events of module m when the system is executing function f. Exhibit 7 shows an example of the ASSIGNS relation for the four functions presented in Exhibit 5. In this example we can see that the function f_1 has been implemented in the program modules m_1 and m_2. One of these modules, m_1, will

Exhibit 7. Example of the ASSIGNS Relation

$F \times M$	m_1	m_2	m_3	m_4	m_5	m_6	m_7	m_8
f_1	T	T						
f_2	T		T		T			T
f_3	T		T	T	T	T		
f_4	T		T		T	T	T	

Exhibit 8. Example of the p Relation

$p(f,m)$	m_1	m_2	m_3	m_4	m_5	m_6	m_7	m_8
f_1	1	1	0	0	0	0	0	0
f_2	1	0	1	0	1	0	0	1
f_3	1	0	1	1	0.2	0.3	0	0
f_4	1	0	1	0	1	1	1	0

be invoked regardless of the functionality. It is common to all functions. Other program modules, such as m_2, are distinctly associated with a single function.

Exhibit 8 provides an example of the p relation. These numbers represent the likelihood that each of the program modules will execute when a particular functionality is invoked. Exhibit 8 represents the proportion of time distributed across each of the six hypothetical program modules. We can see, for example, that $p(f_1, m_1) = 1$. This means that whenever functionality f_1 is invoked, module m_1 will always be executed. On the other hand, we can also observe that $p(f_3, m_5) = 0.2$. In this case, there is a relatively low chance that module m_5 will execute, given that functionality f_2 has been invoked.

There is a relationship between program functionalities and the software modules they will cause to be executed. These program modules will be assigned to one of three distinct sets of modules that, in turn, are subsets of M. Some modules may execute under all of the functionalities of S. This will be the set of common modules. The main program is an example of such a module that is common to all operations of the software system. Essentially, program modules will be members of one of two mutually exclusive sets. There is the set of program modules M_c of common modules and the set of modules M_F that are invoked only in response to the execution of one or more functionalities. It is clear, then, that $M_F = M - M_c$.

The set of common modules, $M_c \subset M$ is defined as those modules that have the property:

$$M_c = \{m : M \mid \forall f \in F \bullet \text{ASSIGNS}(f,m)\}$$

All of these modules will execute regardless of the specific functionality being executed by the software system.

Yet another set of software modules may or may not execute when the system is running a particular function. These modules are said to be *potentially involved* modules. The set of potentially involved modules is:

$$M_p^{(f)} = \{m{:}\,M_F \mid \exists\, f \in F \bullet \text{ASSIGNS } (f,m) \wedge 0 < p(f,m) < 1\}$$

In other program modules, there is extremely tight binding between a particular functionality and a set of program modules. That is, every time a particular function *f* is executed, a distinct set of software modules will always be invoked. These modules are said to be *indispensably involved* with the functionality *f*. This set of indispensably involved modules for a particular functionality *f* is the set of those modules that have the property:

$$M_i^{(f)} = \{m{:}\,M_F \mid \forall f \in F \bullet \text{ASSIGNS}(f,m) \Rightarrow p(f,m) = 1\}$$

As a direct result of the design of the program, there will be a well-defined set of program modules M_f that might be used to express all aspects of a given functionality *f*. These are the modules that have the property:

$$m \in M_f = M_p^{(f)} \cup M_i^{(f)}$$

From the standpoint of software design, the real problems in understanding the dynamic behavior of a system are not necessarily attributable to the set of modules M_i that are tightly bound to a functionality or to the set of common modules M_c that will be invoked for all executing processes. The real problem is the set of potentially invoked modules M_p. The greater the cardinality of this set of modules, the less certain we can be about the behavior of a system performing that function. For any one instance of execution of this functionality, a varying number of the modules in M_p may execute.

For each functionality $f \in F$, there exists a relation *c* over $F \times M$ such that $c(f,m)$ defines the cardinality of the set of functionalities that can call a given module. The *c* relation can be used to partition the set of program modules into two distinct sets. One set contains the modules associated exclusively with one and only one functionality.[1] This is the set of uniquely related modules M_u, where:

$$M_u = \{m{:}\,M \mid f \in F, c(f,m) = 1\}$$

The second set contains the modules that might be executed by more than one functionality, that is, the set of shared modules M_s, to wit:

$$M_s = \{m{:}\,M \mid f \in F \bullet c(f,m) > 1\}$$

There are two distinct ways, then, that we can view program modules associated with functionalities. First, given a functionality, we can charac-

Exhibit 9. Module Classification

Among Functionalities	Within a Functionality
Unique	Indispensable
Shared	Potential

Exhibit 10. Modules Associated with Functionalities

	$M_i^{(f)}$	$M_p^{(f)}$	$M_s^{(f)}$	$M_u^{(f)}$
f_1	$\{m_1, m_2\}$	$\{\}$	$\{m_1\}$	$\{m_2\}$
f_2	$\{m_1, m_3, m_5, m_8\}$	$\{\}$	$\{m_1, m_3, m_5\}$	$\{m_8\}$
f_3	$\{m_1, m_3, m_4\}$	$\{m_5, m_6\}$	$\{m_1, m_3, m_5, m_6\}$	$\{m_4\}$
f_4	$\{m_1, m_3, m_5, m_6, m_7\}$	$\{\}$	$\{m_1, m_3, m_5, m_6\}$	$\{m_7\}$

terize each module as indispensably associated with that functionality or potentially associated with it. Second, each program module may or may not be uniquely associated with a given functionality. These two different module classifications are shown in Exhibit 9.

A functionality will, by definition, be required to have at least two modules and that at least one of them is an element of the set of uniquely related modules and not of the set of potentially involved modules. That is:

$$f_i \in F \text{ if } \left\| \{ m : M^{f_i} \mid \exists m_j \in M_u \wedge m_j \in M_i \} \right\| > 1$$

If each program module were distinctly associated with a single functionality, then the dynamic behavior of a system could be readily understood and modeled. The two sets M_i and M_s are tightly bound to a distinct functionality. The real problem resides in the set of shared modules M_s and it increases in severity if those modules also belong to M_p. The greater the cardinality of the set of potentially executable modules, the more difficult the task of determining the behavior of a system performing that functionality. In the extreme case, a functionality could express essentially disjoint sets of modules every time it is executed. (Many programs demonstrate this characteristic and they are extremely difficult to test.)

It is clear that each functionality will exercise a certain subset of modules. To return to our example, we can see from Exhibit 10 that functionality f_1 does invoke two modules: m_1, and m_2. Both modules are indispensable to the execution of functionality f_1. Module m_1 is shared with all other functionalities. Module m_2 is uniquely associated with functionality f_1. In Exhibit 10 we can also see that functionality f_3 has some interesting properties. The set $M_p^{(f_3)}$ is nonempty in this case. Whenever we exercise f_3 we can execute from three to five modules. It will be difficult to test this functionality in relation to all other functionalities. Sometimes it will execute module m_5 and sometimes it will not. Sometimes it will execute module m_6 and sometimes it will not. Sometimes it will execute both modules and sometimes it will not.

Sometimes it will be desirable to know what functionality is executing at any given moment. We have built a system that will make such a deduction very difficult. For example, if we have just observed the execution of module m_1, we cannot deduce which functionality we are executing. Similarly, there is an equivalent problem with module m_3. There is somewhat more information in the observation of the execution of module m_6. If we have just observed this module execute, then we will know that we are executing either f_3 or f_4. The case for module m_2 is very different. Whenever we see this module executing, we know for a fact that we are now executing functionality f_1.

Now let us return to the problem of operations. Users see and perform operations. Functionalities are used by systems designers to implement the set of user operations. From the relationships defined above, we can now clearly establish the relationship between user operations and specific modules that will be exercised in response to a user invoking a particular operation. That is, each operation will be implemented by a specific set of functionalities. These functionalities will, in turn, invoke a specific set of modules when they are executed. Thus, for each operation o, we can clearly establish a set of program modules associated with the expression of that operation at runtime.

Each operation is distinctly expressed by a set of functionalities. If a particular operation o is defined by functionalities a and b, then the set of program modules that are bound to operation o is:

$$M^{(o)} = M^{(f_a)} \cup M^{(f_b)}. \text{ More generally, } M^{(o)} = \bigcup_{i=1}^{n} M^{(f_i)}$$

If one operation is to be distinguished from another, then there must be certain aspects of its implementation in functionalities that will be unique. For an operation to be considered distinct, it will be required to have at least one distinct functionality. That is, $o_i \in O$ if the set of distinct functionalities $F_d^{(o_i)}$ defined as:

$$F_d^{(o_i)} = \{f: F^{(o_i)} \mid \forall j \neq i \bullet IMPLEMENTS(o_j, f) \Rightarrow p'(o_j, f) = 0\}$$

has cardinality greater than one.

If we insist that each operation has at least one distinct functionality, then it is possible to identify a set of modules for each operation that is uniquely associated with that operation. This set of modules for operation o_i is:

$$M_u^{(o_i)} = \{m: M \mid f \in F^{(o_i)}, c(f, m) = 1\}$$

Exhibit 11. Modules Associated with Operations

	$M_i^{(o)}$	$M_p^{(o)}$	$M_s^{(o)}$	$M_u^{(o)}$
o_1	$\{m_1,m_3,m_5,m_8\}$	$\{m_2\}$	$\{m_1,m_3,m_5\}$	$\{m_2,m_8\}$
o_2	$\{m_1,m_3,m_5,m_6,m_7\}$	$\{\}$	$\{m_1,m_3,m_5\}$	$\{m_3,m_4,m_6,m_7\}$

When a program is executing a module m, where $m \in M_u^{(o_i)}$, it is quite clear that the user is expressing operation o_i. If we wish to determine exactly what the user is doing at any point, we have only to instrument the set of modules $M_u^{(o)}$. As we receive telemetry from each of the modules so instrumented, the sequence of user operations will be eminently clear.

We can now map the operations in our example to specific program modules. This mapping is shown in Exhibit 11. The specific value of this mapping is twofold. First, if the specification for operation o_1 must be changed, we can identify which modules are associated with this operation. Second, there are certain modules that tag each operation that is, they uniquely identify the operation. If, for example, we saw either module in the set $\{m_2,m_8\}$, we would then know that operation o_1 was currently being executed by the user.

9.6 CONFIGURATION CONTROL FOR THE REQUIREMENTS

In an ideal world, the operational, functional, and module requirements would be placed under configuration control in the same manner as the source code itself. That is, SCCS or RCS can be used in the same manner as for source code to maintain the various versions of each of the requirements elements. The requirements and software specification constitute a living document in exactly the same manner as the source code itself. As the requirements evolve, they must be tracked and managed in precisely the same manner as the source code. Some requirement elements will come and go. The code representing these eliminated versions will also come and go. As the source code base changes, it is extremely important to know which version of which requirement element is represented by the code base. The operational requirements are constantly changing. The functional requirements will also probably change very rapidly. The design elements for the modules representing the functionalities will change as well. The code base itself is a very dynamic document. Each code module must be linked to the specific design element that it represents. As the code changes, so too must the design element. Each design element, in turn, implements one or more functionalities. As the functionalities change, the design elements must change and the code must change. Every version of every operation must be traceable to specific functionalities that, in turn, are traceable to specific modules.

Exhibit 12. System Operational Overview

```
System_Name
System_Operational_Overview
```

Exhibit 13. System Operational Metaphor

```
System_Name
System_Operational
Metaphor
```

Exhibit 14. System Nonoperational Requirements

```
System_Name
System_Non-Operational_Requirement
System_Non_Operational_Requirement_Version
```

It frequently happens that a large software system is imbued with a substantial amount of dead code. This code implements operations or functionalities that have materially changed or have even been eliminated. Without complete requirements traceability at the version level, it is almost impossible to control the problem of dead code. Without complete requirements traceability at the version level, it is almost impossible to determine whether the source code actually implements the current requirements specifications.

For the operational requirements specification, there are three parts. First is the system overview. This is a text document that describes the system from an operational viewpoint. This document will evolve in the same manner as any source code module. It will have an initial version and then incremental changes to the initial version. The same is true for the second part of the operational requirements, the operational systems metaphor. Finally, each operation is a separate entity. It will be maintained as a separate element or module in the configuration control system. The mapping of operations to functionalities $O \times F$ will also be stored under version control. Each operation is a separate module or file in the configuration control system. Every version of every operation is linked specifically to specific versions of one or more functionalities. From a database perspective there are three distinct tables that we will need to represent operational requirements. These are shown in Exhibits 12 through 15.

The contents of Exhibits 12 and 13 are self-explanatory. The important thing here is that these change over time. Different builds of the software will implement different versions of the operational requirements. Changes

Exhibit 15. System Operation Specification

```
System_Name
Operational_Requirement_Number
Operational_Requirement_Description
Functionality_Vector
Functionality_Number
Functionality_Version
```

Exhibit 16. System Functional Overview

```
System_Name
System_Functional_Overview
```

to the source code base will be driven, in part, by changes in the operational requirements. Necessarily, each build must reflect the operations that it implements. Each system may have multiple nonoperational requirements relating to reliability, availability, security, survivability, and performance. For each of these nonoperational requirements, there will be a separate instance of the system nonoperational requirements relation. This information is reflected in Exhibit 14.

Exhibit 15 is really the meat of the operational requirements code. Each operation is a separately managed requirements element and has a unique requirements number. If, at any point, any one operational requirement is deleted, the original requirement number will still index the old requirement element. Each operation is implemented by one or more functionality. These functionalities will be known by their unique numeric identifiers. Each version of each operation will be implemented by one or more functionalities. These functionalities are also dynamic. They will change and be updated. As any one of the functionalities is updated, any of the operations that it implements must also be updated to reflect the new version of the functionality. In this manner we can ensure that the latest version of each operational specification references the most recent versions of the functionalities that implement it.

The case for the maintenance of the functionalities is similar to that of the operations. Exhibits 16 and 17 essentially duplicate the tables for the operations shown in Exhibits 12 and 13. Again, there may well be nonfunctional requirements that relate to specific implementation environments. These data are associated with the functional overview.

As was the case for the operational requirements, there will generally be system nonfunctional requirements as well. These nonfunctional require-

Exhibit 17. System Functional Metaphor

```
System_Name
System_Functional Metaphor
```

Exhibit 18. System Non-Functional Requirements

```
System_Name
System_Non-Functional_Requirements
System_Non-Functional_Requirements_Version
```

ments will involve such things as the operating systems environment, specific hardware requirements, and hardware/software interface requirements. For each of these requirements there will be an instance of the system nonfunctional requirements relation. This information is shown in Exhibit 18. Again, as a system evolves, it is reasonable to suspect that the nonfunctional requirements will evolve as well. Thus, it is also important to keep version information.

As was the case for each of the operations, each of the system functional specifications is kept as a separate instance in the database. The structure of this relation is different from that of the system operational specification. For the functionalities, there is a bidirectional mapping. This can be seen in Exhibit 5. From this exhibit, we can see that Operation 1 is implemented in Functionalities 1 and 2. Functionality 2, however, is also used in the implementation of Operation 2. Thus, whenever Functionality 2 changes, it gets a new version number and the corresponding system operational specifications (for Operations 1 and 2) are updated with the new version number of Functionality 2. This, in turn, creates a new version of the operational specifications in the system functional specifications. Necessarily, to prevent cyclical updating problems, the operation version numbers must be updated simultaneously with the changes in the functionality requirement description.

There is an instance of the system functional specification for each functionality. The structure of this relation is shown in Exhibit 19. This table entry shows the precise structure of the linkage that will permit the operations to map to functionalities and the functionalities to map to operations. Similarly, this table will provide the structure for the mapping of functionalities to specific modules and modules to functionalities. If a particular functionality is used to implement three operations, then there will be three elements in the `Implements_Operation_Vector` for that functionality. Each element will consist of the identifying number of the operation together with the latest version of that operation. Similarly, if two mod-

Exhibit 19. System Functional Specification

```
System_Name
Functionality_Requirement_Number
Functionality_Requirement_Description
Implements_Operations_Vector
Operation_Number
Operation_Version
Implemented_By_Modules_Vector
Module_Number
Module_Version
```

ules are required to implement a functionality, then there will be two entries in the `Implemented_By_Modules_Vector`.

The contents of the Exhibit 19 embody the mapping for both the $O \times F$ and the $F \times M$. Of greater importance from a software maintenance perspective is the $M \times F \times O$ mapping that is also possible. One of the central problems in altering any low-level design element is trying to determine the scope of the change; that is, which functionalities and operations will be impacted by a change in the design at the module level. It might well be that a change in a functionality will mandate a change in one or more modules. The real question is what other functionalities (and operations) will also be impacted by this change. With the inverse mapping of modules to operations, the impact of any low-level change can easily be determined. Another real maintenance issue solved by this mapping occurs when an operation (or functionality) is removed from the requirements specification altogether. If there are modules that are uniquely associated with a particular operation and that operation is deleted, then all the modules that are unique to this operation must also be deleted. If one or more such modules are left in the build, these will essentially be dead code. There will be no functionality that will exercise them.

Each functionality is implemented by one or more design modules. The design specification for each of these modules is also kept under configuration control in the same manner as the operational requirement specifications and the functional requirements specifications. The relation for the module specification was shown earlier in Exhibit 4. The essential element of the module element pertinent to this discussion is the `Call_Section`. This is a very important section in that the call structure of the program can be found here. As we can see from Exhibit 20, Module 1 can call Modules 2 and 3. Module 3, on the other hand, is called by Module 1 and calls Modules 3 and 5.

As can be seen in Exhibit 20, there is a one-to-one mapping of design module instances to code modules. Each code module implements exactly

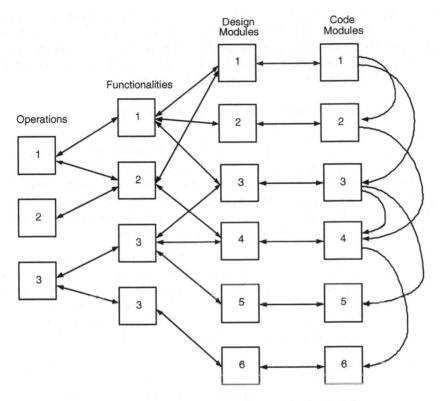

Exhibit 20. Mapping of Operations to Code Modules

the design. There will be little or no need to comment the code module in any way. Anything we wish to know about the code module can be obtained from the design specification (such as domains for local data variables) or the configuration control system (such as developer name).

Just as was the case for the functional specification and the operational specification, each design module instance is kept under version control in precisely the same manner. Each time there are updates to a particular design module, the version change is back-propagated to the affected functionalities. After the design module instance has been modified, then and only then will the associated code module be changed.

Just about any large, modern software system is a maintenance nightmare. This is because there is absolutely no engineering blueprint for the code. It has been carefully crafted by a team (sometimes a hoard) of developers. No modern hardware system would be so crafted. There are elaborate design specifications for modern office buildings. There are astonishingly complex design documents on modern integrated circuits. It would be unthinkable to modify one of these two structures without first updating the blueprints or design documents. It should be equally unthinkable to do this same thing with code. We do not empower carpenters to make design decisions on the buildings we are constructing. They merely implement the design. The same discipline should be enforced on software developers as well.

9.7 MEASURING SOFTWARE DESIGN ALTERNATIVES

From a statistical perspective there are at least three degrees of freedom in the design process. One degree of freedom is attributable to the manner in which the several program modules will be executed. We could, for example, design a program in which all of the functionality is implemented in a small number of the total program modules. On the other hand, we might choose to distribute the functionality across a large number of program modules. The entropy of the design will measure this.

The second degree of freedom in design relates to the complexity of the program modules. We might be able to choose from a series of design alternatives that express the complexity of the set of functionalities in different ways in differing modular structures. This will be measured by the modular complexity of the design. We can think of the design process as one of parsing the functional complexity of our design to particular program modules.

The third degree of freedom is related to the choice of functional alternatives for the high-level design. The interesting thing about the design problem is that there are many different ways to implement a set of operational specifications from a functional viewpoint. The important thing, from a user's perspective, is that all of the different functional approaches create exactly the same operational metaphor. Some of the functional solutions will result in very complex functional metaphors. These complex metaphors will, in turn, create very complex modular structures. A good functional design is one that minimizes the complexity of the functional metaphor or the design functional complexity.

9.7.1 Design Module Complexity

There are many design trade-offs. We can, for example, choose to write a small number of program modules. This will make each module relatively large and very complex. The total module coupling complexity will be very small in this case. At the other extreme, we can decompose our task into lots of very small program modules. In this case, the complexity of each module will tend to be very low. The total system coupling complexity will, however, be astonishingly large. This type of design alternative is one that very naturally emerges in the object-oriented design metaphor.

Unfortunately, we do not know the consequences of the various design alternatives. We do not know, for example, whether low coupling complexity and high module complexity is to be preferred over high coupling complexity and low module complexity. The science simply has not been done. If we are to make sound engineering decisions about our design alternatives, then we must first do the necessary science to evaluate the various alternatives.

9.7.2 Design Functional Complexity

As previously indicated, there are a number of metrics that we can gather from the low-level modular design of a system. We can begin to measure some very important properties of control flow complexity, coupling complexity, and data structures complexity. More often than not, it is not entirely apparent to us, when we are at the early stage of design, which of the many functional design alternatives are most suitable for our operational metaphor. If we choose the wrong (inappropriate) functional metaphor during the design stage, we can potentially pay a very high price for this choice over the life of the software product we are developing.

We now have at our disposal a means of measuring the complexity of a design specifically in terms of the potential total fault burden of that design. The fault index (FI) presented in Chapter 5 is a criterion measure that we can use in this regard.

As per the earlier discussion of FI, it can be seen that it is possible to characterize a program module by a single value such as FI. Many of the metrics we will use to form FI are, in fact, available to us when we have finished our specification of the low-level design at the module specification stage. We can begin our measurement process at this stage, in advance of actually creating the code. The preliminary FI measure ρ of a module is a leading indicator. When a program is executing, not every one of its modules will receive the same level of exposure. This is evident in the concept of execution profile. Some executions might result in very complex program modules being executed. Other program input stimuli may cause the program to execute only its least complex modules.

There is, then, a dynamic aspect to program complexity that is related to its entropy under a particular test scenario. The design functional complexity ϕ_q of a system with a known functional profile is then:

$$\phi_q = \sum_{j=1}^{n} q_j \rho_j$$

where ρ_j is the fault index of the jth program module and qj is the execution probability of this module under a given functional profile. This is simply the expected value of the fault index under a particular execution profile.

The execution profile for a program can be expected to change across the set of program functionalities. That is, for each functionality, f_i, there is an execution profile represented by the probabilities $p_1^i, p_2^i, p_3^i, \cdots, p_n^i$. As a consequence, there will be a functional complexity ϕ_i for each function f_i execution, where:

$$\phi_i = \sum_{j=1}^{n} p_j^i \rho_j$$

This is distinctly the case during the test phase when the program is subjected to numerous test suites to exercise differing aspects of its functionality. The functional complexity of a system will vary greatly as a result of the execution of these different test suites.

Given the relationship between complexity and embedded faults, we would expect the failure intensity to rise as the functional complexity increases. If an application is chosen in such a manner that there are high execution probabilities for the complex modules, then the functional complexity will be large and the likelihood of a failure event during this interval will be relatively high. In Exhibit 20, the operation of a hypothetical software system executing various functionalities across time is presented. From this exhibit we would expect the software failures to be directly related to those periods when the functional complexity is high.

There are two degrees of freedom in the determination of system functional complexity. First, the functional complexity will vary in accordance with the functionality being executed. It will also vary as a function of the reconstitution of the software over builds. Thus, the functional complexity for function f_i, at the jth build represented by v^j will be:

$$\phi_i^j = \sum_{k=1}^{N_j} p_k^i \rho_k^{v_k^j}$$

where N_j represents the cardinality of v^j and v_k^j is the kth element of this vector.

It is possible to simulate the functional complexity for various execution profiles for different design alternatives and thus measure their likely failure intensity. To model correctly the reliability of a software system we will necessarily have determined the functionality of the program and how these functions will interact as the program executes. The latter information not only directs the formation of test suites but also provides the information necessary to formulate execution profiles. The functionalities that imply execution profiles which cause the functional complexity to increase merit our attention because these are the conditions that will increase failure rates for a given design.

9.7.3 Testability

Testability is a term that has been much used and little defined in the software testing community. We can now begin to define and quantify this term in terms of our understanding of the distribution of functionality to program modules. If we were to write a system that always exercised all of its modules, it would be a relatively simple matter to test all of the modules in the system. On the other hand, if we were to build a system that seldom or occasionally used some of the constituent program modules, then it would be pretty difficult to test this system because the circumstances that would cause our shy modules to execute might be obscure or ill defined.

Remember that the cardinality of the set of potentially invoked modules for a functionality f_i was denoted by $\left\| M_p^{(f_i)} \right\|$. Then, for a system of k functionalities, we can find the set M_p of all modules that are potentially invoked by at least one functionality; that is, by

$$M_p = \bigcup_{i=1}^{k} M_p^{(f_i)} .$$

We can also identify the set of those modules M_i that are indispensable to at least one functionality; that is, by

$$M_i = \bigcup_{j=1}^{k} M_i^{(f_j)} .$$

Now we wish to identify the set of modules M_p' that are also not in the set of indispensable modules for at least one functionality. There is a set of modules M_a that are in the intersection set $M_a = M_p \cap M_i$. If we remove this intersection set M_a from the set of modules M_p, we are left with the set M_p' to wit: $M_p' = M_p - M_a$. The cardinality of the set M_p' is $l = \left\| M_p' \right\|$.

The cardinality l of M_p', in relation to the total number of program modules n, is certainly one attribute dimension of the concept of testability. We could formalize this as $\tau = l / n$. A system where τ is relatively small will have a relatively high testability attribute, testability being inversely related to the cardinality of the set of modules M_p'.

The concept of testability is a multidimensional problem. There are many attributes for testability. One attribute dimension certainly relates to poor design choices that create large sets of modules M_p'. As we progress in our understanding of measurement, other aspects of program testability will become clear.

9.8 MAINTAINABILITY

The term "maintainability" has been widely used in the software engineering literature. It is clear from this discussion that maintainability is certainly a desirable property for a system to have. The main problem with maintainability is that no one really knows what it means. As a result, it is a difficult term to quantify. In the past, many people thought that the number of comment statements in code were somehow related to maintainability although there were no scientific studies to support this conclusion. Alternatively, the amount of documentation (presumably measured in kilograms) that a program had was supposed to relate directly to maintainability although, again, there were no scientific studies to this effect.

There are really three different aspects of software maintenance: adaptive, corrective, and perfective.[2] In the case of adaptive maintenance, the code base will change because the requirements, functional or operational, have changed. In the case of corrective maintenance, the code or requirements change because they were not the correct ones. The simplest case is where the code does not implement the module specification. In the case where the requirement is at fault, then the corrective maintenance problem means that the change might propagate from an operational requirement to one or more functional requirements, to multiple module specifications, and thence to a host of code modules. Finally, there is perfective maintenance. In this case the operational requirements and functional requirements are adequate but that certain nonfunctional system requirements such as performance can be enhanced. This will likely occur through a change in an algorithm in one or more module specifications.

We would like to be able to quantify the term "maintainability." It is clear that a system will have good maintainability if we can perform adaptive, corrective, and perfective updates to the system with a minimum of human effort. We can take a cue from modern engineering practice in this regard. A modern office building has a vast complex of blueprints that describe how its various systems are laid out. Good building maintenance discipline suggests that anytime there is a change in any of the subsystems, the blueprints will be modified to reflect the changes that have been made. The larger the building, the more complex the maintenance task. Regardless of how large and complex the building might be, future maintenance efforts are mitigated by maintaining the precise mapping between the building blueprints and the building as it currently exists.

With the mapping of operations to functionalities to modules, it is clear that we can know which modules are used to implement each functionality and each operation. Should we need to change either an operational requirement or a functional specification, we can know which modules will be impacted with this change. Similarly, if a code module does not function

Exhibit 21. Maintainability Attributes

- Requirements traceability
- Number of system operational specifications
- Number of system functional specifications
- Number of system module specifications
- Operation to functionality mapping
- Functionality to module mapping
- Number of arcs in the call graph
- Average number of arcs in module flowgraphs
- Average number of nodes in module flowgraphs

appropriately, we can know which functional or operational specifications are linked to that code module. In this context, each source code module can be linked directly to a single design module specification. Further, each data declaration in the source code module is linked to a data description in the design module. We can also insist that each source code statement be linked to a particular statement or element in the design module algorithm pseudo-code.

With the configuration control for the design specification as discussed in Section 9.6, it is now possible to identify and quantify the attributes of software maintainability. These are listed in Exhibit 21.

The question of operational granularity always arises. It is clearly possible to define a system with one operation implemented with one functionality implemented by one huge design module, in turn implemented by one huge FORTRAN main program. Life is full of trade-offs. The greater the granularity of the operational definition of the system, the more complex the average module flowgraphs become. Granularity of specification is not really the issue that it might seem. Quite simply, specifications should be parsed until they can be parsed no further. At the lowest level, the module, parsing a module into two components will certainly decrease the flowgraph complexity of the module. It will also increase the coupling complexity of that module.

9.8.1 Requirements Traceability

The foundation of requirements traceability is that every attribute of a source code module can be mapped to a specific requirement. Furthermore, each operational requirement can be mapped directly to a set of source code modules. In that we have to start somewhere, we will first look at the mapping from the source code module to the design.

1. Every variable in a source code module is defined in the low-level design module with a variable declaration.

241

2. Every statement in the source code module has a pseudo-code equivalent in the module specification.
3. Every called module in the source code module is listed in the `Call_Section` of the module specification.
4. Some elements of the module design specification are not obvious from the source code.Every module that can call a module is listed in the `Call_Section` of the module specification.

Next, we will turn our attention to the mapping at the functional level.

5. Every design module specification will be referenced by at least one system functional specification.
6. That reference will contain the most current version of the design module specification.
7. Every system functional specification will reference at least one operational specification.
8. The reference to each operational specification will contain the most current version number.

At the level of the system operational specification, we would like to ensure that the links are in place for the mapping to the system functional specifications.

9. Every system operational specification will reference at least one functional specification.
10. The reference to each functional specification will contain the most current version number.

It will not be possible to measure the completeness of the traceability mapping from operations to modules or modules to operations. Sometimes, missing links are made visible through the evolution process when code modules appear that are not traceable to operational specifications or operational specifications that have no associated code modules.

9.8.2 Operational Specification

A very simple system will have but one operation in it. Most logically, this operation would probably read something like this: STOP. Every other system that we might conceive will be more complex than this one. A simple count of the number of user operations is a good leading indicator of the maintainability of a system. That is, maintainability is inversely related to the number of operations that the system can perform.

9.8.3 Functional Specification

Each operation must have at least one functionality associated with it. In most cases, there will probably be many functionalities associated with each operation. Thus, as the operational complexity increases, so too will the functional complexity of the maintenance task. It is clear, then, that the maintainability of a system is also inversely related to the number of functionalities required to implement the set of operations.

9.8.4 Module Specification

Each functionality must have at least one module specification associated with it. Again, there will probably be many modules associated with each functionality. Thus, as the operational complexity increases, so too will the functional complexity, which will also cause an attendant increase of module complexity and, hence, of the maintenance task. It is clear, then, that the maintainability of a system is also inversely related to the number of modules required to implement the set of functionalities.

9.8.5 First-Order Mapping

There are really two levels of first-order mapping between operations and modules: (1) the mappings of operations to functionalities, and (2) the mapping of functionalities to modules. We can represent each operation, functionality, and module as one node in a graph. Each node in the set of operations is connected by an arc to at least one node in the set of functionality; this is a first-order mapping. Similarly, each functionality is similarly connected by an arc to at least one module.

In the most simple case, each operation with be implemented with exactly one functionality and that functionality will be implemented with precisely one module. In this case, for a system of n operations, there will be $2n$ nodes in the first-order mapping from operations to functionalities and n arcs between these nodes. As the system becomes more complex, there will be an increase in the complexity of the connections between the operations and functionalities. This will no longer be a simple one-to-one connection and there will be $m > n$ arcs in the graph. When m is substantially greater than n, it is clear that the complexity of the relationship between operations and functionalities has risen. Anytime a functionality is modified, this change will impact more than one operation. Hence, m is a good indicator of this maintainability attribute. Again, the maintainability of the system is inversely related to m.

Exactly the same argument can be made for the first -order mapping of functionalities to modules. If there are n functionalities, then the simplest mapping to modules will lead to n modules. If there are more modules, say k, than functionalities, then there must be at least k arcs connecting these two sets. As the relationship between the set of functionalities and modules increases in complexity, the number of arcs will also increase. Let l represent this new value of arcs where $l > k$. This new value l representing the number of arcs is also a measure of the maintainability of the system. Maintainability is inversely related to l as well.

9.8.6 Second-Order Mapping

There is also a second-order mapping of operations to modules. We can characterize this relationship with a graph of n_1 operations, n_2 functionalities, and n_3 modules, for a total of $N = n_1 + n_2 + n_3$ nodes. Connecting the sets of operations and functionalities, there are m_1 arcs. Connecting the sets of functionalities and modules there are m_2 arcs, for a total of $M = m_1 + m_2$ arcs. Intuitively, the maintainability of the complete system will be inversely proportional to both N and M.

9.8.7 Call Graph Structure

As the structure of a program becomes more complex, the modules interact to an increasing extent with one another. This interaction can be represented through a call graph as discussed in Chapter 5. The simplest call graph of a software system composed of n modules will have n nodes and $n-1$ arcs connecting them. There will be but one main program module and one leaf node module in this graph. All other nodes will have one entering edge and one exiting edge. From the standpoint of intramodule complexity, this is the most simple call graph structure, the most easily understood, and, thus, the most maintainable. The complexity of the call graph can only get worse. The number of nodes in this call graph is fixed. The number of arcs is not. If c represents the actual number of arcs in the flowgraph, where $c > n-1$, then the call graph maintainability attribute is inversely proportional to c.

9.8.8 Module Flowgraph Structure

As previously discussed for a problem of fixed computational complexity, there is a trade-off between the modularity of the implementation of the problem and the internal flowgraph complexity of the module. That is, we can build a program with but one very complex module or we can have a program with a lot of very simple modules with regard to their internal structure. A module with a very bushy control flowgraph will be very difficult to maintain. This complexity was represented by the number of *Nodes, Edges,* and *Paths* and in the flowgraph representation of the program module. It is clear that these values are, in a sense, complementary to the call graph values. They are inversely related.

9.8.9 Measuring Maintainability Attributes

There are clearly several distinct maintainability attributes. The above list is probably not at all exhaustive. What we have done, however, is to define maintainability attributes that can be measured. That is the first step in understanding the nature of the maintainability beast. We should be wise enough at this point to know that we cannot simply add the maintainability attribute values together to compute some arbitrary maintainability index.

Each attribute has its own measure. These attribute domains are, in fact, potential dependent variables in the modeling process that we will engage in to understand how maintainability might be related to other software quality attributes.

References

1, Elbaum, S.G. and Munson, J.C., Investigating Software Failures with a Software Blackbox, *Proceedings of the 2000 IEEE Aerospace Applications Conference,* IEEE Computer Society Press, November 2000.

2. Pigoski, T.M., *Practical Software Maintenance*, John Wiley & Sons, New York, 1997.

Chapter 10
Dynamic Software Measurement

10.1 INTRODUCTION

Measuring software that is running is a very expensive proposition. The data bandwidth of this process is very large. Unless these data can be filtered in some meaningful way, just the simple task of saving them for future reference can consume a vast number of compute cycles. Data mining on-the-fly will be prohibitively expensive. We must know why we are measuring before we start.

There are a couple of very good reasons to measure systems that are running. First, we can monitor their activity in real-time to ensure that the software is performing in a normal way. If users are forcing a system into some new execution territory, at best they may be inadvertently pushing the system into new and uncertified execution territory and at worst they may be trying to penetrate the security of the system. Second, it is very useful to know what code we have touched during the course of the execution of a specific test. Any observation of code activity, however, must be seen for what it is. The activity that we observe in the code is a reflection of user activity. We will be measuring the code to determine how it is being used. We are not measuring the code for code coverage. That is measurement for measurement's sake. We do not care that all code in a program has been touched in some way during its certification. We do care that the code can do what the user will request of it. Our interest in code measurement will be in what we will learn about the functionality of the program.

By keeping track of the state transitions from module to module and operation to operation we can learn exactly where a system is fragile. This information, coupled with the operational profile, will tell us just how reliable the system will be when we use it as specified. Programs make transitions from module to module as they execute. These transitions can be observed and we can model these transitions as a stochastic process. Ultimately, by developing a mathematical description for the behavior of the software as it transitions from one module to another driven by the operations that it is performing, we can effectively measure what the user is doing with the system.

247

As a program is exercising any one of its many operations in the normal course of execution of the program, the user will apportion his time across a set of operations.[1] The proportion of execution activity that the user spends in each operation is the *operational profile* of the program. The proportion of time that a program spends in each of its functionalities is the *functional profile* of the program. Further, within the functionality, it will apportion its activities across one to many program modules. This distribution of processing activity is represented by the concept of the execution profile. That is, if we have a program structured into n distinct modules, the *execution profile* for a given functionality will be the proportion of program activity for each program module while the function is being expressed.

10.2 A STOCHASTIC DESCRIPTION OF PROGRAM OPERATION

When a user begins the execution of an operation, say o_1, we can envision this beginning as the start of a stochastic process. The execution of o_1 will be followed by a sequence of operations chosen by the user from the set of all operations, O. Each of these operations, in turn, will be implemented at the functional level by a set of functionalities, as per the discussion in Chapter 9. Each of the functionalities will initiate a cascade of activity in an associated set of program modules. The nature of the activity in the set of program modules is determined directly by the sequence of operations that the user elects to do. In short, a sequence of operations performed by the user will cause a sequence of modules to execute.

10.2.1 The Concept of an Epoch

The sense of real-time (or clock time) does not really exist for computer software. Time is relevant only to the hardware on which the software will execute. A given piece of software can run in many different environments on many difference machines. Some machines may be fast while others are very slow. The consequences of execution of the software will be the same in each of these environments. The notion of clock time in this highly variable environment is neither pertinent nor relevant. The simple fact is that computer software does not exist in our four-dimensional world.

We will, however, need to have some sense of the order in which activities occur. We will use the term "epoch" to provide this order. The transition in the user's environment from one operation to another will be an operational epoch. The transition from one functionality to another will be a functional epoch. Finally, the transition from one module to another is a module epoch. We will measure the duration of a user's interaction with the system in terms of operational epochs. We will measure the duration of system activity in terms of module epochs.

10.2.2 Program Execution as a Stochastic Process

The transition from one mutually exclusive element of the system to another can be described as a *stochastic process*. The system elements, of course, can be user operations, expressions of functionalities, or module executions, in which case we can define an indexed collection of random variables $\{X_t\}$, where the index t runs through a set of non-negative integers, $t = 0,1,2,\ldots$, representing the epochs of the process. At any particular epoch the software is found to be executing exactly one of its M possible elements. The fact of the execution occurring in a particular element of a set of operations, functionalities, or modules is a *state* of the system. For this software system, the system is found in exactly one of a finite number of mutually exclusive and exhaustive states that can be labeled $0,1,2,\ldots,M$. In this representation of the system, there is a stochastic process $\{X_t\}$, where the random variables are observed at epochs $t = 0,1,2,\ldots$ and where each random variable may take on any one of the $(M+I)$ integers, from the state space $A = \{0,1,2,\ldots,M\}$, the set of program modules. The elements of **P** are then $P_{ij} = \Pr[X_n = j \,|\, X_{n-1} = i]$.

Interestingly enough, for all software systems there is a distinguished event that represents the start of the stochastic process. In the case of a set of program modules, for example, the main program module that will always receive execution control from the operating system. If we denote this main program as module 0, then, $\Pr[X_0 = 0] = 1$ and $\Pr[X_0 = i] = 0$ for $i = 1,2,\ldots,M$. Further, for module epoch 1, $\Pr[X_1 = 0] = 0$, in that control will have been transferred from the main program module to another function module.

10.3 THE PROFILES OF SOFTWARE DYNAMICS

When a system is exercised by a particular user, this person will exhibit a characteristic distribution of activity across the set of operations O. Some of the operations will occur with a greater likelihood than others. The distribution of user activity across the set of operations will constitute the *operational profile* of that user. The operational profile is a characteristic of the user. Each operation, in turn, will cause the activity of a certain set of functionalities as described by the $O \times F$ mapping. Therefore, a particular operational profile will induce a particular distribution of activity on the program functionalities. This distribution of activity across the set of functionalities is called the *functional profile*. The functional profile is dependent on the operational profile. Each module is exercised by one or more functionalities, as described by the $F \times M$ mapping. The functional profile will induce a particular distribution of activity on the set of program modules. This distribution of activity in the module is called the *module profile*. The module profile is dependent on the functional profile, which is, in turn, dependent on the operational profile. If we simply monitor the distribution of the activity of a program among its program modules for an arbitrary number of module epochs, we can characterize the operation of the system during this interval in an *execution profile*.

10.3.1 Operational Profile

When a software system is constructed by the software developer, it is designed to fulfill a set of specific business requirements. The user will run the software to perform a set of perceived operations. In this process, the user will typically not use all of the operations with the same probability. The *design operational profile* of the software system is the set of unconditional probabilities of each of the operations O being executed by the user. Let Z be a random variable defined on the indices of the set of elements of O. Then, $o_l = \Pr[Z = l], l = 1, 2, \ldots, \|O\|$ is the probability that the user is executing an operation l as specified in the business requirements of the program and $\|O\|$ is the cardinality of the set of operations. A user can only be executing one operation at a time. The distribution of $\boldsymbol{o}$, then, is multinomial for programs designed to fulfill more than two distinct operations.

As we will discover, considerable effort should be directed toward understanding just what the software should do for the user (the set of operations) and how the user will select among the operations. The prior knowledge of this distribution of the operational profile should be a principal guide to the software design process.[2] It seems improbable that we would not wish to know how a system will be used before we build it. Imagine, if you will, if the designers of the Golden Gate Bridge had lacked this foresight when they built that bridge. They clearly had to anticipate both the projected traffic for the bridge and the weight of that traffic on the bridge to build the right bridge.

The design operational profile is a single point in an n-dimensional space. It is, in fact, the centroid in a range of possible departures from the design operational profile. That is, each user will use the system in a slightly different manner. This will create a slightly different operational profile represented by a different point. Let O^d represent the design operational profile. Each user will have a slightly different behavior represented by an operational profile, say O^u. It is possible to compute the distance between a user's operational profile and the design operation profile as

$$d = \sum_{i=1}^{n} \left(o_i^d - o_i^u \right)^2$$

where n represents the number of operations and $0 \le d \le 2$.

In that no two users will use the system in exactly the same way, it is necessary to understand the distribution of the distances, d. Let d_i represent the distance between a particular operational profile for user, i, and the design operational profile. We can then talk about the average distance

$$\bar{d} = \frac{1}{m} \sum_i d_i$$

for a group of m users and the variance of this distance across all users,

$$Var(d) = \frac{1}{m} \sum_i (d_i - \bar{d})^2$$

The real problem, from a design perspective, is that we really do not know what the mean and variance of these distances will be when the system is developed. There are two distinct solutions to this dilemma. First, we can conduct a controlled experiment to develop reasonable estimates of what these statistics will be. Second, we can design a *robust* system. A robust system is one that will work reliably in the face of large values of *Var(d)* when the system is deployed.

10.3.2 Functional Profile

When a software system is constructed by the software developer, it is designed to fulfill a set of specific functional requirements. The user will run the software to perform a set of perceived operations. In this process, the user will typically not use all of the functionalities with the same probability. The functional profile of the software system is the set of unconditional probabilities of each of the functionalities F being executed by the user. Let Y be a random variable defined on the indices of the set of elements of F. Then, $q_k = \Pr[Y = k], k = 1, 2, \ldots, \|F\|$ is the probability that the user is executing program functionality k as specified in the functional requirements of the program and $\|F\|$ is the cardinality of the set of functions. A program executing on a serial machine can only be executing one functionality at a time. The distribution of q, then, is multinomial for programs designed to fulfill more than two specific functions.

The q_k are dependent on how the user distributes his time across the suite of system operations. We can observe and understand the conditional probability distribution of the functionalities to wit: $w_{kl} = \Pr[Y_n = k | Z = l]$. That is, if we know the particular operation being performed, then we can determine the distribution of activity among the various functionalities.

The joint probability that a given operation is being expressed and the system is exercising a particular functionality is given by:

$$\Pr[Y_n = j \cap Z = l] = \Pr[z = l]\Pr[Y_n = j | Z = l] = o_l w_{jl}$$

where k is the index for the set of functionalities and l is the index for the set of operations. Thus, the unconditional probability q_i of executing functionality i under a particular operational profile is:

$$q_i = \Pr[Y_n = i]$$

$$= \sum_k \Pr[Y_n = i \cap Z = l]$$

$$= \sum_k o_l w_{il}$$

As was the case for the functional profile and the execution profile, only one module can be executing at any one time. Hence, the distribution of q is also multinomial for a system consisting of more than two modules.

10.3.3 Module Profiles

The manner in which a program will exercise its many modules as the user chooses to execute the functionalities of the program is determined directly by the design of the program. Indeed, this mapping of functionality onto program modules is the overall objective of the design process. The module profile p is the unconditional probability that a particular module will be executed based on the design of the program. Let X be a random variable defined on the indices of the set of elements of M, the set of program modules. Then, $p_k = \Pr[X = j], y = 1, 2, \ldots \|M\|$ is the unconditional probability that the user is executing program module k as specified in the functional requirements of the program and $\|M\|$ is the cardinality of the set of functionalities. The problem is that the module profile is not known. We can, however, determine the conditional probability of execution of a module, $u_{jk} = \Pr[X_n = j | Y = k]$. It can be observed by causing each of the functionalities to execute.

The joint probability that a given module is executing and the program is exercising a particular function is given by:

$$\Pr[X_n = j \cap Y = k] = \Pr[Y = k]\Pr[X_n = j | Y = k] = q_k u_{jk}$$

where j is the index of the module and k is the index of the functionality. Thus, the unconditional probability p_i of executing module j under a particular design is:

$$p_i = \Pr[X_n = i]$$

$$= \sum_k \Pr[X_n = i \cap Y = k]$$

$$= \sum_k o_k u_{ik}$$

As was the case for the functional profile and the operational profile, only one event, in this case a module, can be executing at any one time. Hence, the distribution of q is also multinomial for a system consisting of more than two modules.

It is clear that p_i is dependent on the functional profile. The functional profile is, in turn, dependent on the operational profile. Remember that $q_i = \sum_l o_l w_{il}$ and that $p_i = \sum_k q_k u_{ik}$. It then follows that:

$$p_i = \sum_k u_{ik} \sum_l o_l w_{kl}$$

10.3.4 Test Profiles

It often happens that software test activity is not based on the operational view of the system. Indeed, specific functionalities are exercised during these test activities quite independent of the distribution of the operational profile. The objective of this test activity is to verify or certify a functional aspect of the system as opposed to an operational aspect. During this test activity several functionalities may be exercised as a unit as a specific test case in a test plan. The specific module activity during this test activity will be described by a *test profile*.

When a program is executing a given functionality, say f_k, it will distribute its activity across the set of modules, M_{f_k}. At any arbitrary module epoch n, the program will be executing a module with a probability $u_{ik} = \Pr[X_n = i \mid Y = k]$. The set of conditional probabilities where $k = 1,2,\ldots,\#\{F\}$ constitute the test profile for function f_k. As was the case with the functional profile, the distribution of the test profile is also multinomial for a software system consisting of more than two modules.

Both the module profile and the test profile describe the activity of the system in terms of module granularity. The module profile represents the steady-state behavior of the system under a given operational profile. This is very different from the test profile. The test activity is driven by functional test objectives and not the operational profile. A test profile, then, is an artifact of a particular test and not an artifact of the software architecture and use.

Remember that as a function of the design of a program, there may be a nonempty set $M_p^{(f)}$ of modules that may or may not be executed when a particular functionality is exercised. This will, of course, cause the cardinality of the set M_f to vary. Some test activity, for example, may cause a particular module in the set $M_p^{(f)}$ to execute while other test activity exercising the same functionality will not cause this module to be expressed. In one extreme case, the test activity may not invoke any of the modules of $M_p^{(f)}$. On the other hand, all of the modules in $M_p^{(f)}$ may participate in the execution of a test scenario. Among other things, this variation in the cardinality of M_f within the execution of a single functionality will contribute significantly to the amount of test effort that will be necessary to test such a functionality.

The test profiles will map the activity of a system when it has been tested in a particular way. It will show us what modules have executed and the relative proportion of test activity attributed to each. This is part of the picture for the evaluation of a test. Static measurement is the other part of the test picture. Dynamic measurements will tell us where we executed; static measurements will tell us where the faults are likely to be. By combining these two measurements we will be able to evaluate the effectiveness of a particular test.

10.4 ESTIMATES FOR PROFILES

Now we know what our measurement objectives are. We wish to know the operational, functional, and module profiles. Unfortunately, these data are known only to Nature, who is not anxious to share her knowledge of these profiles with us. We can never know the real distribution of these three things. We can, however, develop reasonable estimates for the profiles.

The focus will now shift to the problem of understanding the nature of the distribution of the probabilities for various profiles. We have thus far come to recognize these profiles in terms of their multinomial nature. This multinomial distribution is useful for representing the outcome of an experiment involving a set of mutually exclusive events. Let

$$S = \bigcup_{i=1}^{M} S_i$$

where S_i is one of M mutually exclusive sets of events. Each of these events would correspond to a program executing a particular module in the total set of program modules. Further, let

$$\Pr(S_i) = w_i$$

$$w_T = 1 - w_1 - w_2 - \cdots - w_M$$

where $T = M + 1$. In this case, w_i is the probability that the outcome of a random experiment is an element of the set S_i. If this experiment is conducted over a period of n trials, then the random variable X_i will represent the frequency of S_i outcomes. In this case, the value n represents the number of transitions from one program module to the next. Note that:

$$X_T = n - X_1 - X_2 - \cdots - X_m$$

This particular distribution will be useful in the modeling of a program with a set of k modules. During a set of n program steps, each of the modules can be executed. These, of course, are mutually exclusive events. If module i is executing, then module j cannot be executing.

The multinomial distribution function with parameters n and $w = (w_1, w_2, \ldots, w_T)$ is given by:

$$f(x_1, x_2, \cdots, x_{k-1}) = \begin{cases} \dfrac{n!}{x_1! x_2! \cdots x_{k-1}!} p^{x_1} p^{x_2} \cdots p^{x_{k-1}}, & (x_1, x_2, \cdots, x_{k-1}) \in S \\ 0 & \text{elsewhere} \end{cases}$$

where x_i represents the frequency of execution of the ith program module.

The expected values for the x_i are given by:

$$E(x_i) = \bar{x}_i = nw_i, i = 1, 2, \ldots, k$$

the variances by:

$$Var(x_i) = nw_i(1 - w_i)$$

and the covariance by:

$$Cov(w_i, w_j) = -nw_i w_j, i \neq j$$

We would like to come to understand, for example, the multinomial distribution of a program's execution profile while it is executing a particular functionality. The problem here is that every time a program is run, we will observe that there is some variation in the profile from one execution sample to the next. It will be difficult to estimate the parameters $w = (w_1, w_2, \ldots, w_T)$ for the multinomial distribution of the execution profile. Rather than estimating these parameters statically, it would be far more useful to us to get estimates of these parameters dynamically as the program is actually in operation. In essence, we would like to watch the system execute, collect data, and stop when we know that we have enough information about the profiles to satisfy our needs.

Unfortunately, for the multinomial distribution, the probabilities are the parameters of the distribution. We cannot know or measure these. We can, however, observe the frequency that each module has executed. Thus, it is in our interest to choose a probability distribution whose parameters are related to the things that we can measure.

To aid in the understanding of the nature of the true underlying multinomial distribution, let us observe that the family of Dirichlet distributions is a conjugate family for observations that have a multinomial distribution (see Reference3). The probability density function for a Dirichlet distribution, $D(\alpha, \alpha_T)$, with a parametric vector $\alpha = (\alpha_1, \alpha_2, \ldots \alpha_{k-1})$ where $(\alpha_i > 0; i = 1, 2, \ldots, k-1)$ is:

$$f(x_1, x_2, \ldots, x_{k-1}) = \frac{\Gamma(\alpha_1 + \alpha_2 + \cdots + \alpha_n)}{\Gamma(\alpha_1)\Gamma(\alpha_2) \cdots \Gamma(\alpha_{k-1})} x_1^{\alpha_1 - 1} x_2^{\alpha_2 - 1} \cdots x_{k-1}^{\alpha_{k-1} - 1}$$

where $(w_i > 0;\ i = 1, 2, \ldots, M)$ and $\sum_{i=1}^{M} w_i = 1$. The expected values of the w_i are given by:

$$E(w_i) = \mu_i = \frac{\alpha_i}{\alpha_0} \tag{1}$$

where $\alpha_0 = \sum_{i=1}^{T} \alpha_i$. In this context, α_0 represents the total epochs. The vari ance of the w_i is given by:

$$Var(w_i) = \frac{\alpha_i(\alpha_0 - \alpha_i)}{\alpha_0^2(\alpha_0 + 1)} \tag{2}$$

and the covariance by:

$$Cov(w_i, w_j) = \frac{\alpha_i \alpha_j}{\alpha_0^2(\alpha_0 + 1)}$$

Obtaining confidence intervals for our estimates of the parameters for the Dirichlet distribution is not a very tractable problem. To simplify the process of setting these confidence limits, let us observe that if $\mathbf{w} = (w_1, w_2, \ldots, w_M)$ is a random vector having the M-variate Dirichlet distribution, $D(\alpha, \alpha_T)$, then the sum $z = w_1 + \ldots + w_M$ has the beta distribution:

$$f_\beta(z \mid \gamma, \alpha_T) = \frac{\Gamma(\gamma + \alpha_T)}{\Gamma(\gamma)\Gamma(\alpha_T)} z^\gamma (1 - z)^{\alpha_T}$$

or alternately:

$$f_\beta(w_T \mid \gamma, \alpha_T) = \frac{\Gamma(\gamma + \alpha_T)}{\Gamma(\gamma)\Gamma(\alpha_T)} (1 - w_T)^\gamma (w_T)^{\alpha_T}$$

where $\gamma = \alpha_1 + \alpha_2 + \ldots + \alpha M$.

Thus, we can obtain $100(1 - \alpha)$ percent confidence limits for:

$$\mu_T - a \leq \mu_T \leq \mu_T + b$$

from

$$F_\beta(\mu_T - a \mid \gamma, \alpha_T) = \int_0^{\mu_T - a} f_\beta(w_T \mid \gamma, \alpha_T)\, dw = \frac{\alpha}{2} \tag{3}$$

and

$$F_\beta(\mu_T + b \mid \gamma, \alpha_T) = \int_0^{\mu_T + b} f_\beta(w_T \mid \gamma, \alpha_T)\, dw = 1 - \frac{\alpha}{2} \tag{4}$$

Where this computation is inconvenient, let us observe that the cumulative beta function, F_β, can also be obtained from existing tables of the cumulative binomial distribution, F_b, by making use of the knowledge from Raiffa[4] that:

$$F_b(\gamma \mid \mu_T - a, \gamma + \alpha_T) = F_\beta(\mu_T - a \mid \gamma, \alpha_T) \tag{5}$$

and

$$F_b(\alpha_T \mid 1 - (\mu_T + b), \gamma + \alpha_T) = F_\beta(\mu_T + b \mid \gamma, \alpha_T)$$

The value of using the Dirichlet conjugate family for modeling purposes is twofold. First, it permits us to estimate the probabilities of the module transitions directly from the observed module frequencies. Second, we are able to obtain revised estimates for these probabilities as the observation process progresses.

Let us now suppose that we wish to obtain better estimates of the parameters for our software system, the execution profile of which has a multinomial distribution with parameters n and $\mathbf{W} = (w_1, w_2, \ldots, w_M)$, where n is the total number of observed module transitions and the values of the w_1 are unknown. Let us assume that the prior distribution of $\mathbf{W}$ is a Dirichlet distribution with a parametric vector $\alpha = (\alpha_1, \alpha_2, \ldots, \alpha_M)$, where $(\alpha_i > 0; i = 1, 2, \ldots, M)$. In this case, α_i is the observed frequency of execution of module i over $\sum_i \alpha_i$ epochs. If we were to let the system run for an additional, say, $K = \sum_i x_i$ epochs, then we would get better estimates for the parameters for the cost of the observation of these new epochs. Then the posterior distribution of $\mathbf{W}$ for the additional observations $\mathbf{X} = (x_1, x_2, \ldots, x_M)$ is a Dirichlet distribution with parametric vector $\alpha^* = (\alpha_1 + x_1, \alpha_2 + x_2, \ldots, \alpha_M + x_M)$ (see also Reference 5).

As an example, suppose that we now wish to measure the activity of a large software system. At each epoch (operational, functional, or module) we will increment the frequency count for the event. As the system makes sequential transitions from one event to another, the posterior distribution of $\mathbf{W}$ at each transition will be a Dirichlet distribution. Further, for $i = 1, 2 \ldots, T$ the ith component of the augmented parametric vector α will be increased by one unit each time a new event is expressed.

10.5 CODE INSTRUMENTATION

We can measure software systems either invasively by modifying the code to put software instrumentation points in it, or we can monitor the activity of the code through hardware probes. It is by far and away cheaper and easier to modify the code than it is to modify the hardware for measurement purposes. We will continue to pay a performance price for the life of the software should we choose to insert our measurement probes into the software. Life is full of trade-offs.

Should we choose to obtain our measurements from software instrumentation points, there are two ways to do this. First, we can insert new code in the source code of the program modules to do our work. We do not always have access to the source code however. This does not preclude measurement. We can modify the binary code for a program to capture the information that we need. In either case we will need only to know that we have reached a certain point in the program. Each instrumentation point in the code will contain its own unique identifier. When that instrumentation point is encountered, it will transmit its identifier to a receiving module, together with whatever data we wish to capture at the point.

10.5.1 Source Code Instrumentation Process

A software probe or instrumentation point at the source code level is simply a function call to a new source code function module that will capture the telemetry from the instrumentation point. We will probably want to know which instrumentation point was transmitting to us and perhaps capture some data as well. In C, this instrumentation point might look something like:

```
Clic(Point_No, Data);
```

The module being called `Clic` we will add to the source code base to capture in the information supplied in the argument list. Each instrumentation point will transmit its own telemetry. The first argument, `Point_No`, will be a unique number for this instrumentation point so that we can identify the source of the telemetry. The second argument will possibly be a data structure, `Data`, that will capture the essential information we wish to record at the point of call.

There are several different strategies that can be used to place software instrumentation points in source code. The number of points will be a factor in the instrumentation process. A large number of points can be expected to significantly degrade the performance of the software that is being measured. On the other hand, if too few points are used, then we may not achieve the degree of resolution that we need for our monitoring purpose.

The location of instrumentation points in the code will be a function of what we wish to learn from the measuring process. Instrumentation points can be placed in the source code essentially at random, or they can be systematically placed according to the structure of the program. With random instrumentation, probes are simply inserted at random points throughout the system. If we merely want to capture the essential behavior of the software, then random instrumentation should serve this function quite well. In this case, we will determine the degree of resolution that we wish to achieve in this monitoring process and choose the minimum number of points that will achieve this resolution. For some types of statistical monitoring processes, this random probe insertion process will work quite well.

Another approach to the placement of software probes is by module location. This will permit us to track the transition of program activity throughout the call graph representation of the program. There are two different instrumentation strategies that can be employed. We can instrument the software at the beginning of each module call. This instrumentation strategy will permit the frequency count of each module to be developed over an observation interval. This will permit us to generate profiles of module activity *among* program modules. Let us look at this from the data collection process in the data collection module. What we wish to do is to accumulate the frequency count for each module execution. To do this we will set up a vector in the data collection module with one element for each instrumented module. Each time a module is executed during an observation interval, we will increase the frequency count for that module by one. Periodically, the data collection module will transmit the execution profile out of the system for analysis or storage.

The problem with instrumenting a single point at the beginning of each module is that it is not possible to know when control has passed out of a module. That is, we cannot know with any degree of certainty the calling sequence of modules. If we do need to have access to this information, then we will have to instrument the return statements from each program module as well. This is somewhat more difficult than just putting some executable code at the beginning of a program module. There may be multiple `return` statements in a single C program module. Perhaps the easiest way to insert our `Clic` probes is to wrap the `return` statement with a do-while as follows:

```
do {Clic(Point_No, Data); return ((a+b/c));}while(0);
```

We have replaced one statement (the `return`) with another statement (the `do-while`). This means that we will have to run an instrumentation preprocessor through the code before we compile it.

The execution profile can be emitted by our `Clic` module at the end of a real-time observation interval, say every millisecond. This will allow us to see the distribution of program activity as a function of time. Unfortunately, these temporal observations are generally of little utility in measuring software behavior, in that different machines both within and among hardware architectures differ greatly in their performance characteristics. To eliminate this uncontrolled source of variation, a superior strategy is to standardize each profile vector so that each profile represents the same frequency count. That is the basic notion behind the concept of an epoch, which represents the transition from one observation point to the next.

That is, we can set the observation interval to, say, 1000 epochs. Every 1000 epochs we will emit the execution profile and reset the contents of the new execution profile to zeros.

The objective in dynamic measurement is to minimize the number of instrumentation points and still be able to obtain the information needed for decision making. In some circumstances, however, it will not be possible to get the necessary resolution on the phenomenon we wish to study at the module entry and exit level, or the call graph level. For those cases demanding increased resolution on program behavior, we may choose to instrument the control structure *within* each program module. We will call this the *flowgraph instrumentation level.*

To perform flowgraph instrumentation we need to capture information relating to the decision paths of the module that is executing. Experience has shown that instrumenting cycles can create some serious data bandwidth problems and provide little or no valuable information about program behavior. Thus, we choose to instrument only the decision paths in if statements or case statements. We will instrument the path from the if statements for the true predicate outcome. We could also instrument the false or else path but the two paths are mutually exclusive. It is questionable whether the incremental information to be gained from instrumenting both paths merits the additional bandwidth in telemetry.

In C we will modify the predicate clause to contain our software probe. Consider the following if statement:

```
if (a < b || c = = d) <stmt>;
```

We will insert the Clic probe in the predicate clause as follows:

```
if (Clic(Point_No, Data) && a < b || c = = d &&
Clic(Point_No, Data)) <stmt>;
```

For the case statement, we can simply add a statement to each case statement as follows:

```
case 'b' : Clic(Point_No, Data); <stmt>
```

It is very cheap to instrument software with these software probes in terms of human effort. We can write a tool that will preprocess the code and drop it in. We will continue to pay a relatively high performance cost over the life of the software for having elected to take this cheap initial solution. If performance is an issue, then hardware instrumentation should be seriously considered as a viable alternative to software instrumentation.

10.5.2 Binary Code Instrumentation

Binary code can also be modified to insert instrumentation points. In this case we are somewhat more constrained. Without a painful amount of reverse-engineering it will not be possible to capture much data. We will have to be satisfied just learning which instrumentation points fire as the code is executed. For most purposes this level of instrumentation will be more than adequate.

To instrument binary code we must be aware that transitions among program modules at runtime will be implemented by p-capturing instructions. These are instructions that capture the contents of the program counter before they alter it. Within the Intel X86 architecture, for example, there are the absolute CALL instructions. These instructions will push the CS and EIP registers onto the stack and take the jump to the appropriate function module address.

Before we modify the binary code base, we must first monitor the activity of the system to find areas of memory that are used as heap space for dynamic memory allocation by the running system. Our objective in this analysis is to identify a place where we can insinuate our own monitoring code and not affect the operation of the system we are monitoring.

The next step in the process is to identify and capture program call statements (opcodes 9A and FF in the case of Pentium X86). We will substitute these function calls with a call to our own module. The function call that we are replacing will be placed at the end of our telemetry capture module. It will be the last thing we execute in our own code. We will not, of course, ever execute a return statement. We must be careful not to destroy or alter the return information (the CS and EIP register contents) so that the user's function will return control to the appropriate place in the code. Again, any registers that are altered in our telemetry capture module must be saved and restored before we exit the procedure.

For embedded code, sometimes this process can be a little tricky. Some embedded code is time dependent. We might accidentally insert our probe in a sequence of code that must execute under tight time constraints. When additional code is added to this sequence, it is quite possible that the code will fail as a result. In modern software systems, this is much less a factor than it was in the past.

10.6 INSTRUMENTING FOR THE PROFILES

The instrumentation techniques discussed to this point relate to the capture of execution frequency data. To capture execution frequency data, a vector equal in length to the number of modules (or functionalities) is allocated and initialized to zero. We will call this vector the execution frequency vector, EFC. Each time a module is called, a corresponding element in the EFC is incremented. We can monitor and record the entire operation of a system from the time it is initiated until it is terminated in the EFC. Alternatively, we can periodically save the contents of the EFC and reinitialize its elements to zero. This will yield a sequence of EFCs. Each EFC will represent a certain number of epochs. We could, for example, elect to store the contents of the EFC every 1000 epochs.

The data in the EFC is collected independent of the knowledge of what the system might be doing. It speaks only to the execution of the code points that were captured during a particular observation interval. In a sense, there is considerable confounding in these data. An EFC that is generated by observing an arbitrary number of epochs (e.g., 1000) may contain module execution data from the execution of one functionality, it may span from one functionality to another, or it may contain data from several functionalities. Extracting a signal from this noisy data is very difficult. It would be far better to collect execution data that relates to the specific activities, functionalities or operations, of the system.

10.6.1 Module Profile

A module profile is the multinomial probability distribution for the execution of modules on our system under a given operational profile. To create a module profile, we will construct an EFC equal in length to the number of modules in a system. Each element of the EFC will represent the execution frequency of exactly one module. Each module in the system will be instrumented to increment this frequency when the module is first entered. As per our earlier discussion on software instrumentation, the definition of a module must first be nailed down. A module, for example, may be a block of code that is the destination of a CALL machine instruction. It may also be a block of code that is entered through a conditional branch instruction.

A module profile can be derived from an EFC by dividing each entry in the observation profile by the total number of epochs represented in the EFC. From the Dirichlet distribution we observe that our estimate for the probability of execution p_i of the ith program module is the ratio of the number of times this module has executed to the total epochs of observation to wit:

$$E(p_i) = \mu_i = \frac{\alpha_i}{\alpha_0}$$

where α_i is the current module frequency count and α_0 is the total epoch count.

10.6.2 Functional Profile

It is relatively easy to collect data at the module level. We have either source code or machine code that we can easily modify to insert the necessary software instrumentation. We cannot instrument for functionality if this has not first been specified. This will always be a liability. The number of software systems currently in service or in development throughout the world for which complete and current functional specifications are maintained could be easily tallied on the fingers and toes of a single person. This is a particularly astonishing fact when the amount of safety-critical or mission-critical software currently in service is considered. It is possible, however, to retrofit systems with sufficient instrumentation to recapture their underlying functionality (Hall,[6] Elbaum[7]).

To collect data to construct a functional profile, the software system must be instrumented to do this. Unfortunately, functionalities do not really physically exist in code. Therefore, they cannot be directly instrumented. Let us observe that each functionality, by definition, must contain a nonempty set of program modules M_u that are uniquely associated with that functionality. Further, there must be a nonempty set of program modules that are indispensably associated with the functionality. This means that there must be at least one element in the intersection set $M_d = M_u \cap M_i$. Any one of the modules in the intersection set M_d may be instrumented and will represent the expression of the functionality.

In this instrumentation strategy, there will by an EFC equal in length to the number of system functionalities, one entry for each functionality. Exactly one of the modules in M_d will be instrumented. Whenever a new functionality is expressed, the instrumented module associated with this functionality will cause the EFC element associated with this functionality to be incremented. The basic problem with this instrumentation strategy is that there may be a significant latency, in epochs, between the initiation of the functionality and the registration of this event in the EFC. It might well be that the instrumented module falls at the end of a long sequence of module executions that constitute the set of modules $M^{(f)}$ that might execute when this functionality is invoked.

Perhaps the best way to instrument for the functional monitoring is to introduce this measurement task into the design stage of software development. In this case we will insist that a module $m_i \in M_d$ be the first in the sequence of a modules that will express the functionality. In essence, each functionality will excise a subgraph from the execution call graph for the program. There will always be a root module for this subgraph. In this instrumentation strategy we will insist that this module be an element of M_d.

As was the case for the module profile, the functional profile can be derived from the EFC for the functionality. In this case, the elements of the EFC represent the frequency of execution of each functionality.

10.6.3 Operational Profiles

If the number of programs worldwide that have viable functional specifications is very small, then the subset of these that have usable operational specifications as well is even smaller. It is, however, relatively easy to retrofit a viable set of operational specifications from a set of functional specifications. Each operation is a legitimate operation if and only if it has at least one distinct functionality. That is, each operation must have some unique functionality. There must be some services performed by the system that are distinctly associated with a particular user operation.

From Chapter 9 we identified the set of functionalities $F_d^{(o_i)}$ that were distinctly associated with each operation o_i. Further, if we insist that each operation has at least one distinct functionality, then there exists a set of modules $M_u^{(o_i)}$ within this set of functionalities that is unique to that operation. As we observed before, when a program is executing a module m where $m \in M_u^{(o_i)}$, it is quite clear that the user is expressing operation o_i. Thus, if we instrument any one of the elements of $M_u^{(o)}$, there will by an EFC equal in length to the number of user operations, one entry for each operation. Whenever a new operation is invoked by the user, the instrumented module associated with this operation will cause the EFC element associated with this operation to be incremented. Again, the basic problem with this instrumentation strategy is that there may be an even more dramatic latency, in epochs, between the initiation of the operation and the EFC update to reflect that activity.

A more direct instrumentation strategy could be derived in the same manner that we developed for instrumenting the functionalities. Let us observe that the set of distinct functionalities $F_d^{(o_i)}$ associated with each operation are mutually exclusive functionalities. In this set of functionalities, there is one functionality that will always be executed first. Just as we did with the instrumentation of the functionalities, we can design the system so that one particular module is invoked whenever this initial functionality is expressed. By instrumenting just this one module at the head of a call graph structure for the operation, we can then collect the operation EFC data in a timely manner.

As was the case for the functional profile, the actual operational profile can be derived from the EFC for the system operation. In this case, the elements of the EFC represent the frequency of execution of each operation. Remember that our design quality standards dictated that we have some estimate for the prior distribution of the operation profile before we designed the system in the first place. Our subsequent observations on new operational profiles as the system is placed into service will serve either to validate our initial prior distribution of the operational profile or to indicate a need to revisit the design and testing process should a new operational profile emerge.

10.7 PARTIAL COMPLEXITY

Except in the most trivial case, whenever a program module executes, only a subset of execution paths from the start node of the flowgraph to the terminal node will actually execute. In the flowgraph definition in Chapter 5, essentially all of the executable source code in a program module will map to the processing nodes of the flowgraph. The instrumentation methodology described in Section 10.5.1 will allow us to determine just exactly which of these processing blocks have been touched during the execution of each functionality. Once we know which processing blocks have executed, we can then determine exactly which source code statements have executed for that functionality.

In essence, each functionality will select a particular subset of executable source code from each module in the subset of modules $M^{(f)}$ that implement the functionality. The functionality clearly does not execute all of the code in each module. A more accurate representation of the complexity of each module, then, would be to identify just the code that executed and then measure the code attributes of that source code subset. A program module, for example, might contain 100 executable statements. When this module is exercised by a particular functionality, say f_5, only 25 of these statements will actually execute. Thus, the partial attribute complexity for Exec for functionality f_5 is 25.

Consider the program example shown in Exhibit 1. This function module will take an integer (4 bytes) and return the same integer (4 bytes). The essential structure of this program is very similar to that used to interrogate the contents of status words checking for particular bit settings. This program function module has 2^{32} or 4,294,967,296 paths. Necessarily, its path complexity is very high. From the standpoint of control flow complexity, it is a heinous module.

Now let us assume that at runtime, the function module shown in Exhibit 1 is passed the value of 2 as its only argument. The actual code that will execute, in this case, is shown in Exhibit 2. There are exactly two paths through this code. It is a very simple program from the standpoint of control flow complexity.

In one sense, the generalized FI measure is really pessimistic. A much more realistic approach would be to identify the particular subset of code that is actually used under a particular operational profile and measure just that for fault potential. This will yield a partial FI value $\xi_i^{(o)}$ for each program module under an operational profile **o**. We will explore this notion at length in Chapter 11.

The bottom line of the notion of partial complexity is that it is possible to measure the static attributes of the actual pieces of program module that were executed.

Exhibit 1. Function Module Return Same 4-Byte Integer

```
unsigned int test (unsigned int status)
{
    unsigned int power;
    unsigned int cum;
    power = 1;
    if (status & power)
    cum = 1;
    else
    cum = 0;
    power * = 2;
    if (status & power)
    cum + = power;
    power * = 2;
    if (status & power)
    cum + = power;
    power * = 2;
    if (status & power)
    cum + = power;
    power * = 2;
    if (status & power)
    cum + = power;
    power * = 2;
    if (status & power)
    cum + = power;
    power * = 2;
    if (status & power)
    cum + = power;
    power * = 2;
    if (status & power)
    cum + = power;
    power * = 2;
    if (status & power)
    cum + = power;
    power * = 2;
    if (status & power)
    cum + = power;
    power * = 2;
    if (status & power)
    cum + = power;
    power * = 2;
    if (status & power)
    cum + = power;
    power * = 2;
    if (status & power)
    cum + = power;
    power * = 2;
    if (status & power)
    cum + = power;
    power * = 2;
    if (status & power)
    cum + = power;
    power * = 2;
    if (status & power)
    cum + = power;
    power * = 2;
```

Exhibit 1. Function Module Return Same 4-Byte Integer (continued)

```
        if (status & power)
        cum + = power;
        power * = 2;
        if (status & power)
        cum + = power;
        power * = 2;
        if (status & power)
        cum + = power;
        power * = 2;
        if (status & power)
        cum + = power;
        power * = 2;
        if (status & power)
        cum + = power;
        power * = 2;
        if (status & power)
        cum + = power;
        power * = 2;
        if (status & power)
        cum + = power;
        power * = 2;
        if (status & power)
        cum + = power;
        power * = 2;
        if (status & power)
        cum + = power;
        power * = 2;
        if (status & power)
        cum + = power;
        power * = 2;
        if (status & power)
        cum + = power;
        power * = 2;
        if (status & power)
        cum + = power;
        power * = 2;
        if (status & power)
        cum + = power;
        power * = 2;
        if (status & power)
        cum + = power;
        power * = 2;
        if (status & power)
        cum + = power;
        power + = 2;
        if (status & power)
        cum + = power;

        return (cum);
    }
```

Exhibit 2. Code Executed

```
unsigned int test (unsigned int status)
{
    unsigned int power;
    unsigned int cum;
    power = 1;
    if (status & power)
    cum = 1;
    power * = 2;
    if (status & power);
    power * = 2;
    if (status & power);
    power * = 2;
    if (status & power);
    power * = 2;
    if (status & power);
    power * = 2;
    if (status & power);
    power * = 2;
    if (status & power);
    power * = 2;
    if (status & power);
    power * = 2;
    if (status & power);
    power * = 2;
    if (status & power);
    power * = 2;
    if (status & power);
    power * = 2;
    if (status & power);
    power * = 2;
    if (status & power);
    power * = 2;
    if (status & power);
    power * = 2;
    if (status & power);
    power * = 2;
    if (status & power);
    power * = 2;
    if (status & power);
    power * = 2;
    if (status & power);
    power * = 2;
    if (status & power);
    power * = 2;
    if (status & power);
    power * = 2;
    if (status & power);
    power * = 2;
    if (status & power);
    power * = 2;
    if (status & power);
    power * = 2;
    if (status & power);
    power * = 2;
    if (status & power);
```

Exhibit 2. Code Executed (continued)

```
power * = 2;
if (status & power);
power * = 2;
if (status & power);
power * = 2;
if (status & power);
power * = 2;
if (status & power);
power * = 2;
if (status & power);
power * = 2;
if (status & power);
power * = 2;
if (status & power);
power * = 2;
if (status & power);
power + = 2;
if (status & power);

return (cum);
}
```

As an aside, the function module shown in Exhibit 1 is flawed. The statement following the penultimate if statement should read, power * = 2; . This means that exactly one half the integers that may be returned by this module will be wrong. Put another way, one half of the *possible* executions of this module will result in a failure event. It is highly unlikely, however, that a typical user will ever experience this failure. Most people do not use large integers in their daily life. Only a very small fraction of *probable* executions will expose this fault.

10.8 A MEASURE OF COHESION

The term "cohesion" is used frequently in the software engineering literature, mostly without a clear definition; that is, a definition that lends itself to quantification. In general, a module is said to be cohesive if all of the module parts work toward some common goal or function. That is, each module with good cohesion will tend to use all of its parts to the solution of a particular function whenever it is invoked. If we were to write a C function called trig that would return the sine, cosine, or tangent of an angle given as a parameter depending on the value of yet another parameter, then this module would obviously not have good cohesive properties. Sometimes it would compute the sine and return that value; sometimes it would compute the tangent and return that value; etc. Different code segments in the module would be responsible for each of the trigonometric functions. Each of the code segments would operate more or less independently of the others. Although this is a relatively extreme example, in most cases we simply will not know how well we have performed in creating modules that have this property of cohesion until we actually begin to run the code.

It is clear, then, that a measure of software module cohesion will be a dynamic property of that module. Basically, each time a module is executed, it will select a subset of paths from its flowgraph. If the set of arcs executed from this flowgraph is essentially the same from one epoch to another, then the module will have this property of cohesion. Actually, we are not interested in all of the arcs in the program. We are interested only in those that are exiting edges from predicate nodes.

We can measure the execution of the arcs with the instrumentation methodology discussed in Section 10.5.1. For the purposes of assessing the cohesiveness of a module, we are only interested in whether or not an arc executed during one module execution epoch. Let $a_{i,j}^{(k)}$ represent the execution of an arc j in module i on the kth execution epoch. If, during epoch k, arc j in module i was expressed, then we will represent the arc contact by letting $a_{i,j}^{(k)} = 1$, otherwise $a_{i,j}^{(k)} = 0$. After the execution of l epochs, then, the average $a_{i,j}^{(k)}$ will be

$$\bar{a}_{i,j} = \frac{1}{l} \sum_{k=1}^{l} a_{i,j}^{(k)} = \frac{c}{l}$$

where c is the number of times that this arc was executed during the l epochs. The variance of $a_{i,j}^{(k)}$ will be

$$\delta_a^2 = \frac{1}{l} \sum_{k=1}^{l} \left(a_{i,j}^{(k)} - \bar{a}_{i,j} \right)^2 = \frac{c}{l} \left(1 - \frac{c}{l} \right)$$

It is clear, then that if the same arcs of module i execute over all epochs, the variance δ_a^2 will be zero for all arcs. This is the point of maximum cohesion. A module will have demonstrated less cohesion if δ_a^2 is relatively large.

Clearly, the larger the module, the more complex it will become. As its complexity increases, so too will the complexity of the flowgraph for the module. The number of paths through a flowgraph will also tend to follow this trend. Quite naturally, then, we would expect a reasonable correlation between δ_a^2 and any of our module size metrics such as $Exec$.

10.9 ENTROPY

The specific implications for software design of the execution profile can be drawn from information theory. In this case, each scenario under which the program can execute has its own set of execution profiles. Each of the execution profiles can be measured in terms of its functional entropy, defined as follows:

$$h_k = \sum_{i=1}^{n} p_i^k \log_2 p_i^k$$

where p_i^k represents the execution profile of the kth functionality.

The design entropy that represents the particular manifestation of all of the program's functionalities, as articulated in the functional design specifications, can be described as:

$$h = \sum_{i=1}^{m} q_i \log_2 q_i$$

where m is the number of functionalities and q_i represents the functional profile.

The point of maximum entropy will occur when all modules will execute with an equal probability, in which case $h_{max} = n \log_2 n$. This point of maximum entropy will occur in a circumstance where all modules of a program are executed for precisely the same amount of time under a given input scenario. It is a point of maximum surprise. There is no way of guessing where the program is likely to be executing at any point. At the other extreme, the point of minimum entropy, 0, is the point at which the program will execute in only one of its modules. The probability of executing this one module will be 1.0. The probability, therefore, of executing any other module will be 0.

The concept of entropy can also be used to evaluate a design in terms of its modularity. We can see from the standpoint of the entropy measure that the maximum effect of a decision to increase the number of modules in a design from n to $n+1$ is basically the difference between $\log_2 n$ and $\log_2(n+1)$. For small n, this difference might be substantial. For large n, the incremental effect of the additional module is not that great.

10.10 TESTABILITY REVISITED

In Chapter 9, the notion of testability was introduced. It was noted that testability was a multidimensional concept. It had many different attributes. It turns out that the entropy measure is yet another attribute dimension of testability. Low-entropy systems will be very difficult to test. By their very nature, such systems distribute a disproportional amount of their total epochs to a relatively small set of program modules. It is very difficult to impossible, under these circumstances, to create operational (or functional) test cases that will distribute their execution across all modules. The vast majority of test activity will always be spent in a small number of modules. A program module that is executed with a very low probability will perhaps require a large number of epochs to ensure it executes. Object-oriented design, by its very nature, tends to generate very low entropy systems. Testing in this environment can be very costly.

References

1. Munson, J.C., Software Measurement: Problems and Practice, *Annals of Software Engineering,* 1(1), 255–285, 1995.

2. Munson, J.C. and Ravenel, R.H., Designing Reliable Software, *Proceedings of the 1993 IEEE International Symposium of Software Reliability Engineering,* IEEE Computer Society Press, Los Alamitos, CA, 1993, pp. 45–54.

3. Wilks, S.S., *Mathematical Statistics,* John Wiley & Sons, New York, 1962.

4. Raiffa, H. and Schlaifer, R., *Applied Statistical Decision Theory,* Studies in Managerial Economics, Harvard University, Boston, 1961.

5. DeGroot, M.H., *Optimal Statistical Decision,* McGraw-Hill, New York, 1970.

6. Hall, G.A., Usage Patterns: Extracting System Functionality from Execution Profiles, Ph.D. thesis, University of Idaho, Moscow, ID,1997.

7. Elbaum, S.G. and Munson, J.C., Software Black Box: An Alternative Mechanism for Failure Analysis, *Proceedings of the 2000 IEEE International Symposium of Software Reliability Engineering,* San Jose, CA, November 2000.

Chapter 11
The Measurement of Software Testing Activity

11.1 INTRODUCTION

Sometimes there is ambiguity in the goals and objectives of the software testing process. For our purposes, we would like to remove this ambiguity. The objective of the test process will be to certify a software system for a range of behaviors thought to be representative of a typical user's operation profile. In this guise, the software should perform reliably as long as it is operated within the limits of behavior that we have certified. Our real objective in this process is to be able to guarantee the reliable operation of our software. The test process will be used to achieve this objective.

We are rapidly coming to the close of the Wild West days of software development. The corporate survivors in the new world of software development will be those that can certify and guarantee the safe and reliable operation of their software. Sound engineering practice is essentially the only way that a guarantee of reliable software operation can be made. The one thing that we have learned over the years is that it is not possible to use the software test process to achieve reliability. By the time the system arrives in the tester's hands, the damage has been done. Bad software process cannot be redeemed during testing. That will not be an objective of the testing process. Rather, the testing process will be used to certify that the software will perform reliably within the context of a well-defined operating environment.

Each test activity will exercise one or more functionalities. This will, in turn, cause subsets of code modules to be executed. Not all modules are equal. Some are potentially fault prone while others are not so fault prone. The astonishing level of complexity of modern software will guarantee that we will not have the resources to identify all possible faults and fix them. Further, as we have seen, an attempt to fix one fault might well introduce additional faults. We would like, then, to have the ability to marshal our resources so that we can have the greatest impact for the very limited resources that

273

will be available to the test activity. The test activity is perhaps the most resource-poor activity in the entire software development cycle. We need to know how to get the biggest bang for the limited test dollars.

The results of each test activity can be quantified. It is possible to evaluate that test activity in terms of the benefit derived from it. It would be pure folly to devote test resources to an activity that provides little or no exposure to latent faults in the system. The test measurement enterprise will allow us to quantify and evaluate each test. This knowledge will guide us in our future test activities.

In Chapter 8 we saw that an evolving software system is very difficult to manage, measure, and describe. A family of software modules may lay quiescent in the system for many build cycles, having received little or no attention from developers. As a result, the reliability of these modules will probably increase over time. We will learn to accept the reliability of this family and devote our test resources to other, more active code. All of a sudden, the attention of the developers may well turn to this code backwater. In the face of heavy change activity, our code family that was once reliable may now begin to inherit more and more faults. This code family must now be promoted to be a center of attention for future test activity. In that the code base is not static, there can be no static test plan. A test plan must be a living document that changes as the code base changes.

11.2 STATIC AND DYNAMIC MEASUREMENT

It is clear, by now, that static software measurements will give a clear indication as to where the potential faults in a system might be. It is one thing to know where the potential faults in code might be. It is quite another thing to see whether the program actually executes in the region where the faults are. Static software measurement is like one-hand clapping. Dynamic software measurement, then, is the other hand clapping. Static measurement is useful in that it shows where the potential problems are in the source code. Dynamic code measurement shows what code got executed and how intensively. Both static and dynamic measurements come together in the measurement of the software testing enterprise. It is vital to be able to measure program behavior at runtime to determine our exposure to the potential faults in the code. If we are to be able to test a software system, we must know both the location of the faults and whether the software test execution profiles match where the faults are likely to be. The testing process should be monitored and controlled by simple engineering standards. All test activity should be measured as it is occurring.

It seems entirely reasonable that if we know where the faults in the code are likely to be, then our test activity should exploit this information. Unfortunately, the code base is a moving target. Most software systems will evolve very rapidly from the first build to the last. This means that there are essentially two different types of faults that we must deal with during the testing process: (1) faults that were introduced in the initial code as it was first built, and (2) faults that have been introduced in subsequent builds.

It will help clarify our thinking about the testing process if we can establish some reasonable test objectives. Here we will draw from the centuries of test experience from hardware and electronic engineering enterprises. We do not care that our software has faults in it. No matter how careful we are, there will always be faults in our code. As we attempt to remove old faults, we run the risk of adding new faults. It is entirely possible to remove an innocuous fault only to introduce a severe one in the repair process. Removing all of the software faults, then, is neither a viable nor practical goal. We would just like to remove those faults that will impair the way that the system is used when it is deployed.

The first step, then, in the software test process should center on who will be using the system and how will they be using it. When we know how the system will be used when it is deployed, we can then concentrate our efforts on certifying that it will not break when it is used in a fashion specified by a suite of operational profiles.

There are significant flaws in essentially all hardware systems regardless of the level of engineering expertise brought to bear on the design and manufacture of the product. A concrete building column may, for example, have substantial voids in it where the concrete failed to fill the form correctly as it was being poured. If we have done our engineering correctly, the building will not collapse because of this void. If the void occurs in a structurally significant section of the column where either compression or tension forces are concentrated, it may cause the column to fail. We simply cannot build a building without voids in the concrete structures. We can test to be sure that these voids are not structurally significant. The cost of a perfectly cast concrete structure is prohibitive. The cost of a fault-free program is equally prohibitive. We must learn to focus our test energies on those activities that are vital to our customer and learn to ignore those that do not meet this criterion. The worst thing that we could do is to remove a fault that will not affect the functionality of our code and insert a fault in the replacement code that will impact the functionality of the system.

11.3 A METAPHOR FOR TEST ACTIVITY

A software system can be viewed as a set of program modules that are executing a set of mutually exclusive functionalities. If the system executes a functionality expressed by a subset of modules that are fault-free, it will not fail. If, on the other hand, the system is executing a functionality expressed in a subset of fault-laden modules, there is a very high probability that it will fail. Each test of the software will exercise particular functionalities that drive the system into regions of code (i.e., modules) of differing complexities (i.e., fault proneness).

Each software test will generally execute a subset of the total program functionality. As a result, the test will cause a subset of the program modules to execute. As each test is run to completion, we can accumulate the distribution of test activity in a test execution frequency vector (TEFV). Each element in this vector will represent the total number of times that a particular test has executed. From this vector we can generate a *test execution profile* for each test in the same manner as we developed the module profiles in Chapter 10.

Each test scenario will excise a subset of program modules for execution, depending on the test functionality. There will be a call graph for the tested modules that represents a sub-call graph of the entire program. The systematic transition between module pairs in this call graph can be modeled as a stochastic process, where we define an indexed collection of random variables $\{X_t\}$, where the index t runs through a set of nonnegative integers $t = 0,1,2,\cdots$ representing the epochs of the test process. At any particular epoch, the software is found to be executing exactly one of its M modules. The fact of the execution occurring in a particular module is a *state* of the system. For a given test case, the system will be executing exactly one of its M modules. In this representation of the system, there is a stochastic process $\{X_t\}$ where the random variables are observed at epochs $t = 0,1,2,\cdots$ and where each random variable may take on any one of the M integers from the state space $A = 1,2,\cdots M$. The probability that a particular module will execute depends entirely on the set of functionalities that each test in the test suite will exercise.

As a test plan is developed for a software system, a set of T individual test cases will be developed. Let Y be a random variable defined on the indices of the set of all test elements of T, the complete test suite for the software system. Then:

$$p_i^{(k)} = \Pr[X_t = i \mid Y = k]$$

where $k = 1,2,\ldots,\|T\|$ represents the execution profile for a set of modules that can execute during a particular test k. In other words, for each test t_i, there is an execution profile represented by the profile $\mathbf{P}^{(i)} = < p_1^{(i)}, p_2^{(i)}, p_3^{(i)}, \cdots, p_n^{(i)} >$.

11.4 MEASUREMENT-BASED TESTING

Deterministically testing a large software system is virtually impossible. Trivial systems, on the order of 20 or 30 modules, often have far too many possible execution paths for complete deterministic testing. This being the case, we must revisit what we hope to accomplish by testing the system.

Our goal might be to remove all of the faults within the code. If this is our goal, then we will need to know when we have found all of these faults. Given unlimited time and resources, identification and removal of all faults might be a noble goal but real-world constraints make this largely unattainable. The problem is that we must provide an adequate level of reliability in light of the fact that we cannot find and remove all of the faults. Through the use of software measurement, we hope to identify which modules contain the most faults and, based on execution profiles of the system, how these potential faults can impact software reliability. The fundamental principle is that a fault that never executes, never causes a failure. A fault that lies along the path of normal execution will cause frequent failures. The majority of the testing effort should be spent finding those faults that are most likely to cause failure.[1]

The first step in this testing paradigm is the identification of those modules that are likely to contain the most faults. We can know this through our static measurement techniques. In the current state, the objectives of the software test process are not clearly specified and sometimes not clearly understood. An implicit objective of a deterministic approach to testing is to design a systematic and deterministic test procedure that will guarantee sufficient test exposure for the random faults distributed throughout a program. By ensuring, for example, that all possible paths have been executed, then any potential faults on these paths will have had the opportunity to have been expressed.

We must, however, come to accept the fact that some faults will always be present in the code. We will not be able to eliminate them all, nor should we try. The objective of the testing process should be to find those faults that will have the greatest impact on the reliability/safety/survivability of the code. Using this view of the software testing process, the act of testing may be thought of as conducting an experiment on the behavior of the code under typical execution conditions. We will determine, *a priori,* exactly what we wish to learn about the code in the test process and conduct the experiment until this stopping condition has been reached.

11.4.1 Simple Measures for the Test Process

At the completion of each test case, we would like to be able to measure the performance of that test activity. There are many different aspects of the test activity, so there will also be a host of different measurements that we can make. The important thing is that the test activity must be measured and evaluated. We must learn to evaluate every aspect of the test activity. Our objective is not just to drive the code until it fails or fails to fail; we want to know exactly what the test did in terms of the distribution of its activity and where potential faults are likely to be.

The first measure that we will use in this regard will examine how the test activity was distributed across the modules actually exercised by the test. The distribution of the activity will be an important assessment of the ultimate testability of the program. If each of the tests distributes all of the activity on a small subset of the modules, the majority of program modules will not be executed. If, on the other hand, the test activity is distributed evenly across each module, then each of the modules will have had equal exposure during the test. A very useful measure of program dynamics is the program entropy measure discussed in Chapter 10; that is:

$$h = -\sum_{i=1}^{n} p_i \log_2 p_i$$

Each test will generate a different test execution profile. Hence, entropy is a good measure of how the test effort was distributed among the various program modules. For the test execution profile $\mathbf{P}^{(i)}$, the test entropy will be:

$$h^{(i)} = -\sum_{i=1}^{n} p_i^{(i)} \log_2 p_i^{(i)}$$

where n is the cardinality of the set of all program modules. A low entropy test is one that will spend all its time in a relatively small number of modules. Maximum entropy is, of course, $\log_2 n$ for a test suite of n program modules.

Some tests will have a low entropy value and others will have a high entropy value. A large entropy value would indicate that the test tended to distribute its activity fairly evenly across the modules of the system. A small entropy value would indicate that only a small number of modules received the majority of the test activity.

The process of measuring the test process for evolving software systems is very complicated. Existing systems are continually being modified as a normal part of the software maintenance activity. Changes will be introduced into this system based on the need for corrections, adaptations to changing requirements, and enhancements to make the system perform faster and better. The precise effects of changes to software modules, in terms of number of latent faults, is now reasonably well understood. From a statistical testing perspective, test efforts should focus on those modules that are most likely to contain faults. Each program module that has been modified, then, should be tested in proportion to the number of anticipated faults that might have been introduced into it. Thus, the second measure of test activity will relate to the location of potential faults in the system.

In the face of the evolving nature of the software system, the impact of a single test can change from one build to the next. Each program module has a fault index (FI) value ρ_i. Again, FI is a fault surrogate. The larger value of the FI, the greater fault potential that a module has. If a given module has a large fault potential but limited exposure (small profile value), then the *fault exposure* of that module is also small.[2] One objective of the test phase is to maximize our exposure to the faults in the system. Another way to say this is that we wish to maximize fault exposure ϕ, given by:

$$\phi_i^{(k)} = \sum_{j=1}^{n} p_j^{(k)} \rho_j^i$$

where ρ_j^i is the FI of the jth module on the ith system build and $\mathbf{p}^{(k)}$ is the test execution profile of the kth test suite.[3] In this case, $\phi_i^{(k)}$ is the expected value for ϕ under the kth test case profile.

We know that the average ρ is 100 for the baseline system. This is so because we scaled the fault index to make it have a mean of 100. The maximum value for $\phi_i^{(k)}$ is simply the maximum value for ρ_j^i. A unit test of this module j would yield this result. In this case, we would spend 100 percent of the test activity in this single module. By the same reasoning, the minimum $\phi_i^{(k)}$ is simply the least of the ρ_j^i.

We now have two relatively simple measures of test outcomes: the test entropy measure $h^{(k)}$ will tell us about how each test case distributes its activity across modules, and the fault exposure measure $\phi^{(k)}$ will tell us how well the test activity was distributed in terms of where the potential faults are likely to be. The main point is that we should learn to measure the test outcomes of individual tests and evaluate them as we perform each test case. Unfortunately, the current measurement in use in most organizations is a binary outcome: the test failed or the test succeeded.

These two measures will serve well to introduce the notion of test measurement. We must remember, however, that the code base is constantly changing. New modules are entering the code base, modules are being modified, and modules are being deleted. A single test case applied over a series of sequential builds may well produce very different values, depending on the nature of the changes that have occurred and the total code churn.

11.4.2 Cumulative Measure of Testing

Each test activity will generate a TEFV. This vector represents the frequency that each module will have been exercised in a particular test. At the conclusion of each test we can add each element of that TEFV to a cumulative test execution frequency vector (CTEFV). The CTEFV, then, will contain the frequency of execution of each module over the entire lot of test cases that have been executed to date. From this CTEFV we can compute a cumulative test execution profile $\mathbf{p}^{(c)}$. This will show the distribution of test activity across all program modules to date. We can easily compute the cumulative test entropy to date and our cumulative fault exposure $\phi^{(c)}$. The CTEFV is a vector that will contain only the module frequencies for modules in the current build.

Let us assume, for the moment, that our test objectives are strictly to find faults. The measure ϕ is clearly a measure of exposure to potential faults in the program. Therefore, a test that will maximize ϕ would be an optimal test. It turns out, however, that the maximum value of ϕ is obtained when the one module with the highest FI is executed to the exclusion of all others. This is also a point of minimum entropy.

A fair test, on the other hand, is one that will spread its activity across all modules, not just the ones that are most likely to contain faults. A single fault in a module with a very low FI will have exactly the same consequences as a fault in a module with a much higher FI when either of these modules is executed by a user. Each module, then, should receive test activity in proportion to the relative likelihood that it will have faults that can be exposed by testing. Remember from Chapter 8 that the proportion of faults in the module on the jth build of the system was determined to be

$$r_i^j = (\rho_i^0 + \nabla_i^{0,j}) \Big/ (R^0 + \nabla^{0,j})$$

A fair test of a system is one in which $p_i^{(c)} = r_i^j$ for all i. In other words, each module should be tested in proportion to its potential contribution to the total fault count.

We would like to measure the difference between how we have distributed our test activity and where the potential faults might be. Let $\varphi_i^j = \left| p_i^{(c)} - r_i^j \right|$ represent the difference between the test activity on module i and the relative fault burden for that module. A measure of the overall test effectiveness of our test effort to date will then be:

$$\Gamma^{(j)} = \sum_{i=1}^{n_j} \varphi_i^j = \sum_{i=1}^{n_j} \left| p_i^{(c)} - r_i^j \right|$$

where n_j is the cardinality of the set of modules in build j. The maximum value for $\Gamma^{(j)}$ will be 2.0 and its minimum will be 0.0. This minimum will be attained in the case where the cumulative test profile exactly matches the projected fault burden of the program modules. The maximum value will be attained when there is a complete mismatch between the cumulative test profile and the projected fault burden. This could happen, for example, if $p_i^{(c)} = 1.0$ and $r_i^j = 0.0$.

One thing that is immediately apparent in the computation of these cumulative measures of testing is that they involve an incredible amount of data that must be accumulated over the evolving history of the system. It would be literally impossible for a single human being to begin to manage these data. This is one of the primary reasons that the test effort at most software development organizations is run strictly by *gut feeling*. Unless there is a suitable infrastructure in place to collect and manage the measurement data, the quantification of test outcomes will be impossible. Chapter 13 discusses a system for the management of these data.

One of our principal concerns in the test process is that the system should work when the customer uses it. It is not particularly relevant just how many faults are in the system when it is placed in the user's hands for the first time. The important thing is that the user does not execute the residual faults that are in the code. Remember that each user will distribute his or her activity on the set of operations according to an operational profile. Each operational profile will, in turn, generate a functional profile, which ultimately will create a distinct module profile for that operational profile. Our total test activity will be a success if we have tested and certified the software in a manner consistent with how it will be used. That is, $\mathbf{p}^{(c)} = \mathbf{o}$. In other words, our test activity ultimately reflects the user operational profile. It would be a good idea for us to know something about the user operational profile before we ship our software.

11.4.3 Delta Testing

As the software evolution process progresses, new faults will likely be added to the system in proportion to the changes that have been made to affected modules. This means that the distribution of faults in the code will change as the software system evolves. Our measurement data will show us this shifting distribution of fault distribution. This means that we can know which modules are most likely to contain faults. The real problem will be to craft test cases that will expose these faults. Constructing these test cases will be very difficult if we do not know what the system is supposed to do or how it does what it is supposed to do. That is the reason we must insist on having good requirements traceability. In Chapter 9 we developed a system for mapping user operations to specific code modules, $O \times F \times M$. This means that we can identify either specific functionalities that exercise certain sets of modules for functional testing, or we can identify specific user operations that exercise certain modules for operational level testing.

The initial phase of the effective functional testing of changed code is to identify the functionalities that will exercise the modules that have changed. Each of these functionalities thus designated will have an associated test suite designed to exercise that functionality. With this information it is now possible to describe the efficiency of a test from a mathematical/statistical perspective. A delta test is one specifically tailored to exercise the functionalities that will cause the changed modules to be executed. A delta test will be effective if it does a good job of exercising changed code. It is worth noting, however, that a delta test that is effective on one build may be ineffective on a subsequent build. Thus, the *effectiveness* of a delta test between any two builds i and j is given by:

$$\tau_{i,j}^{(k)} = \sum_{a=1}^{m} p_a^{(k)} \chi_a^{i,j}$$

where m represents the cardinality of the modules in build as defined earlier. In this case, $\tau_{i,j}^{(k)}$ is simply the expected value for code churn under the profile $\mathbf{p}^{(k)}$ between builds i and j.

This concept of test effectiveness permits the numerical evaluation of a test on the actual changes that have been made to the software system. It is simply the expected value of the fault exposure from one build to another under a particular test. If the value of τ is large for a given test, then the test will have done a good job of exercising the changed modules. If the set of τs for a given release is low, then it is reasonable to suppose that the changed modules have not been tested well in relation to the number of probable faults that were introduced during the maintenance changes.

Given the nature of the code churn from one build to another, one simple fact emerges with great clarity. That is, there is no such thing as a standard delta test suite. Delta testing must be tailored to the changes made in each build. The functionalities that will be most impacted by the change process are those that use the modules that have been changed the most.

For practical purposes, we need to know something about the upper bound on test effectiveness. That is, if we were to execute the best possible test, what then would be the value of test effectiveness? A *best* delta test is one that will spend the majority of its time in the functionalities that contain the modules that have changed the most from one build to the next. Let,

$$X^{i,j} = \sum_{a=1}^{n} \chi_a^{i,j}$$

This is the total code churn between the i and j builds. To exercise each module in proportion to the change that has occurred in the module during its current revision, we will compute this proportion as follows:

$$q_a^{i,j} = \chi_a^{i,j} \Big/ X^{i,j}$$

This computation will yield a new hypothetical profile called the *best profile*. That is, if all modules were exercised in proportion to the amount of change they had received, we would then theoretically have maximized our exposure to software faults that may have been introduced.

Finally, we seek to develop a measure that will relate well to the difference between the actual profile that is generated by a test and the best profile. To this end, consider the term $\left| p_i^{(k)} - q_i \right|$. This is the absolute value between the best profile and the actual profile for test case k. This value has a maximum value of 1 and a minimum of 0. The minimum value will be achieved when the module best and actual test profiles are identical. A measure of the *efficiency* of a test (task or program) is:

$$\theta^{(k)} = \left(1 - 0.5 \sum_a \left| p_a^{(k)} - q_a^{i,j} \right| \right) \times 100\%$$

This coverage value has a maximum value of 100 percent when the best and the actual profiles are identical, and a value of 0 when there is a complete mismatch of profiles.

In a rapidly evolving software system, there can be no standard suite of delta test cases. These test delta cases must be developed to ensure the operability of each functionality in direct response to modules that implement that functionality.

11.4.4 Delta Test Results: A Case Study

The following discussion documents the results of the execution of 36 instrumented tasks on two sequential builds of a large embedded software system (which we will refer to as the RTJ system) written in C++ for a large mass storage disk subsystem at a major supplier of disk storage subsystems. In this specific example, a module is a task. The perspective of this discussion is strictly from the standpoint of delta testing. That is, certain program modules have changed across the two sequential builds. The degree of this change is measured by code churn. As has been clearly demonstrated on the Cassini spacecraft project, the greater the change in a program module, the greater the likelihood that faults will have been introduced into the code by the change.[4] Each of the delta tests, then, should attempt to exercise these changed modules in proportion to the degree of change. If a changed module were to receive little or no activity during the test process, then we must assume that the latent faults in the module will be expressed when the software is placed into service.

All of the tasks in the RTJ system were instrumented with our Clic tool. This tool will permit us to count the frequency of execution of each module in each of the instrumented tasks and thus obtain the execution profiles for these tasks for each of the tests. In the C++ environment, the term *module* is applied to a method or a function. These are the source code elements that are reflected in the code that actually executes. Each task typically contains from 10 to 30 program modules. In this case, the granularity of measurement has been ratcheted up from the module level to the task level.

The execution profiles show the distribution of activity in each module of the instrumented tasks. For each of the modules, the code churn measure was computed. For the purposes of this investigation, the FI distribution was set to a mean of 50 and a standard deviation of 10. The code churn values for each module reflected the degree of change of the modules during the most recent sequence of builds. The cumulative churn values for all tasks are shown in the second column of Exhibit 1. A churn value of zero indicates that the module in question received no changes during the last build sequence. A large churn value (>30) indicates that the module in question received substantial changes.

For the subsequent analysis, two profile values for each test will be compared. The *actual profile* is the actual execution profile for each test. The *best profile* is the best hypothetical execution profile given that each module would be tested directly in proportion to its churn value. That is, a module whose churn value is zero would receive little or no activity during the regression test process.

From Exhibit 1 we can see that the A and B tasks have received the greatest change activity. The total churn values were 2028.31 and 487.26 respectively. The code churn values were used to establish the Best Profile column. The Profile Difference column represents the difference between the theoretical best profile and the actual test activity reflected by the actual profile. From the profile difference we can derive the test efficiency for this test, which is 9.04 percent. From the Actual Profile column we can see that the test entropy was 1.87. Maximum entropy for the 36 modules in a test that would exercise each of the modules equally would be 5.17.

The last two columns in Exhibit 1 contain the expected value for the code churn of the task under the best profile and also under the actual profile. These columns are labeled Maximum Test Effectiveness and Actual Test Effectiveness. The maximum test effectiveness with the code churn introduced between the builds being measured under the best profile is 1311.50. The actual test effectiveness for all tasks was measured at 89.44. In percentage terms, the actual test effectiveness of this test was 6.82 percent of a theoretical maximum exposure to software faults.

All the data point to the same problem. The tests spent a disproportionate amount of time in modules that had not substantially changed during this build interval. In essence, the bulk of the test resources are being devoted to modules that have not changed and have already been thoroughly tested. We can clearly see this if we plot the differences between the best profile and the actual profile. This difference is shown in Exhibit 2 for the tasks A through AJ. We can see that considerable test effort was invested in tasks D, K, and Q, each of which had relatively little change activity. This is shown by the fact that the difference is negative.

Exhibit 1. Test Summary by Task

Task	Churn	Best Profile	Actual Profile	Profile Difference	Maximum Test Effectiveness	Actual Test Effectiveness
A	2028.31	5.96E-01	1.94E-02	5.77E-01	1208.26	39.29
B	487.26	1.43E-01	7.97E-03	1.35E-01	69.73	3.88
C	154.72	4.54E-02	8.94E-04	4.45E-02	7.03	0.14
D	150.77	4.43E-02	2.71E-01	2.27E-01	6.67	40.89
E	150.71	4.43E-02	2.67E-03	4.16E-02	6.67	0.40
F	126.46	3.71E-02	3.17E-03	3.39E-02	4.69	0.40
G	121.00	3.55E-02	2.79E-03	3.27E-02	4.29	0.34
H	117.2	3.44E-02	8.15E-04	3.36E-02	4.03	0.10
I	14.38	4.23E-03	2.96E-04	3.93E-03	0.06	0.01
J	9.11	2.68E-03	4.97E-05	2.63E-03	0.02	0.00
K	6.84	2.01E-03	4.99E-01	4.97E-01	0.01	3.42
L	6.27	1.84E-03	4.42E-05	1.80E-03	0.01	0.00
M	5.64	1.66E-03	2.83E-03	1.17E-03	0.01	0.02
N	5.17	1.52E-03	7.46E-05	1.45E-03	0.01	0.00
O	3.92	1.15E-03	1.47E-04	1.00E-03	0.01	0.00
P	3.90	1.15E-03	2.27E-03	1.12E-03	0.00	0.01
Q	3.20	9.42E-04	1.72E-01	1.71E-01	0.00	0.55
R	2.28	6.70E-04	2.12E-06	6.68E-04	0.00	0.00
S	1.85	5.44E-04	7.07E-04	1.63E-04	0.00	0.00
T	1.84	5.42E-04	6.40E-05	4.78E-04	0.00	0.00
U	1.19	3.52E-04	4.48E-04	9.60E-05	0.00	0.00
V	0.84	2.49E-04	8.63E-04	6.14E-04	0.00	0.00
W	0.68	2.02E-04	1.17E-04	8.50E-05	0.00	0.00
X	0.54	1.60E-04	3.81E-03	3.65E-03	0.00	0.00
Y	0.26	7.82E-05	3.50E-03	3.42E-03	0.00	0.00
Z	0.22	6.75E-05	1.86E-04	1.19E-04	0.00	0.00
AA	0.09	2.83E-05	6.34E-05	3.51E-05	0.00	0.00
AB	0.08	2.01E-05	1.55E-05	1.00E-05	0.00	0.00
AC	0.04	1.30E-05	6.54E-07	1.23E-05	0.00	0.00
AD	0.00	0.00E+00	1.09E-05	1.09E-05	0.00	0.00
AE	0.00	0.00E+00	3.75E-06	3.75E-06	0.00	0.00
AF	0.00	0.00E+00	3.71E-03	3.71E-03	0.00	0.00
AG	0.00	0.00E+00	3.91E-07	3.91E-07	0.00	0.00
AH	0.00	0.00E+00	2.15E-04	2.15E-04	0.00	0.00
AI	0.00	0.00E+00	4.57E-07	4.57E-07	0.00	0.00
AJ	0.00	0.00E+00	2.85E-06	2.85E-06	0.00	0.00
Total	3404.77				1311.50	89.44

Test entropy	1.87	
Test efficiency	9.04%	
Test effectiveness		6.82%

Exhibit 3 summarizes the performance of the best 24 of a total suite of 115 instrumented tests. Only those tests whose test efficiencies exceeded 10 percent of a theoretical total are shown. Again, the test efficiencies shown in this exhibit were computed from the difference between the actual profile and the best profile for that test. It is clear even in the best circumstances that not all tests will exercise all modules. Therefore, the test efficiency was computed only for those modules whose functionality was included in the test. From a delta test perspective, we now know that we have a testing problem.

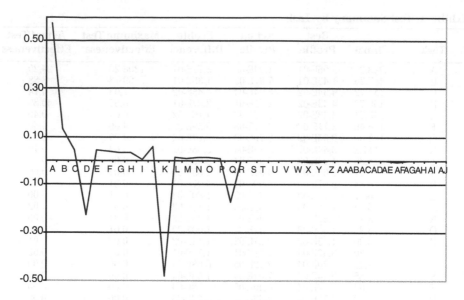

Exhibit 2. Actual versus Best Test Profile Activity

Exhibit 3. Individual Test Summaries

Test No.	Test Efficiency	Test No.	Test Efficiency
28	20.6	177	11.7
18	19.0	31	11.6
14	18.2	3	11.5
12	16.9	167	11.5
47	14.8	59a	11.4
49	14.8	2	11.3
169	14.7	159	11.3
156	13.2	1	10.9
20	13.1	38	10.8
39	12.9	180	10.7
9	12.2	33	10.6
158	12.2	137	10.2

None of these tests do a really good job in executing the code most likely to contain the newly introduced faults. Furthermore, we now have a good clear indication as to how to fix the problem.

In a second investigation at this same organization, two major measurement initiatives were established, this time for a new system we will refer to as the QTB system. This is a real-time embedded system consisting of 120 modules of C++ code. During the test process whose activities are reported here, the QTB system was driven through five sequential test suites of the system on four successive builds of system, called build 10, 11, 12, and 13. For this sequence of builds, build 10 was chosen as the baseline build. All of the metrics for this test series were baselined on this build.

Each of the five test suites was designed to exercise a different set of functionalities. Each of the functionalities, in turn, invoked a particular subset of program modules. Thus, as each of the tests executed, only a limited number of the total program modules received execution control. For Test 1, only 49 of the 120 modules in the QTB task were executed. For Test 2, only 25 of the 120 modules were executed. Of the 120 modules, only 16 were executed in all five tests.

The specific test outcomes for Tests 1 and 2 are shown in Exhibits 4 and 5, respectively. These two tests were chosen for discussion in that their characteristics are very different. The functionalities invoked by Test 1 caused 44 modules to be executed. Test 2, on the other hand, only executed 25 program modules. The baseline system for this test series was chosen to build 10. The metrics for each of the program modules in Tests 1 and 2 were baselined on this build.

The second column of Exhibits 4 and 5 displays the FI value, relative to build 10, for each of the modules that received at least one execution in each of the tests. The total system FI for all 120 modules is 6014. The total FI for all the modules that executed in Test 1 is 2585, or 43 percent of the total system FI. Another way to look at this value is that Test 1 will have exposure to about 43 percent of the latent faults in the system. Test 2 similarly provided exposure for only about 22 percent of the latent faults.

The third column of Exhibit 4 labeled $\mathbf{p}^{(1)}$, contains the actual profile data for each test. The fourth column of this table, $\phi^{(1)}$, is the product of the FI and the profile value. This represents the failure exposure of capabilities of Test 1 on the baseline system. The total value for this column is the total test failure exposure. It is the expected value of FI under the profile, $\mathbf{p}^{(1)}$. If all of the modules in the entire system were to have been executed with equal frequency, this value would have been 50. A value less than 50 means that the test ran less exposure to latent faults than average. In this case $\phi = 52.68$, which is slightly better than average fault exposure for this test. On Test 2, the results of which are shown in Exhibit 5, the expected fault exposure is 55.94, an even better fault exposure.

The fifth column of Exhibit 4, $\chi^{10,11}$, contains the code churn value for the changes between build 10 and build 11. For most of the modules in this exhibit, this value is zero. They did not change from build 10 to build 11. The greatest change was in a new program module not executed by this test. A good delta test for the changes that were made to this module would cause it to be executed with high probability. This module did not execute at all. A delta test suite would be effective with respect to maximizing our exposure to potentially introduced faults if the product of the profile and the churn value is large. The test effectiveness for Test 1 is shown in the column labeled $\tau_{10,11}^{(1)}$. The upper bound on test effectiveness will be achieved in the case where the module with the greatest change is exe-

Exhibit 4. Test Results for Test 1

Module	ρ^{10}	$P^{(I)}$	$\phi^{(10)}$	$\chi^{10,11}$	$\tau^{(I)}_{10,11}$	$\chi^{11,12}$	$\tau^{(I)}_{11,12}$	$\chi^{12,13}$	$\tau^{(I)}_{12,13}$
1	44.23	0.023	1.01	0.00	0.00	0.00	0.00	0.00	0.00
2	48.41	0.002	0.09	0.00	0.00	0.00	0.00	0.00	0.00
3	49.05	0.004	0.19	0.00	0.00	0.00	0.00	0.00	0.00
4	56.30	0.059	3.33	0.00	0.00	0.04	0.00	0.00	0.00
7	54.93	0.004	0.21	0.00	0.00	0.00	0.00	0.00	0.00
8	54.25	0.017	0.93	0.00	0.00	0.00	0.00	0.00	0.00
9	51.48	0.002	0.10	0.00	0.00	0.00	0.00	0.00	0.00
10	50.75	0.017	0.87	0.00	0.00	0.00	0.00	0.00	0.00
12	61.25	0.004	0.23	1.99	0.01	0.00	0.00	1.18	0.00
13	53.12	0.017	0.91	0.57	0.01	0.00	0.00	0.00	0.00
14	51.10	0.013	0.68	0.00	0.00	0.00	0.00	0.00	0.00
15	49.08	0.002	0.09	0.00	0.00	0.00	0.00	0.00	0.00
16	49.92	0.055	2.76	0.00	0.00	0.00	0.00	0.00	0.00
17	55.08	0.004	0.21	0.00	0.00	0.00	0.00	0.00	0.00
18	47.32	0.048	2.26	0.00	0.00	0.00	0.00	0.00	0.00
19	54.14	0.006	0.31	0.00	0.00	0.00	0.00	0.00	0.00
21	44.47	0.044	1.95	0.00	0.00	0.00	0.00	1.13	0.05
22	49.12	0.004	0.19	0.00	0.00	0.00	0.00	0.00	0.00
23	56.82	0.004	0.22	0.00	0.00	0.00	0.00	0.00	0.00
24	57.30	0.021	1.20	0.00	0.00	0.00	0.00	0.00	0.00
25	53.98	0.017	0.93	0.00	0.00	3.13	0.05	1.22	0.02
26	36.52	0.004	0.14	0.00	0.00	0.00	0.00	0.00	0.00
31	50.90	0.017	0.87	0.00	0.00	0.00	0.00	0.00	0.00
52	46.66	0.008	0.36	0.00	0.00	0.00	0.00	0.00	0.00
53	46.11	0.010	0.44	0.00	0.00	0.00	0.00	0.00	0.00
54	46.11	0.011	0.53	0.00	0.00	0.00	0.00	0.00	0.00
56	54.87	0.006	0.31	0.00	0.00	0.00	0.00	0.63	0.00
57	46.74	0.004	0.18	2.66	0.01	0.00	0.00	0.00	0.00
60	58.28	0.004	0.22	0.00	0.00	0.07	0.00	0.07	0.00
63	50.43	0.002	0.10	0.00	0.00	0.00	0.00	0.00	0.00
64	70.82	0.053	3.78	0.00	0.00	0.00	0.00	0.00	0.00
71	55.48	0.128	7.09	0.00	0.00	0.00	0.00	0.00	0.00
75	55.29	0.044	2.43	0.00	0.00	0.00	0.00	0.00	0.00
76	50.99	0.002	0.10	0.00	0.00	0.00	0.00	0.00	0.00
77	52.55	0.002	0.10	0.62	0.00	0.00	0.00	0.00	0.00
80	56.82	0.021	1.19	0.61	0.01	0.00	0.00	1.89	0.04
95	54.93	0.004	0.21	0.00	0.00	0.00	0.00	0.00	0.00
96	58.55	0.006	0.34	0.00	0.00	0.00	0.00	0.00	0.00
97	36.38	0.006	0.21	0.00	0.00	0.00	0.00	0.00	0.00
98	56.44	0.013	0.75	0.00	0.00	0.07	0.00	0.07	0.00
100	57.46	0.002	0.11	0.00	0.00	0.00	0.00	0.00	0.00
103	47.54	0.025	1.18	0.00	0.00	0.00	0.00	0.00	0.00
106	75.43	0.002	0.14	0.00	0.00	0.00	0.00	0.34	0.00
107	50.74	0.006	0.29	0.00	0.00	0.00	0.00	0.00	0.00
110	59.45	0.002	0.11	0.00	0.00	0.00	0.00	0.00	0.00
111	68.39	0.004	0.26	0.00	0.00	0.00	0.00	0.00	0.00
114	49.94	0.193	9.63	0.00	0.00	0.02	0.00	0.02	0.00
115	46.32	0.017	0.80	1.75	0.03	0.76	0.01	0.00	0.00
118	52.86	0.040	2.12	0.00	0.00	0.00	0.00	0.00	0.00
Total	2585.10		52.68	8.20	0.07	4.10	0.07	6.54	0.12
System total	6014.15			67.24		77.52		124.32	

cuted exclusively. The maximum effectiveness for this particular test will be 67.24, the code churn value for the module with the greatest churn value. We can see that the total effectiveness, then, for Test 1 on build 11 is

Exhibit 5. Test Results for Test 2

Module	P^{10}	$P^{(2)}$	$\phi^{(2)}$	$\chi^{10,11}$	$\tau^{(2)}_{12,13}$	$\chi^{11,12}$	$\tau^{(2)}_{11,12}$	$\chi^{12,13}$	$\tau^{(2)}_{12,13}$
3	49.05	0.010	0.48	0.00	0.00	0.00	0.00	0.00	0.00
4	56.30	0.039	2.19	0.00	0.00	0.04	0.00	0.00	0.00
6	48.48	0.039	1.88	0.00	0.00	0.00	0.00	0.00	0.00
14	51.10	0.019	0.99	0.00	0.00	0.00	0.00	0.00	0.00
18	47.32	0.029	1.38	0.00	0.00	0.00	0.00	0.00	0.00
20	47.68	0.019	0.93	0.00	0.00	0.00	0.00	0.00	0.00
21	44.47	0.049	2.16	0.00	0.00	0.00	0.00	1.13	0.05
23	56.82	0.058	3.31	0.00	0.00	0.00	0.00	0.00	0.00
24	57.30	0.019	1.11	0.00	0.00	0.00	0.00	0.00	0.00
26	36.52	0.010	0.35	0.00	0.00	0.00	0.00	0.00	0.00
37	53.51	0.039	2.08	0.00	0.00	0.07	0.00	0.07	0.00
64	70.82	0.136	9.63	0.00	0.00	0.00	0.00	0.00	0.00
66	61.98	0.097	6.02	0.00	0.00	0.02	0.00	0.02	0.00
69	48.46	0.019	0.94	0.00	0.00	0.13	0.00	0.13	0.00
71	55.48	0.097	5.39	0.00	0.00	0.00	0.00	0.00	0.00
77	52.55	0.029	1.53	0.62	0.02	0.00	0.00	0.00	0.00
79	57.34	0.019	1.11	0.00	0.00	0.07	0.00	0.07	0.00
80	56.82	0.058	3.31	0.61	0.04	0.00	0.00	1.89	0.11
83	73.44	0.010	0.71	0.39	0.00	0.00	0.00	0.00	0.00
95	54.93	0.019	1.07	0.00	0.00	0.00	0.00	0.00	0.00
96	58.55	0.019	1.14	0.00	0.00	0.00	0.00	0.00	0.00
103	47.54	0.019	0.92	0.00	0.00	0.00	0.00	0.00	0.00
109	49.05	0.010	0.48	0.00	0.00	0.61	0.01	0.61	0.01
114	49.94	0.117	5.82	0.00	0.00	0.02	0.00	0.02	0.00
118	52.86	0.019	1.03	0.00	0.00	0.00	0.00	0.00	0.00
Totals	1338.32		55.94	1.62	0.06	0.96	0.01	3.93	0.18

0.07, or less than 1 percent of the maximum. The efficiency of this test is less than 4 percent. This is neither an effective nor efficient test of the changes made between builds 10 and 11.

The next four columns of Exhibit 4 contain the code churn values and the test efficiency values for Test 1 on builds 12 and 13, respectively. We can see that the absolute effectiveness of Test 1 on builds 12 and 13 does, in fact, increase. However, when we look at the effectiveness of each of the tests as a percentage of the maximum, we can see that the test effectiveness really declines rather than increases. The test efficiency of Test 1 was never above 4 percent across the three build deltas.

The last row of Exhibit 4 contains the total system values for system FI and also for the total code churn for the three successive build events. We can see, for example, that the total churn for the build 10–11 sequence is 67.24. Test 1 only executed modules whose total churn was 8.2, or 12 percent of the total value. We can see that the greatest change occurred between builds 12 and 13 in that the total system churn was 124.32 for this build.

Similar data is reported for Test 2 in Exhibit 5. Test 2 is a very different test from that of Test 1. We can see from the fourth column in Exhibit 5 that the failure exposure ϕ of the modules actually invoked during Test 2 is somewhat greater than that of Test 1, 55.94 versus 52.68. In that sense, Test

Exhibit 6. Test Results Summary for Tests 1 through 5

Test	Build 10–11 $\chi^{\%10,11}$	$\tau_{10,11}$	Build 11–12 $\chi^{\%11,12}$	$\tau_{11,12}$	Build 12–13 $\chi^{\%12,13}$	$\tau_{12,13}$
1	12	0.07	5	0.07	5	0.12
2	2	0.06	1	0.01	3	0.18
3	6	0.07	6	0.08	5	0.10
4	2	0.04	0	0	2	0.09
5	11	0.07	4	0.05	4	0.07

2 will be more likely to expose latent faults in the base code than will Test 1. Test 2, however, is a very much weaker test suite for the set of modules that it exercises. The test effectiveness for this test is very low. What is interesting to note in Exhibit 5 is that while Test 2 is not an effective test suite for the changes that were made from build 10 to 11 and from build 11 to 12, this test suite is a more effective test suite for the nature of the changes to the system between builds 12 and 13.

We are now in a position to use the summary data to evaluate test outcomes for other test applications. In Exhibit 6 the test results for all five tests are summarized. Each of the five test activities represented by the contents of this table is summarized by two numbers. The first number is in the column labeled $\chi^\%$. It represents the percentage of the total code churn. We would have to conclude that none of the tests did a sterling job for the delta test based on this value for $\chi^\%$. These tests simply did not execute the right modules, those that had changed the most.

The second global test evaluation criterion is τ, or test effectiveness. None of the tests could have been considered to be really effective by this criterion. Even among the modules that were executed that had changed during the successive builds, these tests did not distribute their activity well.

Unless we are able to quantify test outcomes, our impressions of the testing process will likely be wrong. The five tests whose outcomes we evaluated in this study were, in fact, part of a "standard regression test" suite. They are routinely run between builds. We can see that they routinely do not do a good job of identifying and exercising modules that might well have had new faults introduced into them.

When a program is subjected to numerous test suites to exercise differing aspects of its functionality, the test risk of a system will vary greatly as a result of the execution of these different test suites. Intuitively — and empirically — a program that spends a high proportion of its time executing a module set of high FI will be more failure prone than one driven to executing program modules with complexity values. Thus, we need to identify the characteristics of test scenarios that cause our criterion measures of χ and τ to be large.

11.5 FRACTIONAL MEASURES

Up to this point in our discussion of testing, we have regarded a program module as atomic. That is, it was not decomposable. As our need for increased resolution in the test activity begins to be an important factor, we can actually look within a program module and study how the parts of the module interact whenever it is invoked. One thing is clear for most program modules. Not all of the code in the module will execute when it is invoked. If the module is lacking in cohesion, only a very small subset of the executable statements in the module will, in fact, execute.

One thing is quite clear, however. Whatever subset of code that does execute when a module is called is a complete and viable program module in its own right. Thus, a module lacking in cohesion may well be seen as three or more very distinct program modules, depending on how the module is invoked. Each functionality, then, will effectively extract a subset of executable statements from the modules that are invoked in that functionality. We can, in fact, determine, *a posteriori,* which code segments have executed and measure just these code segments. Thus, if a functionality were to execute, say, 12 executable statements out of a total of 48 executable statements in a module, we could measure just the source code attributes of the 12 statements that did execute. This subset of the code would give us a very different view of the program module and its fault liability. It may very well be that the very code constructs that might make a module potentially fault prone are strictly avoided by functionality. The *fractional FI* of the code executed by that module by a particular functionality will consist of measurements of source code attributes of the subset of source code executed.

11.5.1 The FI of the XC Modules

For the purposes of exploring the notions of fractional complexity and its impact on the test process, a small open-source program called XC was chosen for an investigation on the assessment of test activity on fractional code segments.[5] XC is an asynchronous communications program for the UNIX environment. It supports xmodem, ymodem, xmodem-g, ymodem-g, and cis_b+ internal file transfer protocols. Use of external zmodem is also supported with auto-triggering of downloads. XC is a text-mode or command line application written in the C programming language.

For this study, the UX metric tool was employed to measure each of the15 modules of the XC program. A set of nine metrics was obtained from the UX metric measurement tool. These metrics are shown in Exhibit 7. This is a reduced set of metrics obtained from the measurement process.

Exhibit 7. Metrics and Their Definitions

η_1	Halstead's count of the number of unique operators
η_2	Halstead's count of the number of unique operands
N_1	Halstead's count of the total number of operators
N_2	Halstead's count of the total number of operands
Stmt	Count of total noncommented source statements
LOC	Count of the total number of noncommented lines of code
Blks	Count of the total number of program blocks
Span	Average span of a variable reference
$V(g)$	Nodes - Edges + 2

Exhibit 8. FI Values for XC Modules

Module	7	1	6	4	9	3	8	13	15	14	11	10	12	2	5
ρ	119	118	112	104	102	102	101	101	94	93	93	92	90	90	89

They constitute the set of primitive measures that we have found to be the most closely related to software faults. These nine metrics were obtained for each of the fifteen program modules.

While this reduction in the number of metrics has simplified the problem somewhat, we will further simplify the metric values for each module by computing their individual FI values, ρ_i. This static measure of FI for the 15 program modules, ρ, is shown in Exhibit 8.

In its capacity as a fault surrogate, the program modules shown in Exhibit 8 are ordered from the most complex to the least complex. We can see from this arrangement that modules 7, 1, and 6 have disproportionately high values of the FI. Previous validation studies support the conclusion that these are the modules that have the greatest potential for faults.[6] However, when we get to executing the actual modules, we will discover that not all of module 7, for example, ever executes when the module receives control. Some statements will execute and others will not. The design of module 6, on the other hand, may result in all of the code in this module being executed every time it is entered. Thus, there is a dynamic aspect to the complexity of the module. The dynamic complexity of a module, like module 7, may be much less than its static complexity.

It can be seen from Exhibit 8 that there is a great deal of variability in the complexity of these 15 modules. For example, module 7 has an FI of 119, two standard deviations above the mean. Conversely, module 5 has an FI of 89, one standard deviation below the mean. From these static measurements, and the high correlation of FI with software faults, it can be surmised that there are likely to be more faults in module 7 than in module 5. However, this fact does not indicate the likelihood of the system failing. Module 7 rarely, if ever, executes during normal operation. Module 5, on the other hand, executes frequently. Because of this great difference in the exposure each of these two modules receives during execution, we may well observe more

Exhibit 9. C Code Segment 1

```
if (i > j)
    {
    i = i + j;
    printf (i);
    }
  else
    printf (i);
```

Exhibit 10. C Code Segment 2

```
if (i > j)
    {
    i = i + j;
    printf (i);
    }
```

failures attributable to faults in module 5 than we do faults in module 7. To develop an understanding of this failure potential, we must develop a means of characterizing the functional behavior of a system in terms of how it distributes its activity across a set of modules. This requires knowing what the program does, its functionalities, and how these different functionalities allocate time to the modules that comprise the system.

11.5.2 Fractional Complexity

In the usual computation of static software complexity, the complexity of the entire module is computed for each program module. This static measure may be very misleading. As the code in each program module executes, only a small number of the possible paths through the module may execute, in which case the complexity of the *functionality* has been exaggerated by an amount equal to the complexity of the code that did not execute. Hence, it only seems reasonable in the computation of dynamic program complexity to assess the complexity of just that code that executed for each of the distinct functionalities. As a program executes each of the sets of its functions, it will select a subset of statements from each module. The code in this reduced statement set will be a complete and fully functional program in its own right. It will not have the functionality of the entire program in that only a subset of the source code has been selected by the particular functionality. An example of this can be seen in Exhibits 9, 10, and 11. In Exhibit 9 we have a code segment of C code. To compute the FI of this segment we will measure the entire segment. In all, there are seven lines of code, five statements, and seven total operands. When this code is executed, however, there are two outcomes based on the predicate clause. In Exhibit 9 we will assume that the variable i is greater than j when the code

Exhibit 11. C Code Segment 3

```
if (i > j)
    printf (i);
```

is executed. If we measure just the code segment that executed, there are now five lines of code, four statements, and six total operands. In Exhibit 11 we will assume that the predicate is false. Now there are just two lines of code, two statements, and three total operands. The complexity of this code segment depends on the outcome of the evaluation of the predicate clause.

In the dynamic program complexity view, the complexity of a program module will vary in accordance with the code that is selected for execution. Under this view, the complexity of the system will vary by function as well. The metric values for a single program module can no longer be characterized by a single vector of values. In this new view there will be a set of vectors of metrics values, one vector for each functionality. As each functionality is executed, a different subset of code will be excised by the functionality. Thus, every time a new functionality is executed, we will re-measure that code and extract a new set of raw metrics for that subset.

A significant problem arises in the computation of the orthogonal metric sets and, subsequently, FI, in that many different subsets of code will be selected by the varying functionalities. A solution to this problem is to use the original transformation matrix that was calculated for the domain metrics for the entire program. If this is the case, the raw metrics of each module will be bounded above by the raw metric values of the entire module. The FI of any of the subsets of the module code will also be bounded above by the FI of the entire module. Thus, the baseline established for the initial computation of FI will also serve as the baseline for the computation of the complexity of the functional code subsets. As was the case for the model of evolving software discussed in Chapter 8, the baseline established for fractional code measurement will consist of the set of means and standard deviations obtained for the original raw metrics and the transformation matrix. We standardize the raw metrics of the functional code subsets with these means and standard deviations of the full program measures.

Each distinct test scenario to a program will cause a subset of the program and each of its modules to execute. The source code subset of the original program represented by the code subset of a module m_i will have its own FI as the functionality changes. To differentiate between the system FI and the FI of each of the functional code subsets, this new FI of the ith module executing the jth function will be denoted as $\xi_i^{(j)}$. This *fractional* FI value will represent the FI of *just the code that was executed* when the jth functionality was exercised.

Exhibit 12. Functionalities of XC

Function	Functionality Description
f_1	Routing output
f_2	Cross-referencing reserved words
f_3	Processing nested include files
f_4	Generate listing only
f_5	Extended debugging facility
f_6	Cross-referencing user-defined identifiers

Exhibit 13. Functional Module Subsets of XC

F	M_c	M_i	M_p
f_1	$\{m_1\}$	$\{m_3\text{-}m_{12}, m_{14}, m_{15}\}$	$\{m_2, m_{13}\}$
f_2	$\{m_1\}$	$\{m_3\text{-}m_{12}, m_{14}, m_{15}\}$	$\{m_2, m_{13}\}$
f_3	$\{m_1\}$	$\{m_3\text{-}m_8, m_{11}, m_{14}, m_{15}\}$	$\{m_2\}$
f_4	$\{m_1\}$	$\{m_3\text{-}m_8, m_{11}, m_{14}, m_{15}\}$	$\{m_2\}$
f_5	$\{m_1\}$		$\{m_2\text{-}m_{15}\}$
f_6	$\{m_1\}$	$\{m_3\text{-}m_{12}, m_{14}, m_{15}\}$	$\{m_2, m_{13}\}$

From a measurement perspective, it is not always easy to extract the code segments that have executed when a particular functionality is exercised. Necessarily, the software will have to be instrumented to permit this introspection. In some languages, such as C, there are available code coverage tools, such as ATAC, capable of isolating code sequences associated with particular tests.[n] When these code segments are so isolated, they can then be measured by existing metric analysis tools.

To demonstrate the concept of the fractional complexity of functionalities with the software test process, the *XC* system was monitored and measured by a modified version of the ATAC tool. Our modified ATAC tool was used to identify the specific C source statements that had executed for each test activity. The source code elements that were thus identified by the modified ATAC tool were measured by the UX metric tool.

From the standpoint of the highest-level granularity of functionality, the XC tool consists of six basic functions. These functionalities are summarized in Exhibit 12. At any given epoch of the execution of a functionality, it will be executing only one of the modules involved in expressing that functionality. As each functionality executed, it would exercise a subset of program modules. For the six basic functionalities of XC, the corresponding module subsets are depicted in Exhibit 13.

A total of 12 test suites were designed to test this basic set of functionalities. These test functions are show in Exhibit 14. In this table are the descriptions of each of the tests, together with the functionalities exercised by that test in the column labeled $T \times F$. The 12 test suites were designed by the test staff to ensure 100 percent block coverage in the code during the test. The net effect of executing all the program blocks is that all

Exhibit 14. Test Suites for the *XC* Program Functionalities

Test No.	Function	T × F
1	Enable the debug option with the -d switch.	f_5, f_6
2	Flip the -d switch in the case statement in main to exercise the debug option of this program with the output being written to a file with the -o option. It also tests for cross referencing of reserved words -r and emits a printer initialization string with the -e option.	f_1, f_2, f_5, f_6
3	Overflow the hash table in function put_token that is limited to 749 identifiers.	f_6
4	Raise the use_err in main if the command line arguments are less than two.	f_5, f_6
5	Generate a listing only with the -l option and to enable file inclusion with -i.	f_3, f_4, f_6
6	Raise the use_err in main for an illegal file name option.	f_1
7	Raise the use_err in main when the second argument is a '-' instead of a filename.	f_5
8	Raise the use_err in main when -o option is used without giving a legal filename.	f_1
9	Raise the use_err in main if the -o option is invoked followed by another switch with no file name in between.	f_1
10	Raise the use_err in main if a switch is used without preceding it with a '-'.	f_5
11	Raise the use_err in main if an illegal switch is used.	f_5
12	Raise the use_err in proc_file if an illegal or nonexistent filename is given as the second argument.	f_5, f_6

of the program functionality would also be exercised. Because the stopping criterion for the test staff was related to the block coverage, many exception conditions had to be exercised. In most cases (see Tests 7 through 11), the execution of the code that raised the exception conditions only accessed a limited number of program functionalities.

In the case of Test 1, all of the modules, except for module 2, are executed. The execution results of the Test 1 suite are shown in Exhibit 15. The average FI of only the modules that were involved in this execution was 100.7, slightly above the average system FI of 100. If we add the FI values of the modules involved, and then divide by the total number of modules in the system, we get an assessment of the exposure to the complexity of the system that was manifested by this test. If all of the modules are executed in their entirety, then there will be 100 percent exposure to the complexity of the system. In the case of Test 1, this computation yields a value of 97 percent. This appears at face value to be a realistic test.

As mentioned earlier, the failure of a software system is related not only to the complexity of a module, but also to the amount of time spent executing that module. To get a better assessment of the effectiveness of a software test, we need to incorporate this concept of time. For this purpose, we will examine the number of transitions within the system. At this point we will concern ourselves only with the number of times a specific module is called during a particular execution of the system. The frequency with which a module is called will be divided by the total number of calls in the

Exhibit 15. Functional Complexity for Test 1

Module	ρ	Frequency	Profile	φ
1	118	1	0.00002	0.002
2	90	0	0.0	0.0
3	102	1	0.00002	0.002
4	104	1323	0.02923	3.039
5	89	25369	0.56055	49.888
6	112	13785	0.30459	34.114
7	119	1319	0.02914	3.467
8	101	958	0.02116	2.137
9	102	150	0.00331	0.337
10	92	150	0.00331	0.304
11	93	254	0.00561	0.521
12	90	808	0.01785	1.606
13	101	1	0.00002	0.002
14	93	20	0.00044	0.040
15	94	1118	0.02470	2.322
Total	1500	45257	1.0	97.787

entire system in order to determine the probability that at a given epoch of the process, execution will be taking place within that module.[7] This execution profile for Test 1 is shown in Exhibit 15. It represents the proportion of time spent in each of the 15 modules by executing Test 1. We can see, for example, that modules 5 and 6 will receive a disproportionate amount of time in this test, whereas modules 1, 2, 3, and 13 will receive little or no exposure. Similarly, the most complex module, module 7, also gets little exposure in this test, yet it is the one most likely to contain faults. The functional complexity of each of the modules under Test 1 can be found in the column labeled φ in Exhibit 15. It is derived by multiplying the FI, ρ_i, of each module by its probability of execution, or profile, under Test 1. Effectively, the functional complexity of Test 1 is the expected value of FI for the modules that are exercised by Test 1 under the Test 1 execution profile. The frequency data shown in Exhibit 15 was obtained from the C profiler and were extracted for each of the test executions.

By taking into consideration the execution frequency of each of these modules, a more refined assessment of the complexity exercised by Test 1 can be obtained. Now, instead of the initial average module complexity of $\bar{\rho} = 100.7$, we take into account the proportion of time spent in each of the modules of varying complexity. This will yield an expected value for fractional complexity of $\phi^{(1)} = 97.787$. The functional complexity of the test is less than the average system FI. The view of the system as established by this test shows fewer potential faults than the actual number of faults in the whole system. However, even this estimate is still not realistic. It is based on the naive assumption that every time a module is called, the entire module (and thus all of its complexity) is executed. By measuring only the code of a module that executes during a given test, we can better assess the true potential for a test to expose the software to its potential faults. The measurement technique of fractional complexity was developed for this purpose.

11.6.3 Operational Complexity

It is now clear that each function has an associated execution profile. This execution profile, once again, can be expected to change across the set of program functionalities. This will result in a concomitant variation in the *operational complexity* of the function. As was the case in the definition of functional complexity, each functionality f_j has an execution profile represented by the probabilities $\rho^{(j)}$. The operational complexity $\overline{\omega}^{(j)}$ for the execution of each function f_i is the expected value of the fractional complexity under an execution profile as follows:

$$\overline{\omega}^{(j)} = \sum_{i=1}^{n} p_i^{(j)} \xi_i^{(j)}$$

This is the fractional complexity analog of the earlier concept of functional complexity. Operational complexity has the virtue that it reflects the concomitant variation in both the fractional complexity of the code selected by the execution of a function and the execution profile of that function.

11.6.4 Fractional and Operational Complexity of XC Tests

Each of the 12 tests of the system, as shown in Exhibit 14, was run again, this time under the control of the modified ATAC software system. This would permit the source code that was executed for each test to be extracted. This reduced set of code for each program module was then submitted to the metric analyzer and the nine metrics were computed for each of the twelve functional tests. These raw complexity measures were then standardized using the mean and standard deviation values obtained previously from the full code set. Thus, the metric data from each of the tests was standardized relative to the baseline or total code set. These standardized metric values were then transformed to domain metric values using the original baseline transformation data. Fractional complexities ξ_i were computed using the eigenvalues from the baseline data. Again, the fractional complexities are simply the FI of the reduced code sets from each test.

The fractional complexities ξ_i for each module on each test are shown in Exhibits 16 and 17. The data in these two tables represent the same set of modules. Exhibit 17 is abbreviated in that for these tests, modules 4 through 15 simply were not exercised. Each test consists of the sets M_i and M_p for each of the test functionalities. In the case of the data shown in these exhibits, the set M_c clearly consists of only one program module, in this case, the main program. A large number of table entries are zero. This is because the associated program modules did not execute on the particular test and, thus, none of the complexity of that module was exercised. In

Exhibit 16. Fractional Complexities of Modules on Test Suites

Module	Static ρ	Test No. 1 ξ	2 ξ	3 ξ	4 ξ	5 ξ	6 ξ
1	118	107	114	98	91	104	102
2	90	0	0	0	90	0	0
3	102	98	98	96	0	101	0
4	104	104	104	92	0	104	0
5	89	89	89	88	0	89	0
6	112	92	93	109	0	110	0
7	119	87	88	114	0	103	0
8	101	99	100	101	0	88	0
9	102	102	102	102	0	0	0
10	92	88	89	88	0	0	0
11	93	92	92	92	0	0	0
12	90	90	90	90	0	0	0
13	101	99	100	0	0	0	0
14	93	90	92	90	0	91	0
15	94	91	93	92	0	92	0

Exhibit 17. Fractional Complexities of Modules on Test Suites

Module	Test No. 7 ξ	8 ξ	9 ξ	10 ξ	11 ξ	12 ξ
1	92	98	99	93	97	98
2	90	90	90	90	90	0
3	0	0	0	0	0	90

some cases, it can be seen that there is a high degree of variability in the observed complexity of a module on each execution. In other cases, the complexity of a module, when it is called, is relatively fixed, if not constant. It is the highly variable modules that will require the most attention during testing. The test activity with regard to module 7 is notable in this regard. This is the most complex module ($\rho_7 = 119$). Under Test 1 it is one of the least complex modules ($\xi_7^{(1)} = 87$). Thus, Test 1 only executes a small fraction of the potential complexity of module 7. We can see that of all of the tests, only Test 3 begins to exercise the complexity of the code in module 7 ($\xi_7^{(3)} = 114$).

Although Exhibit 17 incorporates one aspect of dynamic measurement, measuring only the code subsets associated with a given execution, it does not reflect the execution profile of the code. As an example, operational complexity for Test 1 will be computed using the fractional complexity data. The frequency data, and thus the profiles, are no different than in Exhibit 15. The only difference is that between the original FI, fractional complexity, and the resultant operational complexities. The operational complexity for Test 1, using fractional complexity, is provided in Exhibit 18.

Exhibit 18. Fractional and Operational Complexity for Test 1

Module	ξ	Frequency	Profile	ω
1	107	1	0.00002	0.002
2	0	0	0	0
3	98	1	0.00002	0.002
4	104	1323	0.02923	3.040
5	89	25369	0.56055	49.889
6	92	13785	0.30459	28.022
7	87	1319	0.02914	2.535
8	99	958	0.02116	2.095
9	102	150	0.00331	0.338
10	88	150	0.00331	0.291
11	92	254	0.00561	0.516
12	90	808	0.01785	1.607
13	99	1	0.00002	0.002
14	90	20	0.00044	0.040
15	91	1118		
$\bar{\xi}$	94.857		$E(\bar{\omega})$	90.626

To return to the previous case, under Test 1 the static FI of module 7 was $\rho_7 = 119.0$ and its fractional complexity was $\phi_7^{(1)} = 3.467$. When we actually look within this module at the code that is actually expressed by the execution of Test 1, we find that the fraction of code executed by this test as measured by $\xi_7^{(1)} = 87$ is really quite small. Further, the operational complexity $\omega_7^{(1)} = 2.535$ is also small. Test 1 simply does not expose this module to the potential faults that it may contain. Further examination of Exhibit 18 shows exactly where Test 1 was focused. We can see that the operational complexity of modules 5 and 6 are quite a bit larger than other entries in this exhibit. More interesting is the fact that module 5 is the least complex module of the entire set. A considerable amount of the total test effort is focused on this module, which is least likely to contain faults. This observation is quite characteristic of normal test activity. The test process and test outcomes are not intuitive. A stress test of the software is one that will maximize the exposure to latent faults in the system. This stress can be measured directly with either functional or operational complexity. Altogether too often we have seen the stress testing of systems reflect the mental anguish of the tester as opposed to the exercise of the potentially fault-prone code.

Let us now examine other test possibilities. Our objective now will be to maximize our exposure to the faults in the system. A logical activity would be to identify a functionality that would generate a profile giving maximum exposure to those modules whose fractional complexity was large for that functionality. This is a research process. Our objective will be to understand the behavior of the system in this process — not to find faults. This is the principal metaphor shift in the measurement-based approach to testing.

Exhibit 19 summarizes four distinct measures of test activity as the *XC* system was driven through its set of functionalities. Each of these mea-

Exhibit 19. Four Measures of Test Activity

Test No.	Static Measures		Dynamic Measures	
	$\bar{\rho}$	$\bar{\xi}$	ϕ	ω
1	94	89	98	91
2	94	90	98	91
3	87	83	98	96
4	14	12	104	91
5	68	65	96	94
6	8	7	118	102
7	14	12	104	91
8	14	13	104	94
9	14	13	104	94
10	14	12	104	92
11	14	12	104	93
12	15	13	110	94

sures will provide a global assessment of just what the test did to exercise the code within each of the program modules. The second column in Exhibit 19, labeled $\bar{\rho}$, represents the average FI of just the set of program modules that were executed at least once. Only the first three tests provided reasonable exposure to the complete set of modules by this test criterion. At the other extreme is Test 6, with an average FI of 8. The exposure to the full system complexity of this test is clearly trivial.

The third column in Exhibit 19, labeled $\bar{\xi}$, contains the average fractional complexity, again for only those modules that were executed at least once by each of the tests. According to this criterion, none of the tests were really good at exercising the modules to their full extent. The very best of the tests, Test 2, executed a code set whose average complexity was 90, a figure well below the average complexity (100) of all of the program modules.

The fourth and fifth columns in Exhibit 19 contain the dynamic measures of test outcomes. These two columns represent the expected values of FI and fractional complexity under each of the test profiles. The fourth column shows the values of functional complexity for each of the tests. According to this test criterion, Test 6 provided substantial exposure to fault-prone code. However, this fact is somewhat misleading in and of itself. Test 6 only executed program module 1, which had an FI of 118. The final column Exhibit 19 contains the operational complexity of each of the tests. If we exclude the anomalous result of Test 6, we can see that the best test of all of the test activity was on Test 3. This test provided a large exposure to the total system complexity while also yielding the largest operational complexity of all the full tests.

By computing fractional complexity, and then using it to calculate functional complexity, we get a more accurate assessment of Test 1. Where we first had an initial average module complexity of 94 under this test as was shown in Exhibit 18, then a functional complexity based on a module's full FI of 89, we now have a functional complexity of 98. So, by incorporating the dynamic aspects of the test, we obtain a quite different assessment of the average module complexity for Test 1. Furthermore, by dividing the total observed complexity for this execution (1019) by the total complexity for the full system (1500), fractional complexity estimates that 67.93 percent of the full complexity of the system was exercised by this test. Recall that using the FI for the full module provided an estimate of 97 percent. Both the assessment of the average module complexity and the percentage of the full complexity of the system are needed to assess the effectiveness of a test in terms of the potential fault exposure.

11.6 INTRODUCTION TO STATISTICAL TESTING

The reliability of a system is a function of the potential for failure in the software. A software failure event, on the other hand, is precipitated by a software fault in the code. Current thinking in the software development field is that faults in programs are randomly distributed through a software system by processes known only to Nature. For these faults to express themselves as software failures, all the code must be exercised in some meaningful way during the testing process. The success of the testing process is measured in a more or less *ad hoc* fashion by the extent to which all possible paths of a program have been taken at least once, whether the program has succumbed to external input values, etc.

In those program modules that have large values of the fault surrogate measure FI, it is reasonable to suppose that the numbers of faults will also be large. If the code is made to execute a significant proportion of time in modules having large FI values, then the potential exposure to software faults will be great and, thus, the software will be likely to fail.

Software faults and other measures of software quality can be known only at the point the software has finally been retired from service. Then, and only then, can it be said that all of the relevant faults have been isolated and removed from the software system. On the other hand, software complexity can be measured very early in the software life cycle. In some cases, these measures of software complexity can be extracted from design documents. Some of these measures are very good leading indicators of potential software faults. The first step in the software testing process is to construct suitable surrogate measures for software faults.

11.6.1 The Goal of Statistical Testing

The central thesis of statistical testing is that programs will fail because of indigenous faults. These faults are directly related to measurable software attributes. If you can understand the relationship between faults and specific attributes, you will know where to look for faults. Of particular utility, in this role as a fault surrogate, is FI. The important thing for the following discussion is that there exist some measurable program module attribute, say ϕ, that is highly correlated with software faults. Intuitively (and empirically), a program that spends a high proportion of its time executing a module set M_f of high ϕ values will be more failure prone than one that seeks our program modules with smaller values of this attribute.

From the discussion earlier, we see that a program can execute any one of a number of basic functionalities. Associated with each of these functionalities is an attendant value of ϕ_f. At the beginning of the test process, the first step in statistical testing is to understand the nature of the variability of ϕ *between* the functions that the program can execute. The next step in the statistical testing process is to understand the nature of the variance of ϕ *within* functionalities. The greater the variability in the ϕ of a program found during normal test scenarios, the more testing will be required. It is normally presumed that a major objective of software testing is to find all of the potential faults in the software. We cannot presume to believe that a test has been adequate until we have some reasonable assessment of the variability in the behavior of the system.

In this new perspective, the entire nature of the test process is changed. Our objective in this new approach will be to understand the program that has been designed. It may well be that the design of a program will not lend itself to testing in any reasonable timeframe given a high ratio of within-module variability to between-module variability. We cannot hope to determine the circumstances under which a program might fail until we first understand the behavior of the program itself.

The next logical step in the statistical testing process is to seek to identify the precise nature of the mapping of functionality to ϕ_f. That is, we need to identify the characteristics of test scenarios that cause our criterion measure of ϕ_f to be large. Test scenarios whose values of ϕ_f are large are those that will most likely provide maximum exposure to the latent faults in a program. In this new view, a program can be *stress tested* by choosing test cases that maximize ϕ_f.

11.6.2 Estimating the Functional Parameters

The initial stage in the testing process is primarily concerned with developing an understanding of the behavior of the software system that has been created by the design process. As such, all test suites during this phase will be carefully architected to express a single functionality. For each of these program functionalities f_i, let us define a random variable $a^{(i)}$ defined on the domain of values of the functional complexity $\phi_f^{(i)}$ of the ith function. As each test of functionality f_i is conducted, we will have a sample data point $a_j^{(i)}$ on $a^{(i)}$. After a sequence of tests of f_i, we can compute a sample mean $\bar{a}^{(i)} = \sum_j a_j^{(i)}$, an estimate of the parameter $\mu^{(i)}$, and the mean functional complexity of the ith functionality. Similarly, it will be possible to compute the sample variance

$$s_{(i)}^2 = \frac{1}{n} \sum_j (a_j^{(i)} - \overline{a}^{(i)})^2 ,$$

which is an estimate of the parameter $\sigma_{(i)}^2$, the variance of $\phi_f^{(i)}$ for the ith functionality. Note that the contribution in variability of each test is due largely to the set $M_p^{(f)}$. If this is an empty set, the range of the functional complexity for a functionality will be considerably constrained.

Without any loss in generality, let us assume that the $a^{(i)}$ are defined on a normal probability distribution. This distribution is specified succinctly by its mean $\mu^{(i)}$ and its variance $\sigma_{(i)}^2$ of which the sample mean $\overline{a}^{(i)}$ and variance $s_{(i)}^2$ are sufficient statistics. It is now possible to construct a standard error of the estimate $\overline{a}^{(i)}$ as follows:

$$s_{\overline{a}^{(i)}} = \frac{s_{(i)}}{\sqrt{n}} sws$$

for a set of n tests of the ith function.

Once we have initiated a testing phase it would be desirable to be able to formulate a mathematical statement or a stopping rule for determining the conclusion of the test phase. A stopping rule for this first test phase is based on the attainment of an *a priori* condition for b and α that

$$\Pr\left[-b < \frac{\overline{a}^{(i)} - \mu^{(i)}}{\sigma_{(i)} / \sqrt{n}} < b \right] = 1 - \alpha$$

That is, the initial test phase will continue until we have attained an estimate for each of the mean functional complexities of the software system with the $100(1-\alpha)$ percent confidence limits set as a condition of a test plan.

As the test process progresses during this first test phase, it may well emerge that the variation in the functional complexity will be inordinately large. We can begin to see in advance that a significant amount of total test resources will be consumed only on this first parametric estimation phase of the software. In this circumstance it is quite possible that the software system is not testable. This being the case, we are now in a position to specify that the implementation of certain functionalities, specifically those for which the within functionality variability is so large as to demand too many test resources, be redesigned and recoded. Not all software can be reasonably or economically tested.

This view represents a fundamental shift in test philosophy. In the past, software testers were obliged to take their best shot at whatever systems were designed and coded by staff outside the test process. Through the systematic introduction of measurement processes in the testing phase of the life cycle it is now possible to set criteria *a priori* for the testability of software systems.

In looking at the parameter estimation phase of software test, we are working strictly with the within functionality variability of a design. Let us now focus on the variability among the set of all functionalities. The focus in this next phase is on the construction of a sequence of test that will focus on the set of operations O, which will represent the user's view of the system.

11.6.3 The Optimal Allocation of Test Resources

It is our thesis that it would be entirely unrealistic to suppose that it would be possible to construct a fault-free software system or to test a large system exhaustively to find all possible faults in the system. It is not really of interest that a system has faults in it. What is relevant, however, is that there are no faults in the range of functions that the consumer of the software will typically execute. It would take unlimited test resources to certify that a system is, in fact, fault-free. What we would like to do is to allocate our finite test resources to maximize the exposure of the software system to such faults as might be present.

Let us assume that we are investigating a system designed to implement a set of n functional requirements. As a result of the design process, each of these functions f_i will have and associated functional complexity $\phi_f^{(i)}$. From the initial stages of the test process we will have an estimate a_i for $\phi_f^{(i)}$. We can now formulate an objective function for the allocation of test resources as follows:

$$Q = a_1 x_1 + a_2 x_2 + \cdots + a_n x_n$$

where x_i is the amount of test resources (time) that will be allocated to the test of the ith function and Q is a measure proportional to FI (quality). It would be well to remember that functional complexity is an expected value for the FI of the design implementation of each functionality. FI was constructed to be a surrogate for software faults. Thus, a functionality whose functional complexity is large can be expected to be fault prone. By maximizing the value of Q in the objective function above a test plan will be seen to have maximized its exposure to the embedded faults in the system. Clearly the best way to maximize Q is to allocate all test resources to the function f_i whose functional complexity is the largest. That is, allocate all resources to a_i where $a_i > a_j$ for all $j \neq i$.

The real object of the test process at this stage is to maximize our exposure to software faults that will have the greatest impact on what functions the user will be performing with the software. In this sense, the test process is constrained by the customer's operational profile. As per the earlier discussion, a user of the software has a distinct set of operations O that he or she perceives the software will perform. These operations are then implemented in a rather more precise set of software functions F. From this operational profile we can then construct the following constraints on the test process to ensure that each of the user's operations receives it due during the test process.

$$b_{11}x_1 + b_{12}x_2 + \cdots + b_{1n}x_n \leq c_1$$

$$b_{21}x_1 + b_{22}x_2 + \cdots + b_{2n}x_n \leq c_2$$

$$\vdots$$

$$b_{m1}x_1 + b_{m2}x_2 + \cdots + b_{mn}x_n \leq c_m$$

The coefficients bij are proportionality constants that reflect the implementation of an operation in a set of appropriate functions such that:

$$b_{ij} = \begin{cases} p'(o_i, f_j) & \text{if IMPLEMENTS}(o_i, f_j) \text{ is } true \\ 0 & \text{if IMPLEMENTS}(o_i, f_j) \text{ is } false \end{cases}$$

and c_i represents the test resources assigned to the ith operation. The total test effort is simply the sum of time apportioned to each of the functionalities, $\sum_i x_i$.

References

1. Munson, J.C., Software Faults, Software Failures, and Software Reliability Modeling, *Information and Software Technology*, December 1996.

2. Munson, J.C., Dynamic Program Complexity and Software Testing, *Proceedings of the IEEE International Test Conference*, Washington, D.C., October 1996.

3. Munson, J.C. and Elbaum, S.G., A Measurement Methodology for the Evaluation of Regression Tests, *Proceedings of the 1998 IEEE International Conference on Software Maintenance,* IEEE Computer Society Press, pp. 24–33.

4. Nikora, A.P., Software System Defect Content Prediction from Development Process and Product Characteristic, Ph.D. thesis, University of Southern California, Los Angeles, January 1998.

5. Munson, J.C. and Hall, G.A., Dynamic Program Complexity and Software Testing, *Proceedings of the 1995 IEEE International Testing Conference,* IEEE Computer Society Press, Los Alamitos, CA, 1995, pp. 730–773.

6. Horgan, J.R., London, S., and Lyu, M.R., Achieving Software Quality with Testing Coverage Measures, *IEEE Computer,* 27(9), 60–69, 1994.

7. Munson, J.C., A Functional Approach to Software Reliability Modeling, in *Quality of Numerical Software, Assessment and Enhancement*, Boisvert, R.F., Ed., Chapman & Hall, London, 1997.

Chapter 12
Software Availability

12.1 INTRODUCTION

There are as many definitions of software availability as there are authors writing about the subject. In the more traditional hardware sense of the term, *availability* is defined as the ratio of mean time to failure (MTTF) to the sum of MTTF and mean time to repair (MTTR). In the hardware world, a failure event is very easy to observe. A light bulb burned out. A disk drive went south. Consequently, it is easy to measure the precise elapsed time between failure events. Similarly, it is quite easy to measure the interval between when a light bulb burned out and when it was replaced with another. We can actually measure the length of time that it takes for a light bulb to burn out. From this we can compute the average time to failure for light bulbs. Similarly, we can measure how long it takes to change a light bulb; and from this we can compute the average time to repair a failed light bulb.

The concept of availability in the software world is not so clear. For the most part, software failure events are not directly observable. In fact, perhaps only 1 percent of the most catastrophic software failure events can be witnessed. In modern complex software, system failure events may occur hours, days, or even weeks before the consequences of the failure event percolate to the surface to be observed. Thus, the MTTF statistic cannot be determined with any degree of certainty because the underlying failure event is essentially unobservable.

Similarly, the MTTR statistic has even less meaning in the software world. In most cases of an operating system failure, for example, we simply reboot the system and continue working. We do not, and cannot, fix the problem. We simply work around it until the software vendor provides updates to fix the problem. We do not wait for this fix to occur. We try our best to survive with the current problem.

The term *availability* must be redefined when it is applied to software systems. There are clearly four components to availability: (1) reliability, (2) security, (3) survivability, and (4) maintainability. A system will not run correctly if it is hijacked or damaged by intentional misuse. Thus, security is an important component of availability. A system will not run correctly if it is permitted to execute flawed code. Software that has been made corrupt or contains corrupt code will cause a system to operate improperly.

A *reliable* software system is one that does not break when it is placed into service at a customer's site. Reliability, however, is not a static attribute of a software system. Reliability is a function of how that customer will use the software. Some operations of the software will perform flawlessly and forever; other operations of this same software system will be flawed and subject to repeated failure events. Software reliability, then, is determined by the interaction between the structure of the code and the user's operation of the system, as reflected in his or her operational profile.

In the case of embedded software systems, the reliability of the software system depends on both good code and good hardware. If a specific set of software modules is tasked with the responsibility for the operation of a failing hardware component, the first sign of this incipient hardware problem may first appear in the software component. That is, the software behavior will change as a direct result of an evolving hardware failure. The problem might first detected in a disturbance in the software system.

A *secure* system is one that can repulse all attempts for misuse. A software system can be assailed from outside the designated and authorized user community by agents who wish to stop the normal use of our software. An outside agent who exploits the weakness of our defenses for his or her own purposes might also invade a software system. Such misuse might divert financial resources or goods to the agent. The agent might also misuse our software to steal our intellectual property. At the heart of a secure software system is a real-time control infrastructure that can monitor the system activity and recognize invidious behavior and control it before damage is done to the system. From the availability standpoint, the essence of the security problem is that outside agents are actively trying to subvert our system. This will cause our system to fail to perform its normal activities. In the worst case, they can cause our system to fail, destroy system resources, or consume system resources through a denial-of-service attack.

A system that has been developed for *survivability* can identify potential problems as they occur and seek remediation for these problems before the system can fail. Typically, a system that has been tested and certified for certain operational behaviors will run without problems when it is placed into service. When the software is driven into new and uncertified domains by new and certified user activity, it is likely to fail. A system based on principles of survivability will be able to identify new usage patterns by the customer and communicate these new uses to the software developer. The developer then has the ability to recertify the system for its new usage patterns and ship a new release of the software to the customer before the system has the opportunity to fail in the user's hands.

A *maintainable* system is one that is built around the principle of requirements traceability. If you do not know what a piece of code is doing, it is nearly impossible to alter it without having an adverse effect on some undetermined functionality. Similarly, if it becomes necessary to change the system requirements, this becomes an impossible task when we do not know which code modules implement which requirement. Basically, a maintainable system is one that can be fixed or modified very quickly.

At the heart of a highly available system is a control structure built into the software that will monitor the system in real-time for failure potential and for misuse. This control structure will measure the software to ensure that it is performing functions that have been certified by the vendor. It will also detect and blockade noncritical functionalities that will cause the entire system to fail should they execute.

12.2 SOFTWARE RELIABILITY

There have been many attempts made to understand the reliability of software systems through software reliability modeling. These models have become very sophisticated. They are able to predict the past with great accuracy. Unfortunately, these models are essentially worthless for predicting the future behavior of software systems. The reason is really quite simple; most attempts to understand software reliability have attempted to model software in exactly the same manner as one would model hardware reliability. Herein is the nut of the problem. Software and hardware are vastly different.

A hardware system is an integrated and functional unit. When a jet engine, for example, is running, all of the pieces of this jet engine are involved in the process of generating fire and great mayhem. Similarly, when a new computer CPU chip is energized, the whole surface of the chip is engaged in directing the flow of electrons. Further, when either of these systems is manufactured, there will be slight differences in them as a result of the manufacturing process. If nothing else, the atoms that comprise any two CPU chips are mutually exclusive.

Software systems are very different. The control software for a cellular telephone is exactly the same for each telephone set. All telephones with the same release of software will have exactly identical software loads on them. There is exactly zero manufacturing variation in these systems. If there is a fault in one software system, then that same fault will be present in all systems.

Just as a CPU chip has thousands of component parts, so will an equally complex software system. In a CPU chip, all of these systems are working at once. In our software system, only one component is operational at any instant. This is a phenomenally important difference. A software system is not the sum of its parts; it is only its parts. Some of these parts are more flawed than others.

The failure of a software system as it is dependent only on what the software is currently performing: operations that a user is performing. If a program is currently executing an operation that is expressed in terms of a set of fault-free modules, this operation will certainly execute indefinitely without any likelihood of failure. Each operation causes a program to execute certain program modules. Some of these modules may contain faults. A program may execute a sequence of fault-prone modules and still not fail. In this particular case, the faults may lie in a region of the code that is not likely to be expressed during the execution of a function. A failure event can only occur when the software system executes a module that contains faults. If an operation is never selected that drives the program into a module that contains faults, then the program will never fail. Alternatively, a program may well execute successfully in a module that contains faults just as long as the faults are in code subsets that are not executed.

Some of the problems that have arisen in past attempts at software reliability determination all relate to the fact that their perspective has been distorted. Programs do not wear out over time. If they are not modified, they will certainly not improve over time, nor will they get less reliable over time. The only thing that really impacts the reliability of a software system is the operations that the program is servicing. A program may work very well for a number of years based on the operations that it is asked to execute. This same program may suddenly become quite unreliable if the user changes its mission.

Existing approaches to the understanding of software reliability patently assume that software failure events are observable. The truth is that the overwhelming majority of software failures go unnoticed when they occur. Only when these failures disrupt the system by second-, third-, or fourth-order effects do they provide enough disruption for outside observation. Consequently, only those dramatic events that lead to the immediate collapse of a system can be seen directly by an observer when they occur. The more insidious failures will lurk in the code for a long interval before their effects are observed. Failure events go unnoticed and undetected because the software has not been instrumented so that these failure events can be detected. In that software failures go largely unnoticed, it is presumptuous to attempt to model the reliability of software based on the inaccurate and erroneous observed failure data. If we cannot observe failure events directly, then we must seek another metaphor that will permit us to model and understand reliability in a context that we can measure.

Computer programs do not break. They do not fail monolithically. Programs are designed to perform a set of mutually exclusive tasks or functions. Some of these functions work quite well while others may not work well at all. When a program is executing a particular function, it executes a well-defined subset of its code. Some of these subsets are flawed and some are not. Users execute varying subsets of the total program functionality. Two users of the same software might have totally different perceptions as to the reliability of the same system. One user might use the system on a daily basis and never experience a problem. Another user might have continual problems in trying to execute exactly the same program. The reliability of a system is clearly related to the operations that a user is performing on the system.

Another problem found in software reliability investigations centers on the failure event itself. Our current view of software reliability is colored by a philosophical approach that began with efforts to model hardware reliability (see Musa[1]). Inherent in this approach is the notion that it is possible to identify with some precision this failure event and measure the elapsed time to the failure event. For hardware systems this has real meaning. Take, for example, the failure of a light bulb. A set of light bulbs can be switched on and a very precise timer started for the time that they were turned on. One by one the light bulbs will burn out and we can note the exact time to failure of each of the bulbs. From these failure data we can then develop a precise estimate for both the mean time to failure for these light bulbs and a good estimate of the variance of the time to failure. The case for software systems is not at all the same. Failure events are sometimes quite visible in terms of catastrophic collapses of a system. More often than not, the actual failure event will have occurred a considerable time before its effect is noted. In most cases it is simply not possible to determine with any certainty just when the actual failure occurred on a real-time clock. The simplest example of this improbability of measuring the time between failures of a program can be found in a program that hangs in an infinite loop. Technically, the failure event happened on entry to the loop. The program, however, continues to execute until it is killed. This may take seconds, minutes, or hours, depending on the patience and attentiveness of the operator. As a result, the accuracy of the actual measurement of time intervals is a subject never mentioned in most software validation studies. Because of this, these models are notoriously weak in their ability to predict the future reliability of software systems. A model validated on Gaussian noise will probably not do well in practical applications. The bottom line for the measurement of time between failures in software systems is that we cannot measure these time intervals with any reasonable degree of accuracy. This being the case, we then must look to new metaphors for software systems that will allow us to model the reliability of these systems based on things that we *can* measure with some accuracy.

Yet another problem with the hardware adaptive approach to software reliability modeling is that the failure of a computer software system is simply not time dependent. A system can operate without failure for years and then suddenly become very unreliable based on the changing functions that the system must execute. Many university computer centers experienced this phenomenon in the late 1960s and early 1970s when there was a sudden shift in computer science curricula from programming languages such as FORTRAN that had static runtime environments to ALGOL derivatives such as Pascal and Modula that had dynamic runtime environments. From an operating system perspective, there was a major shift in the functionality of the operating system exercised by these two different environments. As the shift was made to the ALGOL-like languages, latent code in the operating system, specifically those routines that dealt with memory management, that had not been executed overly much in the past now became central to the new operating environment. This code was both fragile and untested. The operating systems that had been so reliable began to fail like cheap light bulbs.

Each program functionality can be thought of as having an associated reliability estimate. We may choose to think of the reliability of a system in these functional terms. Users of the software system, however, have a very different view of the system. What is important to the user is not that a particular function is fragile or reliable, but rather whether the system will *operate* to perform those actions that the user will want the system to perform correctly. From a user's perspective, it matters not, then, that certain functions are very unreliable. It only matters that the functions associated with the user's actions or operations are reliable. The classical example of this idea was expressed by the authors of the early UNIX utility programs. In the last paragraph of the documentation for each of these utilities there was a list of known bugs for that program. In general, these bugs were not a problem. Most involved aspects of operation that the typical user would never exploit.

The main problem in understanding software reliability from this new perspective is getting the granularity of the observation right. Software systems are designed to implement each of their functionalities in one or more code modules. In some cases there is a direct correspondence between a particular program module and a particular functionality. That is, if the program is expressing that functionality, it will execute exclusively in the module in question. In most cases, however, there will not be this distinct traceability of functionality to modules. The functionality will be expressed in many different code modules. It is the individual code module that fails. A code module will, of course, be executing a particular functionality associated with a distinct operation when it fails. We must come to understand that it is the operation — not the software — that fails.

We will see that the key to understanding program failure events is the direct association of these failures to execution events with a given operation. A stochastic process will be used to describe the transition of program modules from one to another as a program transitions among operations. From these observations, it will become fairly obvious just what data will be needed to accurately describe the reliability of the system. In essence, the system will be able to apprise us of its own health. The reliability modeling process is no longer something that will be performed *ex post facto*. It can be accomplished dynamically while the program is executing. It is our goal to develop a methodology that will permit the modeling of the reliability of program operation. This methodology will then be used to develop notions of design *robustness* in the face of departures from design operational profiles.

12.2.1 Understanding Software

Computer software is very different from the hardware on which it resides. Software is abstract whereas hardware is real and tangible. There is nothing to suggest that software artifacts share any common attributes with their hardware counterparts, save that they were both created by people. It is unrealistic to suppose that any mathematical modeling concepts that apply to hardware development would relate to software. Consider the case, for example, of the manufacture of pistons for automobile engines. Each piston is uniquely different from its predecessor and its successor on the manufacturing line. Each piston has metallic elements that are not shared with any other piston. Further, the metallic composition of each piston is slightly different from every other piston. Each piston is slightly different in its physical size and shape from its neighbors. We can characterize these differences in degree by the statistical notion of variance. The pistons are designed to an average or expected value and the manufacturing processes then approximate this design value. A good manufacturing process is one that will permit only very small variations in the actual physical and chemical properties of the pistons.

In the manufacture of embedded software systems, there is zero variance among production software systems. If there is a fault in the control software for a single cell phone, then this defect will be present in every cell phone manufactured that contains this particular software release. They will all be flawed. If there is a software fault in the new release of a popular operating system, all of the software systems of that release will be flawed. They are all identical. There is zero variance. In essence, when we construct software, we build only one system, ever. There may be many copies of these systems but they are all perfect clones. Thus, the basic

313

principles of statistical quality control simply do not apply to manufactured software systems.

The manner in which software systems will be used when they are deployed, however, does vary. This means that each user of the system will, in fact, be using a different software system. They will, by their operational profiles, select certain subsets of the code to exercise in ways that do vary from one user to another. Thus, our statistical models must reflect the *context* of the use of the software and not the software system itself. The variance in the software system is induced by the context and is not an intrinsic property of the software.

Physical systems also change with respect to time. Components that move over each other will cause wear and abrasion. Electrical current anomalies will gradually erode the chemical substrate of integrated circuits. Software systems, on the other hand, do not change with respect to time. They are eternal. They quite literally operate in a different universe than the one we occupy. The software universe is devoid of space and time. There is no such thing as gravity. In essence, different rules of physics apply in this timeless universe. Our success in understanding software is predicated on our ability to formulate mathematical models of behavior consistent with the physics of this different universe.

12.2.2 Software Reliability Modeling

It is increasingly evident that the reliability of a software system is largely determined during program design. One distinct aspect of the software design process that lends itself to measurement is the decomposition of the functionality of a system into modules and the subsequent interaction of the modules under a given set of inputs to the software. The actual distribution of execution time to each software module for a given input scenario is recorded in the execution profile for the system. For a given input scenario to a program, the execution profile is a function of how the design of the software has assigned functionality to program modules.

The reliability of a software system can be characterized in terms of the individual software modules that make up the system. From the standpoint of the logical description of the system, these functional components of the larger system are, in fact, operating in series. If any one of these components fails, the entire system will fail. The likelihood that a component will fail is directly related to the complexity of that module. If it is very complex, the fault probability is also large. The system will be as reliable as its weakest component.

For each possible design outcome in a software design effort, there will be a set of expected execution profiles, one for each of the anticipated program functionalities. We should evaluate design alternatives in terms of the variance of functional complexity. If there is high variability in functional complexity, the reliability of the product of the design is likely to be low. A reasonable design objective would be to reduce functional complexity.

At the design stage, quantitative measures correlated to module fault-proneness and product failure provide a means to begin to exert statistical process control techniques on the design of a software system as an ongoing quality control activity. Rather than merely documenting the increasing operational complexity of a software product and therefore its decreasing reliability, one can monitor the operational complexity of successive design adaptations during the maintenance phase. It becomes possible to ensure that subsequent design revisions do not increase operational complexity and especially do not increase the variance among individual module's functional complexity.

It is now quite clear that the architecture of a program will be a large determinant of its reliability. Some activities that a program will be asked to perform are quite simple. Designers and programmers alike will easily understand them. The resulting code will not likely contain faults. If, on the other hand, the specified functionality of a program is very complex and as a result ambiguous, then there is a good likelihood that this functionality will be quite fragile due to the faults introduced through the very human processes of its creation. A more realistic approach to software reliability modeling will reflect the software reliability in terms of the functionality of the software.

12.2.3 Software Module Reliability

To capture the essence of the concept of software failure, let us suppose that each software system has a virtual failure module (VFM), m_{n+1}, to which control is automatically passed at the instant the program departs from its specified behavior. We can easily accomplish this action with assertions built into the code. In essence, we cannot perceive a failure event if we are not watching. Some program activities such as a divide by zero will be trapped by the system automatically. The hardware and operating system, however, cannot know our intentions for the successful execution of a module on a more global scale. We must instrument the code to know whether it is operating correctly. Programming assertions into the code is a very good way to measure for failure events.

There are really three levels of granularity of program reliability. At the lowest level of granularity, there is *module reliability*. The module design process has specified each program module very carefully. We know what it should be doing. We can easily define the parameters for its successful operation. We can know, that is, whether the program module is operating within its design specifications. The moment that it begins to operate outside its design framework, we will imagine that the module will transfer control to the VFM representing the failure state. Thus, if we have a system of n program modules, we will imagine that this system is augmented by a module that will trap all contingencies that arise when any program module has failed.

Each program module, then, will or will not fail when it is executed. We can know this and we can remember these failure events. A program module will be considered reliable if we have used it frequently and it has failed infrequently. A program module will be considered unreliable if we have used it frequently and it has failed frequently. A program module that has been used infrequently is neither reliable nor unreliable.

Any program module can transfer control to the VFM. This transfer, of course, can only happen if the current module has departed from program specifications. With our dynamic instrumentation and measurement technique, we can clearly count the number of times that control has been transferred to each module. Those data can be accumulated in a module execution frequency vector (MEFV). We can also count the number of times that control has been transferred from any module to the VFM. These data can be accumulated in a failure frequency vector (FFV) for each module. A module will be considered reliable if there is a small chance that it will transfer control to the VFM.

Let t_i represent the ith element of the MEFV. It will contain the number of times that module i has received control during the last $\sum_{i=1}^{m} t_i$ epochs. Similarly, let s_i represent the number of times that module i has transferred control to the VFM during the same time period. It is clear that $s_i \leq t_i$. That is, a module could have failed every time it was executed or it could have executed successfully at least once. Our current estimate for the failure probability of module i on the mth epoch is $z_i^{(m)} = s_i^{(m)} / t_i^{(m)}$. This means that of the total $t_i^{(m)}$ epochs that module i has received control, it has worked successfully on $e_i^{(m)} = t_i^{(m)} - s_i^{(m)}$ epochs. The reliability of this module is simply one (1) minus its failure probability: $r_i^{(m)} = 1 - z_i^{(m)}$. From these observations we can construct a vector $z^{(m)} = \langle z_1^{(m)}, z_2^{(m)}, ..., z_n^{(m)} \rangle$ of failure probabilities for each module on the mth epoch.

It is clear that if module i has executed successfully for a large number of epochs, say 100,000, and failed but once over these epochs, then the module will be fairly reliable. In contrast, consider another module j that has executed only ten times and has not failed at all. At face value, the reliability of module j is 1, whereas the reliability of module i is 0.99999. However, we really lack enough information on module j to make a real accurate assessment of its behavior.

What we are really interested in is the current point estimate for reliability and a lower confidence for that estimate. It is clear that we can derive our estimate for the failure probability $z_i^{(m)}$ from $z_i^{(m)} = s_i^{(m)} / t_i^{(m)}$. It is also clear that executing module i will have exactly two outcomes: it will execute successfully or it will fail. The distribution of the outcome of each trial will be binomial. Let us observe that for relatively large n, we can use the binomial approximation to a normal distribution with a mean of np and a standard deviation of $\sqrt{np(1-p)}$.

An estimate a for the $(1-\alpha)w$ upper bound for this failure probability can be derived from the binomial approximation to the normal distribution where:

$$\frac{1}{\sqrt{2\pi}} \int_{-\infty}^{a} e^{-\frac{1}{2}(x-np)/np(1-p)} dx = \alpha$$

If, for example, we wished to find the 9 percent confidence interval $u_i^{(m)}$ for $z_i^{(m)}$, we could compute this from:

$$u_i^{(m)} = \left(s_i^{(m)} + 1.65\sqrt{t_i^{(m)} z_i^{(m)}(1- z_i^{(m)})} \right) / t_i^{(m)}$$

$$= \left(s_i^{(m)} + 1.65\sqrt{t_i^{(m)} \frac{s_i^{(m)}}{t_i^{(m)}} \left(1 - \frac{s_i^{(m)}}{t_i^{(m)}} \right)} \right) / t_i^{(m)}$$

$$= \left(s_i^{(m)} + 1.65\sqrt{s_i^{(m)} \left(1 - \frac{s_i^{(m)}}{t_i^{(m)}} \right)} \right) / t_i^{(m)}$$

where 1.65 is the x ordinate value from the standard normal ($N(0,1)$) distribution for $\alpha = 0.95$. This estimate, $u_i^{(m)}$, is an unbiased estimate for the upper bound of $z_i^{(m)}$. The problem is that if we have executed a particular module only a very few times and it has not failed, then the number of failures $s_i^{(m)}$ for this module will be zero and the estimate for the upper bound $u_i^{(m)}$ will also be zero. This would seem to imply that an untested module is also highly reliable and we are very confident about that estimate. Nothing could be further from the truth.

A more realistic assumption for the reliability of each module is to assume that it is unreliable until it is proven reliable. To this end, we will assume that each module has, at the beginning, been executed exactly once and it has failed. Thus, the number of measured epochs for each module will be increased by one and the number of failures experienced by that module will also be increased by one. Let $s_i'^{(m)} = s_i^{(m)} + 1$ and $t_i'^{(m)} = t_i^{(m)} + 1$. Thus, a more suitable estimate for the initial failure probability for a module is $z_i^{(m)} = s_i'^{(m)} / t_i'^{(m)}$ with an upper bound on this estimate of:

$$u_i^{(m)} = \left(s_i'^{(m)} + 1.65\sqrt{s_i'^{(m)} \left(1 - \frac{s_i'^{(m)}}{t_i'^{(m)}} \right)} \right) / t_i'^{(m)}$$

We can construct a vector $\mathbf{u}^{(m)}$ whose elements are the $(1-\alpha)$ upper bounds on the estimates for the failure probabilities. Thus, with the vector of failure probabilities $\mathbf{z}^{(m)}$ and the vector of upper bounds on these estimates $\mathbf{u}^{(m)}$, we can characterize the failure potential and our confidence in this estimate of set of modules that comprise the complete software system.

As each functionality f_i is exercised, it will induce a module execution profile $p^{(f_i)}$ on the set of n program models. That is, each functionality will exercise the set of program modules differently. Therefore, each functionality will have a different failure potential, depending on the failure probability of the modules that it executes. We can compute an expected value for the functionality failure probability of each functionality on the mth execution epoch as follows:

$$q^{(f_i)} = \sum_{i=1}^{n} p_i^{(f_i)} z_i^{(m)}$$

In matrix form we can represent the vector of functional failure probabilities as $\mathbf{q} = \mathbf{p}\mathbf{z}^{(m)}$, where $\mathbf{p}$ is an $m \times n$ matrix of module execution profiles for each functionality. We can also compute an upper bound on the expected value of the functional failure probabilities as $\mathbf{q}' = \mathbf{p}\mathbf{u}^{(m)}$.

As each operation ω_i in the set of l operations is exercised by the user, it will induce a functional profile $p^{(\omega_i)}$ on the set of k functionalities. That is, for every operation, there will be a vector of conditional probabilities for the execution of each functionality given that operation. Let $\mathbf{p}'$ represent the $l \times k$ matrix of the conditional probabilities of the k functionalities for the l operations.

It is clear that each operation will exercise the set of program functionalities differently. Therefore, each operation will have a different failure potential, depending on the failure probability of the functionalities that it executes. We can compute an expected value for the operational failure probability of each operation on the mth execution epoch as follows:

$$x^{(\omega_i)} = \sum_{i=1}^{k} p_i^{(\omega_i)} q^{(f_i)}$$

In matrix form we can represent the vector of operational failure probabilities as $\mathbf{x} = \mathbf{p}'\mathbf{q}$, where $\mathbf{p}'$ is an $l \times k$ matrix of functional profiles. Substituting for $\mathbf{q}$ we can define $\mathbf{x}$ directly in terms of the measurable module failure probabilities to wit: $\mathbf{x} = \mathbf{p}'\mathbf{p}\mathbf{z}^{(m)}$. We can also establish an upper bound on the operational failure probabilities as $\mathbf{x}' = \mathbf{p}'\mathbf{p}\mathbf{u}^{(m)}$.

The elements of the vector $\mathbf{x}$ represent the failure probabilities for each of the l operations. The reliability of operation ω_i can be derived from its failure probability as follows: $r_i = 1 - x_i$. Thus, we can construct a vector of operational reliability estimates $\mathbf{r} = \mathbf{I} - \mathbf{x}$, where $\mathbf{I}$ is a vector of ones. We can also construct a vector of lower bounds on these reliability estimates: $\mathbf{r}' = \mathbf{I} - \mathbf{x}'$.

The reliability of a software system is therefore not a static attribute of the system. It is an artifact of how the system will be used. There is a different reliability estimate for each operation, depending on how that operation exercises different modules. Furthermore, there is a lower bound on that reliability estimate, depending on how much we know about the modules that comprise that operation. A user's perception of the reliability of our system will depend on how he or she uses that system. The operational profile $\mathbf{o}$ represents the distribution of user activity across the system. Therefore, the user's reliability perception of the system ρ is simply $\rho = \mathbf{or}$ and the lower bound for this estimate is $\rho' = \mathbf{or}'$.

12.2.4 Data Collection for Reliability Estimation

It seems pointless to engage in the academic exercise of software reliability modeling without making at least the slightest attempt to discuss the process of measuring failure events. A failure occurs immediately at the point that the program departs from its specification, not when we first perceive this departure. The latencies between when a system fails and when the user perceives this may be substantial. We could, for example, have a small memory leak in our Web browser. We will have to run this program for some time before it self-destructs, but die it will with this memory leak. The actual failure occurs at the point when the browser software failed to release some memory it had used. The instant when this first happened is when the failure occurred. If we are not watching, we will fail to see this happen. We will see it only when some functionality is first impaired. The user may not see the problem until the Web browser crashes or slows his machine to a crawl.

The basic premise of our approach to reliability modeling is that we really cannot measure temporal aspects of program failure. There are, however, certain aspects of program behavior that we can measure and also measure with accuracy. We can measure transitions to program modules, for example. We can measure the frequency of executions of functions, if the program is suitably instrumented. We can also measure the frequency of executions of program operations, again supposing that the program has been instrumented to do this.

Let us now turn to the measurement scenario for the modeling process described above. Consider a system whose requirements specify a set O of user operations. These operations, again specified by a set of functional requirements, will be mapped into a set F of elementary program functions.

Exhibit 1. Mapping of Operations to Functionalities

Operation	Functionality					
	1	2	3	4	5	6
1	1				1	1
2		1				1
3			1			1
4				1	1	

The functions, in turn, will be mapped by the design process into the set of M program modules.

The software will be designed to function optimally under known and predetermined operational profiles. We will need a mechanism for tracking the actual behavior of the user of the system. To this end we will require a vector O in which the program will count the frequency of each of the operations. That is, an element o_i of this vector will be incremented every time the program initiates the ith user operation as per our discussion in Chapter 10. This is, of course, assuming that the system will perform only operations within the set O. A system that has failed will depart from the specified set of operations. It will do something else. We really do not care what it does specifically. The point is that the system has performed an operation outside of the set O. We know it to have failed as a result. This implies the existence of an additional operational state of the system, a failure state. That is, the system is performing an operation o_{n+1} completely outside the repertoire of the normal set of n specified user operations. This fact has strong implications in the area of computer security. It is clear that if a program is executing within a predefined set of operational specifications, it is operating normally. Once it has departed from this scenario, it is operating abnormally. This likely means that the program is now operating in a potentially unsafe manner.

When we first start using a program we will have little or no information about how its components will interact. The initial test activity is, in essence, the start of a learning process wherein we will come to understand how program components actually work together. To help understand this learning process, let us imagine that we have built a small software system that will perform four simple operations. These operations, in turn, will be implemented by a total of six functionalities. These functionalities will be mapped during the design process to a total of eight program modules. As per the discussion in Chapter 10, we will instrument this program so that we can monitor the transition from one operation to another, from one functionality to another, and from one module to another. Exhibit 1 shows the $O \times F$ mapping for this hypothetical system. Exhibit 2 shows the $F \times M$ mapping.

Let us now assume that we have tested our software and exercised at least some of its capabilities. Exhibit 3 shows the frequency of exposure of

Exhibit 2. Mapping of Functionalities to Modules

| Functionality | Module | | | | | | | |
	1	2	3	4	5	6	7	8
1	1						1	
2		1						1
3			1				1	1
4				1				1
5					1			1
6						1		1

Exhibit 3. Distribution of Functionalities by Operation

| Operation | Functionality | | | | | |
	1	2	3	4	5	6
1	201				1472	1603
2		506				1001
3			602			549
4				332	567	

Exhibit 4. Conditional Probabilities of Functionality Execution by Operation

| Operation | Functionality | | | | | |
	1	2	3	4	5	6
1	0.06	0	0	0	0.45	0.49
2	0	0.34	0	0	0	0.66
3		0	0.52	0	0	0.48
4	0	0	0	0.37	0.63	0

each functionality for each operation. We can see, for example, that functionality 1 was uniquely associated with operation 1 and was invoked 201 times during the operation of the software.

We can now derive the conditional probabilities of each functionality by operation from the data in Exhibit 3. These conditional probabilities are shown in Exhibit 4. They represent the contents of the matrix p' from the previous section.

Let us now assume that we have tallied the execution of each module within each functionality. That is, we will build a matrix of module execution frequencies for each of the functionalities. These data are shown in Exhibit 5.

From the frequency data in Exhibit 5 we can derive the conditional probabilities for the execution of each module given a functionality. Again, these conditional probabilities are derived by dividing the row marginal sums into the individual row entries. The resulting conditional probabilities are shown in Exhibit 6. They represent the contents of the matrix p from the previous section.

Exhibit 5. Distribution of Module Activity by Functionality

| Functionality | Module | | | | | | | |
	1	2	3	4	5	6	7	8
1	4651						2444	
2		32						10
3			9456				987	64
4				761				765
5					5465			1226
6						756		796

Exhibit 6. Conditional Probabilities of Module Execution by Functionality

| Functionality | Module | | | | | | | |
	1	2	3	4	5	6	7	8
1	0.66	0	0	0	0	0	0.34	0
2	0	0.76	0	0	0	0	0	0.24
3	0	0	0.90	0	0	0	0.09	0.01
4	0	0	0	0.50	0	0	0	0.50
5	0	0	0	0	0.82	0	0	0.18
6	0	0	0	0	0	0.49	0	0.51

Exhibit 7. Conditional Probabilities of Module Execution by Operation

| Operation | Module | | | | | | | |
	1	2	3	4	5	6	7	8
1	0.04	0.00	0.00	0.00	0.37	0.24	0.02	0.33
2	0.00	0.26	0.00	0.00	0.00	0.32	0.00	0.42
3	0.00	0.00	0.47	0.00	0.00	0.23	0.05	0.25
4	0.00	0.00	0.00	0.18	0.52	0.00	0.00	0.30

If we multiply the two matrices **p** and **p′**, we will get the product matrix **pp′** shown in Exhibit 7. These are the conditional probabilities of executing a particular module while the user is expressing each operation.

We have instrumented our hypothetical system so that we can keep track of the number of times that each module has failed during the total time we have tested the system. These data are shown in Exhibit 8. In every case, we are going to assert that every module has failed once in epoch 0.

Using the formulas for failure probability derived in the previous section we can compute the failure probability for each module from the data in Exhibit 8. These failure probabilities are shown in Exhibit 9. We can also compute the 95 percent upper confidence intervals for these failure probabilities. These upper bounds are also shown in Exhibit 9. The data are sorted by failure probability. We can see that the most reliable module is module 7, and the least reliable module is module 2. Not only is module 2 the most likely to fail, the upper bound on this estimate is also very large.

We now know something about the failure probability (reliability) of each module. We know very little, however, about the reliability of the sys-

Exhibit 8. Hypothetical Module Executions

Total Epochs	Failures	Successes
4652	6	4646
33	1	32
9457	5	9452
762	4	758
5466	2	5464
757	3	754
3432	1	3431
2862	4	2858

Exhibit 9. Module Failure Probabilities

Module	Failure Probability	Upper Bound
7	0.0003	0.0008
5	0.0004	0.0008
3	0.0005	0.0009
1	0.0013	0.0022
8	0.0014	0.0025
6	0.0040	0.0077
4	0.0052	0.0096
2	0.0303	0.0795

tem. This will depend entirely on how this system is used. If a user were to choose operations that expressed modules 7, 5, and 3, the system would be seen as very reliable. If, on the other hand, the user were to favor operations that heavily used modules 6, 4, and 2, then this same system would very likely fail in the near term.

Now let us assume that there are four different users of our hypothetical system. Each user will exercise the system in his own particular way, represented by an operational profile. Exhibit 10 shows the operational profiles for each of the four users. We can see that user 1, represented by Operational Profile 1, shows a heavy bias to Operation 3, while user 3 exploits Operation 2 and, to a small extent, Operation 4.

If we multiply the contents of Exhibit 10 with the contents of Exhibit 7, **PP'**, we can see how each of the four users' activity will distribute across the modules that comprise the system. This module activity is shown in Exhibit 11. Clearly, there is a distinct pattern of module execution for each of these users (operational profiles).

Exhibit 11 represents a matrix that shows the distribution of module activity for each operational profile. Exhibit 9 is a matrix containing the failure probability of each module and an upper bound for that estimate. The product of these two matrices is shown in the second and third columns of Exhibit 12. We can now associate a failure probability with each operational profile and establish an upper bound for that estimate. The reliabil-

Exhibit 10. Four Sample Operational Profiles

Operational	Operation			
Profile	1	2	3	4
1	0.00	0.04	0.86	0.10
2	0.05	0.43	0.05	0.48
3	0.05	0.69	0.01	0.26
4	0.49	0.01	0.01	0.49

Exhibit 11. Distribution of Module Activity under Four Operational Profiles

Operational	Module Activity							
Profile	1	2	3	4	5	6	7	8
1	0.00	0.01	0.41	0.02	0.05	0.21	0.04	0.26
2	0.00	0.11	0.02	0.09	0.26	0.16	0.00	0.35
3	0.00	0.18	0.00	0.05	0.15	0.23	0.00	0.38
4	0.02	0.00	0.01	0.09	0.43	0.12	0.01	0.32

Exhibit 12. Distribution of Module Activity under Four Operational Profiles

Operational Profile	Failure Probability	Upper Bound	Reliability	Lower Bound	Difference
1	0.0018	0.0037	0.9982	0.9963	0.0019
2	0.0050	0.0119	0.9950	0.9881	0.0069
3	0.0071	0.0173	0.9929	0.9827	0.0102
4	0.0017	0.0033	0.9983	0.9967	0.0016

ity of each operational profile is simply one minus the failure probability. Thus, the fourth column represents the reliability of the system under each operational profile. The fifth column (Lower Bound) shows the lower bound for each of the reliability estimates. This is, of course, simply one (1) minus the estimate for the upper bound of the failure probability.

By inspection of Exhibit 12, we can see that user 4, represented by Operational Profile 4, will use the system in the most reliable manner. That is because this user is exploiting modules with the highest reliability. Similarly, user 3 will have the dubious privilege of discovering problems with the software in that he is running the least reliable system.

The very nature of the milieu in which programs operate dictates that they will modify the behavior of the individuals who are using them. The result of this is that the user's initial use of the system, as characterized by the operational profile, will not necessarily reflect his or her future use of the software. There may be a dramatic shift in the operational profile of the software user, based directly on the impact of the software or due to the fact that the users' needs have changed over time. A design that has been established to be robust under one operational profile may become less than satisfactory under new profiles. We must come to understand that some systems may become less reliable as they mature, due to circumstances external to the program environment.

The continuing evaluation of the execution, function, and module profiles over the life of a system can provide substantial information as to the changing nature of the program's execution environment. It is clear that as we execute a particular piece of software, we will continue to collect data on the execution of the system. In all likelihood, the system will run quite well for many thousands of epochs. Thus, our perceptions of the reliability of our system will tend to be enhanced the more we work with the system. Also, our confidence in these estimates will grow over time as well.

12.3 AVAILABILITY

A major cause of failures in the field of any software system is that the software is used in a different manner in the field than the developers had anticipated and that testers have validated. Also, it frequently happens that a software system will function with high reliability in the field until a substantial change in the system activity causes these reliable systems to fail. We recently witnessed, for example, an astonishing number of failures in the field of a fault-tolerant storage device built by one of the manufacturers of large fault-tolerant file servers. These failure events were attributable to a new release of a database management system being run on these systems. This new software release was determined to make use of a host of features that had not been adequately tested when the software was developed. What really happened, in other words, was that there was a major shift in the operational profile of the system after the system had been in operation. This shift in operational profile caused an attendant shift in the reliability of the system.

To ensure the continuing reliable operation of a system, our objective should be to monitor the activity of our software system in real-time. In this operating mode, a baseline operational profile can be used to initialize an instrumented software system with a standard for certified behavior. When this system is deployed to a user's site, the activity of the system will be monitored dynamically as it is exercised by the user. When the system is placed in service, its activity will be monitored constantly through a sequence of execution profiles. The profile summaries of these module epochs will be sent to an analytical engine. This analytical engine will compare this profile against a nominal database to ensure that each profile is within the bounds of nominal behavior; i.e., that the current activity of the system is in conformance with the system behavior that has been tested by the vendor during its test and validation process.

Perhaps the greatest threat to the reliable operation of a modern software system is that the customer will exercise a system in an unanticipated fashion. That is, the customer will shift to the use of an operational profile different from that certified by the software developer. As a consequence, the system will shift from a reliable one to an unreliable one in this context.

Our ultimate objective of dynamic measurement availability assessment is to provide a methodology that can easily be incorporated into its software system, one that can:

- Monitor the activity of any piece of software
- Identify the novel uses of this software
- Call home (to the software developer) to notify testers of the new behavior
- Describe, in sufficient detail, the precise nature of the new behavior

We accept the proposition that no software system can be thoroughly or exhaustively tested. It is simply not possible to do this because of the complexity of our modern software system. We can, however, certify a range of behaviors for this software. These behaviors, in turn, are represented by certified operational profiles. If a user induced new and uncertified behavior on a system, then the reliability of the system might decline. It is also possible that the new behavior might well be sufficiently reliable but our level of certainty about this reliability estimate may be too low.

In the event that a user does depart from a certified operational profile, it will be important to know just what the new behavior is so that we can test the system and possibly certify it for the new behavior. If the software system is suitably instrumented, as was the case in our simple example in Section 12.3.4, then we will have sufficient information at our disposal to reconstruct the user's activity and certify the system components associated with that behavior.

The main objective of our dynamic measurement methodology for availability is to trap in real-time any behavior that is considered uncertified. We want to observe the software modules and their behavior to determine, with a certain level of confidence, the future reliability of a system under one or more certified operational profiles.

In the event that a system is determined to be operating out of the nominal range, the analytical engine must:

- Capture the execution profiles that represent the aberrant behavior
- Map this behavior to specific user operations
- Call home to report the specifics of the new behavior, including:
  - The specific modules involved
  - The operations exercised
  - The duration of the activity

With these data in hand, the software vendor can take the necessary steps to duplicate the activity, fix any problems that occur in this new operational context, recertify the software, and ship a new release to the customer *before* the software in the field *breaks*.

The availability measurement instrumentation can be installed at any level of granularity on a computer: the system kernel, the network layer, the file system, the shell, and the end-user application. At the kernel level, the operating system will generate and display a normal level of activity, as shown in its nominal execution profile. When this profile shifts to an off-nominal profile, something new and potentially unreliable is occurring on the system. At the file system level, each user accesses different files, in different locations, with different frequencies that describe certain patterns that can be represented in a profile. At the shell level, each user generates a standard profile representing the normal activities that are customary for that person. Finally, each application generates profiles of characteristic nominal behavior for each activity.

In any of these levels, when a user profile begins to differ from a nominal profile by a preestablished amount, an alarm is activated. Two things might be wrong: (1) a hardware component on which the system is running is beginning to fail; or (2) a current user is driving the system into operations that have not been certified. For complete availability monitoring capability, all software running on a system must be monitored in real-time.

Essentially, all developers of large software systems have come to realize that the past reliability of a piece of software is not a very good determinant of its future reliability. A system may function well in the field until its users begin to use it in new and unanticipated ways. In particular, developers of software for Internet applications are painfully aware of this phenomenon. The Internet and all its clients is a rapidly changing environment. Further, it is relatively difficult to forecast just how the system will evolve. In that we really cannot predict the future behavior of our software clients, we can never know for certain just how they will use our products. Thus, we are perennially vulnerable to failure events in this environment. These failure events are not particularly critical for Internet browsers. You can always reboot. The consequences of failure in a safety-critical software system are very different. No software vendors can or want to assume this kind of cyber-liability.

We have sought to introduce a little science into the world of software development. We exploit dynamic measurement techniques to analyze the internal software behavior. Our research has shown that internal behavior analysis has an enormous potential as an effective means to detect abnormal activities that might constitute threats to the availability of a system. Through the real-time analysis of the internal program activities, we can detect very subtle shifts in the behavior of a system. In addition, based on the initial experiments, we can now presume that each system abnormality has a particular internal behavior profile that can be recognized.

The dynamic availability measurement technology permits us to measure, in real-time, the behavioral characteristics of the software. These measurements, in turn, allow us to make inferences as to whether a software system is executing certified user operations or is being pushed into new uncertified behavior domains. Of utmost importance is the fact that we can capture this data and submit it to a software vendor in a timely fashion with an eye toward (1) understanding the new uses of the software, (2) recertifying the software for the new observed behaviors, and (3) replacing the software on the user's system before it has a chance to fail. With this capability in place, a software vendor has the capability of fixing a software system before it breaks.

12.4 SECURITY

When we monitor systems that are executing, their patterns of execution of program modules readily become apparent. This is not surprising. We saw in Chapter 9 that there is a direct mapping from what a user does to a specific set of program modules. That is, when a user exercises an operation, this operation will be implemented by one or more system functionalities. One or more program modules will, in turn, implement these functionalities. The pattern of activity of the modules under each user operation becomes the *behavior* of the system. Each user will ultimately generate an operational profile that describes how he or she has used the system. At the module level, there will be a rather small set of module profiles that characterize this operation profile. These profiles constitute the normal system behavior.

Most of the computer security methods now in place attempt to characterize the abnormal conditions that occur during each security violation. Signatures of this abnormal activity can be developed for the behavior of the system such that whenever we recognize a certain pattern of behavior, we will know that we are under attack by the Manama virus or the Blorch Buffer Overflow exploit. The basic problem with this approach is that the state space for abnormal behavior is unknowably large. This creates a real advantage for the attacker who would exploit our system. The state space for normal behavior in a typical operating system or any other large software system is really quite small. We can know and understand this normal behavior quite well. If we know what a system's normal activity is, we can quite easily determine when the system is no longer operating within the bounds of normal activity.

The vast majority of security vulnerabilities in software are there for a very simple reason: the software has not been engineered. It has been crafted. It would be difficult to conceive of a nuclear power plant that was operated without process monitoring hardware in place. It would be equally difficult to imagine an oil refinery that could safely operate without extensive process monitoring probes in place. In both of these hardware systems, vital information is monitored in real-time for all aspects of plant operation. This information is obtained in a sufficiently timely manner to react to operating conditions that exceed normal parameters. In essence, both of these systems are operating under real-time feedback control systems.

Modern operating systems are far more complex than most oil refineries or nuclear power plants. Modern command and control software is far more complex than the hardware systems controlled by these C4I systems, yet no modern software systems have any form of process control built into them. They are essentially running out of control. It is not surprising, therefore, that even a novice hacker can gain control of these complex systems. No one is watching. No mechanism has been provided to exercise the necessary restraints to prevent unwanted incursions into these systems.

Software systems have been created by developers who have not been schooled in basic engineering principles. Each software system is hand-crafted by software craftsmen. These craftsmen are simply not aware of the concepts of dynamic software measurement or control systems. It is not surprising that the systems that they build are vulnerable and fragile. These handcrafted systems are not constructed according to the most fundamental principles of sound engineering practice.

The solution to the current crisis in software security and reliability lies in the application of basic engineering principles that have dominated mechanical, electrical, and civil engineering for some time. Software systems simply need to be measured as they are designed and tested. They must have the basic real-time controls built into them that we have come to enjoy in our microwave ovens and automobiles. It would be very difficult to sabotage a military installation because of the real-time monitoring that is built in to protect it. It is relatively easy to render this same installation inoperable in that the software that forms the nucleus of the entire system is not subject to the same level of engineering discipline.

In essence, we do not have a security problem. We have a control problem. Interested parties can hijack our software because we are not watching its operation. Similarly, we do not have a software reliability problem. We have a monitoring problem. Software is allowed to perform uncertified functions that will certainly increase the risk of its failure. Our current problems with software security can easily be eliminated when we understand the need for building real-time controls into these systems.

12.5 MAINTAINABILITY

We will need to change a piece of software for one of two reasons. First, our needs may have changed. We will need to implement new features or operations for the users. Alternatively, the operating milieu of the software has changed. New or different hardware may be added to the environment in which the software is running. In this case, the set of user operations will not change but the set of functionalities will change in response to this new operating environment.

The second reason that we will have to change a system is that we have observed it failing. We will know that the system has failed in that it has departed in some measure from its specifications. In the simplest case we could simply insist that the software system merely meet the nonfunctional requirement that it not cease to operate for any reason. That is, if it suffers from a catastrophic collapse (the blue screen of death), then we will know that the system has failed.

The vast majority of software systems currently in operation or under development do not really have a set of specifications that control their development. They have been or are being lovingly crafted by small groups of people who do not really communicate with each other. This makes the failure determination problem significantly more difficult. If we do not have a precise set of software specifications for a given system, then any behavior of the system other than outright failure is really acceptable behavior. This is so in that a software failure of a program will be recognized at the point of its departure from its specified behavior. Absent a set of specifications, any behavior of this system is as good as any other. It might, for example, trash the system password file whenever it is run. If we have not specified exactly what the system should be doing, then trashing the password file is probably as acceptable as any other behavior.

Reference

1. Musa, J.D., *Software Reliability Engineering*, McGraw-Hill, New York, 1998.

Chapter 13
Implementing a Software Measurement Plan

13.1 THE SOFTWARE MEASUREMENT PROCESS

Measurement is something that we must learn how to do. The very worst thing that we can do in the measurement process is to presume that all of the tools necessary to perform the required measurement are handily available, that all we need to do is just find them. We would like very much for the measurement effort to be someone else's problem. We would like to buy a miracle. That is, we would like to find the ideal measurement toolset that would automatically install on our software development hardware and provide instant feedback on our software process. Unfortunately, there are no miracles. We have watched software developers acquire many different miraculous metric tools in the past. The end game has always been the same. The miracle just did not happen. If we are going to learn how to do measurement-based software engineering, we are going to have to roll up our sleeves and do some serious investment of our own labor. You simply cannot buy good engineering practice. You must work to make it happen.

Measurement tools simply produce numbers. These numbers are simply data. For the numbers to be made meaningful, they must first be converted to information. This information can, in turn, be used to monitor and change the software development information process. There are really three parts, then, to a measurement system. First, we must have tools that generate the measurement data. Hopefully, the data produced will be meaningful and valid. Second, we must have in place a strategy to manage the data. The data must be sent to a data repository where it can be structured in relation to other data for easy access in the future. Finally, we must have tools in place to convert the data to information.

There is also the misconception that simple is best. If we could just find the right snake oil salesman, we could buy an answer to our measurement problems. Measurement is not just a question of finding the right metric.

Exhibit 1. Misuse of Measurement Data

Cyclomatic Complexity	Risk Evaluation
1–10	A simple program, without much risk
11–20	More complex, moderate risk
21–50	Complex, high risk program
>50	Untestable program (very high risk)

From the Software Enginering Institute, Carnegie Mellon University

We have clearly seen that measuring the static attributes of a software system is a multivariate problem. Computer programs are extremely complex entities. The people who create them are even more complex. Any attempt to oversimplify the measurement process will certainly contribute to our misunderstanding of the software development process. One of the most egregious misuses of measurement data can be seen in Exhibit 1. Here we see that one metric, cyclomatic complexity, is the unique determinant of program risk (whatever that might be). When this metric is applied to a program module, we can clearly see that a module with cyclomatic complexity greater than 20 will create high risk. The obvious solution is to split the module into two or more modules, each of which will have less complexity than the first. What this does is to shift the complexity from a domain that is being measured, ostensibly control flow complexity, to one that is not being measured, coupling complexity. It might well be that this decision would result in a program whose net complexity across all attribute domains will increase. This is a very good example of how incomplete information can result in exactly the wrong decision.

The most important concept in the establishment of an effective software measurement process is simplicity. Start with a simple process and get it right. The focus should be on the process itself, and not on the tools. It is possible to have the best tools that money can buy and still not have a viable software measurement system. If we have designed an effective software measurement process, it will be possible to insert tool enhancements at will. The process should not depend on the tools. We would expect to build better tools as our understanding of the measurement process matures. If the process is a good one, the tools can be plugged into or unplugged from it without disruption.

The measurement process should be continuous. With the aid of a software measurement database, the measurement data should be timely. That is, the information in the database should reflect exactly the system as it is *right now*. Measurement is an integral part of the software development process. Just as is the case with other engineering disciplines, all design decisions and development decisions should be based on measurement outcomes. Many times during the initial stages, we will not have the information we need to make the decisions we will need to make. In this case, we will have to design experiments to understand the nature of the problem we are trying to solve. This will naturally lead to the integration into the measurement database of new measurement data as an aid to the development process.

Inherent in the measurement process should be a mechanism for measurement process improvement. We propose that the measurement system should begin with a very simple set of measurement tools and processes. We will then institutionalize a process of measurement process improvement. In this chapter, we will sketch out such a simple system and show some fundamental elements of this system. What we will discover in this design process is that the measurement structure should be woven out of whole cloth. That is, the source code measurement system should integrate with the source code control system, which should also be used to manage the evolving requirements specification. The software testing process should be integrated into the measurement process at a very early stage. Ultimately, all aspects of the software development of a new software system — from cradle to retirement — should operate under the scrutiny of the measurement system. That is what engineering is all about.

The most difficult obstacle to overcome in the transition from the world of software craftsmanship to the engineering discipline will be from the software management staff. They know how to manage software craftsmen. They do not know how to do engineering, much less manage an engineering process. Unless there is a high degree of management buy-in, any attempt to initiate a software measurement is doomed to failure. This may mean that substantial training in the use of measurement data must occur within the management staff. The typical manager has made decisions by seat-of-the-pants methodology for his entire management lifetime. Managers must be trained to use the information that the measurement system yields. That is part of the process of beginning a new measurement-based development system.

Finally, for there to be a successful transition to a software engineering system, the notion of engineering discipline is paramount. All software measurement and reporting systems must be rigorously followed and there must be processes in place to enforce this discipline. Nothing, for example, can undermine a fault tracking system any faster than the pocket program trouble report (PTR). In this case, a developer may well discover faults in a program module that he or she has written. In that the developers are aware that faults are now being tracked to individual developers, there will be an attempt to hide or disguise faults on the part of the developers. One way to do this is the pocket PTR. In this case, a developer discovers a fault in code that he or she has written, and rather than report this problem, the developer will simply note the problem on a piece of paper that is filed in his or her pocket. The developer will then hold the informal

PTR until a problem is found in the same module that was introduced by another developer. When the developer applies a fix to the new problem, he or she will simply introduce the fix for the pocket PTR, thus disguising the original fault.

The use of the pocket PTR by developers indicates that there are several things wrong with the development process. First, the developer thinks that he or she owns the code. In fact, the code base belongs to the company. It is in the company's interest that the code is fixed. A system that punishes the developer for faults will only encourage the faults to be hidden. This, in turn, results in real distortions in the fault measurement system. Developers should be rewarded for finding faults — not punished.

Second, the fault got into the code because the software development process failed, not because the developer introduced it. The process that led to the introduction of the fault in the first place should be the focus of interest in the etiology of the fault. If, for example, a developer introduced a fault that resulted in a divide exception, then it is possible that other developers have done the same thing. We might then elect to introduce a check for division operations in all new code as an item on an inspection protocol for future software review processes. Even more important, if a developer introduced a division operation that resulted in a divide exception, it is likely that there are other instances of this problem in the code as well. A code inspection process should be initiated that will cause the code base to be reviewed for other similar problems.

Third, there was no review process to ensure change integrity. Code should only be changed in response to a single PTR or a single change request. Each code update should address exactly one PTR or one change request. A review committee should audit all proposed code changes before they are committed to the source code control system.

We can use metric tools to measure software code with a high degree of precision. Other measurement activities, such as the fault tracking system, depend heavily on human cooperation. It will do little good to have very precise code measurements and very imprecise and inaccurate fault data. Thus, the majority of the emphasis in the establishment of an effective software measurement system should be on those measurement activities that involve humans in the process. These human beings are, in fact, measurement tools. They must be manufactured (trained) with the same precision as the automated measurement tools, such as source code metric tools.

13.2 BUILDING A MEASUREMENT PROCESS

The initial focus in the development of a measurement system should be on the process itself. There are some key requisites for the measurement process to succeed, including:

- The measurement activity should be transparent.
- The actual measurement tools should be pluggable into this process.
- The measurement data should reside in a common repository or database.
- Information from the database should be restricted to a need-to-know basis.
- Software measurement will have to earn a position in the software development process.

Any measurement process that demands extra resources allocated to the measurement function will not succeed. Everyone in the software development process is painfully aware that their resources are stretched to the limit with an already impossible task and impossible deadlines. Any additional workload imposed by the measurement activity will be sufficient reason to slip delivery deadlines or eliminate the measurement activity itself. At the outset, there is no perceived benefit for software measurement by the troops on the frontlines of software development. No activity that demands resources without immediate payoff will last for long in this environment. Unfortunately, there will be a significant latency between the start of the measurement process and the first significant return on this measurement investment. Measurement is completely unnecessary and unwanted in the world of the software craftsman. It will have to be bootlegged in its incipient stages. If the measurement activity is embedded in the day-to-day operations of the software development processes, it can be made invisible.

13.2.1 Building an Initial Measurement System

Every system and every process has a beginning. Perhaps the best beginning for a software engineering measurement system is to begin by measuring source code. This will be the least disruptive of just about any other thing that can be measured. We will prime the measurement pump by building the first software measurement tool for our software. The primitive software metrics discussed in Chapter 5 would be a very good start for this process. Actually, the size metrics discussed in this chapter will be an adequate start. It should take less than 100 staff hours of one or two competent programmers to build such a tool. An alternative to building a tool would be to acquire one from the public domain of open source software. The downside of this strategy is that the tool must be certified to meet the standard for the appropriate enumeration of operators, operands, statements, etc. It is quite likely that each tool will have its own standard. These tools must be rebuilt to conform to the evolving measurement standard suggested in Chapter 5.

The initial measurement tool can be regarded as a cipher. Its real value is to hold the place for a more competent tool that will be added later. For

Exhibit 2. Module Version Data

- Module_Name
- Date
- Time
- Developer_Name
- Revision_Number
- CR or PTR_Number
- Vector of Source_Code_Metrics

the moment, the sole objective is to get the measurement activity going. It is far better to collect data on a very few valid and standard metrics than it is to collect a lot of metrics of highly questionable value. Our basic measurement tool will collect its metric data at the source code module level. The tool will be integrated into the source code control system, such as the RCS or SCCS that is used for a project. Every time a source code module is checked into RCS, our metric tool will be invoked. The module metric data will be captured at the point of the save. There are many different source code control systems in place today other than RCS. The important aspect of the measurement tool is that the code be measured for every change. The main objective of this level of integration of the measurement tool with the configuration control system is that the code measurements be as current as the source code. There is no latency of measurement. The current measurement data reflects the current state of the source code base.

Let us now turn our attention to the data that is available at the point that each module is measured. First of all, we have the name and revision number of the module from RCS. Second, we have a vector of metrics data for the module. Third, we know who made the changes. Fourth, we can know the date and time of the change. Finally, we can know why the changes were made. If the changes were made in response to a program trouble report (PTR), we can capture the trouble report number at this point. If the change was made in response to a particular change request (CR) document, we can capture the change request document number. All changes to code after the initial check into RCS will be made for exactly one of these two reasons. We can summarize the data available at each measurement point as shown in Exhibit 2. This data is bound together for each measurement event. It will be placed into our measurement database.

The next step in the measurement process development will be to take our simple measurement database and put in place processes that will convert the data stored there to information. The first thing we might want to do is to get a handle on the rate of change and code churn in the database. To do this we will design a process to capture build information in the database. Each build can be characterized by the information shown in Exhibit 3. We will now implement processes to ensure that this data is added to the measurement database. If we know nothing more than the date and time of

Exhibit 3. Build List

- Build_Number
- Build_Date
- Time
- Build_List of
- Module_Name
- Revision_Number

Exhibit 4. Baseline Data

- Baseline_Build_Number
- Vector of Metric_Means
- Vector of Metric_Standard_Deviations
- Vector of Metric_Eigenvalues
- Matrix of Metric_Transformation_Coefficients

each build, we can easily reconstruct which modules actually went to the build from the code repository.

With the build data and the source code module metric data alone, we have a tremendous information capability at hand. We can actually increase the utility of this data if we are able to baseline the data so that we can easily compare across builds. In Chapter 6, the fault index (FI) measure was introduced to serve as a fault surrogate. In Chapter 8 we learned how we could use the FI metric, or some other suitable quality criterion metric, to compare data across builds. To that end we will now create a baseline build record to store the necessary information for a baseline build. This record will contain the data shown in Exhibit 4.

We will obtain the baseline data through the statistical analysis of the modules that comprise the baseline build. The means and standard deviations are simple descriptive statistics. The eigenvalues and transformation coefficients can be obtained from a principal components analysis (PCA) of the metric data in the baseline build.

The initial metric data collected by the initial measurement system will be far from comprehensive. The focus of this initial stage should be on the processes surrounding the measurement devices, and on the storage and maintenance of the data that streams from the measurement processes.

13.2.2 Building a Measurement Reporting System

The measurement processes discussed in the previous section will generate an astonishing amount of data. These data must be sent to the measurement database as they are generated as part of the automated measuring process. The next logical step is to build the processes that will convert these data into information. The first such process will be one that will build FI values for each of the versions of each of the modules in the database. The next logical step is to build a set of SQL procedures to build new and meaningful relationships among the data elements.

The baseline build is not necessarily a static position in the build sequence. The baseline build is merely a reference point. It can be changed at any point. However, once the baseline build is changed, then the FI values must be recalculated for all versions of the modules. FI, remember, is constructed from the baseline means, standard deviations, and eigenvalues of the baseline build. If this baseline build changes, so too will the statistics associated with the build. Also, it must be remembered that each build will probably differ in terms of the sets of modules that comprise the build.

After very few builds of a moderate-sized software system there will be an astonishingly large amount of data in the database. We will now turn our attention to the process of converting these data to information. From a global perspective, the first thing we might wish to know is just how the system has changed from its inception to the present. The code churn value discussed in Chapter 8 is a very good indicator of the total system code change. We can compute each system build code churn for any two builds by taking the module versions from the build list of the two builds in question and computing the difference in FI for each module pair in the two builds. In doing so, we must remember that, in all likelihood, there will be some modules in the first such build that are not in the second, and vice versa. Code churn values can be established for any two builds in the database. It would be logical to create some standard SQL procedures for computing the code churn for all sequential build pairs in the database. We can then see, at a glance, how much the system has changed over its entire development history.

From a global or system perspective, the FI values for all modules in each build can be summed. For the baseline build, the average FI was set to 100. If there are 1000 modules in this build, then the total system FI would be 100,000. If, on a subsequent build, the total system FI increases, then it will be apparent that the net complexity and hence the net fault burden of the system are increasing. Similarly, we can sum the code churn values for all modules in each build. These code churn modules would represent the net change in a system from one incremental build to the next. If a system is relatively stable and has changed little from one build to the next, then the net code churn will tend to zero. A system that has a large net code churn is far from being ready for deployment.

We are now, for the first time, in a position to track process measures. Faults are introduced into software systems by people operating under formal or informal software development processes. What we would really like to know is the actual rate at which these faults are being introduced. In Exhibit 2 we now have two relevant pieces of data: a module version number and a PTR number. With the module version number we can go to the source code control system and retrieve the changes that we made between the version number associated with the PTR number and the previous version of the module in the system. This will permit the actual number of faults to be determined, as per the discussion in Chapter 5. For each PTR and associated module version number, it is possible to compute the total fault count for each PTR. Once the specific lines of source code associated with each PTR have been identified, it is then possible to track backward through the source control system to find exactly when those lines first appeared in the system.

From Chapter 8 we realize that there are two distinct sources of faults in any system. There are those faults that were put into the code during the initial software development prior to the first system build. These faults are put into the code by people following regular institutionalized software development processes. The second type of fault is one that was introduced later in the software evolution process by change activity. This can be a very different type of process from the initial software development process. In Chapter 5 we introduced two proportionality constants, k and k', that represented the relative proportion of faults introduced during the initial development process (k) and the relative proportion of faults introduced by subsequent maintenance activity (k'). In the case of both proportionality constants, a smaller value represents a better software process. This provides a solid foundation to measure the relative effect of a change in software process that can be introduced during the development of any system. If a new software process is so introduced, there should be a diminution in the maintenance activity constant k'. Let k_0' represent the initial proportionality constant for the initial software process. When a new software maintenance process is introduced, there will be a new proportionality constant, k_1'. If the new process does, in fact, represent an improvement over the old one, then we would expect $k_1' < k_0'$.

In Exhibit 2, we recorded the developer name. This is absolutely the most inflammatory information in the metric database and it is the most easily misused. It must be remembered that people introduce faults into code because they are following specific processes, either formal or informal. The process directly determines the rate at which people introduce faults. When software systems are late in shipping or have reliability problems, it is far too easy to comb the database for an individual to "sack." Individuals should never be the subjects of scrutiny. There is exactly nothing to be gained in the analysis of information from a single individual. Individuals do not fail; processes do. There is nothing that can create failure of an incipient software measurement system faster than to use this data to analyze individual performance.

There are really two entwined issues relating to developer introduction of faults. The first relates to variability. If there is a very tightly controlled software development process with equally tight audit procedures built into it, then there will be little or no variation in the rate at which different developers introduce faults into code. The very first sign of a poor software development process is visible in the variation in fault rate across developers. This is perhaps the most singularly important information that we can extract from our measurement database to this point. It would be pointless, and indeed meaningless, to attempt to introduce a change in an already bad process. Before new software development processes are considered, we must first seek to gain control of the current processes. Our first clear indication that we have begun to gain the high ground of good software process is that the *variation* in rate of fault introduction across individual developers is very low. Then, and only then, can we begin to consider changing the underlying software development process. Thus, the first statistic that we will extract from our new measurement database that involved people will be the variation in the individual rate of fault introduction. It is relatively easy to obtain this information. We have at our disposal all the modules that have been changed by an individual. This can be obtained from the source control system. We also have at our disposal a very precise means of determining exactly which code elements have been changed by this person. The FI values of each of the program modules will allow us to compute the code churn for these changes. Of these changes, we can easily measure the number of faults introduced by this individual during the change process. Again, we must accept the fact that the rate of fault introduction by a single individual has little or no meaning. It is the variation in rate across all developers that will tell us how much work we will have to do to eliminate these sources of variation.

It is very difficult to gain control of a process that has run amok. A process clearly out of control is one that has a large variation in the rate of fault introduction across individuals. As an example of such a bad process, we can imagine a system in which a single individual consistently forgets to check the range of a divisor, resulting in code with zero divide exceptions. Another developer consistently forgets to free memory for data structures no longer in use, resulting in memory leaks. Yet another developer consistently forgets to initialize pointer values. There is absolutely no excuse for a zero divide exception. One way to gain control of this problem is to fire the guilty party. We could also use this same strategy to eliminate memory leaks. Sooner or later, we would have no staff left and our rate of fault introduction would fall to zero. Regrettably, so too would our code production. Zero divide exceptions are very easy to deal with at the process level. Perhaps one of the easiest ways to eliminate them is to institute inspection and review processes that will ensure that there is adequate range checking for each divisor before the divide operation is performed. It is very reasonable to assume that if one divide operation produced a divide exception, then every other divide operation in the program is an equally likely candidate for a divide exception. They must all be examined. Any new division operations that are subsequently introduced will be subject to the same level of review.

The second issue of a developer's rate of fault introduction as a measure of process is the variation within each developer's rate. Not all faults are equal. In Chapter 5 we learned that there can be many structural elements in code that will have to change to fix a single problem. By the same token, there can be relatively little code that will have to change in response to a PTR. This means that there may be substantial *within-developer* variation. Some code that a particular developer writes may be fraught with faults, while other code may be quite clean. Again, this is a process issue. There are many different attributes that a code module can have. Some modules are compute intensive with substantial mathematical computation; some modules are highly interactive with the operating system; and other modules are I/O intensive. It is reasonable to believe that if we assign a developer who is mathematically naive to a task of coding a complex numerical algorithm, that person is doomed to struggle through the coding task with great difficulty. People have attributes just as do the program modules. Matching people to tasks is a very simple measure that can be taken to eliminate within-developer variation.

There are many other ways in which the data in Exhibits 2 through 4 can be combined to produce very useful management information. If the data is precise and accurate, then the information that can be extracted from this data will be meaningful. At this early stage of building a measurement system, considerable attention must be given to the nature of the reporting process.

13.2.3 Measurement for Testing

Once the processes for gathering static information about the code base, code evolution, and preliminary developer information are in place, the next logical place to focus is the test process. As indicated in Chapter 11, static source code measurement is like one-hand clapping. Perhaps the greatest utility of the static measures of the code base will come in the testing phase. Here we would like to install the basic elements of a system that will collect information on test activity. This will be the *dynamic* measurement system.

There are many different levels of granularity that can be used for dynamic granularity. Consistent with the level of granularity of source code measurement, all source code should also be measured at the module level. Each test activity will exercise a subset of the code. The code will be suitably instrumented to generate the test execution profile. As discussed in Chapter 10, the test execution profile is simply a vector equal in length to the cardinality of the set of all modules that have ever been in any build.

Exhibit 5. Test Execution Data

- Test_ID
- Test_Date
- Test_Case_ID
- Test_Case_Version_Number
- Test_Time
- Tester_Name
- Build_Number
- Test_Execution_Vector

Each module in every build will have a unique integer identifier that will distinguish it from every other module. As each test is run, each module exercised by that test will cause a corresponding element in the test execution profile to be incremented every time the module is entered. At the conclusion of the test, the test execution profile will contain the frequencies of execution of each module exercised by that test. These data, together with the test case, possible test ID, test date, build number, and tester, will be added to the measurement database. These new data elements are shown in Exhibit 5.

With these data, we can now compute the test statistics presented in Chapter 11. First would be test entropy. A low entropy test will concentrate its energies on a small number of program modules, whereas a high entropy test will distribute its attention to a much broader range of modules. A test execution profile can be computed using the test execution vector. This execution profile will show the proportion of time spent in each program module during the test activity. These data, in conjunction with code churn data, can be used from a delta testing perspective to compute both the test effectiveness and test efficiency of the specific test represented by the Test_ID.

At any point, the test execution vectors for all tests to date can be summed into a single cumulative test execution frequency vector (CTEFV), as discussed in Chapter 11. From the CTEFV, a cumulative execution profile can be computed, spanning all test activity to date. These data, together with the FI values for the current build number, will yield cumulative measures of test effectiveness and efficiency.

Each test activity will also have a binary outcome. Either a failure was noted while the code was run or no failure occurred. If the test failed, then the failure event will be resolved to a fault in a particular program module. Directly corresponding to the CTEFV we also have the failure frequency vector (FFV), as discussed in Chapter 12. Each time a failure is resolved to a particular program module, the element of the FFV corresponding to the program module will be incremented by one. From these data we can then work out the current reliability of the system for a given operational profile.

Thus, the dynamic metric data will permit us to evaluate each individual test and the cumulative test activity for the entire system. In addition, we will also have a working estimate of the overall system reliability.

13.2.4 Requirements Tracking System

Chapter 9 introduced the notion of tracking in the evolution of software requirements. This tracking system should be online and accessible to all software developers. For the purposes of this discussion, we are going to include this management system in our measurement database. Of interest to us from the measurement perspective are the system operational specifications as shown in Chapter 9, Exhibit 14; the system functional specifications as shown in Chapter 9, Exhibit 17; and the design module specification as shown in Chapter 9, Exhibit 4. The current requirements definitions are a necessary and vital part of the software testing system.

13.2.5 Software Test System

The basic objective of the software testing process is to ensure that the software meets the basic quality standards. On the quality side, the reliability of the software is of great importance to the software test activity. In particular, there must be some assurance that the software will not fail in a predetermined user environment. As previously discussed, it is a very unrealistic goal of the test process that all software faults will be found and eliminated. New faults are continually being added to systems as they evolve, even as old faults are found and removed. What is important is that the faults that remain are quiescent. The typical user will not expose them in his or her use of the system. Also of interest is the fact that the system can be certified to meet the nonoperational and nonfunctional requirements articulated in the software requirements specification.

13.2.5.1 Delta Testing. Chapter 11 introduced the notion of delta testing. At each new build, code will be added or deleted. Each of these changes will create the opportunity for new faults to be introduced into the code. The likelihood of introduction will be proportional to the measure of code churn. For each build it is easy to extract from the measurement system the values of code churn for that build. This will show the distribution of the changes that have been made to the code. The code churn, $\left\langle \chi_1^{k,k+1}, \chi_2^{k,k+1}, \ldots, \chi_n^{k,k+1} \right\rangle$, between builds k and $k+1$ will clearly reflect where the greatest changes have occurred. From Chapter 11, if we were to execute the best possible test for this changed code, we would construct an execution profile that will spend the majority of its time in the functionalities that contain the modules that have changed the most from one build to the next. Let

Exhibit 6. Functional Test Case Specification

- Test_Case_ID
- Test_Case_Name
- Test_Setup
- Input_Data_Requirements
- Execution_Steps
- Expected_Outcome
- Functionalities_Vector
- Functionality_Requirement_Number
- Functionality_Version_Number

$$X^{k,k+1} = \sum_{i=1}^{n} \chi_i^{k,k+1}$$

This is the total code churn between builds k and $k+1$. For delta test purposes we would like to exercise each module in proportion to the change that has occurred in the module during its current revision. Again, we will compute this proportion as follows:

$$q_i^{k,k+1} = \chi_i^{k,k+1} \Big/ X^{k,k+1}$$

The distribution of $q_i^{k,k+1}$ clearly shows where we must distribute our test activity to create maximum exposure for the faults that may have been introduced on the new build $n+1$. If each of the modules were exercised in proportion to the amount of change that they had received, we would maximize our exposure to software faults to these new faults.

Constructing tests that will distribute test activity to modules in a particular fashion is a very difficult to impossible task to accomplish without a suitable measurement database. Fortunately, in our measurement database we will have the requirements specifications that show the mapping between functionalities (and operations) and specific program modules. With this mapping information it will be relatively simple to design tests that will cause specific modules to be executed.

13.2.5.2 Functional Testing. A functional test of a software system is a test activity designed to exercise one or more functionalities. To initiate this process, test cases will be derived from the program functional specifications. Each test case will evolve just as the requirements evolve. The test case specification elements are shown in Exhibit 6. These specifications should be maintained by a configuration control system in the same fashion as the source code and the software requirements specifications. It is clear that the functionalities will change over time. As these functionalities change, the test cases related to the functionalities must also change. Some functionalities may be deleted. Those test cases that reference these deleted functionalities must either be modified or deleted. The entire software structure of requirements and code is a living system. It is in a con-

344

stant state of change. This implies that there is no such thing as a *standard* test case. Test cases are evolving documents as well.

Each test case will have a test case ID and name. It will also have the canonical test information, such as test setup information, input data requirements, execution steps, and expected outcomes. These data will be placed under some type of document revision control system. The functionalities vector contains one or more pairs of numbers representing the functionalities that the test case is design to exercise. Whenever any of the functional requirements represented in the functionalities vector for each test case are updated, so too should the corresponding test cases be updated. Whenever a test case is modified, it may well represent a new test activity altogether.

Each functional test case will generate a test execution profile when it is executed. These data are, of course, stored in the test execution data on the database, as is shown in Exhibit 5. It is vital that the test execution data shown in this table distinguish between the test case versions.

In addition to the set of functionalities, there may also be a number of nonfunctional requirements that the software must meet. Therefore, test cases must be constructed that will assess these requirements. The documentation for these test cases would be very similar to that of Exhibit 6.

13.2.5.3 Operational Testing. An operation test of a system is a test activity designed to exercise one or more system operations. The case for managing the test cases for operational testing is very similar to that of functional testing. The requisite data for each of these tests are shown in Exhibit 7. Again, these data are dynamic. As was the case for the functional test case specification, the operation test case specification also contains a vector of operations exercised by the test case. As each operation is changed as the operational requirements evolve, the corresponding test cases must also be updated to contain the version data from the affected operations.

Associated with each operation test case specification is, of course, the test case ID. These ID numbers will permit the test case results to be parsed correctly to their functional or operational test execution profiles. Also, as was the case with the functionalities, there may be a family of nonoperational specifications. This will mandate the certification of the software to these nonoperational specifications. The test cases for the nonoperational specifications would be very similar in nature to the contents of Exhibit 7.

13.2.5.4 Software Certification

The final stage of the test process is the certification process. Prior to the design of the software, it is imperative that we understand just how it will be used when it is deployed. The essence of this use is embodied in the

---

Exhibit 7. Operational Test Case Specification

- Test_Case_ID
- Test_Case_Name
- Test_Setup
- Input_Data_Requirements
- Execution_Steps
- Expected_Outcome
- Operations_Vector
- Operation_Requirement_Number
- Operation_Version_Number

---

operational profile. A typical user will not randomly distribute his activities across the suite of operations. He will distribute his activities according to an operational profile. Prior to the delivery of any software system, the final test exercise should validate that the system will perform flawlessly under the projected operational profile. That is the first step. Test cases should be developed that will mimic this operational profile as closely as possible.

The second step in the software certification process is the validation of the operational profile. As the software system is deployed to the field for a limited beta test, each system should be instrumented so that the actual operational profile of the system in the field can be closely monitored. If the actual use of the system in the field is consistent with the projected operational profile, the software will have passed the final level of certification. If, on the other hand, the field operational profile is significantly different from the design operational profile, then the software must be recertified for the actual or observed operational profile.

There will, of course, be no standard operational profile. Each user will use the system in a slightly different manner. That is, there will be some variation in the operational profile from user to user. As per the discussion in Chapter 10, we can measure the distance between each user's observed operational profile and the design operational profile. If the average distance $\bar{d}$ between the observed behavior in the field and the design operational profile is sufficiently large, then the certification process must be reinitiated. Similarly, if the observed variation in the departures from the design operational profile is too large, $Var(d)$, the software must be reevaluated from the standpoint of its robustness.

13.2.6 Program Trouble Reporting System

In order that faults might be tracked correctly, there must be some mechanism to report problems that develop as a software system evolves. There are several ways that problems in the execution of the code can occur. In every case, however, the program will fail to perform its execution of the requirements correctly. The initial purpose of the program trouble reporting (PTR) system is to document the departure of the program execution

Exhibit 8. The Program Trouble Report

- System_Name
- PTR_ID
- Build_Number
- Reporter_ID
- Date
- Time
- Test_Case_ID
- Failure_Analysis
- Severity
- Priority
- Apparent_Cause
- Resolution

from an established standard. Once the departure (or apparent departure) of the program from standard behavior is observed, the problem must be reported for subsequent analysis.

At the point when a problem is evident, certain information must be captured. The initial capture data is shown in Exhibit 8. First, let us observe that anyone in the universe can report a problem, not just testers or developers. In the resolution process, not all PTRs will result in one or more faults being recorded. Many times, the person reporting the apparent problem will incompletely understand the specified behavior of the system.

The purpose of the PTR is to report apparent or incipient failures in the system. The PTR tracking system will track trouble reports, perhaps on multiple systems. As each PTR is entered on the system, it is automatically assigned a unique PTR_ID by the tracking system. For the purposes of the measurement system, this identification number is the most important data that will be collected. It will link all subsequent change activity that will spin from this PTR. The next most important item will be the system build number. Each build is characterized by a set of specific code modules, functionalities, and operations. As the features of a system change from build to build, the problem reported in the PTR may become obsolete with regard to the latest system build.

There are four different types of source documents that must be managed in the software development process: (1) the operations requirements specification, (2) the functional requirements specifications, (3) the low-level design elements, and (4) the source code. A PTR may be filed against any of these four systems. The code may be working perfectly correctly according to its design. The system may be functionally correct. It may not, however, be doing what the user wants it to do, in which case a PTR would be filed and the appropriate operational specifications would be altered to reflect the user's requirements. In this case, the fault is in the operational specification, not in the code or functionality of the system. Assuming that the code is working as specified, it will

Exhibit 9. The Change Report

- System_Name
- CR_ID
- Build_Number
- Requester_ID
- Date
- Time

not change under a PTR. Only the system operational specification will change under the PTR. All other documents will change under a change request. Simply stated, a PTR will resolve to a fault in one of the four types of documents. If other system documents are altered, they must be altered under a change request.

13.2.7 Program Change Request System

Programs will change as a result of evolving requirements changes in either operations or functionalities. Operations and functionalities can be added, modified, or removed from the system. If a new operation is added to the system, necessarily there must be at least one new functionality added, plus at least one new program module. Similarly, if there is one new functionality added to the functional specifications, then there must be a least one module added to the design and source code as well. This will also mean that at least one operational requirement must change as well. Any changes to operations, functionalities, design, or source code elements must reference the change request (CR) number, as shown in Exhibit 9.

After the first build of any system, any alteration of any system document should have a reason for that alteration. If the document is flawed and contains one or more faults, then the revision control data for the new version must reflect either a PRT or a CR. No change to any document should be made without the authorization of a review process and a PTR or CR. This may seem like an overly bureaucratic process but is a necessary part of the engineering discipline that must be instituted for a successful software engineering program to be established. In the construction of modern aircraft, it would be absolutely unthinkable for a worker on the assembly floor to make an undocumented change in an aircraft airframe. It should be equally unthinkable that a software developer should be empowered to make undocumented changes to a software system.

13.2.8 Measuring People

It is not recommended that people attributes be part of an initial software development measurement system. The potential for misuse of these data is far too great to justify any potential value they might have. It is too easy, for example, to look at people as the source of faults in code. It is really very simple to find out which developers, designers, or requirements analysts contributed which problems to the system. This information, for immature systems, will inevitably contribute to a witch-hunt. Faults are, indeed, put into documents by people. However, it is the processes followed by those people that caused them to put the faults in the code and leave them there. It is the process that failed to trap the potential fault before it created problems in the design or in the code. In the initial stages of the development of or measurement system, the entire focus should be on process issues — not people.

13.3 MEASUREMENT PROCESS IMPROVEMENT

Quite clearly, we must develop a software measurement process. We must build a measurement system capable of measuring software products, process, people, and environments. That is a given. Once this measurement process is in place, we must take the next critical step. We must institutionalize the measurement process improvement process. The first rulers that we build will be crude instruments. The first software metric tool will be very simple. It will probably only measure a subset of the potential metrics that we think might be important. The first telescope ever made was a very primitive instrument by today's standards. However simple it might have been, it revolutionized the world of science. It opened the world of science to the notion that we are members of a vast universe. From that first very primitive instrument, incremental gains were made in the resolving power of the telescopes. With each improvement in resolution, our understanding of our physical universe also grew. We must be very careful just how complex we make our measurement tool. It can easily provide much more information than we are capable of digesting in our growth of understanding in software measurement. Imagine, if you will, the improbabilities of sharing the latest photographs from the Hubble space telescope with Galileo. He simply would not have been able to grasp the notion of the photograph itself, much less the image that it represented. Science evolves in very slow evolutionary steps. Each time a new telescope technology was introduced into the astronomical world, it took substantial time to assimilate the basic concepts of the new universe revealed by these new, more powerful instruments. It was suggested earlier that the initial metric tool should probably only measure a handful of size metrics. If this measurement is done accurately and precisely, the data that this metric tool will yield, in conjunction with the other data that we are also accumulating, will result in a quantum leap forward in the software development process.

13.3.1 Tools Refinement

In the case of astronomy, each new advance in telescope resolving power permitted astronomers to look farther back in time. This, in turn, allowed them to make new discoveries and expand their knowledge of the universe. Each incremental improvement of the telescope occurred at the right time for the knowledge base of that time. Each new technological advance in telescope construction represented an evolutionary enhancement in the observational technology. The images from the Hubble telescope would probably have been incomprehensible to astronomers as recently as 75 years ago. The same path must be followed in the evolution of software measurement tools. There is real value, for example, in a source code measurement tool that measures a few simple source code attributes such as those presented in Chapter 5.

After the initial tool has been inserted in the measurement process, we will seek to learn that which we do not yet know. The modeling techniques discussed in Chapter 7 will serve as a guide for identifying the directions that this new research should take. We will always know exactly what sources of variation we are measuring, and we will know how well we are measuring these attributes. Once we have clearly established what we are measuring, it will become increasingly clear what we are *not* measuring. It is clear, for example, that there are no metrics in Chapter 5 that deal directly with the object-oriented (O-O) design metaphor. This is a very complicated environment to measure. Great caution and considerable research will have to be performed before this metaphor can be well understood, let alone measured effectively. One of the major problems confronting us with this particular metaphor is that we must parse our measurement activity carefully into the O-O metaphor constructed for the user precompilation and the part of that metaphor that persists at runtime. From the standpoint of testing and dynamic measurement, a great deal of the O-O metaphor vanishes during compilation. Therefore, measurement of these attributes would be pointless from the standpoint of testing.

In essence, our measurement tools will be refined by an orderly sequence of experiments. Each experiment will be designed to identify new sources of variation in program attributes that contribute to our understanding of one or more criterion attributes. One of the major thrusts of our own research has been in the area of predicting the fault liability in source code constructs. An improvement in our measurement tool, therefore, would be one that would significantly increase the amount of explained variation in software faults. Exactly the same process would be followed for different criterion measures such as maintainability or availability. A better tool is one that explains more variation in one or more criterion measures. It is just that simple. Our initial objective is to build a simple, good tool to prime the measurement process. We will then institute experimental processes that will lead to subsequent improvements in this tool.

13.3.2 Measurement Process Enhancement

Part of the measurement process enhancement will occur directly from the simple and consistent improvement of the measurement tools around which we have initially built the measurement system. Clearly, our initial system has incorporated only a very small set of metrics with a small number of tools. The tools produced data in that they were part of a measurement process that drove the data capture. There is plenty of room for enhancement from our initial system in how these data will be captured, analyzed, and reported.

Even the most primitive kind of measurement system, as sketched above, has a tremendous amount of information in it. It would be pointless to take the next step in the enhancement of the measurement process if we did not take the requisite time to educate the development, test, requirements analysis, and management staff in the effective use of the information now at their disposal. Therefore, a vital step in the enhancement of the measurement system is the establishment of a training program in the correct uses of the information now available from the measurement and analysis system.

The next logical step in the measurement process enhancement is to expand on the number of attribute domains being measured for each of the people, process, product, and environment measurement domains. Initially, for example, we shied away from direct measurement of the people in the software process. This was principally because of the potential land mines in the misuse that this information might bring to bear. It is far too easy to draw exactly the wrong conclusions from data. Only after there has been sufficient training of the personnel who will have access to the measurement information should these potentially volatile sources be measured in the first place.

The most important consideration in the measurement enhancement process is that more is not better. Our objective is not to mine new sources of data just because they exist; it is far more important to have quality information than quantity. Also, no data should be added to the measurement system until there is a complete understanding of how these new data will be converted to useful information.

13.4 INSTITUTIONALIZING MEASUREMENT PROCESS IMPROVEMENT

Once a commitment has been made to build a good software development measurement system, the initial focus should be on building an effective measurement process. Around this measurement process we will systematically add new measurement tools, enhance the software measurement database, build a larger SQL framework to add value to the data that are constantly flowing into the database, and increase the exposure of the development staff to the contents of the measurement system through a training program.

There must next be a regular process created to improve the measurement process itself. The purpose of this process improvement process is to review and analyze the measurement process. The criterion measures for the measurement process are that the measurement process must:

- Be transparent
- Be timely
- Be cost effective
- Produce accurate and precise data
- Produce useful information
    - For project planning purposes
    - For managing the software development process
    - For future project planning

Once we understand just precisely how we are going to use the information from the measurement process, then we can institute a process to ensure that its objectives are met.

Perhaps the best way to conceptualize the measurement process improvement process is for us to think of the improvement occurring in a set of discrete steps. We will think of each of these potential improvement steps as an experiment. First we will formulate a hypothesis that suggests that our understanding of a single criterion measure would be enhanced if we were to make a change to the measurement process. That, after all, is why we are measuring things in the first place. We do not wish to make any change to the process that will not somehow make it better. We will not be able to make this assertion unless we have a controlled experiment to show the effect of change. We definitely want to steer clear of the Hawthorn effect. The essence of the Hawthorn effect is that change activity of just about any type will induce a short-term positive effect on the process that is being altered. Thereafter, the process will return to normal.

As a side note in the institutionalization of the change process, it is worth noting that the best source of potential improvements in the process will come from the people who are using the information provided by the measurement database. Far too often, experts are brought in to suggest changes to a process with which they are unfamiliar. The real experts are the consumers of the information.

The second step in this process will subject the experimental design to a critical review process of a team of people familiar with sound experimental design principles, software measurement processes in general, and the target software process. The purpose of this panel review process is to ensure the scientific and commercial integrity of the proposed changes to the measurement system.

The third step is to institute the proposed process change in a controlled environment. This will serve as a good pilot project for instituting the change on a more massive scale should the process change prove advantageous. Data collection during this trial phase will be subject to the rigors of a scientific experiment. Data will be collected for the new and improved process as well as the old and unimproved measurement process.

Finally, the process improvement must demonstrate significantly better understanding of the selected process criterion measure. If, for example, we wanted a more cost-effective measurement system, then a successful experimental outcome would be that the new measurement process would produce the same flow of information at reduced expense.

13.5 A NETWORK-BASED MEASUREMENT SYSTEM

It should be eminently clear, at this point, that measuring the evolution of a software system is a very complex process. There is an astonishing amount of data that generates from this measurement process. Teams of software developers are constantly modifying the code base. Testers are continually testing the evolving systems. Requirements are constantly changing. For a large system, the total data flow can easily amount to several megabytes per week. These data must be organized and managed in a database so that they can be converted into information for software development managers, software test managers, and software quality assurance staff.

We have developed a system called Darwin, after the father of evolution, that is designed to manage the measurement data for evolving software systems. The Darwin system is a very good example of how a measurement system can be integrated into a software development system. Darwin is a software engineering management system for tracking the progress of evolving software systems. It is a repository for all of the engineering data surrounding software development and software test. It is a Web server that permits developers and testers to interact with the system. It is an analytical tool that provides the measurement capabilities for both software development and software test. All management aspects of the software development and testing process are to be maintained by the Darwin system.

There are two criteria that must be satisfied for the measurement program to be a success. First, the measurement process must be automated. Second, it must be made invisible. Software developers have little or no experience with static software measurement. If they are confronted with the measurement, they will simply fail to do it. Software testers have little or no experience with dynamic software measurement. If they are also confronted with the additional task of measurement, they too will resist the additional effort.

At the core of the Darwin system is the software measurement database. All information surrounding the daily changes made to a system and the activities surrounding the test of that system will be recorded in the database. All measurement processes are automated and transparent. The Darwin system also provides a framework for software failure tracking and for software fault resolution. Finally, Darwin has an integrated software requirements tracking capability to aid in the regression test process.

13.5.1 Network Appliance

The Darwin software system was designed to reside in a network appliance (NA) computer attached to the local intranet connecting systems analysts, software developers, software testers, software managers, and software quality staff. The measurement database, the metric tools, and all the ancillary support software for Darwin are serviced from this machine. To interact with the system, a user will visit a Web site on the server and will then be linked through Web pages provided by the appliance to the appropriate application. This NA approach greatly simplifies the problem of instituting a measurement program, in that it obviates the need to port the software measurement infrastructure from one platform to another.

Different people in the development group will interact with the NA in different ways. A software manager will query the database to retrieve the latest status of the evolving software system. A build manager will inform the NA of the modules and versions of the modules for each of the builds. A software tester will retrieve test cases for the test process from the NA. A test manager will query the test database for the status of the test process to date.

Of greatest importance to the entire development process is the cogency of the information. A development manager can see the status of the development process essentially in real-time. Specific reports on change activity can assist in the process of setting milestones and reviews. A test manager can evaluate the status of a test process, again in near-real-time. The NA is a visible aid to developers, managers, and testers. All of the engineering data about the evolving software is managed from this location.

13.5.2 The Measurement Infrastructure

On the static measurement side, Darwin is designed to track changes to code and faults reported against specific code modules. The measurement of specific changes to the source code system can be a very complex process, in that a typical large software system may have many developers working with the same code base at the same time. It is possible to track changes to code at the individual version level. However, experience has shown that this kind of resolution is seldom, if at all, necessary. What is of primary interest to developers and managers is the code that constitutes a build.

At the point of a new build, a build manager will develop a new build index vector. This build index vector will determine which source code elements actually go to the build. On completion of the build index vector, Darwin can be requested to measure the source code for the build. Currently, the Darwin NA can supply measurement tools for C and C++ with the Extended C Metric Analyzer (ECMA), or for Java with the Java Metric Analyzer (JMA). The measurement tools are a component of the Darwin NA.

With the contents of the build index vector, Darwin will systematically retrieve the appropriate source code elements from the configuration control system with the updated versions of this code. Each source code module will then be measured by the appropriate measurement tool and the raw metrics for that module will be incorporated into the database. It is important to observe that the only modules that are measured by the system are those that will result in executable code. All header files and compiler directives will have been resolved before the measurement process begins.

Just as important as the process of measuring code is the process of maintaining specific fault reports. Each fault report will report on exactly one fault on one managed document. These fault reports are served from the NA as Web pages and are tracked by Darwin. For each change to a system, there can be exactly two reasons for the change: a fault has occurred or there has been a change in the program specifications. Darwin must track all program document changes relative to faults.

On the dynamic measurement side, Darwin will track failure reports and test execution profiles. As we are working on a developing system, faults will be introduced. Some of these faults will result in the failure of the system. This failure will be recorded in the failure reporting system. The specifics of this report will vary from one installation to another but will typically contain information similar to that listed below in the Failure Report Relation for a typical Darwin database. As the failure report is examined and mapped to one or more specific problems in the requirements, design, or code, the appropriate fault reports are completed. Each failure report is resolved by the creation of one or more fault reports.

To monitor the code when it is executing, some languages (such as C and C++) will have to be instrumented with software probes prior to their test so that their execution can be profiled. Other language environments, such as Java, already support profiling as a built-in feature of the runtime environment. The Darwin NA currently has the capability of instrumenting both C and C++ with our Clic toolset. It also can link to and receive information from the Java Virtual Machine Profile Interface.

From a test outcomes measurement standpoint, the result of a test is a test execution profile. As each test is completed, the test measurement database is updated with the test execution profile and the information surrounding the test, such as the test case number, the tester, the test date and time, etc.

The entire Darwin NA measurement infrastructure was designed to make the measurement process both automatic and invisible. We have listened to the sad stories of legions of software developers, software development managers, and software testers. Their stories seem to indicate that they are some of the world's most harried employees. The mere thought of adding incremental responsibilities to their work list brings instant resistance. Software engineering measurement will not occur in this environment unless it is made painless and transparent.

13.5.3 The Software Engineering Maintenance Problem

The Darwin NA plays another significant role in the software development environment. It also serves a maintenance function. The NA will serve as a repository for the software requirements and also for the test plan and specific test cases.

There are two distinct classes of requirements that must be separately maintained. First, there are the operational requirements. These address *what* the software will do from a user's perspective. These operational requirements are a mutually exclusive set of distinct operations that the system is capable of performing. The second set of requirements includes the functional requirements or the design requirements. They address *how* the software will perform each of the operations. Again, this is a set of mutually exclusive functionalities that express exactly the activities that the system will perform to implement each of the operations.

The most important aspect of the requirements database is that each of the operational requirements is linked to the functionalities that will implement it. Further, each of the functional requirements is linked to the program modules that will implement it. This linkage will ensure complete requirements traceability. Starting at any one operation, it is possible to know what program modules actually implement that operational requirement. Similarly, beginning at the module level, it is possible to identify all of the functionalities that invoke that module and all of the operations that invoke those functionalities. With Darwin, we can easily identify the modules that have had the greatest code churn between builds. To know that fact and to be able to design a test case that would specifically test those modules is something very different. With the requirements traceability made manifest in the requirements database, we can easily develop test cases around the operations that will cause those modules to be expressed.

The second aspect of maintenance that is also performed within the Darwin database is the maintenance of the test cases. As each test case is designed, it is placed into the database. This gives a complete overview to everyone in the development and test organizations as to the completeness of the test case design. Further, as each test case is executed, the evaluation of that test case from the standpoint of functional coverage, test effectiveness, and test efficiency can be evaluated instantly.

13.5.4 The Darwin Reporting System

The Darwin system is equipped with a set of standard SQL generated reports that reflect the more typical database inquires that will be made by most managers. Darwin tracks changes in source code across builds. We have shown that change activity in the examples of the Space Shuttle PASS (Primary Avionics Software System) and the Cassini project. Software systems can be characterized for reporting purposes in terms of changes to the structure of the code in the attribute domains and also in terms of the fault burden of the system as measured by the system fault index (FI), code churn, and code deltas. This gives us considerable insight into where existing faults might be and continuing processes that are potentially introducing new faults. These data are useful for prioritizing the software review processes. We can devote our software review team energies to those regions of the code where the greatest problems are likely to be. In a sense, this is like one hand clapping, as indicated earlier.

The dynamic code measurements from the test activities give us a good, clear idea of how the test activity is distributed across the modules that comprise the system. In conjunction with the functional requirements, it will provide solid information as to the extent of coverage of the set of functional and operational requirements in the system to date. It will also give some limited insight into the ability of the test activity to enter regions of code where faults might be. This dynamic measure assessment is the other hand clapping.

When we combine the static measurement capability with the dynamic measurement capability in the report generation system of the Darwin NA, we will have both hands clapping. The static measures identify the potential fault problems; the dynamic measures indicate what code has executed. Together, they tell us how well the test activity has focused on the problems that are likely to be in the code.

Identifying the extent to which the potential faults have been exposed is but one part of the problem. It is all well and good to learn that modules 27, 105, and 231 were fault prone and were not executed; it is quite another to know what it will take to execute them. With the requirements traceability features built into the Darwin database, the answer can be developed from a simple SQL statement. This is so because functional specifications are linked to specific program modules. Operational specifications are linked to functional specifications. It is a very simple process to construct a new test suite that will operationally exercise modules 27, 105, and 231.

A case does not need to be made for the reporting capabilities of the Darwin system. This reporting capability is inherent in any database system. What is important is that the Darwin NA contains the relevant information to make informed decisions about the software development process and the software quality/testing process.

13.5.5 The Darwin Database

The structure of a schema for a generic database for Darwin is outlined in Exhibit 10. The strong influence of development work on this database at JPL is evidenced by the module naming conventions. This is not intended to be a universal database for all potential applications. It can easily be tailored to suit the needs of individual organizations.

There are two parts to the schema. The first part, the Domains, defines the attributes that we will keep in the database. The Relations show how the entities will be created to convert the flow of data into the database into meaningful information. In each relation the key fields are underlined. This sample schema is the underlying framework for a Darwin system currently in operation at Sun Microsystems and at the JPL.

Exhibit 10. Generic Database for Darwin

DOMAINS
People
   Name
      Last
      First
      MI
   Employee Code
   Position Code
   Activity Code
Process
   Event
      Failure
         Failure ID
         Severity
         Priority
         Apparent Cause
         Resolution
      Fault
         Location
         Functions Affected
         Etiology of Error
         How Discovered
         Fault Classification
         Fault Resolution Code
      Change
         Change Request Number
         Modules Affected
         Reason
         Design Element
   Staff Hours
   Software Process Methodology
   Testing
      Test Suite
      Test Iteration
Product
   Software Module Name
      CSCI
      CSC
      CSU
   Operational Requirement Number
   Operational Requirement Text
   Functional Requirement Number
   Functional Requirement Text
   Build Number
   Version Number
   Static Metrics
      Metric Primitives
         Comments
         Executable Statements
         Nonexecutable Statements

Exhibit 10. Generic Database for Darwin (continued)

        Total Operators
        Unique Operators
        Unique Nonoverloaded Operators
        Function Operators
        Total Operands
        Unique Operands
        Nodes
        Edges
        Paths
        Maximum Path Length
        Average Path Length
        Cycles
        System Fan-Out Explicit
        Unique System Fan-Out Explicit
        C++ Library Fan-Out
        Unique C++ Library Fan-Out
        System Fan-Out Implicit
      Derived Metrics
        Fault Index
        Code Delta
        Net Fault Change
    Dynamic Metrics
      Module Frequency Count
Environment
  Building
  Work Area
Organization
  Department
  Project
  Group
Time
  Date
    MM
    DD
    YY
  Time
    HH
    MM
    SS
RELATIONS
Operational Requirement
  Operational Requirement Number
  Operational Requirement Text
  Implemented_by_Functional_Requirement Vector (Array
  [1..m] of Functional Requirement Number)
Functional Requirement
  Functional Requirement Number
  Functional Requirement Text
  Implemented_in_Module Vector (Array [1..m] of Software
  Module Name)

Exhibit 10. Generic Database for Darwin (continued)

Operational Profile
    Operation (Array [1..m] of Profile)
Failure Report
    Program (CSC)
    Build Number
    Tester (Employee Code)
    Date
    Time
    Test Suite
    Test Iteration
    Failure
        <u>Failure ID</u>
        Severity
        Priority
        Apparent Cause
        Resolution
Module Fault Resolution
    CSCI
    <u>CSC</u>
    <u>CSU</u>
    <u>Version Number</u>
    Fault Classification
    Failure ID
    Fault Resolution Code
Module Measurement Element
    CSCI
    CSC
    CSU
    Version Number
    Metric Primitives
    Fault Index
Module Descriptor Element
    <u>Module Name</u> (CSU)
    <u>Program Name</u> (CSC)
    System Name (CSCI)
    Developer (Employee Code)
    Start Date (Date)
    Finish Date (Date)
Module Change History
    <u>Module Name</u> (CSU)
    <u>Change Request Number</u>
    Date
    Developer (Employee Code)
    Developer Time (Staff Hours)
    Unit Tester (Employee Code)
    Test Time (Staff Hours)
Module Fix History
    <u>Module Name</u> (CSU)
    <u>Fault Resolution Code</u>

Exhibit 10. Generic Database for Darwin (continued)

Date
Developer (Employee Code)
Unit Tester (Employee Code)
Test Metric Report
   <u>Program</u> (CSC)
   <u>Build Number</u>
   <u>Test Suite</u>
   <u>Test Iteration</u>
   Date
   Module Frequency (Array [1..n] of Module Frequency Count)
Baseline Build Data
   <u>Build Number</u>
   <u>Program</u> (CSC)
   Date
   Mean Vector (Array [1..m] of real)
   Std Vector (Array [1..m] of real)
   Eigenvalues (Array [1..k] of real)
   Transformation Matrix (Matrix [1...k;1...m] of real)
Build Metrics
   <u>Program</u> (CSC)
   <u>Module</u> (CSU)
   <u>Build Number</u>
   Code Delta
   Net Fault Change
Build Modules
   <u>Module Name</u> (CSU)
   <u>Build Number</u>
   <u>Version Number</u>
Developers
   Name
      Last
      First
      MI
   <u>Employee Code</u>
   Position Code
   Activity Code
Testers
   Name
      Last
      First
      MI
   Employee Code
   Position Code
   Activity Code
Change Request
   <u>Change Request Number</u>
   Date
   Reason

Chapter 14
Implementing a Software Research Plan

The Law of the Hammer: Give a child a hammer and everything in his or her environment becomes a nail.

The Law of C++: Give a programmer access to C++ and everything in his or her environment becomes a C++ application.

14.1 WHAT IS SOFTWARE RESEARCH?

Much of what we *know* about software development is purely conjectural. The literature abounds with new software processes that promise miracles, new software development methodologies that border on the extreme, or new language metaphors whose object is unclear. There is little or no empirical research to support any of these new approaches. That, in and of itself, is not bad. What is most depressing is that no one appears to be seeking validation of these claims. The validation process has at its foundation empirical research.

In a typical modern hardware development organization, approximately 10 percent of the development budget is typically devoted to basic research. This is research that is not designed to produce an immediate product. An example of such a research facility was the long-standing example of AT&T Bell Laboratories. There were many people employed within this organization that were doing research on theoretical areas that were far removed from the mechanics of a production line. The intellectual property that resulted from this investment was truly astonishing. It produced, among many other things, the transistor that, in turn, fundamentally changed the world in which we live.

Curiously, it is difficult, if not impossible, to point to a similar organization devoted to basic research in the area of software engineering (computer science, informatics, etc.). It is even stranger, in that a lion's share of development cost of any new product with embedded software is the software itself. Most organizations have the attitude that software is just something that you add in when the product has been built. It is odd to hear from development organizations that are using embedded software systems that the cost of software development has now exceeded that of hardware development. These same organizations are not listening to their own message. They continue to devote substantial resources to hardware research and zero resources to software research.

We start our software research program on the premise that little or nothing is known about software development methodology. We are on a quest to create the foundation for this knowledge within our own organization. We can learn little from the work that others have done in the area because of the lack of measurement standards. A group might report, for example, that a typical developer in their organization could produce 20 C statements per day. We learn nothing from this data because we simply do not know what a statement means to the people reporting the result. The 20 statements might well include an average of 10 comment statements, for example. If we were to use these data to insist that our developers produce 20 executable statements per day based on the results of this report, then we would be seeking to achieve a level of productivity twice that of the reporting organization.

The best way to kill an incipient software research plan is to form a committee to study the process. If there is to be a software research effort, it will have to have its impetus at the top of the corporate food chain. There must be commitment at the highest level in the company. Software research should be a line item in the operating budget of every department. Audit systems should be put in place to ensure that the money budgeted actually winds up in the hands of the people doing the research.

14.1.1 How We Got This Way

It is clear that there has been very little empirical research in what we call computer science. In fact, computer science is really a very odd term. There has been really little empirical science in computer science. We have much theory; that is because most of the early founders in the field came from mathematics. In fact, most computer science programs had their origins in departments of mathematics. A typical mathematician has had little or no training in the scientific method. There is no reason to have this preparation. The concept of empirical validation of theoretical constructs is about as far from a mathematician's thinking process as you can get. It is completely understandable, then, that there has been little impetus in computer science curricula to teach students about scientific methodology. The first serious chemistry course that a chemistry major will take is called quantitative methods. In this course, students learn how to measure things for laboratory research. Psychology students are exposed early in their academic careers to a course in the design of experiments. A careful analysis of computer science curricula throughout the United States will not reveal a single course in either measurement or the design of experiments. It would be unrealistic, therefore, to presume that people with computer science backgrounds could begin to formulate an empirically based research program. They will have received no training in the conduct of scientific inquiry, nor will they have the statistical preparation to assist them in this regard.

There is an emerging discipline of software engineering. It is now relatively common to see software engineering curricula at the undergraduate and graduate levels in universities throughout the world. Unfortunately, students in these curricula are not exposed to the notions of the basic engineering discipline. At the beginning of every term at every university that supports a mechanical engineering program, you will see prospective engineers out around campus with their survey instruments, trying to find the locations of various points of interest throughout the university. This is a most important course. Students learn how to measure and they also learn a great deal about accuracy and precision. This knowledge is vital to their success as mechanical engineers. Measurement and the discipline associated with measurement are fundamental principles of the engineering discipline. However, there are no similar measurement courses for software engineering undergraduates. Whatever the discipline of software engineering might be, it is not an engineering discipline.

For the moment, then, the software development industry will have to play a leading role in empirical software research. In essence, these organizations will have to develop their own training programs to teach computer scientists to do science and software engineers to do engineering. Some software development organizations have gone so far as to recruit only mechanical, computer, or electrical engineers for their software engineering staff. It is far more cost effective to teach a mechanical engineer the essentials of software development than it is to try to teach a software engineer about an engineering discipline. A typical mechanical engineer will have four to five years of training in what it means to be an engineer. A typical new software engineer will have had no training in any engineering discipline.

14.1.2 Empirical Research

Empirical research is a scientific means of investigating the validity of theoretical research. It is also the driving force behind the discipline of engineering. In the field of mathematics, there is only theory. The notion that theory might in some sense have practical value is preposterous. Theory exists for theory's sake. Practical relevance was far from Whitehead and Russell's thinking when they did the *Principia Mathematica*.

Mathematicians, and consequently computer scientists, are theoreticians and that is that. It is not reasonable, therefore, to expect that the typical computer scientist will have the necessary training or interest to do empirical research.

A real case could be made that considerable investment has been made in empirical research programs in software, particularly in the aerospace industry. There is a great difference, however, between empirical research in an application domain and empirical research on software development. The current work in speech recognition and prosody is a very good example of empirical research in an application area. In this context, there has been a very substantial research investment on the part of quite a number of companies. There is great interest in speech processing, voice recognition, and speaker intonations. A considerable amount of research money is now pouring into this area. Unfortunately, these research dollars are being invested in the application domain, and not in the software domain. There is very little interest in the nature of software development to do speech recognition. Very soon we will have speech recognition technology that will be able to recognize the speaker and make an assessment of his mental attitude. We will have little information, however, about how to develop software for this application. It will probably be written in the universal language, C++.

The defining element of empirical software research is the controlled experiment. In the controlled experiment environment, potential sources of variation are first identified. Some of these sources of variation will be controlled so that they do not impact the sources of variation that will be manipulated by the experiment. If, for example, we wanted to compare programming language A with programming language B for use in an application C, begin by identifying one or more criterion variables such as complexity, maintainability, or reliability that will serve as the basis for comparison. We would then seek to identify sources of variation not related to the criterion variable(s) that would influence the outcome of the experiment. One such source of variation might be programmer experience with language B. We might have a development staff that is completely familiar with language B but has little or no familiarity with language A. In this case, we would expect that language B will turn out to be the language of choice, not because it is intrinsically better for application C, but because our programming staff does not really have the same degree of expertise with language A that they have with language B.

The focus of this experiment is on the language comparison, not on the application. We seem to be quite willing to invest research money in solving application-specific problems but not on software-specific questions. Most of the programming languages in common use today were simply hacked out by a small group of individuals. They are then deployed in safety-critical or high-availability applications. It is not possible to produce reliable code with a language system that is, in and of itself, unreliable.

14.2 IMPLEMENTING A RESEARCH PLAN

Most of what we need to know about software development methodology is simply not known. We choose language systems such as Java and C++ strictly, but strictly based on current trends and fads. The choice of these programming languages has resulted in some incredible performance and reliability problems for those who have unwisely chosen to use them in inappropriate contexts. The problem is that we really do not know what are good applications, if any, to apply these programming languages. We do know that it will be literally impossible to construct reliable and precisely defined systems based on programming languages fraught with syntactic and semantic ambiguities such as C++. It might well be that C++ is really the language of choice for some applications. The disturbing fact is that we do not know what that context might be. Even more disturbing is the fact that there seems to be little real interest in discovering what that context might be.

14.2.1 Software Research Training Program

It is clear that there will be very little expertise to draw on to develop a software research program within today's corporate computer development organizations. We are confronted with the problem that there is very little academic preparation in the disciplines of software engineering, computer science or informatics in the conduct of empirical inquiry. There will be very limited opportunities to hire a research staff with empirical research credentials from individuals with this academic preparation. There are other disciplines, such as chemistry and physics, where training in empirical research is an integral part of academic preparation. Unfortunately, the individuals with the requisite background in empirical research have little formal knowledge of software engineering.

Given this dilemma, the obvious strategy is to institute a software research training program. It will be the objective of this training program to take individuals with cognate preparation in software engineering or computer science and bring them up to speed in the conduct of empirical research. Not every software developer needs to participate in this training program to the same degree. There should probably be three levels of training programs in a typical software development organization. These three levels would probably correspond directly to the individuals having the bachelor's degree, the master's degree, and the doctoral degree.

The first level of training in empirical research should be at the recognition level. Individuals trained to this level will be equipped to *recognize* sound empirical research. What little empirical research is currently available in the published literature is astonishingly weak. The experimenters reporting the research have failed to meet the simplest criterion for published science. That is, the reported research must be reproducible. Any outside observer should be able to read the published research and replicate the experiment precisely. The essence of science is that reported research results should be reproducible. The research training at the recognition level should equip the software developer to at least recognize science.

The second level of training takes the research process one step forward. Training at this level will involve the ability to conduct simple experiments to answer immediate questions in the software development process. This research process is simply scaled so that it can be performed by a small group of developers within a limited budget.

The third level of research training will equip an individual with the ability to design experiments in basic software research. Perhaps the most effective means to deliver this type of training is the mentoring system. Each novice researcher would be assigned to understudy a person, a mentor, who has recognized research experience.

14.2.2 Research and the Decision-Making Process

Many of the decisions governing today's software development processes are capricious and ill-considered. The decision to implement applications in different programming language metaphors is a very good example of this. For example, we really do not know whether it is better to use C, C++, Java, or even FORTRAN for certain applications. It is clear that there is no panacea as far as programming languages are concerned. No one language is clearly the best language for all applications. It might well be that C is to be preferred to C++ for certain classes of applications. Unfortunately, we do not know for which applications C might be the language of choice. Again, there are multiple concomitant criteria that must all be investigated simultaneously. We might wish to look at performance, reliability, maintainability, and security as criteria in evaluating a language. When we turn to the computer science or software engineering literature to seek guidance in the decision-making process to select a language for a new project, we find little or no help. There are plenty of anecdotal stories about languages in given applications, but no real science.

If we make the wrong decision in the choice of a language, we will possibly pay horrible consequences for this decision. What is worse about the initial bad decision is the fact that there are no processes in place to monitor the effect of having made the wrong decision. Any manager who has made a development decision will go to great lengths to guarantee that everyone clearly understands that the proper choice was made. A manager may have decided, for example, to use Java for a new application. The case might have been made that using Java would reduce the total system development time. After the system is up and running, it is then discovered that the new system is incredibly slow. To run it effectively will require investment in new hardware with sufficient processing speed to overcome the inherent performance hit taken by Java. The cost of this new hardware is the hidden cost of the manager having made a very bad decision in choosing a language. Meanwhile, the manager is basking in glory for having delivered a system on time and under budget.

In essence, to make sound engineering decisions about the software development process is going to mean that the first step in the process will be to invest in the necessary basic research to provide the information necessary to make informed and cost-effective decisions. Scientific inquiry should be an integral part of the software development process. Much of what we need to know to make effective decisions about software development is simply not known. What is worse is that the nature of the applications that we are developing is also rapidly evolving.

14.2.3 Institutional Research Reporting Mechanism

It is one thing to conduct a simple experiment that results in valuable insight into the mechanics of the software development process. It is quite another to be able to share this result across the corporate software development structure. Without appropriate reporting mechanisms, most of the results of simple experiments conducted on the software development floor will either be lost to history or replicated again and again by other software development groups. With today's level of connectivity through the Internet and on intranets, it is possible to share research results very widely and rapidly. This is an excellent mechanism for recording and sharing the results of corporate research projects.

14.2.4 Institutionalize the Research Review Process

If research results of homegrown microexperiments are to be widely distributed, there must be some type of peer review process instituted to filter this dissemination of information. The consequences of making software development decisions based on poorly conducted or ill-conceived experiments are too great. The entire nature of the peer review process has changed dramatically. The traditional peer review process is much too slow and labor intensive to provide the timely feedback necessary for a corporate research program. Again, the connectivity provided by local communication networks can provide the solution to the peer review process.

As the results of each research effort are made accessible through the local communication network, provisions should be made for online commentary. Each person who reads an article should have the ability to make a rebuttal to the article. These commentaries are then appended to the original article. Criticism of a critical and constructive nature should be invited. One of the major drawbacks to yesterday's research reporting was that the reader never had the opportunity to review the results of the peer review process. Once an editorial decision was made to publish an article, the contents of the article then became fact, regardless of the objections that any one of the reviewers might have had.

What immediately becomes obvious is the distinction between bad research and controversial research. Whenever new ideas are first introduced, there is a real reluctance on the part of the research community to embrace these new ideas. Hubble's work on the idea that the universe was not a static place but was rapidly expanding brought him the scorn of many of his colleagues. This new idea represented too great a threat to the established view of the astronomical community. In the long run, however, the notion of an expanding universe was empirically validated. Science prevailed. Franz Joseph Gall, on the other hand, developed the science of phrenology. In the world of phrenology, it was believed that by examining the shape and unevenness of a head or skull, one could discover the development of the particular cerebral organs responsible for different intellectual aptitudes and character traits. This theory could not be empirically validated. In the past, it took a very long time for the technical review process. It took even longer for the validation process. With today's communication capabilities, this whole process has been accelerated many orders of magnitude.

So, not only should a company invest in the research process, but it should also provide the infrastructure for reporting the research results and a forum for the review and analysis of research results.

14.2.5 Provide Kudos for Research Investigations

Unless some level of corporate recognition is built into the research process at the grass-roots level, research activities will either not get off the ground in the first place or will rapidly diminish. If research is seen as an increment to the daily grind, it simply cannot succeed. A nurturing environment must be created for a research program to succeed. In a research-friendly environment, research activities will be part of a job assignment. Employees can propose a simple research project, submit the project for peer and management review, and perform the research activity, all as part of their assignment.

It is clear that employees who are providing a research contribution in addition to their work commitment should be singled out for reward. Not everyone will be able to do research. Those who are capable should be encouraged to participate. There are two incentives that can be used very effectively here. First, there are financial rewards. Bonuses can be given for each published research result. A personal and privileged parking space might well be at the top of the list of motivators. Second, the researcher can be recognized in department-level meetings. Peer recognition is a very important process in the social structure of any organization.

14.3 DEFINING SOFTWARE RESEARCH OBJECTIVES

In the beginning, a new software research program will need some clearly defined research objectives. These, of course, will vary from organization to organization. The best strategy, perhaps, is to focus on those issues that will have the greatest financial impact on the software development process. If a clear case cannot be made for the benefits obtained from the initial investment in the research program, the research effort will die on the vine. Therefore, empirical research issues that can demonstrate value *a priori* should be considered. There are some real hot buttons in the software development process that come to mind immediately.

Time-to-market issues are central in software development. Many different obstacles arise that cause projects to be delayed. Any research program that can potentially ameliorate any of these obstacles can be seen to be of real and near-term benefit. A few small successes in simple research studies in this area will provide great interest in continuing and fully funding future research projects.

Software project planning is another area that has great potential for a new research program. It is very difficult to plan software projects. Any research project that can leverage the experience gained from past projects to plan for future projects is a clear winner. Much of this research will involve mining and measuring previous projects to learn how they have evolved. These data can be used for modeling and projecting costs for future projects.

The most important objective of a new research program, then, is to demonstrate the value of the program to the company bottom line.

14.4 BUDGETING FOR SOFTWARE RESEARCH

There are two types of software research: basic research and product development research. They are very different. Basic research is not intended to have immediate practical relevance. A company cannot convert the results of this research to cash in the near term. Product development research, on the other hand, focuses on a specific technology application. Specially trained development or maintenance staff will perform this product development research as part of their normal duties.

14.4.1 Basic Research

Basic software research is not application specific. There should be no expectation that the results of a basic software research program will enhance the company bottom line in the near term. It is an investment in the future. We intend to make the transition from the world of software craftsmanship to a new world based on sound engineering practice. There simply is not the knowledge base to do that now. Basic research will provide that foundation.

We do not know, for example, what is the best programming language metaphor for a particular application. We do not know how developers think. There are many different metaphors. Perhaps some are better than others; perhaps different developers are better with some metaphors and not so good with others; or perhaps developers are good at some programming applications and not so good at others. How should we match developers to applications? We really would like to have maintainable software. We just do not know what this means. Some topics that are clearly within the purview of basic research relate to the evaluation of:

- Design objectives
- Testability of software
- Reliability of software systems
- Hardware–software interface
- Human–software interface

Basic research will provide the foundation for these and other fundamental questions that must have answers relatively soon. We are very rapidly approaching a software crisis. Modern, large software systems cannot be handcrafted; they must be engineered. No one individual can begin to understand the mechanics of a system that consist of over one million lines of code. No single group of people can begin to understand the mechanics of these huge systems. They will clearly have to be engineered. Basic software research will provide the necessary information for future software systems to be engineered.

One of the principal products of the basic research program will be intellectual property. Many companies in the computer-related sector now derive a significant portion of their revenue from their intellectual property base. The return on investment (ROI) for basic research is a strong factor in the budget for basic research. The time has come to learn to budget for basic research in software with the same expectation of ROI on the research expenditures.

14.4.2 Product Development Research

Product development research is very different from basic research. It is problem solving at its most basic level. The focus of product development research is on the here and now. There is a product on the floor and a deadline to ship the product. Research in this case will focus on solving problems specifically related to the product being developed. Again, a distinction must be made between research done on the application domain and research on the software development domain. Software product development research is entirely on the processes that will develop the software and not on the specific application domain.

Each software development or test department should have a product research budget. This budget should be used to fund release time and the hard costs of employees participating in the research program. By budgeting these monies, corporate commitment to the product development research effort will have clearly been established. By auditing the expenditure of these monies, guarantees can be given that the money is being invested wisely, if at all. If, for example, a manager is allocated 10 percent of the total departmental budget for product development research, then there is an expectation that there will be observable research results for this budget.

14.5 RESEARCH PAYS

There is a mentality that has developed over the years in the computer hardware industry that hardware is the most important aspect of a computer system. Once the hardware is designed, it is tossed over the wall for the software developers to do something with it. This was clearly the mentality of the developers of the IBM PC. IBM thought that building the box was the most important aspect of the project. So pervasive was this mentality that IBM decided to give the operating system component of the system to the "kid in Seattle." That single decision made IBM an also-ran of the computer industry. Microsoft could easily acquire IBM.

The nature of the computer industry has changed. Software is now king. The bulk of the revenues have shifted to the software side of the house. Unfortunately, this news does not seem to have penetrated very far into the upper reaches of the bastions of the hardware companies. Most of these companies invest heavily in basic hardware research. These same companies have no formal software research program. The upper-level management of these organizations came from the hardware side of the house. They clearly think that people are buying hardware. The customer's focus, however, is clearly on functionality. This functionality is provided by software, not hardware.

It is clear that there is substantial return on investment for monies spent in hardware research. This research creates intellectual property. The resulting intellectual property can be developed into a product within the company or it can return substantial revenue under licensing agreements. A case does not have to be made to justify the benefits derived from both basic research and product-oriented research. The case that does have to be made is that investment in software research is equally important.

The state of the software discipline in regard to research funding in the commercial and governmental sectors is abysmal. The need for serious funding in this area is great. Software now drives the control systems for safety-critical applications. The liabilities are far too great to discount the importance of software reliability. The opportunities for revenue enhancement through software are also very great. Someday in the near future, computer companies will proudly show off their new multibillion-dollar software research facilities. Software quality and security will soon be the driving force behind the successful survivors in the competition for the consumer dollar. Those companies that are best able to respond to these needs will be those that have a future. It is clear that we have reached the technological limits of handcrafted software systems. The time has come to make a serious investment in software research to provide a solid foundation for the development of engineered software systems.

Appendix 1
Review of Mathematical Fundamentals

A1.1 MATRIX ALGEBRA

A matrix is a rectangular array of numbers. These numbers are organized into rows and columns. A matrix X of n rows and m columns is said to be of order $n \times m$. We will represent this matrix as follows:

$$\mathbf{X} = \begin{pmatrix} x_{11} & x_{12} & \cdots & x_{1m} \\ x_{21} & x_{22} & \cdots & x_{2m} \\ \vdots & \vdots & \vdots & \vdots \\ x_{n1} & x_{n2} & \cdots & x_{nm} \end{pmatrix}$$

The transpose of X is a new matrix $\mathbf{X}^T$ derived from X by interchanging the rows and columns of X. Thus,

$$\mathbf{X}^T = \begin{pmatrix} x_{11} & x_{12} & \cdots & x_{1n} \\ x_{21} & x_{22} & \cdots & x_{2n} \\ \vdots & \vdots & \vdots & \vdots \\ x_{m1} & x_{m2} & \cdots & x_{mn} \end{pmatrix}$$

We can form the sum of two matrices X and Y if they are of the same order. In such a case, a new matrix Z containing the sum is formed as follows:

$$\mathbf{Z} = \mathbf{X} + \mathbf{Y} = \begin{pmatrix} x_{11} + y_{11} & x_{12} + y_{12} & \cdots & x_{1m} + y_{1m} \\ x_{21} + y_{21} & x_{22} + y_{22} & \cdots & x_{2m} + y_{2m} \\ \vdots & \vdots & \vdots & \vdots \\ x_{n1} + y_{n1} & x_{n2} + y_{n2} & \cdots & x_{nm} + y_{nm} \end{pmatrix}$$

The following shorthand notation will be used to simplify this operation:

$$\mathbf{Z} = \mathbf{X} + \mathbf{Y} = (x_{ij}) + (y_{ij}) = (x_{ij} + y_{ij}) \text{ for all } i \text{ and } j$$

The product of two matrices is defined if the matrices are conformable. The matrices X and Y are conformable if the number of columns of X equals the number of rows of Y. Thus, if X is of order $n \times m$ and Y is of order $m \times p$ and they are conformable, then the product is defined to be:

$$\mathbf{XY} = (x_{ij})(y_{ij}) = \sum_{j=1}^{m} x_{ij} y_{jk}, \quad i = 1,2,\ldots,n, \quad k = 1,2,\ldots,p$$

A matrix is a square matrix if it has an equal number of rows and columns. A square $n \times n$ matrix X is a symmetric matrix if $x_{ij} = x_{ji}$, for all $i,j = 1,2,\ldots,n$. The trace of a square matrix X is the sum of the diagonal elements of X. Thus, the trace of X is defined by:

$$\text{trace}(\mathbf{X}) = \sum_{i=1}^{n} x_i^j$$

It follows that:

$$\text{trace}(\mathbf{XX^T}) = \sum_{i=1}^{n} \sum_{j=1}^{m} x_{ij}^2.$$

A1.1.1 Determinants

To simplify the discussion of determinants, a brief discussion of nomenclature is necessary concerning the notion of permutations. If we take the set consisting of the first four counting numbers, $\{1,2,3,4\}$, there are 4! or 24 different ways that these four number can be ordered. Let J represent a vector containing a permutation of these four numbers, where $J = <j_1, j_2, j_3, j_4>$. Thus, if j_1 has the value of 3, then j_2 can only assume one of the values 1, 2, or 4. Let t represent the number of transpositions to convert the set of integers $<1,2,3,4>$ to the new permutation $<j_1, j_2, j_3, j_4>$. Let $\varepsilon^t = +1$ if the number of transformations is even and $\varepsilon^t = -1$ if the number of transformations is odd.

The determinant of the matrix X is denoted by $|X|$. It can be formed from the elements of X by the following computation:

$$|\mathbf{X}| = \sum_{k \in J} \varepsilon^t \prod_{i=1}^{n} x_{ij_i}$$

where n is the number of rows and columns in the matrix. In the simplest case, where we have a 2×2 matrix, $|X| = x_{11}x_{22} - x_{12}x_{21}$.

The cofactor X_{ji} of an element x_{ij} of $\mathbf{X}$ is the product of $(-1)^{i+j}$ and the determinant of reduced matrix of $\mathbf{X}$ whose ith row and jth column have been deleted. We can then represent the determinant of X as:

$$|\mathbf{X}| = \sum_{j=1}^{n} x_{ij} X_{ji} ,$$

where i can be any value $i = 1, 2, \ldots, n$.

A1.1.2 Matrix Inverses

If the determinant of $\mathbf{X}$ exists, that is $|\mathbf{X}| \neq 0$, then there is a unique matrix $\mathbf{Y}$ such that $\mathbf{XY} = \mathbf{I}$, the identity matrix. The matrix $\mathbf{Y}$ is the inverse of matrix $\mathbf{X}$. It is sometimes represented as $\mathbf{X}^{-1}$. Each element y_{ij} of the inverse matrix $\mathbf{Y}$ is derived from $\mathbf{X}$ as:

$$y_{ij} = \frac{X_{ji}}{|X|}$$

where X_{ji} is a cofactor of $\mathbf{X}$.

A1.1.3 Eigenproblems

The eigenvalues of a square matrix X are the roots of the determinantal equation:

$$e(\lambda) - |\mathbf{X} - \lambda \mathbf{I}| = 0$$

The n roots of $e(\lambda)$ are $\lambda_1, \lambda_2, \ldots, \lambda_n$. For each $i = 1, 2, \ldots, n$, observe that $|\mathbf{X} - \lambda_i \mathbf{I}| = 0$. Thus, $\mathbf{X} - \lambda_i \mathbf{I}$ is singular and there exists a nonzero vector $\mathbf{e}_i$ with the property that:

$$\mathbf{Xe}_i = \lambda_i \mathbf{e}_i$$

Any vector with this property is called an *eigenvector* of $\mathbf{X}$ for the eigenvalue λ_i.

A1.1.4 Spectral Decomposition

Any symmetric matrix $\mathbf{X}$, such as a variance-covariance matrix or a matrix of correlation coefficients, can be written as:

$$\mathbf{X} = \mathbf{E\Lambda E}'$$

where $\mathbf{\Lambda}$ is a diagonal matrix of the eigenvalues of $\mathbf{X}$ and $\mathbf{E}$ is an orthogonal matrix whose columns are the associated eigenvectors of each of the eigenvalues in $\mathbf{\Lambda}$. This result is called the spectral decomposition of $\mathbf{X}$. If the eigenvalues of a variance-covariance matrix $\mathbf{X}$ are extracted from the largest eigenvalue to the smallest, the resulting spectral decomposition will produce the *principal components* of $\mathbf{X}$.

A1.2 SOME NOTIONS OF PROBABILITY

Programs, people, and processes, as entities, have attributes. These attributes, in turn, are defined on particular measurement scales. For each attribute there is a set of values, or domain, that defines the possible values for that attribute. For example, the sex attribute of a person is defined on the set male and female, which is nominal. It will be useful to define the term "variable" to use on the instantiations of the attributes. A sex variable can then assume the values of Male or Female, depending on the sex of the person that the variable represents.

A *random variable,* or stochastic variable, is a variable that assumes each of its definite values with a definite probability. This concept of a random variable will be quite useful in our evolving view of the software process as a nondeterministic one. The domain on which a random variable is defined can be discrete or continuous. Thus, there are two distinct types of random variables. A discrete random variable is one that has only a countable number of possible values. This countable number can either be finite or infinite.

A1.2.1 Discrete Random Variables

Only events have probabilities. Thus, from a measurement perspective we can define an event that we have selected a male; or if x is a random variable, then we will denote this event as $\{x = \text{Male}\}$. Our random variable x is a real-valued function on the probability space. The random variable x makes correspond to each elementary event a real number $x(a)$, the value of the random variable at the event a.

Now let us take this concept of a random variable and apply it to two different contexts. Let us assume that the event space is as above, where the random variable x was defined for the event space $\{x = \text{Male}\}$ and $\{x = \text{Female}\}$. Now let us look at this concept as applied to two distinctly different populations of students at a typical university. First suppose that the population in question is the set of Home Economics majors at a large land-grant university. In this case, the $\Pr\{x = Male\}$ is very small indeed. Certainly it will be the case that $\Pr\{x = Male\} < \Pr\{x = Female\}$. Now, if we were to change the population so that we are now considering the population of mechanical engineering students, then the reverse would probably be true and $\Pr\{x = Male\} > \Pr\{x = Female\}$.

Now consider a set of discrete events $\{a_1, a_2, \cdots, a_n\}$ or $\{a_1, a_2, \cdots\}$. The random variable x induces a probability space on the set of real numbers in which the finite set $\{a_1, a_2, \cdots, a_n\}$ and the infinite set $\{a_1, a_2, \cdots\}$ of real numbers has a positive probability. Let p_i be the probability that x will assume the value a_i; then, $p_i = Pr(\mathbf{x} = a_i)$ for $i = 1, 2, \cdots, n$ or $i = 1, 2, \cdots$. Further, $\sum_i p_i = 1$. The *probability distribution* of x is defined by the values a_i and the probabilities p_i. The *probability function* of x is generally stated in terms of a variable x, where:

$$f(x) = \Pr(\mathbf{x} = x)$$

and $x = a_1, a_2, \cdots, a_n$ or $x = a_1, a_2, \cdots$. Again, it follows that:

$$\sum_i f(x) = 1$$

The *distribution function* $F(x)$ of the random variable x is defined by:

$$F(x) = \Pr(\mathbf{x} < x)$$

It represents the cumulative probability of the initial set of events $a_1, a_2, \cdots, a_k$, where $x = a_{k+1}$.

A1.2.2 Continuous Random Variables

If the random variable is continuous, then the probability that the random variable will assume any particular value is zero, $\Pr\{\mathbf{x} = a\} = 0$. There are essentially no discrete events. In this case, it only makes sense that we discuss intervals for the random variable such as:

$$\Pr[\mathbf{x} < a]$$

$$\Pr[a < \mathbf{x} < b]$$

$$\Pr[\mathbf{x} \geq a]$$

If $f(x)$ is the *probability density function* of x, then:

$$\Pr(a < \mathbf{x} < b) = \int_a^b f(x)dx$$

Again, it follows that:

$$\int_{-\infty}^{\infty} f(x)dx = 1$$

The *distribution function* $F(x)$ of x is given by:

$$\Pr(\mathbf{x} < x) = F(x) = \int_{-\infty}^{x} f(x)dx$$

A1.3 DISCRETE PROBABILITY DISTRIBUTIONS

There are a number of probability distributions that will prove useful to us in the pursuit of software engineering measurement. These are grouped into two categories based on the nature of the random variables they represent. First there is the case of the discrete random variable that assumes a countable number of possible values. Second is the case where the random variable is continuous and can assume values from an interval of real numbers. There are a very large number of probability distributions. Some of these are more relevant to our software engineering investigations than others. There follows a discussion about three discrete probability distributions and four continuous probability distributions that are particularly relevant to our needs in this book.

A1.3.1 The Binomial Distribution

Many discrete events that we wish to model have only two possible outcomes. Consider the example of a program in test. The program will run successfully, $\Pr(x = S) = p$, or it will fail during test, $\Pr(x = F) = 1 - p$. After the program has been tested n times, the number of successful executions x in these tests is given by the probability function:

$$f(x) = \frac{n!}{x!(n-x)!} p^x (1-p)^{n-x}, \quad x = 0, 1, 2, \cdots, n$$

$$= 0 \quad \text{elsewhere}$$

The mean of this distribution is:

$$\mu = np$$

and the variance is:

$$\sigma^2 = np(1-p)$$

A1.3.2 The Multinomial Distribution

Let

$$S = \bigcup_{i=1}^{k} S_i$$

where S_i is one of k mutually exclusive sets of events. Further, let $\Pr(S_i) = p_i$ and $p_k = 1 - p_1 - p_2 - \cdots - p_{k-1}$. In this case, p_i is the probability that the outcome of a random experiment is an element of the set S_i. If this experiment is conducted over a period of n trials, then the random variable X_i will represent the frequency of S_i outcomes. Note that $X_k = n - X_1 - X_2 - \cdots - X_{k-1}$

This particular distribution will be useful in the modeling of a program with a set of k modules. During a set of n program steps, each of the modules can be executed. These, of course, are mutually exclusive events. If module i is executing, then module j cannot be executing.

The multinomial distribution function for this execution scenario is given by:

$$f(x_1, x_2, \cdots, x_{k-1}) = \begin{cases} \dfrac{n!}{\displaystyle\prod_{i=1}^{i-1} x_i!} p^{x_1} p^{x_2} \cdots p^{x_{k-1}}, & (x_1, x_2, \cdots, x_{k-1}) \in S \\ \end{cases}$$

$$= 0 \ \text{elsewhere}$$

where x_i represents the frequency of execution of the ith program module.

The mean values for the x_i are given by:

$$\mu_1 = np_1$$
$$\mu_2 = np_2$$

$$\bullet$$
$$\bullet$$
$$\bullet$$

$$\mu_k = np_k$$

and the variances by

$$\sigma_1^2 = np_1 q_1, \quad q_1 = 1 - \sum_j p_j, \quad \forall j \neq 1$$

$$\sigma_2^2 = np_2 q_2, \quad q_2 = 1 - \sum_j p_j, \quad \forall j \neq 2$$

$$\bullet$$
$$\bullet$$
$$\bullet$$

$$\sigma_k^2 = np_k q_k, \quad q_k = 1 - \sum_j p_j, \quad \forall j \neq k$$

A1.3.3 The Poisson Distribution

Yet another discrete probability distribution that is used very frequently in modeling applications in the operating systems environment is the Poisson distribution. It is frequently used to model events of a temporal nature. For example, we might wish to model the number of I/O interrupts in a particular time interval t. The probability that there will be x such calls in an interval dependent on λ is:

$$f(x) = \frac{\lambda^x e^{-\lambda}}{x!}, \quad x = 0, 1, 2, \cdots$$

where $\lambda > 0$. This distribution has the remarkable property that:

381

$$\mu = \sigma^2 = \lambda$$

This interesting property greatly simplifies a number of queuing model scenarios.

This distribution raises an interesting specter. Sometimes, a probability distribution will be used for modeling purposes, not because we observe that nature has chosen that probability distribution but rather because it makes the modeling process much easier. Solutions of this nature are called Procrustean solutions after an ancient Greek who invented them. Old Procrustes, as the story goes, ran a motel in ancient Greece. He was most concerned about the comfort of his guests. Although all the beds in every room in his motel were the same size, not all of the guests were of a size to fit the beds. So, Procrustes hit upon an interesting solution. Those guests who were too tall for his beds, he simply cut off a little of the legs of these guests. Those guests who were too short, he put upon a rack and stretched them out a bit. The long and short of this story is that Procrustes made each person fit his beds. Similarly, queuing theorists tend to see all queuing problems in a Poisson light.

A1.4 CONTINUOUS PROBABILITY DISTRIBUTIONS

A1.4.1 The Normal Distribution

A teacher of mine once observed that there never is, nor ever was, such a naturally occurring thing as a normal probability density function. However, this distribution is the foundation of much of the discipline of statistics. If there were such an artifact in Nature, it would have a pdf like this:

$$f(x) = \frac{1}{\sigma\sqrt{2\pi}} e^{-\frac{(x-\mu)^2}{2\sigma^2}}$$

The mean of this distribution is μ and its variance is σ. This is an interesting distribution in that it is completely specified by just these two parameters. While we do know that:

$$F(\infty) = \int_{-\infty}^{\infty} f(x)dx = 1$$

there are not too many random variables in Nature that have this range $(-\infty, \infty)$. For example, it is often stated that the height of the population of the country is normally distributed. This being the case, we would certainly expect to find some individuals with a height of −200 cm or perhaps even 2000 cm. This, however, is not the case. People do not come in those heights.

In that a truly normal distribution is an improbable event in its own right, we must learn to adjust to this fact. The assumption of normality is very important. What we must learn to think about is not that the population we are modeling is not really normal. Rather, we must always worry about how *robust* the statistical procedures we are using are in relation to potential departures from the assumption of normality. Some techniques are very sensitive about these departures. Other techniques are not so sensitive and, as a result, are said to be robust.

A1.4.2 The χ^2 Distribution

The χ^2 distribution scarcely has a life of its own. Only rarely will this distribution be used by itself for modeling purposes. We will use it primarily as a building block for the t distribution and the F distribution, both of which we will use frequently. The pdf

$$f(x) = \frac{1}{2^{k/2}\Gamma(k/2)} x^{(k/2)-1} e^{-x/2}$$

is a χ^2 distribution with k degrees of freedom. This distribution is defined on the interval $[0, \infty)$.

The mean of this distribution and its variance depend entirely on the degrees of freedom of the distribution as follows:

$$\mu = k$$

$$\sigma^2 = 2k$$

There is an interesting relationship between the χ^2 distribution and the normal distribution. That is, if the random variable X has a normal distribution with a mean of μ and a variance is σ, then the random variable

$$V = \left(\frac{X - \mu}{\sigma}\right)^2$$

has a χ^2 distribution with one degree of freedom.

A1.4.3 The t Distribution

Let W be a random variable where $W \sim N(0,1)$ and V be a random variable that has a χ^2 distribution with k degrees of freedom. Under the condition that W and V are stochastically independent, we can define a new random variable T where

$$T = \frac{W}{\sqrt{V/r}}$$

A *t distribution* with n degrees of freedom can be defined as that of the random variable T symmetrically distributed about 0. Then, $f(x) = \Pr(T = x)$ and

$$f(\pm x) = \frac{\Gamma((n+1)/2)}{\sqrt{2\pi}\,\Gamma(n/2)}\left(1 + \frac{x^2}{n}\right)^{-(n+1)/2}$$

A1.4.4 The F Distribution

Now consider two independently distributed random variables U and V having n_1 and n_2 degrees of freedom, respectively. We can define a new random variable

$$F = \frac{U/n_1}{V/n_2}$$

Then,

$$f(x) = \Pr(F = x)$$

and

$$f(x) = \begin{cases} \dfrac{(n_1/n_2)^{n_1/2}\Gamma((n_1+n_2)/2)}{\Gamma(n_1/2)\Gamma(n_2/2)}\dfrac{x^{(n_1/2)-1}}{(1+n_1 x/n_2)^{(n_1+n_2)/2}}, & 0 < x < \infty \\ 0 & \text{elsewhere} \end{cases}$$

A1.4.5 The Beta Distribution

A random variable X has a beta distribution with parameters α and β (α, $\beta > 0$) if X has a continuous distribution whose pdf is:

$$f(x \mid \alpha, \beta) = \begin{cases} \dfrac{\Gamma(\alpha+\beta)}{\Gamma(\alpha)\Gamma(\beta)}x^{\alpha-1}(1-x)^{\beta-1}, & 0 < x < 1 \\ 0, & \text{otherwise} \end{cases}$$

The expected value of X is given by:

$$E(X) = \frac{\alpha}{\alpha+\beta}$$

and the variance of X is given by:

$$Var(X) = \frac{\alpha\beta}{(\alpha+\beta)^2(\alpha+\beta+1)}$$

This distribution will be particularly useful because of its relationship to the binomial distribution, as shown in Chapter 10.

A1.4.6 The Dirichlet Distribution

The pdf for a Dirichlet distribution, $D(\alpha, \alpha_T)$, with a parametric vector $\boldsymbol{\alpha} = (\alpha_1, \alpha_2, ..., \alpha_M)$, where $(\alpha_i > 0;\ i = 1, 2, ..., M)$, is:

$$f(w \mid \boldsymbol{\alpha}) = \frac{\Gamma(\alpha_1 + \alpha_2 + \cdots + \alpha_M)}{\prod\limits_{i=1}^{M} \Gamma(\alpha_i)} w_1^{\alpha_1 - 1} w_2^{\alpha_2 - 1} \cdots w_M^{\alpha_M - 1}$$

where $(w_i > 0;\ i = 1, 2, ..., M)$ and $\sum\limits_{i=1}^{M} w_i = 1$. The expected values of the w_i are given by:

$$E(w_i) = \mu_i = \frac{\alpha_i}{\alpha_0}$$

where $\alpha_0 = \sum_{i=1}^{T} \alpha_i$. In this context, α_0 represents the total epochs. The variance of the w_i is given by:

$$Var(w_i) = \frac{\alpha_i(\alpha_0 - \alpha_i)}{\alpha_0^2(\alpha_0 + 1)}$$

and the covariance is given by:

$$Cov(w_i, w_j) = \frac{\alpha_i \alpha_j}{\alpha_0^2(\alpha_0 + 1)}$$

This distribution will be particularly useful because of its relationship to the multinomial distribution as was shown in Chapter 10.

A1.5 STATISTICS

A1.5.1 Measures of Central Tendency

Measures of central tendency are used to describe, as succinctly as possible, the attributes of a population or a sample from that population. We might use, for example, the average height of the students at a school to represent the entire population. This single number represents some measure of the center point or central tendency of the population. There are several possible measures of central tendency.

   A1.5.1.1 Mean. Because of the very nature of populations in the real world, we will seldom, if ever, have access to the entire population. We will be obliged to work with small sets or *samples* drawn from the larger population. We will use these samples to draw inferences about measurable aspects of the population called *parameters*. Before the sample is actually taken from the population, the sample values are considered to be random variables. Thus, if we wish to obtain m sample points from a population induced by a random variable x, then we will have the sample random variables $\mathbf{x}_1, \mathbf{x}_2, \cdots, \mathbf{x}_n$. The sample *mean* $\bar{\mathbf{x}}$ is also a random variable defined as:

$$\bar{\mathbf{x}} = \frac{1}{n} \sum_{i=1}^{n} \mathbf{x}_i$$

and is an estimator of the population mean. Such functions of random variables are called *statistics*.

Once a sample is taken we will now have an observation vector $x_1, x_2, \cdots, x_n$ from $\mathbf{x}_1, \mathbf{x}_2, \cdots, \mathbf{x}_n$. The sample mean $\bar{x}$ will be computed from this sample point as follows:

$$\bar{x} = \frac{1}{n} \sum_{i=1}^{n} x_i$$

A1.5.1.2 Median. The problem with the mean as a measure of *central tendency* is that it represents the distribution of the mass of the probability distribution. All of the members of a sample might, for example, be tightly clustered together in value, with the exception of one value that is very much larger. This single value would distort our view of where the majority of the mass is actually located. Yet another example of where the mean as a statistic would be misleading would be in the economic arena. Consider, for example, the mean per-capita income in a country like Mexico. This mean is strongly influenced by a small number of individuals who have enormously large incomes in comparison to the near poverty level of most of the citizens. In this case we are more interested in a measure of central tendency that will be more representative of where the per-capita income is located in terms of its *frequency* or occurrence in the population.

The median of a sample $x_1, x_2, \cdots, x_n$ can be obtained by sorting the observations and then choosing x_M such that $M = \frac{n}{2}$. In the special case that $n \bmod 2 = 1$, we might wish to interpolate such that the median:

$$x_M = \frac{x_{\lfloor \frac{n}{2} \rfloor} + x_{\lceil \frac{n}{2} \rceil}}{2}$$

Thus, the median as a measure of central tendency has half of the population frequency on either side of the median value.

A1.5.1.3 Mode. The mode is simply the most frequently occurring value in a sample. If we were to take a sample of students and measure their heights. and find that all of the sample points were different except for three people whose heights were 170 centimeters, then the mode for this sample would be 170. Sometimes in continuous probability distributions we refer to the maximum value in the probability density function as the

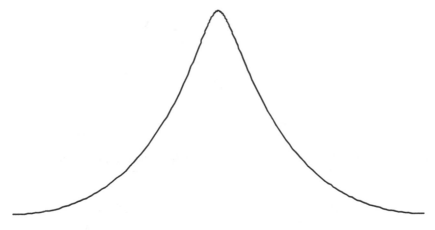

Exhibit 1. Distribution Concentrated near the Mean

Exhibit 2. Distribution Less Centrally Located

modal value. In some samples there may be two modal points. In which case the sample distribution is said to be bimodal. In the case were there are several modal values, the distribution will be called multi-modal.

A1.5.2 Measures of Moment

One of the difficulties of the measures of central tendency is that they convey, in most cases, insufficient information as to the actual location of the mass of a distribution in relation to a measure of central tendency. Consider the case of the pdfs shown in Exhibits 1 and 2. In the case of Exhibit 1, most of the mass of the distribution is concentrated right around the mean. In the case of the distribution represented in Exhibit 2, the mass is much less centrally located. Now consider the pdfs represented in Exhibits 3 and 4. In Exhibit 3, we see that the mass is not symmetrically distributed about the mean. In the example of Exhibit 4, the mass is evenly distributed about the mean but is bimodal: the mass of the distribution is concentrated in two nodes that are separated from the

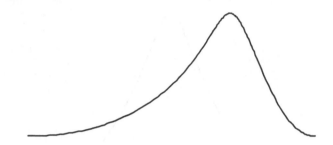

Exhibit 3. Mass not Symmetrically Distributed about the Mean

Exhibit 4. Bimodal Distribution

mean. To capture these characteristics of probability distributions, we will need additional statistics.

A1.5.2.1 Variance. Each observation x_i in a sample $x_1, x_2, \cdots, x_n$ will differ from the mean by an amount $(x_i - \bar{x})$ called the mean deviation. With these mean deviations we can construct a set of *moments* about the mean. Let $M(x,r)$ represent the rth moment about the mean. Then:

$$M(x,r) = \frac{\sum_{i=1}^{n} (x_i - \bar{x})^r}{n}$$

The first moment about the mean, of course, will be zero in that:

$$\frac{\sum_{i=1}^{n} (x_i - \bar{x})}{n} = \frac{1}{n} \sum_{i=1}^{n} x_i - \frac{1}{n} \sum_{i=1}^{n} \bar{x} = \bar{x} - \bar{x} = 0$$

The second moment about the mean is the sample variance:

$$s^2 = Var(x) = \frac{\sum_{i=1}^{n} (x_i - \bar{x})^2}{n}$$

In that the sample variance tends to be rather large, the sample standard deviation is sometimes used in its stead, as follows:

$$s = \frac{1}{n}\sqrt{\sum_{i=1}^{n}(x_i - \bar{x})^2}$$

If a distribution is not symmetrical, the mode may be to the left or right of the mean and either close to the mean or relatively far from it. This will represent the *skewness* of the distribution. We can compute a coefficient of skewness c_s as follows:

$$c_s = \frac{M(x,3)}{s^3}$$

where s is the sample standard deviation defined above. If c_s is negative, then the modal point will lie to the left of the mean; the magnitude of c_s is a measure of this distance. Similarly, if c_s is positive, then the modal point will lie to the right of the mean. Again, the magnitude of c_s is a measure of this distance.

The degree to which a distribution is flattened (see also Exhibit 4) can be assessed by a measure of *kurtosis* c_k, which is defined as follows:

$$c_s = \frac{M(x,4)}{s^4}$$

In this case, if there is a tendency toward bimodality (platykurtic), then $c_k > 1$. If, on the other hand, $c_k < 1$, the distribution of the mass of the distribution is very close to the mean (leptokurtic).

A1.5.2.2 Standard Error of the Mean. Another measure of variation that is very important to us relates to the variation in $\bar{x}$, the estimate of the population mean. Returning, for a moment, to the sample random variables $\mathbf{x}_1, \mathbf{x}_2, \cdots, \mathbf{x}_n$, the variance of:

$$\bar{\mathbf{x}} = \frac{1}{n}\sum_{i=1}^{n}\mathbf{x}_i$$

is:

$$Var(\bar{\mathbf{x}}) = Var\left(\frac{1}{n}\sum_{i=1}^{n}\mathbf{x}_i\right) = \frac{1}{n^2}Var\left(\sum_{i=1}^{n}\mathbf{x}_i\right) = \frac{1}{n^2}\left(\sum_{i=1}^{n}Var(\mathbf{x}_i)\right)$$

Observe that each of the random variables $\mathbf{x}_i$ has the same distribution as $\mathbf{x}$; therefore:

$$Var(\mathbf{x}_i) = Var(\mathbf{x}) = \sigma^2$$

Thus:

$$Var(\overline{x}) = \sigma_{\overline{x}}^2 = \frac{1}{n^2}\left(\sum_{i=1}^{n}\sigma^2\right) = \frac{\sigma^2}{n}s$$

The standard deviation of $\overline{x}$, using the sample estimate s^2 for σ^2, is known as the standard error of the estimate of the mean and is defined as:

$$s_{\overline{x}} = \frac{s}{\sqrt{n}}$$

In general, we can see from this relationship that as the sample size increases, the standard error of the estimate for the mean will decrease.

A1.6 TESTS OF HYPOTHESES

A1.6.1 Basic Principles

Many of the basic decisions confronting software engineering are binary; there are just two distinct courses of actions that can be taken. If the software engineer had complete information, then the appropriate course of action would be obvious. The purpose of statistics is to provide some information that can be used in making a reasonable decision between the two possible actions. The possible perceived states of Nature are said to be *hypotheses* about Nature. Further, each of the states is said to be a *simple hypothesis*. It is possible to form a set of simple hypotheses into a *composite* hypothesis that will be true if some of the simple hypotheses are true.

One of the major challenges in the field of research is the formulation of questions that have answers. We might, for example, formulate a hypothesis that the population on which a random variable X is defined has a mean of 50. We could then design an *experiment* that would test this simple hypothesis. In this process we would collect a sample set of observations, compute the mean of the sample, compare this sample mean with the population mean, and either accept the simple hypothesis or reject it. If, on the other hand, we were to form the hypothesis that X is normally distributed, then we would have a composite hypothesis. This is so because a normal distribution is defined by its mean and variance. The actual composite hypothesis is that $X \sim N(\mu,\sigma)$. To specify a normal distribution, we must know both the mean and the variance.

In general then, the strategy is to partition the decision space into two actions A and B, depending on two alternate hypotheses H_0 and H_1. The first hypothesis, H_0, is often called the *null hypothesis*, in that it very often means that we will not change our current strategy based on the acceptance of this hypothesis. Most experimental designs are centered only on H_0. That is, we will accept H_0 or we will reject H_0, which implies the tacit acceptance of H_1.

We might wish, for example, to test the value of a new design methodology such as object-oriented (O-O) programming . We would formulate a hypothesis H_0 that there would be no significant difference between an *ad hoc* program design and O-O with respect to the number of embedded faults in the code as observed in the test process. We would then conduct the experiment and if we found that there were no differences in the two design methodologies, we would then accept the null hypothesis H_0. If, on the other hand, we found significant differences between the two groups, we would then reject the null hypothesis in favor of H_1.

In arriving at a decision about the null hypothesis H_0, two distinct types of error can arise. We can be led to the conclusion that H_0 is false when, in fact, it is true. This is called a Type I error. Alternatively, we can accept H_0 as true when the alternate hypothesis H_1 is true. This is called a Type II error. There will always be some noise in the decision-making process. This noise will obscure the true state of Nature and lead us to the wrong conclusion. There will always be a nonzero probability of our making a Type I or Type II error. By convention, α will be the probability of making a Type I error and β the probability of making a Type II error. From the standpoint of responsible science, we would much rather make a Type II error than a Type I error. Far better is it to fail to see a tenuous result than it would be to be led to the wrong conclusion from our experimental investigation.

At the beginning of each experiment, the values of α and β are determined by the experimenter. These values remain fixed for the experiment. They do not change based on our observations. Thus, we might choose to set $\alpha < 5.05$. That means that we are willing to accept a 1-in-20 chance that we will make a Type II error. A *test of significance* is a statistical procedure that will provide the necessary information for us to make a decision. Such a statistical test can, for example, show us that our result is significant at $\alpha < 0.035$. If we have established our *a priori* experimental criterion at $\alpha < 0.05$, then we will reject the null hypothesis. As a matter of form, a test is either significant at our *a priori* level of α or it is not. If we were to observe two tests, one significant at $\alpha < 0.03$ and the other at $\alpha < 0.02$, we would never report the former test as *more* significant than the latter. They are both significant at the *a priori* level of $\alpha < 5.05$.

The determination of the probability β of making a Type I error is a little more tenuous. It is dependent on the statistical procedures that we will follow in an experiment. We might, for example, be confronted in an experimental situation with two alternative procedures or tests. If two tests of simple H_0 against simple H_1 have the same α, the one with the smaller β will dominate and is the preferred test of the two. It is the more *powerful* of the two tests. In general then, the power of a test is the quantity $1-\beta$.

It is possible to conceive of two simple experiments A and B that are identical in every respect except for the number of observations in each. B might have twice as many observations in its sample as A. Within a given test of significance, the test for B will be more powerful than that for A. It would seem, then, that the best strategy is to design large experiments with lots of observations. This is not desirable in software engineering for two totally different reasons. First, we will learn that experimental observations in software engineering are very expensive. More observations are not economically better. Even worse is the prospect that we run the risk of proving the trivial. As a test increases in power, the more resolving power it will have on *any* differences between two groups, whether these differences are related to the experiment or not. More is not better. Rather, we must identify a procedure that will allow us to determine just how many observations we will need for any experiment. Intuitively, in any experiment there is the signal component that represents the information that we wish to observe. There is also a noise component that represents information added to the experiment by Nature that will obscure our signal event. The ratio of the signal strength to the noise component will be a very great determinant in our evolving sense of experimental design.

A1.6.2 Test on Means

The tests of hypotheses in statistics are rather stereotyped. Experiments, in general, are formulated around hypotheses that relate either to measures of central tendency (mean) or to measures of variation. The formulation of hypotheses in this manner is a large part of the craft of experimental design. Any unskilled person can ask questions. Most questions, however, do not have scientific answers. It takes a well-trained person in experimental design to postulate questions that have answers.

Hypothesis testing in its most simple form occurs when we have identified an experimental group that we think is different from (or similar to) a control group, either because of some action that we have taken or because of some *ex post facto* evidence that we have collected. If the members of the experimental group sample are different from the population, then the *statistics* describing our experimental group will differ from the control group. In particular, the mean of the experimental group, $\bar{x}_1$, will be different from the mean of the control group, $\bar{x}_2$. We will conveniently assume that the samples are drawn from normally distributed populations with means of μ_1 and μ_2 and a common variance of σ^2. The null hypothesis for this circumstance is:

$$H_0: \mu_1 - \mu_2 = 0$$

The case for the alternate hypothesis is not so clear. Depending on the nature of the experimental treatment, there are three distinct possibilities for H_1 as follows:

$$H_1^{(1)}: \mu_1 - \mu_2 > 0$$

$$H_1^{(2)}: \mu_1 \neq \mu_2$$

$$H_1^{(3)}: \mu_2 - \mu_1 > 0$$

If we now consider the new random variables $\bar{X}_2 - \bar{X}_1$, where $\bar{X}_1$ and $\bar{X}_2$ are sample means of the two populations, this sum also has a normal distribution, its mean is $\mu_2 - \mu_1$, and its standard deviation is:

$$\sqrt{Var(\bar{X}_2) + Var(\bar{X}_1)} = \sqrt{\sigma^2/n_2 + \sigma^2/n_1}$$

Then:

$$W = \frac{((\bar{X}_2 - \bar{X}_1) - (\mu_2 - \mu_1))}{\sigma\sqrt{\dfrac{1}{n_2} + \dfrac{1}{n_1}}}$$

is distributed normally such that $W \sim N(0,1)$.

Now, if S_1^2 and S_2^2 are random variables representing the sample variances, then $\frac{n_1 S_1^2}{\sigma^2}$ and $\frac{n_2 S_2^2}{\sigma^2}$ have the χ^2 distribution with $n_1 + 1$ and $n_2 + 1$ degrees of freedom. Their sum

$$V^2 = \frac{n_1 S_1^2 + n_2 S_2^2}{\sigma^2}$$

also has the χ^2 distribution with $n_1 + n_2 - 2$ degrees of freedom. Therefore:

$$T = \frac{W\sqrt{n_1 + n_2 - 2}}{V}$$

has the t distribution with $n_1 + n_2 - 2$ degrees of freedom. Substituting for W and V we have:

$$T = \frac{((\bar{X}_2 - \bar{X}_1) - (\mu_2 - \mu_1))\sqrt{n_1 + n_2 - 2}}{\sigma\sqrt{\dfrac{1}{n_2} + \dfrac{1}{n_1}}} \Bigg/ \sqrt{\frac{n_1 S_1^2 + n_2 S_2^2}{\sigma^2}}$$

$$= \frac{((\bar{X}_2 - \bar{X}_1) - (\mu_2 - \mu_1))}{\sqrt{n_1 S_1^2 + n_2 S_2^2}} \sqrt{\frac{n_1 n_2 (n_1 + n_2 - 2)}{n_1 + n_2}}$$

We will assume now that the null hypothesis is true. This being the case, $\mu_1 - \mu_2 = 0$. The actual value of the t distribution that will be used as a criterion value of the acceptance of the null hypothesis will be derived from:

$$t = \frac{((\bar{x}_2 - \bar{x}_1)\sqrt{n_1 n_2 (n_1 + n_2 - 2)}}{\sqrt{n_1 s_1^2 + n_2 s_2^2 (n_1 + n_2)}}$$

Now let us return to the three alternate hypotheses to understand just how to construct a criterion value for the test of the null hypothesis from the t distribution. First, let us set an *a priori* experimental value for $\alpha < 0.05$. If we wish to employ $H_1^{(1)}$, then we wish to find a value a such that $\Pr(T > a) = 0.05$ or

$$F(a) = \int_{-\infty}^{a} f(x)dx = 0.95$$

for the t distribution with $n_1 + n_2 - 2$ degrees of freedom. To simplify this notation for future discussions, let us represent this value as $t(n_1 + n_2 - 2, 1 - \alpha)$. In the case that we wish to use the alternate hypothesis $H_1^{(3)}$, we would use precisely the same value of t. Tests of this nature are called *one-tailed* t tests in that we have set an upper bound a on the symmetrical t distribution.

In the special case for the second hypothesis $H_1^{(2)}$, we have no information on whether $\mu_1 > \mu_2$ or $\mu_1 < \mu_2$; consequently, we are looking for a value of a such that $\Pr(-a < T > a) = 0.05$. Given that the t distribution is symmetrical, $\Pr(-a < T > a) = 0.05$ is equal to $2\Pr(T_1 > a)$. Thus, for this *two-tailed* t test we will enter the table for $t(n_1 + n_2 - 2, 1 - \frac{1}{2}\alpha)$.

A1.7 INTRODUCTION TO MODELING

An important aspect of statistics in the field of software engineering will be for the development of predictive models. In this context we will have two distinct types of variables. We will divide the world into two sets of variables: independent and dependent. The objective of the modeling process is to develop a predictive relationship between the set of independent variables and the dependent variables. Independent variables are called such because they can be set to predetermined values by us or their values may be observed but not controlled. The dependent or criterion measures will vary in accordance with the simultaneous variation in the independent variables.

A1.7.1 Linear Regression

There are a number of ways of measuring the relationships among sets of variables. Bivariate correlation is one of a number of such techniques. It permits us to analyze the linear relationship among a set of variables, two at a time. Correlation, however, is just a measure of the linear relationship, and nothing more. It will not permit us to *predict* the value of one variable from that of another. To that end, we will now explore the possibilities of the method of least squares or regression analysis to develop this predictive relationship.

The general form of the linear, first-order regression model is:

$$y = \beta_0 + \beta_1 x + \varepsilon$$

In this model description, the values of x are the measures of this independent variable. The variable y is functionally dependent on x. This model will be a straight line with a slope of β_1 and an intercept of β_0. With each of the observations of y there will be an error component ε that is the amount by which y will vary from the regression line. The distributions of x and y are not known, nor are they relevant to regression analysis. We will, however, assume that the errors ε do have a normal distribution.

In a more practical sense, the values of ε are unknown and unknowable. Hence, the values of y are also unknown. The very best we can do is to develop a model as follows:

$$\hat{y} = b_0 + b_1 x$$

where b_0 and b_1 are estimates of β_0 and β_1, respectively. The variable $\hat{y}$ represents the predicted value of y for a given x.

Now let us assume that we have at our disposal a set of n *simultaneous* observations $(x_1, y_1), (x_2, y_2), \cdots, (x_n, y_n)$ for the variables x and y. These are simultaneous in that they are obtained from the same instance of the entity being measured. If the entity is a human being, then (x_i, y_i) will be measures obtained from the ith person at once. There will be many possible regression lines that can be placed through this data. For each of these lines, ε_i in

$$y_i = \beta_0 + \beta_1 x_i + \varepsilon_i$$

will be different. For some lines, the sum of the ε_is will be large and for others it will be small. The particular method of estimation that is used in regression analysis is the method of least squares. In this case, the deviations ε_i of y_i will be:

$$S = \sum_{i=1}^{n} \varepsilon_i^2 = \sum_{i=1}^{n} (y_i - \beta_0 - \beta_1 x_i)^2$$

The objective now is to find values of b_0 and b_1 that will minimize S. To do this we can differentiate first with respect to β_0 and then β_1 as follows:

$$\frac{\partial S}{\partial \beta_0} = -2 \sum_{i=1}^{n} (y_i - \beta_0 - \beta_1 x_i)$$

$$\frac{\partial S}{\partial \beta_1} = -2\sum_{i=1}^{n} x_i (y_i - \beta_0 - \beta_1 x_i)$$

The next step is to set each of the differential equations equal to zero, and substitute the estimates b_0 and b_1 for β_0 and β_1:

$$\sum_{i=1}^{n} (y_i - b_0 - b_1 x_i) = 0$$

$$\sum_{i=1}^{n} x_i (y_i - b_0 - b_1 x_i) = 0$$

Performing a little algebraic manipulation, we obtain:

$$\sum_{i=1}^{n} y_i - nb_0 - b_1 \sum_{i=1}^{n} x_i = 0$$

$$\sum_{i=1}^{n} x_i y_i - b_0 \sum_{i=1}^{n} x_i - b_1 \sum_{i=1}^{n} x_i^2 = 0$$

These, in turn, yield the set of equations known as the *normal equations:*

$$nb_0 + b_1 \sum_{i=1}^{n} x_i = \sum_{i=1}^{n} y_i$$

$$b_0 \sum_{i=1}^{n} x_i + b_1 \sum_{i=1}^{n} x_i^2 = \sum_{i=1}^{n} x_i y_i$$

These normal equations will first be solved for b_0 as follows:

$$b_0 = \frac{\sum_{i=1}^{n} y_i - b_1 \sum_{i=1}^{n} x_i}{n} = \bar{y} - b_1 \bar{x}$$

Next, we will solve for b_1 as follows:

$$(\bar{y} - b_1 \bar{x}) \sum_{i=1}^{n} x_i + b_1 \sum_{i=1}^{n} x_i^2 = \sum_{i=1}^{n} x_i y_i$$

$$n\bar{x}\bar{y} - nb_1 \bar{x}^2 + b_1 \sum_{i=1}^{n} x_i^2 = \sum_{i=1}^{n} x_i y_i$$

$$b_1 = \frac{\sum\limits_{i=1}^{n} x_i y_i - n\overline{x}\,\overline{y}}{\sum\limits_{i=1}^{n} x_i^2 - n\overline{x}^2} = \frac{\sum\limits_{i=1}^{n} (x_i - \overline{x})(y_i - \overline{y})}{\sum\limits_{i=1}^{n} (x_i - \overline{x})^2} = \frac{Cov(x, y)}{Var(x)}$$

A1.7.1.1 The Regression Analysis of Variance. It is possible to use the least squares fit to fit a regression line through data that is perfectly random. That is, we may have chosen a dependent variable and an independent variable that are not related in any way. We are now interested in the fact that the independent variable varies directly with the independent variable. Further, a statistically significant amount of the variation in the independent variable should be explained by a corresponding variation in the independent variable. To study this relationship we will now turn our attention to the analysis of variance (ANOVA) for the regression model.

First, observe that the residual value, or the difference between the predicted value $\hat{y}_i$ and the observed value y_i can be partitioned into two components as follows:

$$y_i - \hat{y}_i = (y_i - \overline{y}) - (\hat{y}_i - \overline{y})$$

Now, if the two sides are squared and summed across all observed values, we can partition the sum of squares about the regression line $(y_i - \hat{y}_i)^2$ as follows:

$$\sum_{i=1}^{n} (y_i - \hat{y}_i)^2 = \sum_{i=1}^{n} [(y_i - \overline{y}) - (\hat{y}_i - \overline{y})]^2$$

$$= \sum_{i=1}^{n} [(y_i - \overline{y})^2 + (\hat{y}_i - \overline{y})^2 - 2(y_i - \overline{y})(\hat{y}_i - \overline{y})]$$

$$= \sum_{i=1}^{n} (y_i - \overline{y})^2 + \sum_{i=1}^{n} (\hat{y}_i - \overline{y})^2 - \sum_{i=1}^{n} 2(y_i - \overline{y})(\hat{y}_i - \overline{y})$$

Now observe that:

$$\hat{y}_i - \overline{y} = b_1(x_i - \overline{x})$$

Thus, the last term in the equations above can be written as:

$$-\sum_{i=1}^{n} 2(y_i - \bar{y})(\hat{y}_i - \bar{y}) = -\sum_{i=1}^{n} 2(y_i - \bar{y})b_1(x_i - \bar{x})$$

$$= -2\sum_{i=1}^{n} b_1^2(x_i - \bar{x})^2$$

$$= -2\sum_{i=1}^{n} (\hat{y}_i - \bar{y})^2$$

If we substitute this result into the previous equation, we obtain:

$$\sum_{i=1}^{n} (y_i - \hat{y}_i)^2 = \sum_{i=1}^{n} (y_i - \bar{y})^2 - \sum_{i=1}^{n} (\hat{y}_i - \bar{y})^2$$

which can be rewritten as:

$$\sum_{i=1}^{n} (y_i - \bar{y})^2 = \sum_{i=1}^{n} (y_i - \hat{y}_i)^2 + \sum_{i=1}^{n} (\hat{y}_i - \bar{y})^2$$

From this equation we observe that the total sum of squares about the mean (SS_{tot}) can be decomposed into the sum of squares about the regression line (SS_{res}) and the sum of squares due to regression (SS_{reg}):

$$SS_{tot} = \sum_{i=1}^{n} (y_i - \bar{y})^2$$

$$= \sum_{i=1}^{n} y_i^2 - \frac{\left(\sum_{i=1}^{n} y_i\right)^2}{n}$$

$$SS_{reg} = b_1\left(\sum_i x_i y_i - \frac{1}{n}\left(\sum_i x_i\right)\left(\sum_i y_i\right)\right)$$

$$SS_{res} = SS_{tot} - SS_{reg}$$

In essence, the above formula shows how the total variance about the mean of the dependent variable can be partitioned into the variation about the regression line, residual variation, and the variation directly attributable to the regression. We will now turn our attention to the analysis of this variation or the regression ANOVA. The basic question that we ask in the analysis of variance is whether we are able to explain a significant amount of variation in the dependent variable or is the line we fitted likely to have occurred by chance alone.

We will now construct the mean squares of the sums of squares due to regression and due to the residual. This will be accomplished by dividing each term by the degrees of freedom of each term. This term is derived from the number of independent sources of information needed to compile the sum of squares. The sum of squares total has $(n-1)$ in that the sum of $y_i - \bar{y}$ must sum to zero. Any of the combinations of $(n-1)$ terms are free to vary but the nth term must always have a value such that the sum is zero. The sum of squares due to regression can be obtained directly from a single function b_1 of the y_is. Thus, this sum of squares has only one degree of freedom. The degrees of freedom, then, for the residual sum of squares can be obtained by subtraction and is $(n-2)$. Thus, $MS_{reg} = SS_{reg} / 1$ and $MS_{res} = SS_{res} / (n-2)$. Now let us observe that SS_{reg} and SS_{res} both have the χ^2 distribution. Therefore:

$$F = \frac{MS_{reg} / 1}{MS_{res} / (n-2)}$$

has the F distribution with 1 and $(n-2)$ degrees of freedom, respectively. Therefore, we can determine whether there is significant variation due to regression, if the F ratio exceeds our *a priori* experiment wise significance criterion of $\alpha > 0.05$ from the definition of the f distribution:

$$G(F) = \int_0^F g(x)dx = 0.95$$

where $g(x)s$ is defined in Section A1.4.4. As with the t distribution, actually performing this integration for each test of significance that we wished to perform would defeat the most determined researchers among us. The critical values for $F(df_1, df_2, 1-\alpha)$ can be obtained from the tables in most statistics books.

The coefficient of determination R^2 is the ratio of the total sum of squares to the sum of squares due to regression, or:

$$R^2 = \frac{SS_{reg}}{SS_{tot}}$$

It represents the proportion of variation about the mean of y explained by the regression. Frequently, R^2 is expressed as a percentage and is thus multiplied by 100.

A1.7.1.2 Standard Error of the Estimates. As noted when we computed the mean of a sample, this statistic is but an estimate of the population mean. Just how good an estimate it is, is directly related to its standard error. Therefore, we will now turn our attention to the determination of the standard error of the slope, the intercept, and the predicted value for y.

The variance of b_1 can be established as follows:

$$Var(b_1) = \frac{\sigma_x^2}{\sum_i (x_i - \bar{x})^2}$$

The standard error of b_1 is simply the square root of the variance of b_1 and is given by:

$$\sigma_{b_1} = \frac{\sigma_x}{\sqrt{\sum_i (x_i - \bar{x})^2}}$$

In most cases, however, we do not know the population variance. In these cases we will compute the estimated standard error of b_1 as follows:

$$s_{b_1} = \frac{s_x}{\sqrt{\sum_i (x_i - \bar{x})^2}}$$

The variance of b_0 can be obtained from:

$$Var(b_0) = Var(\bar{y} - b_1\bar{x}) = \frac{\sigma_x^2 \sum_i x_i^2}{n \sum_i (x_i - \bar{x})^2}$$

Following the discussion above for b_1, the standard error of b_0 is then given by:

$$\sigma_{b_0} = \sigma_x \sqrt{\frac{\sum_i x_i^2}{n \sum_i (x_i - \bar{x})^2}}$$

By substituting the sample standard deviation for the population parameter, we can obtain the estimated standard error for b_0 as follows:

$$s_{b_0} = s_x \sqrt{\frac{\sum_i x_i^2}{n \sum_i (x_i - \bar{x})^2}}$$

To obtain the standard error of $\hat{y}$, observe that:

$$\hat{y} = \bar{y} + b_1(x - \bar{x})$$

The variance of $\hat{y}$ can then be obtained from:

$$\sigma^2_{\hat{y}_k} = Var(\bar{y} + b_1(x_k - \bar{x}))$$

$$= Var(\bar{y}) + (x_k - \bar{x})^2 Var(b_1)$$

$$= \frac{\sigma^2}{n} + \frac{(x_k - \bar{x})^2 \sigma^2}{\sum_i (x_i - \bar{x})^2}$$

$$= \sigma^2 \left(\frac{1}{n} + \frac{(x_k - \bar{x})^2}{\sum_i (x_i - \bar{x})^2} \right)$$

As before, substituting the sample variance for the population parameter, the estimated standard error of $\hat{y}$ is then given by:

$$s_{\hat{y}_k} = s \left(\frac{1}{n} + \frac{(x_k - \bar{x})^2}{\sum_i (x_i - \bar{x})^2} \right)$$

A1.7.1.3 Confidence Intervals for the Estimates. Once the standard error of the estimate for b_0 has been established, we can compute the $(1-\alpha)$ confidence interval for b_0 as follows:

$$b_0 \pm t(n-1, 1 - \tfrac{1}{2}\alpha)s_{b_0}$$

We may wish to test the hypothesis that $\beta_0 = 0$ against the alternate hypothesis that $\beta_0 \neq 0$, in which case we will compute the value

$$t = b_0 / s_{b_0}$$

to see whether it falls within the bounds established by $t(n-1, 1 - \tfrac{1}{2}\alpha)$. In a similar fashion, the $(1-\alpha)$ confidence interval for b_1 is as follows:

$$b_1 \pm t(n-1, 1 - \tfrac{1}{2}\alpha)s_{b_1}$$

Sometimes it will occur that we are interested in whether the slope b_1 has a particular value, say 0 perhaps. Let γ be the value that we are interested in. Then, the null hypothesis is H_0: $\beta_0 = \gamma$ and the alternate hypothesis is H_1: $\beta_0 \neq \gamma$. We will compute the value

$$t = (b_1 - \gamma) / s_{b_1}$$

to see whether $|t|$ falls within the bounds established by $t(n-1, 1 - \tfrac{1}{2}\alpha)$.

We would now like to be able to place confidence intervals about our estimates for each of the predicted values of the criterion variable. That is, for each observation x_j, the model will yield a predicted $\hat{y}_k$. We have built the regression model for just this purpose. We intend to use it for predicting future events. If the model is good, then our prediction will be valuable. If only a small portion of the variance of y about its mean is explained by the model, the predictive value of the model will be poor. Thus, when we use the model for predictive purposes, we will always compute the experimentally determined $(1-\alpha)$ confidence limits for the estimate:

$$\hat{y} \pm t(n-2, 1-\tfrac{1}{2}\alpha)s_{\hat{y}}$$

The purpose of this section has been to lay the statistical foundation that we will need for further discussions on modeling.

Appendix 2
A Standard for the Measurement of C Programming Language Attributes

A2.1 INTRODUCTION

In this appendix, we will develop precise rules for the standard measurement of 19 program attributes for the C programming language. Moses did not come down from the mountain to give us our new 19 rules. They are not holy. They are, however, intended to be unambiguous and completely reproducible by others. That is the intent of a standard. It is hoped that this standard will serve as a framework for new measures for C program attributes and also as a framework for the development of similar standards for other programming languages.

This standard is meant to capture the metrics at the C function level. These are the smallest compilable C program units. This standard is carefully defined from the C compiler perspective. It will assume that all compiler directives have been resolved prior to the measurement process. Header files (the .h files) will have been resolved prior to measurement as well.

The proposed measurement standard will identify procedures for the precise enumeration of 19 metrics:

1. Comments
2. Executable statements
3. Nonexecutable statements
4. Operators
5. Unique operators
6. Unique nonoverloaded operators
7. Total operands
8. Unique operands

9. Unique actual operands
10. Nodes
11. Edges
12. Paths
13 Maximum path length
14. Average path length
15. Cycles
16. Total system fan-out
17. Unique system fan-out
18. Total standard C fan-out
19. Unique standard C fan-out

Each of these 19 metrics will be described in an unambiguous manner so that new measurement tools written to this standard will all produce identical results. That is the whole notion of a standard. These definitions will be organized into the four basic measurement groups: style and statement metrics, lexical metrics, control flowgraph metrics, and coupling metrics.

A2.2 COMPILER DIRECTIVES

The measurement process is applied only to post-processed C code. The C preprocessor will be invoked before any measurement will occur. The rationale behind this is that we wish to measure the source code as it will be compiled for execution on the machine. That is, the source code presented to the measurement process will be the same code that will execute at runtime. A list of compiler directives can be found in the "Definitions" section.

A2.3 STYLE AND STATEMENT METRICS

A programmer may have a strong influence over the manner in which a program is constructed. Some programmers use many comment statements to document their activities. Other programmers think that their code must be self-explanatory. Some programmers tend to write very short statements while others might implement the same design specification in very few lines. Some programmers are very terse in their use of declarations. Other programmers will be very expressive with their use of declared variables. The first class of metrics we wish to define are those that relate to the frequency of use of comments, executable program statements, and nonexecutable statements.

A2.3.1 Comments

Comments are delimited by "/*" and "*/". Each occurrence of the comment delimiter pair is counted. Global comments will not be counted. They are clearly outside the scope of any function module. Nested comments and comments delimiters found within comment strings are ignored.

Exhibit 1. Examples with Executable Statements

Examples	Executable Statements
`int a;`	0
`a = b + c;`	1
`for(i=1; I<50; i++)`	4
`  b[i] = ';';`	
`while(a=b<c)`	2
`  a++;`	

A2.3.2 Executable Statements

The character ';' is used to delimit some statements in C. An executable statement is a statement that will change the state of the program at runtime. In C, executable statements can stand alone, in which case they are delimited by <;>. They can also be embedded in predicate clauses such as:

```
while (j = k < 1)
```

in which case they are delimited by <)>. They can also occur in declarations, such as:

```
{
    int j = 1, k = 2;
}
```

In this case, the statement `j = 1` is delimited by <,>.

A compound statement delimited by <{> and <}> may or may not contain declarations within its body. If it does contain declarations, it is a block. The declarations that differentiate a block from a compound statement will cause the compiler to build an activation stack at runtime. Therefore, a block is an executable statement in its own right.

The executable statement count must not be modified in the following cases (see Exhibit 1):

- Within a string constant
- Within a character constant
- Within a comment
- At the end of a nonexecutable statement
- As a separator in a `for` structure

A2.3.3 Nonexecutable Statements

Nonexecutable statements are present in variable declarations, structures, unions, enumerated declarations, and type definitions. If a variable is declared, the declaration is considered a nonexecutable statement. Very simply, nonexecutable statements will not result in executable code at runtime.

Exhibit 2. Examples with Nonexecutable Statements

Examples	Nonexecutable Statement
`int i;`	1
`int i = 3 ;`	1
`typedef int bool;`	1
`struct time`	3
`{`	
`  int hour;`	
`  int minute;`	
`};`	
`typedef struct time`	4
`{`	
`  int h our;`	
`  int minute;`	
`}timetype;`	
`timetype a, b, *c;`	

The nonexecutable statement metric must not be modified in the following cases (see Exhibit 2):

- Within a string constant
- Within a character constant
- Within a comment
- Type definition

A2.4 LEXICAL METRICS

The lexical analysis of a C source program module will resolve the strings of characters on the input stream to a sequence of tokens. These tokens can be classified into the two mutually exclusive classes of operators and operands. There are two distinct ways to enumerate both of the categories of operators and operands. We can count the total times that a particular operator or operand has been used or we choose to enumerate only the first time it occurs. In a language such as C, and operator may be overloaded. That is, it may be called to serve many different duties. Take, for example, the operator "+". This operator can be used for integer operands or for real operands. Further, it can be used as a unary operator or as a binary operator. Thus, there are two distinct ways in which the unique operator count can be computed. First, we will enumerate the token "+". This will yield the metric value η_1. Next we will parse the C program to determine the context in which the "+" operator has been used and reclassify each new occurrence of this operator as an integer "+", a floating point "+", etc. This will yield a nonoverloaded count of the "+" operators. The nonoverloaded operator count will be known as η_3.

Exhibit 3. Examples with Operators

Examples	Operator
`{ }`	2 operators: `{ }`

`{`
`  int a, b;`
`  char c = 'O';`
 	
`  a = 1;`
`  b = a + a;`
`}`
	13 operators:
	`{`
	`int`
	`,`
	`;`
	`char`
	`=`
	`;`
	`=`
	`;`
	`=`
	`+`
	`;`
	`}`

`{`
`  int a;`
`  int b;`
 	
`  int c = 1 + 2;`
`  a = 2;`
`  printf("%d", a + c);`
`}`
	18 operators:
	`{`
	`int`
	`;`
	`int`
	`;`
	`int`
	`=`
	`+`
	`;`
	`=`
	`;`
	`printf`
	`(`
	`+`
	`,`
	`)`
	`;`
	`}`

A2.4.1 N_1

The occurrence of any token classified by the parser as an operator will cause N_1 to increase by one. It represents the total operator appearances in a module. Function calls are considered operators (as well as operands; see Exhibit 3).

A2.4.2 η_1

Each occurrence of a new and distinct operator causes an increase in η_1. An operator is counted independently of the adjoining operands (see

Exhibit 4. Examples with Unique Operators

Examples	Unique Operators

`{  }`	2 operators:
	`{`
	`}`

`{`
`  int a, b;`
`  char  c = 'O';`
 	
`  a = 1;`
`  b = a + a;`
`}`
	8 unique operators:
	`{`
	`int`
	`'`
	`;`
	`char`
	`=`
	`+`
	`}`

`{`
`  int a;`
`  int b;`
 	
`  int c = 1 + 2;`
`  a = 2;`
`  printf("%d", a + c);`
`}`
	10 unique operators:
	`{`
	`int`
	`;`
	`=`
	`+`
	`printf`
	`(`
	`'`
	`)`
	`}`

Exhibit 4). Function calls play a dual role. On the one hand, they are operators; on the other hand, they return values and thus are also operands.

A2.4.3 η_3

There are two ways that unique operators can be enumerated: overloaded and nonoverloaded. η_3 is a special variation of the count of the number of unique operators. It represents the count of unique nonoverloaded operators. The counting rules are similar to η_1. In addition, the concept of operator overloading is taken into consideration. η_3 distinguishes operators that appear to be identical but are intrinsically different because of the operands they work with (see Exhibit 5).

The following rules apply when computing this metric:

- An assignment has always the type of its left-hand expression.
- If there is an addition or a multiplication operation of the form:

operand-1 operator operand-2

the type of the operator is determined according to the order of precedence. The types of operand-1 and operand-2 are compared and the oper-

Exhibit 5. Example with Overloaded and Unique Operators

Example	η_1	η_3

`{`
`  int i1=1,i2=2,i3;`
`   float`
`f1=1.1,f2=2.2,f3;`
 	
`  i3 = i1 + i2;`
`  f3 = f1 + f2;`
`}`
	8 unique overloaded operators:
	`{`
	`int`
	`=`
	`,`
	`;`
	`float`
	`+`
	`}`
		10 unique operators:
		`{`
		`int`
		`=int`
		`,`
		`;`
		`float`
		`=float`
		`+int`
		`+float`
		`}`

Exhibit 6. Examples with Considerations

Examples	Considerations

`char c1, c2;`
`c1 = c1 + c2;`
`char mod_1()`
`{ }`
	= is a character assignment
	+ is an integer addition

`main()`
`{`
`  mod_1();`
`}`
	A character function call

ation takes the higher type of both within this order. The order of precedence is:

$$\text{double} \Rightarrow \text{float} \Rightarrow \text{long} \Rightarrow \text{int} \Rightarrow \text{short}$$

- Function calls are classified based on the called function's return type.
- Unary operators can also be overloaded.
- A character is considered an integer except in (see Exhibit 6):

  — A character assignment
  — A function declaration

A2.4.4 N_2

The total operand count is represented by N_2. Each occurrence of an operand causes an increase in N_2. Operands can be simple identifiers or complex structures that combine a set of identifiers. According to the C syntax, an operand is an expression. An expression is an operand if it is embedded in an operation; otherwise, only its elements can be operands. The total

Exhibit 7. Total Number of Operands

Examples	Total Number of Operands
`a = b;`	Total of 2:
	a
	b
`a = b + c;`	Total of 3:
	a
	b
	c
`if (a = b + c)`	Total of 3:
	a
	b
	c
`{`	Total of 11:
`    int a, b;`	a
`    int c = 1 + 2;`	b
`     a = 2;`	c
`    printf("%d",a+c);`	1
`}`	2
	a
	2
	printf
	"%d"
	a
	c

number of operands must not be modified in the following cases (see Exhibit 7):

- Within a string constant
- Within a character constant
- Within a comment
- Type definition
- On the left-hand side in a variable declaration (including the "=" and the final ";")

A2.4.5 η_2

The total number of unique operands will be denoted by η_2. Unique operands are characterized by their name and type. Each occurrence of a distinct operand increases η_2 by one. The total number of operands must not be modified in the following cases:

- Within a string constant
- Within a character constant
- Within a comment
- Type definition

410

- On the left-hand side in a variable declaration (including the "=" and the final ";")

Very simply, the collection of all operand tokens is a bag. The collection of unique operations is a set.

A2.5 CONTROL FLOWGRAPH METRICS

A control flowgraph of a program is constructed from a directed graph representation of the program that can be defined as follows:

- A directed graph, $G = (N, E, s, t)$, consists of a set of nodes N; a set of edges E; a distinguished node s, the start node; and a distinguished node t, the exit node. An edge is an ordered pair of nodes (a, b).
- The in-degree $I(a)$ of node a is the number of entering edges to a.
- The out-degree $O(a)$ of node a is the number of exiting edges from a.

The flowgraph representation of a program, $F = (E', N', s, t)$ is a directed graph that satisfies the following properties:

- There is a unique start node s such that $I(s) = 0$.
- There is a unique exit node t such that $O(t) = 0$.

All other nodes are members of exactly one of the following three categories:

- *Processing node.* It has one entering edge and one exiting edge. They represent processing node a, $I(a) = 1$ and $O(a) = 1$.
- *Predicate node.* It represents a decision point in the program as a result of *if* statements, *case* statements, or any other statement that will cause an alteration in the control flow. For a predicate node a, $I(a) \geq 1$ and $(a) > 1$.
- *Receiving node.* It represents a point in the program where two or more control flows join, for example, at the end of a `while` loop. For a receiving node a, $I(a) > 1$ and $O(a) = 1$.

If (a, b) is an edge from node a to node b, then node a is an immediate predecessor of node b and node b is an immediate successor of node a. The set of all immediate predecessors for node a is denoted as $IP(a)$. The set of all immediate successors for node b is denoted as $IS(b)$. No node can have itself as a successor. That is, a cannot be a member of $IS(a)$. In addition, no processing node can have a processing node as a successor node. All successor nodes to a processing node must be either predicate nodes or receiving nodes. Similarly, no processing node can have a processing node as its predecessor.

From this control flowgraph representation, two essential control flow primitive metrics emerge:

- Number of nodes
- Number of edges

A path P in a flowgraph F is a sequence of edges $< \overrightarrow{a_1 a_2}, \overrightarrow{a_2 a_3}, \ldots, \overrightarrow{a_{N-1} a_N} >$ where all a_i ($i = 1, \ldots, N$) are elements of N'. P is a path from node a_1 to node a_n. An execution path in F is any path P from s to t.

The average length of the paths measured in numbers of edges constitutes a second program characteristic. A program that has a large number of relatively short control-flow paths differs greatly in terms of testing or maintenance from one having a few relatively long control-flow paths.

Whether or not a node lies on a cycle relates to the concept of connectedness defined as follows:

- A flowgraph F is weakly connected if any two nodes a and b are connected by a sequence of edges.
- A flowgraph F is strongly connected if each node lies on a cycle.

Any flowgraph might potentially contain weakly connected subsets of nodes that are flowgraphs in their own right. To examine this potential hierarchical structure of the flowgraph representation, the notion of a sub-flowgraph is essential.

A sub-flowgraph $F' = (N'', E'', s', t')$ of a flowgraph $F = (N', E', s, t)$ is a flowgraph if the out-degree of every node in F' is the same as the out-degree of the corresponding node in F with the exception of the nodes s' and t'. All nodes in the sub-flowgraph are weakly connected only to nodes in N''.

A sub-flowgraph of F is a sub-flowgraph with the property that the cardinality of $N'' > 2$ and $F' \neq F$. That is, the sub-flowgraph must contain more nodes than the start and exit nodes and cannot be the same flowgraph.

A flowgraph is an irreducible flowgraph if it contains no proper sub-flowgraph. A flowgraph is a prime flowgraph if it contains no proper sub-flowgraph for which the property $I(s') = 1$ holds. A prime flowgraph cannot be built by sequencing or nesting other flowgraphs, and it must contain a single entrance and a single exit structure. The primes are the primitive building blocks of a program control flow.

In the C language, the primes relate to the basic control structures shown in Exhibit 8.

A2.5.1 Nodes

The node count represents the number of nodes in the flowgraph representation of the program module. The minimum number of nodes that a module can have is three: the start node, a single processing node, and an exit node.

If a module has more than one exit point, then a virtual receiving node must be created to meet the condition that there be but one exit node. This

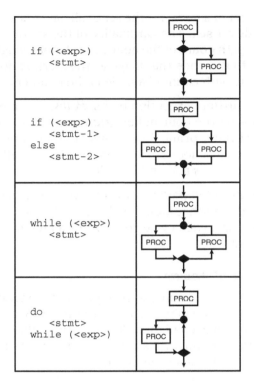

Exhibit 8. C Language and Basic Control Structures

virtual node helps to keep the consistency in the flowgraph by ensuring that there is a unique exit node.

The return statement should be considered a processing node (or as a part of a processing node) because it sets the value of what is been returned to the caller function. The processing node must be followed by an edge to the virtual receiving node if multiple return statements are present.

A2.5.2 Edges

The *Edge* metric represents the number of edges in the control flow representation of the program module. The minimum number of edges that a module can have is two, in that there must be at least one processing node.

A2.5.3 Paths

A path through a flowgraph is an ordered set of edges (*s*, ... , *t*) that begins on the starting node *s* and ends on the terminal node *t*. A path can contain one or more cycles. Each distinct cycle cannot occur more than once in sequence. That is, the subpath (*a*, *b*, *c*, *a*) is a legal subpath but the subpath (*a*, *b*, *c*, *a*, *b*, *c*, *a*) is not permitted.

The total path set of a node a is the set of all paths (s, a) that go from the start node to node a itself. The cardinality of the set of paths of node a is equal to the total path count of the node a. Each node singles out a distinct number of paths to the node that begin at the starting node and end with the node itself. The path count of a node is the number of such paths.

The number of distinct execution paths, *Paths*, is computed by systematically decomposing the control flowgraph representation of a program module into constituent prime flowgraphs, a process that systematically eliminates all predicate nodes. The *Path* metric will tally the number of paths that begin at node s and end at node t.

Cycles are permitted in paths. For each cyclical structure, exactly two paths are counted: one that includes the code in the cycle and one that does not. In this sense, each cycle contributes a minimum of two paths to the total path count.

A2.5.4 Maximum Path Length

This metric represents the number of edges in the longest path. From the set of available paths for a module, all the paths are evaluated by counting the number of edges in each of them. The greatest value is assigned to this metric. This metric gives an estimate of the maximum path flow complexity that might be obtained when running a module.

A2.5.5 Average Path Length

The average path length is the mean of the length of all paths in the control-flow graph. If the average path is not an integer, it is rounded:

- *[x.0, x.499]* average path length = x
- *[x.500, x.999]* average path length = $x + 1$

A2.5.6 Cycles

A cycle is a collection of strongly connected nodes. From any node in the cycle to any other, there is a path of length one or more, wholly within the cycle. This collection of nodes has a unique entry node. This entry node dominates all nodes in the cycle. A cycle that contains no other cycles is called an inner cycle.

The cycles metric counts the number of cycles in the control flowgraph. There are two different types of cycles:

1. Iterative loops are those that result from the use of the `for`, `while`, and `do/while` structures.
2. Control loops are created by the backward reference of instructions. If the label object of a `goto` is above the `goto` and there is a possible path from the label to the `goto` statement, it causes a cycle. Thus,

each occurrence of such a cycle increases the count of the cycle metric.

A2.6 COUPLING METRICS

Coupling reflects the degree of relationship that exists between modules. The more coupled two modules are, the more dependent they become on each other. Coupling is an important measurement domain because it is closely associated with the impact that a change in a module (or also a fault) might have in the rest of the system.

There are many different attributes that relate specifically to the binding between program modules at runtime. These attributes are related to the coupling characteristics of the module structure. For our purposes, we will examine two attributes of this binding process: (1) the transfer of program control into and out of the program module, and (2) the flow of data into and out of a program module.

The flow of control among program modules can be represented in a program call graph. This call graph is constructed from a directed graph representation of program modules that can be defined as follows:

- A directed graph, $G = (N, E, s)$, consists of a set of nodes N, a set of edges E, and a distinguished node s, the main program node. An edge is an ordered pair of nodes (a, b).
- There will be an edge (a, b) if program module a can call module b.
- As was the case for a module flowgraph, the in-degree $I(a)$ of node a is the number of entering edges to a.
- Similarly, the out-degree $O(a)$ of node a is the number of exiting edges from a.

The nodes of a call graph are program modules. The edges of this graph represent calls from module to module and not returns from these calls. Only the modules that are constituents of the program source code library will be represented in the call graph. This call graph will specifically exclude calls to system library functions.

Coupling reflects the degree of relationship that exists between modules. The more tightly coupled two modules are, the more dependent they become on each other. Coupling is an important measurement domain because is closely associated with the impact that a change in a module (or also a fault) might have on the rest of the system. Several program attributes are associated with coupling. Two of these attributes relate to the binding between a particular module and other program modules. There are two distinct concepts represented in this binding: (1) the number of modules that can call a given module, and (2) the number of calls out of a particular module. These will be represented by the fan-in and fan-out metrics, respectively.

A2.6.1 F_1

This metric enumerates the total number of local function calls made *from* a given module. Local functions do not include calls to the C standard library.

A2.6.2 f_1

This metric is a count of the unique number of C function calls made *within* a program module to another C function. This metric is incremented only when a function call appears for the first time. If the same function is called more than once, this metric will remain unchanged.

A2.6.3 F_2

This metric counts the total number of standard C function calls made *into* a given module. It is the total number of times that a module is invoked by all other program modules. There might, for example, be multiple calls into a module from a single program module. Each of these would increment the F_2 metric.

A2.6.4 f_2

This metric counts the unique number of standard C function calls into a given module. This metric is incremented only when the standard C function call appears for the first time in a particular module. If the same function is called more than once within a given program module, the f_2 metric will remain unchanged.

A2.7 DEFINITIONS

A2.7.1 Definition of a String Constant

A string constant is delimited by a starting " and an ending ". For example, the C function `printf()` uses string constants:

```
printf(" Hello World ");
```

The content of the string constant does not play any role in determining the metrics but a string constant itself can be an operand.

A2.7.2 Definition of a Character Constant

A character constant starts with ' and ends with '. For example, the assignment of a character variable:

```
a = 'b';
```

Semicolons and operators appearing in character constants are not relevant for counting the statement or operator metrics.

A2.7.3 Definition of a `for` Structure

A `for` has the following form:

```
for (expression1; expression2; expression3) expression;
```

The semicolons between the brackets do not play a role in determining the statement metric count. They do not delimit a statement but serve to separate expressions.

A2.8 TOKENS

A2.8.1 Operand Tokens

```
Identifier
Constant
String_Literal
Function_Call
```

A2.8.2 Operator Tokens

A2.8.2.1 Keywords

```
auto
break
case
char
continue
const
default
do
double
else
enum
extern
float
for
goto
if
int
long
noalias
register
return
short
signed
sizeof
static
struct
switch
```

417

```
typedef
union
unsigned
volatile
void
while
```

A2.8.2.2 Punctuation

```
:as label operation
;as statement delimiter
```

A2.8.2.3 Blocks

```
{   } as block delimiters
```

A2.8.2.4 Unary Operators

```
&as address operator
*as pointer operator
-as minus operator
+as plus operator
!as not operator
sizeof( ) (<type>)cast operators
~as integer complement operator
++as integer prefix increment operator
++as short prefix increment operator
++as long prefix increment operator
++ as float prefix increment operator
++ as double prefix increment operator
--as integer prefix decrement operator
-- as short prefix decrement operator
--as long prefix decrement operator
--as float prefix decrement operator
--as double prefix decrement operator
++as integer postfix increment operator
++as short postfix increment operator
++as long postfix increment operator
++as float postfix increment operator
++as double postfix increment operator
--as integer postfix decrement operator
--as short postfix decrement operator
--as long postfix decrement operator
--as float postfix decrement operator
--as double postfix decrement operator
```

A2.8.2.5 Function Calls as Operators

```
intfunction call
shortfunction call
longfunction call
```

```
floatfunction call
doublefunction call
charfunction call
voidfunction call
```

A2.8.2.6 Array Operators

```
[
]
```

A2.8.2.7 Structure Operators

```
.as structure operator
->as structure operator
```

A2.8.2.8 Primary Operators

```
(
)
```

A2.8.2.9 Assignment Operators

```
=integer
=short integer
=long integer
=float
=double float
=char
=string
=array
=struct
*=integer multiplication
*=short multiplication
*=long multiplication
*=float multiplication
*=double multiplication
/=integer division
/=short division
/=long division
/=float division
/=double division
%=integer modulus
%=short modulus
%=long modulus
+=integer addition
+=short addition
+=long addition
+=float addition
+=double addition
-=integer subtraction
-=short subtraction
```

```
-=long subtraction
-=float subtraction
-=double subtraction
<<=
>>=
&=
^=
|=
```

A2.8.2.10 Conditional Operators

```
?
:
```

A2.8.2.11 Logical Operators

```
||
&&
|
^
&
```

A2.8.2.12 Relational Operators

```
<
>
<=
>=
==
!=
```

A2.8.2.13 Shift Operators

```
>>
<<
```

A2.8.2.14 Addition Operators

```
+integer addition
+short addition
+long addition
+float addition
+double addition
-integer subtraction
-short subtraction
-long subtraction
-float subtraction
-double subtraction
```

A2.8.2.15 Multiplying Operators

```
*integer multiplication
```

```
*short multiplication
*long multiplication
*float multiplication
*double multiplication
%integer modulus operation
%short modulus operation
%long modulus operation
/integer division
/short division
/long division
/float division
/double division
```

A2.8.3 Compiler Directives

There follows a list of compiler directives that must be resolved before the measurement process can begin.

```
#include
#define
#undef
#if
#ifdef
#ifndef
#else
#endif
#elif
#error
#pragma
#
```

A2.8.4 C Functions

A2.8.4.1 Math

```
abs
acos
asin
atan
ceil
cos
cosh
exp
fabs
floor
log
log10
pow
rand
sin
```

```
sing
sqrt
tan
tanh
```

A2.8.4.2 Memory Allocation

```
calloc
free
malloc
```

A2.8.4.3 Input/Output

```
close
creat
fclose
fgetc
fgets
fopen
fprintf
fputc
fputs
fread
fscanf
fseek
ftell
fwrite
getc
getchar
gets
lseek
open
printf
putc
putchar
puts
read
scanf
sprintf
sscanf
ungetc
```

A2.8.4.4 Type and Conversion

```
atof
atoi
atol
isalnum
isalpha
isascii
isatty
```

```
iscntrl
isdigit
isgraph
islower
isprint
ispunct
isspace
isupper
isxdigit
toascii
tolower
toupper
```

A2.8.4.5 String

```
strcat
strchr
strcmp
strcpy
strcspn
strlen
strncat
strncmp
strncpy
strpbrk
strrchr
strspn
```

A2.8.4.6 Miscellaneous

```
exit
signal
sleep
system
time
```

Index

9 780367 395377